CYBERSECURITY AND CYBERWAR

WHAT EVERYONE NEEDS TO KNOW®

**P. W. SINGER AND
ALLAN FRIEDMAN**

OXFORD

UNIVERSITY PRESS

OXFORD

UNIVERSITY PRESS

Oxford University Press is a department of the University of Oxford.
It furthers the University's objective of excellence in research, scholarship,
and education by publishing worldwide.

Oxford   New York
Auckland   Cape Town   Dar es Salaam   Hong Kong   Karachi
Kuala Lumpur   Madrid   Melbourne   Mexico City   Nairobi
New Delhi   Shanghai   Taipei   Toronto

With offices in
Argentina   Austria   Brazil   Chile   Czech Republic   France   Greece
Guatemala   Hungary   Italy   Japan   Poland   Portugal   Singapore
South Korea   Switzerland   Thailand   Turkey   Ukraine   Vietnam

Oxford is a registered trademark of Oxford University Press
in the UK and certain other countries.

"What Everyone Needs to Know" is a registered trademark of Oxford
University Press.

Published in the United States of America by Oxford University Press
198 Madison Avenue, New York, NY 10016

© P. W. Singer and Allan Friedman 2014

All rights reserved. No part of this publication may be reproduced, stored in a
retrieval system, or transmitted, in any form or by any means, without the prior
permission in writing of Oxford University Press, or as expressly permitted by law,
by license, or under terms agreed with the appropriate reproduction rights
organization. Inquiries concerning reproduction outside the scope of the above
should be sent to the Rights Department, Oxford University Press, at the
address above.

You must not circulate this work in any other form
and you must impose this same condition on any acquirer.

Library of Congress Cataloging-in-Publication Data
Singer, P. W. (Peter Warren)
Cybersecurity and cyberwar : what everyone needs to know / Peter W. Singer,
Allan Friedman.
ISBN 978–0–19–991809–6 (hardback)—ISBN 978–0–19–991811–9 (paperback)
1. Computer security—United States   2. Computer networks—Security
measures—United States.   3. Cyberspace—Security measures—United States.
4. Cyberterrorism—United States—Prevention.   5. Information warfare—United
States—Prevention.   I. Title.
QA76.9.A25S562 2014
005.8—dc23
2013028127

1 3 5 7 9 8 6 4 2
Printed in the United States of America
on acid-free paper

CONTENTS

PART III   WHAT CAN WE DO?   166

CONCLUSIONS 247

INTRODUCTION

Why Write a Book about Cybersecurity and Cyberwar?

"All this cyber stuff."

The setting was a Washington, DC, conference room. The speaker was a senior leader of the US Department of Defense. The topic was why he thought cybersecurity and cyberwar was so important. And yet, when he could only describe the problem as "all this cyber stuff," he unintentionally convinced us to write this book.

Both of us are in our thirties and yet still remember the first computers we used. For a five-year-old Allan, it was an early Apple Macintosh in his home in Pittsburgh. Its disk space was so limited that it could not even fit this book into its memory. For a seven-year-old Peter, it was a Commodore on display at a science museum in North Carolina. He took a class on how to "program," learning an entire new language for the sole purpose of making one of the most important inventions in the history of mankind print out a smiley face. It spun out of a spool printer, replete with the perforated paper strips on the side.

Three decades later, the centrality of computers to our lives is almost impossible to comprehend. Indeed, we are so surrounded by computers that we don't even think of them as "computers" anymore. We are woken by computerized clocks, take showers in water heated by a computer, drink coffee brewed in a computer, eat oatmeal heated up in a computer, then drive to work in a car controlled by hundreds of computers, while sneaking peeks at the last night's sport scores on a computer. And then at work, we spend most of our day pushing buttons on a computer, an experience so futuristic in our parents' day that it was the stuff of *The Jetsons* (George Jetson's job was a "digital index operator"). Yet perhaps the best way to gain even a hint of computers' modern ubiquity is at the end of the day. Lie in bed, turn off the lights, and count the number of little red lights staring back at you.

These machines are not just omnipresent, they are connected. The computers we used as little kids stood alone, linked to nothing more than the wall electricity socket and maybe that spool printer. Just a generation ago, the Internet was little more than a link between a few university researchers. The first "electronic mail" was sent in 1971. The children of those scientists now live in a world where almost 40 trillion e-mails are sent a year. The first "website" was made in 1991. By 2013, there were over 30 trillion individual web pages.

Moreover, the Internet is no longer just about sending mail or compiling information: it now also handles everything from linking electrical plants to tracking purchases of Barbie dolls. Indeed, Cisco, a company that helps run much of the back end of the Internet, estimated that 8.7 billion devices were connected to the Internet by the end of 2012, a figure it believes will rise to 40 billion by 2020 as cars, fridges, medical devices, and gadgets not yet imagined or invented all link in. In short, domains that range from commerce to communication to the critical infrastructure that powers our modern-day civilization all operate on what has become a globalized network of networks.

But with the rise of "all this cyber stuff," this immensely important but incredibly short history of computers and the Internet has reached a defining point. Just as the upside of the cyber domain is rippling out into the physical domain, with rapid and often unexpected consequences, so too is the downside.

As we will explore, the astounding numbers behind "all this cyber stuff" drive home the scale and range of the threats: 97 percent of Fortune 500 companies have been hacked (and 3 percent likely have been too and just don't know it), and more than one hundred governments are gearing up to fight battles in the online domain. Alternatively, the problems can be conceptualized through the tough political issues that this "stuff" has already produced: scandals like WikiLeaks and NSA monitoring, new cyberweapons like Stuxnet, and the role that social networking plays in everything from the Arab Spring revolutions to your own concerns over personal privacy. Indeed, President Barack Obama declared that "cybersecurity risks pose some of the most serious economic and national security challenges of the 21st century," a position that has been repeated by leaders in countries from Britain to China.

For all the hope and promise of the information age, ours is also a time of "cyber anxiety." In a survey of where the world was heading in the future, *Foreign Policy* magazine described the cyber area as the "single greatest emerging threat," while the *Boston Globe* claimed that future is already here: a "cyber world war" in progress that will culminate in "bloody, digital trench warfare."

These fears have coalesced into the massive booming business of cybersecurity, one of the fastest growing industries in the world. It has led to the creation of various new governmental offices and bureaucracies (the US Department of Homeland Security's National Cyber Security Division has doubled or tripled in size every year since its inception). The same is true for armed forces around the globe like the US Cyber Command and the Chinese "Information Security Base" (*xinxi baozhang jidi*), new military units whose very mission is to fight and win wars in cyberspace.

As we later consider, these aspects of "cyber stuff" raise very real risks, but how we perceive and respond to these risks may be even more crucial to the future, and not just of the Internet. As Joe Nye, the former Dean of the Harvard Kennedy School of Government, notes, if users begin to lose confidence in the safety and security of the Internet, they will retreat from cyberspace, trading "welfare in search of security."

Fears over cybersecurity increasingly compromise our notions of privacy and have allowed surveillance and Internet filtering to become more common and accepted at work, at home, and at the governmental level. Entire nations, too, are pulling back, which will undermine the economic and human rights benefits we've seen from global connectivity. China is already developing its own network of companies behind a "Great Firewall" to allow it to screen incoming messages and disconnect from the worldwide Internet if needed. As a Yale Law School article put it, all of these trends are "converging into a *perfect storm* that threatens traditional Internet values of openness, collaboration, innovation, limited governance and free exchange of ideas."

These issues will have consequences well beyond the Internet. There is a growing sense of vulnerability in the physical world from new vectors of cyberattack via the virtual world. As a report entitled "The New Cyber Arms Race" describes, "In the future, wars will not just be fought by soldiers with guns or with planes that drop bombs. They will also be fought with the click of a mouse a half a world away that unleashes carefully weaponized computer programs that disrupt or destroy critical industries like utilities, transportation, communications, and energy. Such attacks could also disable military networks that control the movement of troops, the path of jet fighters, the command and control of warships."

Such a vision of costless war or instant defeat either scares or comforts, wholly dependent on which side of the cyberattack you're on. The reality, as we explore later in the book, is much more complex. Such visions don't just stoke fears and drive budgets. They also are potentially leading to the militarization of cyberspace itself. These visions threaten a domain that has delivered massive amounts of information, innovation, and prosperity to the wider planet, fuel tensions between nations, and, as the title of the aforementioned report reveals, maybe even have set in motion a new global arms race.

In short, no issue has emerged so rapidly in importance as cybersecurity. And yet there is no issue so poorly understood as this "cyber stuff."

Why Is There a Cybersecurity Knowledge Gap, and Why Does It Matter?

"Rarely has something been so important and so talked about with less and less clarity and less apparent understanding.... I have sat in *very* small group meetings in Washington...unable (along with my colleagues) to decide on a course of action because we lacked a clear picture of the long term legal and policy implications of *any* decision we might make."

This is how General Michael Hayden, former Director of the CIA, described the cybersecurity knowledge gap and the dangers it presents. A major part of this disconnect is the consequence of those early experiences with computers, or rather the lack of them among too many leaders. Today's youth are "digital natives," having grown up in a world where computers have always existed and seem a natural feature. But the world is still mostly led by "digital immigrants," older generations for whom computers and all the issues the Internet age presents remain unnatural and often confusing.

To put it another way, few older than fifty will have gone through their university training even using a computer. Even the few who did likely used one that stood alone, not connected to the world. Our most senior leaders, now in their sixties and seventies, likely did not even become familiar with computers until well into their careers, and many still today have only the most limited experience with them. As late as 2001, the Director of the FBI did not have a computer in his office, while the US Secretary of Defense would have his assistant print out e-mails to him, write his response in pen, and then have the assistant type them back in. This sounds outlandish, except that a full decade later the Secretary of Homeland Security, in charge of protecting the nation from cyberthreats, told us at a 2012 conference, "Don't laugh, but I just don't use e-mail at all." It wasn't a fear of security, but that she just didn't believe e-mail useful. And in 2013, Justice Elena Kagan revealed the same was true of eight out of nine of the United States Supreme Court justices, the very people who would ultimately decide what was legal or not in this space.

It is not solely an issue of age. If it was, we could just wait until the old farts died off and all would be solved. Just because someone is young doesn't mean the person automatically has an understanding of the key issues. Cybersecurity is one of those areas that has been left to only the most technically inclined to worry their uncombed heads over. Anything related to the digital world of zeros and ones was an issue just for computer scientists and the IT help desk. Whenever they spoke, most of us would just keep quiet, nod our heads, and put on what author Mark Bowden calls "the glaze." This is the "unmistakable look of profound confusion and disinterest that takes hold whenever conversation turns to workings of a computer." The glaze is the face you put on when you can only call something "stuff." Similarly, those who are technically inclined too often roll their eyes at the foreign logic of the policy and business worlds, scoffing at the "old way" of doing business, without understanding the interactions between technology and people.

The result is that cybersecurity falls into a no man's land. The field is becoming crucial to areas as intimate as your privacy and as weighty as the future of world politics. But it is a domain only well known by "the IT Crowd." It touches every major area of public- and private-sector concern, but only the young and the computer savvy are well engaged with it. In turn, the technical community that understands the workings too often sees the world only through a specific lens and can fail to appreciate the broader picture or nontechnical aspects. Critical issues are thus left misunderstood and often undebated.

The dangers are diverse and drove us in the writing of the book. Each of us, in whatever role we play in life, must make decisions about cybersecurity that will shape the future well beyond the world of computers. But often we do so without the proper tools. Basic terms and essential concepts that define what is possible and proper are being missed, or even worse, distorted. Past myth and future hype often weave together, obscuring what actually happened and where we really are now. Some threats are overblown and overreacted to, while others are ignored.

This gap has wide implications. One US general described to us how "understanding cyber is now a command responsibility," as it affects almost every part of modern war. And yet, as another general put it pointedly, "There is a real dearth of doctrine and policy in the world of cyberspace." His concern, as we explore later, was not just the military side needed to do a better job at "cyber calculus," but that the civilian side was not providing any coordination or guidance. Some liken today to the time before World War I, when the militaries of Europe planned to utilize new technologies like railroads. The problem was that they, and the civilian leaders and publics behind them didn't understand the technologies or their implications and so made uninformed decisions that inadvertently drove their nations into war. Others draw parallels to the early years of the Cold War. Nuclear weapons and the political dynamics they drove weren't well understood and, even worse, were largely left to specialists. The result was that notions we now laugh off as Dr. Strangelovian were actually taken seriously, nearly leaving the planet a radioactive hulk.

International relations are already becoming poisoned by this disconnect between what is understood and what is known. While we are both Americans, and thus many of the examples and lessons in this book reflect that background, the "cyber stuff" problem is not just an American concern. We were told the same by officials and experts from places ranging from China and Abu Dhabi to Britain and France. In just one illustration of the global gap, the official assigned to be the "czar" for cybersecurity in Australia had never even heard of Tor, a critical technology to the field and its future (don't worry, you—and hopefully she—will learn what everyone needs to know about Tor in Part II).

This is worrisome not just because of the "naiveté" of such public officials, but because it is actually beginning to have a dangerous impact on global order. For instance, there is perhaps no other relationship as important to the future of global stability as that between the two great powers of the United States and China. Yet, as senior policymakers and general publics on both sides struggle to understand the cyber realm's basic dynamics and implications, the issue of cybersecurity is looming ever larger in US-China relations. Indeed, the Chinese Academy of Military Sciences released a report whose tone effectively captured how suspicion, hype, ignorance, and tension have all begun to mix together into a dangerous brew. "Of late, an Internet tornado has swept across the world...massively impacting and shocking the globe....Faced with this warm-up for an Internet war, every nation and military can't be passive but is making preparations to fight the Internet war."

This kind of language—which is mirrored in the US—doesn't illustrate the brewing global cyber anxiety. It also reveals how confusion and misinformation about the basics of the issue help drive that fear. While both sides, as we explore later on, are active in both cyber offense and defense, it is the very newness of the issue that is proving so difficult. Top American and Chinese governmental leaders talked with us about how they found cybersecurity to be far more challenging than the more traditional concerns between their nations. While they may not agree on issues like trade, human rights, and regional territorial disputes, they at least understand them. Not so for cyber, where they remain woefully ill-equipped even to talk about what their own nation is doing, let alone the other side. For example, a top US official involved in talks with China on cyber issues asked us what an "ISP" was (here again, don't fret if you don't yet know, we'll cover this soon!). If this had been back in the Cold War, that question would be akin to not knowing what an ICBM was in the midst of negotiating with the Soviets on nuclear issues.

Such matters are not just issues for generals or diplomats but also for all citizens. The general lack of understanding on this topic is becoming a democracy problem as well. As we write, there are some fifty cybersecurity bills under consideration in the US Congress, yet the issue is perceived as too complex to matter in the end to voters, and as a result, the elected representatives who will decide the issues on their behalf. This is one of the reasons that despite all these bills no substantive cybersecurity legislation was passed between 2002 and the writing of this book over a decade later.

Again, the technology has evolved so quickly that it is no surprise that most voters and their elected leaders are little engaged on cybersecurity concerns. But they should be. This field connects areas that range from the security of your bank accounts and online identity to broader issues of who in which governments can access your personal secrets and even when and where your nation goes to war. We are all users of this realm and are all shaped by it, yet we are not having any kind of decent public dialogue on it. "We're not having a really good, informed debate," as one professor at the US National Defense University put it. "Instead, we either punt the problem down the road for others to figure out, or to the small number of people who make important policy in the smoky backrooms." And even that is insufficient, given that most people in today's smoky backrooms have never been in an Internet chatroom.

How Did You Write the Book and What Do You Hope to Accomplish?

With all of these issues at play, the timing and value of a book that tried to tackle the basic issues that everyone should know about cybersecurity and cyberwar seemed ideal. And the format of this Oxford series, where all the books are in a "question and answer" style, seemed to hit that sweet spot.

As we set out to research and write the book, this question-and-answer style then structured our methodology. To put it another way, if you are locked into a Q and A format, you better first decide the right set of Qs.

We tried to gather all the key questions that people had about this field, not only those asked by people working in politics or technology, but also from our interactions and interviews well beyond. This set of questions was backed by what would have previously been called a "literature survey." In the old (pre-Internet) days, this meant going to the library and pulling off the shelf all the books in that section of the Dewey decimal system. Today, on this topic especially, the sources range from books to online journals to microblogs. We were also greatly aided by a series of workshops and seminars at Brookings, the think tank in Washington we work at. These gathered key public- and private-sector experts to explore questions ranging from the efficacy of cyber deterrence to what can be done about botnets (all questions later dealt with in the book). We also held a series of meetings and interviews with key American officials and experts. They ranged from top folks like the Chairman of the Joint Chiefs, the highest-ranking US military officer, and the Director of the National Security Agency down to low-ranking systems administrators, from civilian governors, cabinet secretaries, and CEOs to small business owners and teenaged hackers. Our scope was global, and so the meetings also included leaders and experts from China (the foreign minister and generals from the PLA among them), as well as the UK, Canada, Germany, France, Australia, Estonia, United Arab Emirates, and Singapore. Finally, while it is a virtual world, we also visited key facilities and various cybersecurity hubs in locales that ranged from the DC Beltway and Silicon Valley to Paris and Abu Dhabi.

Over the course of this journey, we noticed a pattern. The questions (and the issues that came from them) generally fell under three categories. The first were questions of the essential contours and dynamics of cyberspace and cybersecurity, the "How does it all work?" questions. Think of these as the "driver's ed" part, which gives the basic building blocks to the online world. The second were questions on the broader implications of cybersecurity beyond cyberspace, the "Why does it matter?" questions. And then there were questions on the potential responses, the "What we can do?" questions. The following sections follow this basic structure.

And with the questions laid out, then came the task of answering them. This book is the result. While the questions are diverse, you'll notice that over the course of answering them, a few themes emerged to run through the book:

- *Knowledge matters*: It is vital we demystify this realm if we ever want to get anything effective done in securing it.
- *People matter*: Cybersecurity is one of those "wicked" problem areas that's rife with complexities and trade-offs. This is in

large part not because of the technical side, but because of the people part. The people behind the machines are inherently inside any problem or needed solution.

- *Incentives matter*: If you want to understand why something is or isn't happening in cyberspace, look to the motivations, the costs, and the tensions at play behind the issue. Indeed, anyone claiming a simple "silver bullet" solution in the cyber realm is either ignorant or up to no good.
- *The crowd matters*: This is not a realm where governments can or should have all the answers. Cybersecurity depends on all of us.
- *States matter*: That said, governments' roles are crucial, especially the United States and China. The reason is not just that these two nations remain powerful and influential, but that the interplay of their often differing visions of cybersecurity are critical to the future of both the Internet and world politics.
- *Cats matter*: In the end, the Internet is what we make of it. And that means while serious "stuff" is at play in it, cyberspace is also a fun, often whimsical realm, with memes like dancing babies and keyboard-playing cats. So any treatment of it should be sure to capture that whimsy.

To put it another way, our goal was to wrestle directly with the "cyber stuff" problem that set us on the journey. This is a book written by two researchers, following rigorous academic guidelines, and published by an esteemed university press. But our intent was not a book only for academics. The best research in the world is worthless if it does not find its way into the hands of those who need it. Indeed, the number of academic papers related to cybersecurity has increased at a compound annual growth rate of 20 percent for well over a decade. Yet no one would say that the broader world is all the more informed.

Instead, we embraced this series' core idea of "what everyone needs to know." Everyone does not need to know the software programming secrets of Stuxnet or the legal dynamics of ISP insurance schemes. But as we all become more engaged in and dependent on cybersecurity, there are certain building blocks of understanding that we all need to have. Ignorance is not bliss when it comes to cybersecurity. Cyber issues affect literally everyone: politicians wrestling with everything from cybercrime to online freedom; generals protecting the nation from new forms of attack, while planning new cyberwars; business executives defending firms from once unimaginable threats, and looking to make money off of them; lawyers and ethicists building new frameworks for right and wrong. Most of all, cybersecurity issues affect us as individuals. We face new questions in everything from our rights and responsibilities as citizens of both the online and real world to how to protect ourselves and our families from a new type of danger.

So this is not a book only for experts, but rather a book intended to unlock the field, to raise the general level of expertise, and then push the discussion forward.

We hope that you find the journey useful, and ideally even enjoyable, just like the world of "cyber stuff" itself.

Peter Warren Singer and Allan A. Friedman,
August 2013, Washington, DC

Part I

HOW IT ALL WORKS

The World Wide What? Defining Cyberspace

"It's not a truck. It's a series of tubes."

This is how the late Alaska senator Ted Stevens famously explained cyberspace during a congressional hearing in 2006. As late-night humorist Jon Stewart noted, that someone who doesn't "seem to know jack BLEEP about computers or the Internet...is just the guy in charge of regulating it" is a near-perfect illustration of how disconnected Washington policymakers can be from technological realty.

While it's easy to mock the elderly senator's notion of electronic letters shooting through tubes, the reality is that defining ideas and terms in cyber issues can be difficult. Stevens's "tubes" is actually a mangling of the idea of "pipes," an analogy that is used by experts in the field to describe data connections.

If he wanted to be perfectly accurate, Stevens could have used science-fiction writer William Gibson's original conception of cyberspace. Gibson first used the word, an amalgam of "cybernetics" and "space," in a 1982 short story. He defined it two years later in his genre-revolutionizing novel *Neuromancer* as "A consensual hallucination experienced daily by billions of legitimate operators, in every nation....A graphic representation of data abstracted from the banks of every computer in the human system. Unthinkable complexity. Lines of light ranged in the nonspace of the mind, clusters and constellations of data." Of course, if the senator had described cyberspace that way, most people would have thought him stoned rather than simply disconnected.

Part of why cyberspace is so difficult to define lies not only in its expansive, global nature, but also in the fact that the cyberspace of today is almost unrecognizable compared to its humble beginnings. The US Department of Defense can be considered the godfather of cyberspace, dating back to its funding of early computing and original networks like ARPANET (more on this soon). Yet even the Pentagon has struggled to keep pace as its baby has grown up. Over the years, it has issued at least twelve different definitions of what it thinks of as cyberspace. These range from the "notional environment in which digitized information is communicated over computer networks," which was rejected because it implied cyberspace was only for communication and largely imaginary, to a "domain characterized by the use of electronics and the electromagnetic spectrum," which was also rejected as it encompassed everything from computers and missiles to the light from the sun.

In its latest attempt in 2008, the Pentagon assembled a team of experts who took over a year to agree on yet another definition of cyberspace. This time they termed it "the global domain within the information environment consisting of the interdependent network of information technology infrastructures, including the internet, telecommunications networks, computer systems, and embedded processors and controllers." It is certainly a more detailed definition but so dense that one almost wishes we could go back to just the "tubes."

For the purposes of this book, we think it's best to keep it simple. At its essence, cyberspace is the realm of computer networks (and the users behind them) in which information is stored, shared, and communicated online. But rather than trying to find the exact perfectly worded definition of cyberspace, it is more useful to unpack what these definitions are trying to get at. What are the essential features that not only compose cyberspace, but also make it unique?

Cyberspace is first and foremost an information environment. It is made up of digitized data that is created, stored, and, most importantly, shared. This means that it is not merely a physical place and thus defies measurement in any kind of physical dimension.

But cyberspace isn't purely virtual. It comprises the computers that store data plus the systems and infrastructure that allow it to flow. This includes the Internet of networked computers, closed intranets, cellular technologies, fiber-optic cables, and space-based communications.

While we often use "Internet" as shorthand for the digital world, cyberspace has also come to encompass the people behind those computers and how their connectivity has altered their society. One of the key features, then, of cyberspace is that its systems and technologies are man-made. As such, cyberspace is defined as much by the cognitive realm as by the physical or digital. Perceptions matter, and they inform cyberspace's internal structures in everything from how the names within cyberspace are assigned to who owns which parts of the infrastructure that powers and uses it.

This leads to an important point often misunderstood. Cyberspace may be global, but it is not "stateless" or a "global commons," both terms frequently used in government and media. Just as we humans have artificially divided our globe into territories that we call "nations" and, in turn, our human species into various groups like "nationalities," the same can be done with cyberspace. It relies on physical infrastructure and human users who are tied to geography, and thus is also subject to our human notions like sovereignty, nationality, and property. Or, to put it another way, cyberspace's divisions are as real as the meaningful, but also imaginary, lines that divide the United States from Canada or North from South Carolina.

But cyberspace, like life, is constantly evolving. The hybrid combination of technology and the humans that use it is always changing, inexorably altering everything from cyberspace's size and scale to the technical and political rules that seek to guide it. As one expert put it, "The geography of cyberspace is much more mutable than other environments. Mountains and oceans are hard to move, but portions of cyberspace can be turned on and off with the click of a switch." The essential features remain the same, but the topography is in constant flux. The cyberspace of today is both the same as but also utterly different from the cyberspace of 1982.

The hardware and software that make up cyberspace, for instance, were originally designed for computers operating from fixed wires and telephone lines. Mobile devices were first the stuff of *Star Trek* and then only for the drug dealers on *Miami Vice* who could afford to have something as exotic as a "car phone." Today, a growing percentage of computing is moving onto mobile devices, so much so that we've seen toddlers punch the screens of desktop computers as if they were broken iPads.

Along with the technology of cyberspace, our expectations of it are likewise evolving. This generates new norms of behavior, from how kids "play" to the even more powerful concept that we should all have access to cyberspace and be able to express our personal opinions within it, on everything from a Hollywood star's new hairdo to what we think of an authoritarian leader.

So what constitutes the Internet itself is evolving before us in an even more fundamental way. It is simultaneously becoming massively bigger (each day some 2,500,000,000,000,000,000 bytes are added to the global supply of digital information) and far more personalized. Rather than passively receiving this onslaught of online information, the individual users are creating and tailoring sites to their personal use, ultimately revealing more about themselves online. These sites range from social networks like Facebook in the United States and RenRen in China to microblogs like Twitter and the Chinese equivalents Tencent and Sina. Indeed, microblogs in China (called Weibo) have taken off to the extent that 550 million were registered in 2012.

Thus, while cyberspace was once just a realm of communication and then e-commerce (reaching over $10 trillion a year in sales), it has expanded to include what we call "critical infrastructure." These are the underlying sectors that run our modern-day civilization, ranging from agriculture and food distribution to banking, healthcare, transportation, water, and power. Each of these once stood apart but are now all bound together and linked into cyberspace via information technology, often through what are known as "supervisory control and data acquisition" or SCADA systems. These are the computer systems that monitor, adjust switching, and control other processes of critical infrastructure. Notably, the private sector controls roughly 90 percent of US critical infrastructure, and the firms behind it use cyberspace to, among other things, balance the levels of chlorination in your city's water, control the flow of gas that heats your home, and execute the financial transactions that keep currency prices stable.

Cyberspace is thus evolving from "the nervous system—the control system of our economy," as President George W. Bush once said, into something more. As *Wired* magazine editor Ben Hammersley describes, cyberspace is becoming "the dominant platform for life in the 21st century."

We can bitch about it, but Facebook, Twitter, Google and all the rest are, in many ways the very definition of modern life in the democratic west. For many, a functioning Internet with freedom of speech, and a good connection to the social networks of our choice is a sign not just of modernity, but of civilization itself. This is not because people are "addicted to the video screen," or have some other patronizing psychological diagnosis. But because the Internet is where we live. It's where we do business, where we meet, where we fall in love. It is the central platform for business, culture, and personal relationships. There's not much else left. To misunderstand the centrality of these services to today's society is to make a fundamental error. The Internet isn't a luxury addition to life; for most people, knowingly or not, it is life.

But just as in life, not everyone plays nice. The Internet that we've all grown to love and now need is increasingly becoming a place of risk and danger.

Where Did This "Cyber Stuff" Come from Anyway?
A Short History of the Internet

"Lo."

This was the very first real word transmitted over the computer network that would evolve into the Internet. But rather than the beginning of some profound proclamation like "Lo and behold," "Lo" was instead the product of a system failure. In 1969, researchers at UCLA were trying to log into a computer at the Stanford Research Institute. But before they could type the "g" in the word "log," the computer at the Stanford end of the network crashed. However, the ARPANET project, so named as it was funded by the Advanced Research Projects Agency (ARPA), would eventually transform how computers shared data and, with that, everything else.

Electronic communication networks have been shaping how we share information since the invention of the telegraph, the device that some now look back on and call the "Victorian Internet." The hype around that old technology were similarly high; contemporaries declared that, with the telegraph, "It is impossible that old prejudices and hostilities should longer exist."

What makes the Internet distinct from prior communication networks like the old telegraphs and then telephone networks, however, is that it is packet-switched instead of circuit-switched. Packets are small digital envelopes of data. At the beginning of each packet, essentially the "outside" of the envelope, is the header, which contains details about the network source, destination, and some basic information about the packet contents. By breaking up flows of data into smaller components, each can be delivered in an independent and decentralized fashion, then reassembled at the endpoint. The network routes each packet as it arrives, a dynamic architecture that creates both flexibility and resiliency.

Packet-switching was not developed to allow the United States to maintain communications even in the event of a nuclear attack, a common myth. It was really just developed to better enable more reliable, more efficient connections between computers. Prior to its rise in the 1970s, communication between two computers required a dedicated circuit, or preassigned bandwidth. This direct link meant those resources could not be used by anyone else, even when no data was being transmitted. By breaking these conversations into smaller parts, packets from multiple distinct conversations could share the same network links. It also meant that if one of the network links between two machines went down mid-communication, a transmission could be automatically rerouted with no apparent loss of connection (since there was never a connection to begin with).

ARPA (now DARPA, with a D for "Defense" added) was an organization developed by the Pentagon to avoid technological surprise by leaping ahead in research. Computers were proliferating in the late 1960s, but even more researchers wanted to use them than was available. To ARPA, that meant finding ways to allow people at different institutions to take advantage of unused computer time around the country.

Rather than have dedicated—and expensive—connections between universities, the vision was a network of shared data links, sharing computational resources. Individual machines would each be connected with an Interface Message Processor that handled the actual network connection. This network was ARPANET, home of the first "Lo" and start of the modern cyber era. That first 1969 link from UCLA to Stanford grew to link forty nodes in 1972. Soon more universities and research centers around the world joined this first network, or alternatively created their own networks.

For the purposes of the modern Internet, a series of packets sent between machines on a single network does not count as an "internet." Internet implies connecting many different networks, in this case these various other computer networks beyond ARPANET that soon emerged but remained unlinked.

The challenge was that different networks used very different underlying technology. The technical problem boiled down to abstracting these differences and allowing efficient communication. In 1973, the solution was found. Vint Cerf, then a professor at Stanford, and Robert Khan of ARPA refined the idea of a common transmission protocol. This "protocol" established the expectations that each end of the communication link should make of the other. It began with the computer equivalent of a three-way handshake to establish a connection, continuing through how each party should break apart the messages to be reassembled, and how to control transmission speeds to automatically detect bandwidth availability.

The brilliance of the model is how it breaks the communication into "layers" and allows each layer to function independently. These packets, in turn, can be sent over any type of network, from sound waves to radio waves to light pulses on a glass fiber. Such Transport Control Protocols, or TCPs, could be used over all sorts of packet protocols, but we now use a type called the Internet Protocol, or IP, almost exclusively in the modern Internet.

This protocol enabled the creation of a network of networks. But, of course, the Internet didn't stop there. The new links excelled at connecting machines, but humans excel at making technology conform to their whims. As people shared machines for research, they started leaving messages for each other, simple files that could be edited to form a conversation. This became clunky, and in 1972 Ray Tomlinson at the technical consulting firm BBN wrote a basic program to read, compose, and send messages. This was e-mail: the first Internet "killer app." Within a year, a majority of traffic across the network originally created for research was e-mail. Now networked communication was about people.

The last step in creating the modern Internet was eliminating barriers to entry. Early use was limited to those who had access to the networked computers at research and defense institutions. These organizations communicated via dedicated data lines. As the evident value of networked communication grew and the price of computers dropped, more organizations sought to join. Modems, which convert data to sound waves and back, allowed basic phone lines to serve as links to other computers.

Soon, researchers outside computer science wanted access, not just to take advantage of the shared computing resources, but also to study the new networking technology itself. The US National Science Foundation then connected the existing supercomputering centers around the country into the NSFnet, which grew so rapidly that the expansion required commercial management. Each upgrade brought greater demand, the need for more capacity, and independently organized infrastructure. The architecture of a "backbone" that managed traffic between the different regional networks emerged as the efficient solution.

This period also saw the introduction of the profit motive in Internet expansion. For instance, by this point Vint Cerf had joined the telecommunications firm MCI. In 1983, he led efforts to start MCI mail, the first commercial e-mail service on the Internet. By the late 1980s, it became obvious that managing the nascent Internet was not the business of the research community. Commercial actors could provide the necessary network services supporting the Internet and become avid consumers as well. So the White House Office of Science and Technology developed a plan to expand and commercialize the backbone services, seeing it as the only way that the new Internet could truly take off.

The planners envisioned a decade-long process, though, with the final stages of commercial handover not completed until the late 1990s. Fortunately, a young senator from Tennessee became convinced it should speed up. In 1989, Al Gore authored a bill calling for quicker privatization of the network. While he would later make a slight overstatement that he "took the initiative in creating the Internet," this move by Congress to accelerate things was crucially important to the Internet's expansion. By the time Gore was Vice President in 1994, the NSF was turning over official control of regional backbone connections to private interests.

This privatization coincided with various new inventions and improvements that then democratized and popularized the Internet. In 1990, a researcher at the European research center CERN in Switzerland took a relatively obscure form of presenting information in a set of linked computer documents and built a new networking interface for it. With this HyperText Transfer Protocol (HTTP), and an accompanying system to identify the linked documents (URLs), Tim Berners-Lee "invented" the World Wide Web as we now look at it. Amusingly, when Berners-Lee tried to present it at an academic conference, his breakthrough wasn't considered worthy enough even to make a formal panel. Instead, he was relegated to showing a poster on it in a hallway. A few years later, researchers at the University of Illinois introduced the Mosaic web browser, which simplified both web design and introduced the new practice of "web surfing" for the general public.

And whether we like to admit it or not, this is the period when the pornography industry proved integral to the Internet's history. A darker domain that some estimate makes up 25 percent of all Internet searches, the smut industry drove both new online users and new online uses like instant messaging, chatrooms, online purchasing, streaming video, trading files, and webcams (and the growing demands each of these placed on bandwidth, driving more underlying business). "Of course pornography has played a key role in the Web," says Paul Saffo, an analyst with the Institute for the Future, a Silicon Valley think tank. "Porn is to new media formats what acne is to teenagers," he said. "It's just part of the process of growing up."

And soon the mainstream media started to wake up to the fact that something big was happening online. As the *New York Times* reported in 1994 (in a printed newspaper, of course!), "Increasing commercialization of the Internet will accelerate its transformation away from an esoteric communications system for American computer scientists and into an international system for the flow of data, text, graphics, sound and video among businesses, their customers and their suppliers."

Lo and behold indeed.

How Does the Internet Actually Work?

For a few hours in February 2008, Pakistan held hostage all the world's cute cat videos.

The situation came about when the Pakistani government, in an attempt to prevent its own citizens from accessing what it decided was offensive content, ordered Pakistan Telecom to block access to the video-sharing website YouTube. To do so, Pakistan Telecom falsely informed its customers' computers that the most direct route to YouTube was through Pakistan Telecom and then prevented Pakistani users from reaching the genuine YouTube site. Unfortunately, the company's network shared this false claim of identity beyond its own network, and the false news of the most direct way to YouTube spread across the Internet's underlying mechanisms. Soon over two-thirds of all the world's Internet users were being misdirected to the fake YouTube location, which, in turn, overwhelmed Pakistan Telecom's own network.

The effects were temporary, but the incident underscores the importance of knowing how the Internet works. The best way to gain this understanding is to walk through how information gets from one place to another in the virtual world. It's a bit complex, but we'll do our best to make it easy.

Suppose you wanted to visit the informative and—dare we say—entertaining website of the Brookings Institution, the think tank where we work. In essence, you have asked your device to talk to a computer controlled by Brookings in Washington, DC. Your machine must learn where that computer is and establish a connection to enable communication.

The first thing your computer needs to know is how to find the servers that host the Brookings web page. To do that, it will use the Internet Protocol (IP) number that serves as the address for endpoints on the Internet. Your machine was most likely automatically assigned an IP address by your Internet service provider or whatever network you are using. It also knows the address of its router, or the path to the broader Internet. Finally, your computer knows the address of a Domain Name System server.

The Domain Name System, or DNS, is the protocol and infrastructure through which computers connect domain names (human memorable names like Brookings.edu) to their corresponding IP addresses (machine data like 192.245.194.172). The DNS is global and decentralized. Its architecture can be thought of as a tree. The "root" of the tree serves as the orientation point for the Domain Name System. Above that are the top-level domains. These are the country codes such as .uk, as well as other domains like .com and .net. Each of these top-level domains is then subdivided. Many countries have specific second-level domains, such as co.uk and ac.uk, to denote business and academic institutions, respectively.

Entry into the club of top-level domains is controlled internationally through the Internet Corporation for Assigned Names and Numbers (ICANN), a private, nonprofit organization created in 1998 to run the various Internet administration and operations tasks that had previously been performed by US government organizations.

Each top-level domain is run by a registry that sets its own internal policies about domains. Organizations, such as Brookings or Apple or the US Department of State, acquire their domains through intermediaries called registrars. These registrars coordinate with each other to ensure the domain names in each top-level domain remain unique. In turn, each domain manages its own subdomains, such as mail.yahoo.com.

To reach the Brookings domain, your computer will query the DNS system through a series of resolvers. The basic idea is to go up the levels of the tree. Starting with the root, it will be pointed to the record for .edu, which is managed by Educause. Educause is the organization of some 2,000 educational institutions that maintains the list of every domain registered in .edu. From this list, your computer will then learn the specific IP address of Brookings's internal name server. This will allow it to address specific queries about content or applications from inside the Brookings domain. Then, the Brookings name server will direct your computer to the specific content it is looking for, by returning the IP address of the machine that hosts it.

In reality, this process is a little more complex. For example, servers often store data locally in caches for future use, so that every query does not have to go to the root, and the protocol includes specific error conditions to handle errors predictably. The rough outline above, however, gives a sense of how it all works.

Now that your computer has the location of the data, how will that data get to your computer? The server at Brookings needs to know that it should send data to your machine, and the data needs to get there. Figure 1.1 illustrates how your computer requests a web page by breaking down the request into packets and sending them across the Internet. First, at the "layer" of the application, your browser interprets the click of your mouse as a command in the HyperText Transfer Protocol (HTTP), which defines how to ask for and deliver content. This command is then passed down to the transport and network layers. Transport is responsible for breaking the data down into packet-sized chunks and making sure that all of

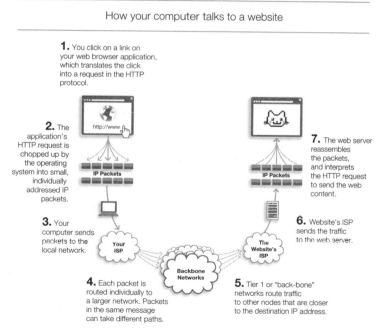

How your computer talks to a website

1. You click on a link on your web browser application, which translates the click into a request in the HTTP protocol.

2. The application's HTTP request is chopped up by the operating system into small, individually addressed IP packets.

IP Packets

3. Your computer sends packets to the local network.

4. Each packet is routed individually to a larger network. Packets in the same message can take different paths.

Your ISP

Backbone Networks

7. The web server reassembles the packets, and interprets the HTTP request to send the web content.

IP Packets

6. Website's ISP sends the traffic to the web server.

The Website's ISP

5. Tier 1 or "back-bone" networks route traffic to other nodes that are closer to the destination IP address.

Figure 1.1

the chunks arrive free of error and reassembled in the correct order for the application layer above. The network layer is responsible for trying its best to navigate the packets across the Internet. If you think of the data you are trying to send and receive as a package of information, the transport layer is responsible for packing and receiving the packages, while the network is responsible for moving them from source to destination. Once at the destination, the packets are reassembled, checked, and then passed back up to the application—in this case, a web server sending you the web content you requested.

But how do the packets know how to get across the Internet to their destination? Like the DNS that helped your computer find the website it was looking for, the organization of Internet networks can be thought of as a hierarchy. Each computer is part of a network, like the network connecting all the customers of an Internet service provider (ISP). ISPs are essentially the organizations that provide access to the Internet, as well as other related services like e-mail or hosting websites. Most ISPs are private, for-profit companies, including a number of the traditional telephone and cable TV firms that began offering Internet access when the field took off, while others are government or community owned.

Those networks, in turn, form nodes called Autonomous Systems (AS) in the global Internet. Autonomous Systems define the architecture of Internet connections. Traffic is routed locally through the AS and controlled by the policies of that organization. Each AS has a set of contiguous blocks of IP addresses and forms the "home" for these destinations. All have at least one connection to another AS, while large ISPs might have many. So routing to a particular IP address is simply a matter of finding its AS.

There's a problem, though: The Internet is big. There are over 40,000 AS nodes on the Internet today, and their interconnections are changing and shifting over time. Given this scale, a global approach to routing everything the same way is impossible.

Instead, the Internet uses a dynamic, distributed system that does not maintain a permanent vision of what the network looks like at any given time. The principle of routing is fairly simple: at each point in the network, a router looks at the address of an incoming packet. If the destination is inside the network, it keeps the packet and sends it to the relevant computer. Otherwise, it consults a routing table to determine the best next step to send the packet closer to its destination.

The devil is in the details of this routing table's construction. Since there is no global address book, the nodes in the network have to share key information with other routers, like which IP addresses they are responsible for and what other networks they can talk to. This process happens separately from the Internet routing process on what is known as the "control plane." Routers also pass along information to their neighbors, sharing up-to-date news about the state of the network and who can talk to whom. Each router then constructs its own internal, temporary model of how best to route the traffic coming through. This new model, in turn, is shared so that a router's neighbors now know how it will pass along new traffic.

If this sounds complex, it's because it is! In just a few pages, we've summed up what it took decades of computer science research to create. The takeaway for cybersecurity is that the entire system is based on trust. It is a system that works efficiently, but it can be broken, either by accident or by maliciously feeding the system bad data.

The Pakistan example shows what happens when that trust is abused. The government censors "broke the Internet" by falsely claiming to have direct access to the IP address that serves YouTube. This was a narrow, local, politically motivated announcement. But because of how the Internet works, soon every ISP in Asia was trying to route all their YouTube traffic to Pakistan, solely because they believed it was closer than the real intended destination. The models they were building were based on false information. As more networks did this, their neighbors also came to believe that YouTube was the Pakistani IP address. The whole mess wasn't resolved until Google engineers advertised the correct routes aggressively across the network.

In sum, understanding the Internet's basic decentralized architecture provides two insights for cybersecurity. It offers an appreciation of how the Internet functions without top-down coordination. But it also shows the importance of the Internet's users and gatekeepers behaving properly, and how certain built-in choke points can create great vulnerabilities if they don't.

Who Runs It? Understanding Internet Governance

In 1998, a computer researcher and a respected leader in the networking community named Jon Postel sent an innocuous sounding e-mail to eight people. He asked them to reconfigure their servers so that they would direct their Internet traffic using his computer at the University of Southern California rather than a computer in Herndon, Virginia. They did so without question, as Postel (who had been part of the team that set up the original ARPANET) was an icon in the field, who served as a primary administrator for the network's naming system.

With that one e-mail, Postel committed the first coup d'état of the Internet. The people he had e-mailed ran eight of the twelve organizations that controlled all the name servers—the computers ultimately responsible for translating a domain name such as "Brookings.edu" into a computer-addressable IP address. And the computer in Virginia that he had steered two-thirds of the Internet's root servers away from was controlled by the US government. While Postel would later say he had only seized control of a majority of the Internet's root servers as a "test," others think that he did so in protest, showing the US government "that it couldn't wrest control of the Internet from the widespread community of researchers who had built and maintained the network over the previous three decades."

Postel's "coup" illustrates the crucial role of governance issues even for a technical space. As the Internet has grown from a small research network to the global underpinning of our digital society, questions of who runs it have become more and more important. Or, as Eric Schmidt (who went on to become the CEO of a little firm known as Google) told a 1997 programmers conference in San Francisco, "The Internet is the first thing that humanity has built that humanity doesn't understand, the largest experiment in anarchy that we have ever had."

Since digital resources are not "scarce" like traditional resources, its governance questions are a bit different. That is, the main questions of Internet governance are of interoperability and communication rather than the classic issue of distribution, which has consumed political thinkers from Socrates to Marx. However, even in a digital world of seemingly endless resources, traditional issues of governance also arise in cyberspace, including representation, power, and legitimacy.

Key decision chokepoints revolve around the technical standards for interoperability, the distribution of IP numbers that gives computers an address allowing them to send and receive packets, and the management of the Internet's naming system. Interestingly enough, it is this final category, the intersection of the technical and nontechnical aspect of naming, that has produced the most conflict.

The operations of the Internet require independent actors to follow basic rules that guarantee interoperability, known as standards. This standards-based approach goes back to the beginning of the Internet, when the engineers building the initial systems published Requests For Comments (RFCs) to seek feedback on proposed standards. Over time, this group of network engineers and researchers grew into an international, voluntary standards organization called the Internet Engineering Task Force (IETF). The IETF develops new Internet standards and protocols and modifies existing ones for better performance. Everything developed by the IETF falls under specific working groups that concentrate on areas like routing, applications, and infrastructure. These groups are open forums that work mostly through mailing lists, and anyone is welcome to participate. Many of the individuals in them are from large technology firms, but no one actor or small party can steamroll the process, which relies on consensus.

Openness, and even a sense of whimsy, is critical to the culture of the IETF. In some working group meetings, the members decide on an issue by humming for or against a proposal. The proposal with the loudest hum advantage wins. While it sounds a bit silly, it is seen as a way of maintaining the original Internet creators' ethic of fostering consensus and reaching decisions relatively quickly. The volume of the humming also helps maintain a level of anonymity, unless you abuse the system: That is, you can hum or not without opening your mouth, but it's hard to hum louder to dominate a vote without being too obvious about it, which would cause backlash.

Despite the sense of fun that can drive working groups members, security is a principle concern in the system. In addition to working groups focused on particular security issues, every proposed standard must have an explicit "Security Considerations" section. Additionally, a security directorate reviews all proposed standards passed from the working groups to the Steering Group.

While the IETF has no official board or formal leadership, the Internet Engineering Steering Group (IESG) offers oversight and guidance for both the standards process and the standards themselves. In turn, the Internet Architecture Board (IAB), which evolved from the technical advisory board of the original ARPANET management in the early 1970s, offers further oversight of the IESG.

Both of these organizations fall under the auspices of the Internet Society, or ISOC, an international group formed in 1992 that oversees most of the technical standards process. The ISOC came about when Internet governance moved beyond just matters of technical coordination. As the web went global and companies began to depend on Internet business, more and more participants had a financial or political stake in the system's evolution in one direction or another. Organizations began to disagree on process, and the US government's central involvement worried many. The ISOC was established as an independent, international organization to offer a formal, legal means to safeguard the independent and open standards processes. ISOC's power derives from its membership; it's open to any individual and, for a fee, any organization. These members then elect trustees who, in turn, appoint leadership to the IAB, which oversees the governance process for the IESG and the working groups' process they guide.

Imagine this alphabet soup all as a mix of informal, semiformal, and formal groups all nested together. This structure promotes a high degree of independence while still allowing for accountability to the Internet community. While there are political and financially motivated disagreements, when it comes to standards development, the process has thus far fostered globally shared interest in maintaining a functioning Internet.

This ethic of shared interest, however, becomes more difficult in dealing with property rights and other scarce resources on the Internet. The Internet may be seemingly infinite in size, but it still has zero-sum games. Identifiers such as IP addresses and domains have to be unique—the Internet wouldn't work if multiple parties attempted to use the same IP address or wanted to resolve a domain name to a competing address. One of the earliest oversight roles was apportioning these numbers and names. What emerged was the Internet Assigned Numbers Authority, a collaborative effort of the US government and the early researchers who had developed the original technology. Yet as the Internet grew, control of this process grew more important. Assigning names and numbers meant control over who could access the Internet and how. Jon Postel's "coup" illustrated the need for a more transparent and accessible governance structure.

The growing pressure for a commercial Internet, and the emerging realization that Americans could not expect to control the network forever, meant that this new structure could not be run by the US government. In 1998, after a survey period that sought input from the public and key Internet leaders and organizations, responsibility shifted to an independent corporation with a governance structure that "reflects the geographical and functional diversity of the Internet." The Internet Corporation for Assigned Names and Numbers, or ICANN, was born.

While chartered in California as a nonprofit, ICANN set in motion a structured way to distribute IP addresses that more appropriately reflected the Internet's global nature. Regional authorities in North America, Europe, and Asia, followed later by Latin America and finally Africa in 2004, took over this task and continue to perform this role today.

Not everything with ICANN is easy. Domains define identity on the Internet, which brings strong commercial and political interests into conflict. Decisions about who gets what Internet identity inherently create winners and losers; adding new top-level domains such as .tech enables new business models but requires more expense for trademark protection to fend off "squatters." Trademarks themselves can pose risks. For example, a process was needed to decide which of the many businesses with "Apple" in their name would get apple.com. At the same time, that process could not be corrupted to deny free speech opportunities, such as <insert whatever trademark name you dislike>sucks.com. This process has even touched on hot issues of national identity. When nations achieve independence or dissolve into civil war, who controls their country's top-level domain? In Western Sahara, both sides of a forty-year-old conflict claim the rights to the top-level domain .eh.

The process and governance of ICANN have drawn even more controversy. Policy scholars use the term "multi-stakeholder process" to describe its organic, open, yet non-representative approach.

Decisions are supposed to be made by consensus, while a host of advisory committees help represent key constituencies in the Internet's smooth operations, such as Internet service providers and the intellectual property community. National interests from around the world are represented through a Governmental Advisory Committee. Yet this multi-stakeholder model strikes some as disposed to favor the powerful. Governments and large commercial interests can afford to pay staff to participate in these forums, while nonprofit civil society groups may lack the resources to sit at the table at all. Many argue that special interests are too heavily represented among the decision-makers. Others want it to be more like traditional international organizations, which tend to follow the United Nations model of "one state, one vote."

And despite efforts to globalize Internet governance, many still see ICANN as captive to US interests. The control of assigning names and numbers still ostensibly belongs to the US Department of Commerce, which it delegates to ICANN by renewable contract. That is, the United States retains overall control, while the management function is held by an industry-led organization. Both have a vested interest in maintaining the status quo.

The challenge, of course, is that no other institution or process could easily replace ICANN. While it is easy to criticize ICANN, there is no practical model for an alternative organization that must represent and balance such a broad range of interests from around the world and across all sides of complex policy issues.

The key takeaway of these governance issues for cybersecurity is not just the important role that trust and open-mindedness have played in the Internet's growth (aspects that are challenged by growing security concerns) but that the Internet has always been recognized as a space that defies traditional governance models. In 1992, Internet pioneer David Clark of MIT set out his bold dictum for the community:

> We reject: kings, presidents and voting.
> We believe in: rough consensus and running code.

This quote has been widely circulated. Less well known is what Clark wrote on his very next slide: "What are we bad at? Growing our process to match our size."

On the Internet, How Do They Know Whether You Are a Dog? Identity and Authentication

Carnegie Mellon University professor Alessandor Acquisti has a fun but scary party trick: show him a picture of your face that is online and he will then guess your Social Security number.

Understanding how Acquisti does this is useful even for non-Americans (who lack these supposedly secret Social Security numbers) because it illustrates the story of identity and authentication and how it can go awry. Acquisti first uses image-matching technology to find your face on a social networking website. If your birthdate and birth city are listed online, as they are for most people, then he can use the patterns that link time and location to the first five of the nine numbers in your Social Security number. Then it is just a numbers guessing game for the remaining digits. If you come from a small state like Delaware, the Social Security number can be determined in less than 10 tries.

In theory, no one should care, since Social Security numbers were never meant to be secret. Before 1972, Social Security cards even said "not for identification" on them. But as we began to use computers to track people, it became critical for computers to differentiate individuals. Using someone's name alone wasn't enough: there are too many John Smiths in the world. Across every database, each record needed to be accessed with some identifier unique to that person. And since every American had a unique Social Security number, it was convenient to use that.

So far, so good. The number was just a means to look someone up in a computer. But this number also became the way for two systems to know they were talking about the same person. Soon the Social Security number began to be used to track bank accounts, tax details, and all other sorts of personal information. Along the way, organizations assumed that, since Social Security numbers weren't published, they weren't public, and if they weren't public, they must be secret. Wrong.

In the computer world, "identification" is the act of mapping an entity to some information about that entity. This can be as mundane as a fantasy football website accepting the association between a person and the name the person claims, or as critical as matching a medical record to an unconscious patient.

It is important to separate identification from "authentication," which is the proof of the identification. This proof has traditionally been defined as "something you know, something you have, or something you are." What you "know" is the basic password model. It is a secret that is known, presumably only by the right person. Something you "have" refers to a physical component with limited access, so that only the right person might have it. With bank ATMs, it is a card, while more recently the mobile phone has become a de facto authenticator for receiving text messages containing a one-time code. By entering this one-time code, people taking action on the Web show that they have control of the verified mobile phone that is receiving the messages. Finally, you can prove who you "are" through something recognizable. Since this often refers to one's person, we call this a "biometric." Biometrics can be as simple as another human recognizing your face or as sophisticated as a sensor that recognizes your eye's retina.

There are weaknesses with these proofs. Passwords can be guessed or broken and require a cognitive load (you have to memorize them). If they are reused across different contexts, then breaking one system allows an attacker into others. Things that you "have" can be stolen or forged. And even biometrics can be compromised. For instance, access readers that require supposedly unique fingerprints have been fooled by forged fingerprints pressed into Gummy Bear candy, or, much more gruesomely, pressing down an amputated finger onto the machine (Russian mobsters ironically don't seem to like cute, bear-shaped candy).

There are various mechanisms to bolster these measures. One is to contact trusted friends to confirm that individuals are who they say they are. The idea is drawn from the old line "It's all about who you know," since a mutually trusted friend can verify that the individual in question conforms to the claimed identity. Other systems factor in the cost of fooling the controls. Anyone can create a website claiming a specific identity, but it requires time and effort to maintain an active and lengthy presence on an associated social media platform like Twitter or Facebook. Here again, these can be hacked or faked, but at a much greater cost to the attacker to pull off.

After authentication is authorization. Now that a system knows who you are, what can you do? In classic computer security, authorization was about giving access to network files, but in our increasingly connected world, gaining authorization can open the doors to practically everything. Authorization is the part that links these technical issues to policy, business, political and moral questions. Is the individual authorized to buy something, like an account on an online gambling site? And even if so, is the individual old enough to participate? Or, at a slightly larger world stage, just because someone has access to a military's classified networks, should the person be authorized to read and copy every file in them (a practice that would haunt the US military in the Bradley Manning and Edward Snowden leaks)?

The entire problem was perhaps best illustrated by one of the most cited cartoons in history. In 1993, *New Yorker* magazine published a drawing by Peter Steiner of two dogs sitting near a computer. One dog tells the other, "On the Internet, nobody knows you're a dog."

Yet this isn't to say that people can't find out private details about you if they want. Every activity on the Internet is data being routed from an Internet Protocol (IP) address. As we saw in the prior section, an IP address is a numerical label that is assigned to an addressable connection in the Internet. For most consumers, the IP address is not permanently assigned to their device. Instead, the IP address will be dynamic. The consumer's Internet service provider will assign an IP address for a period of time, but it might be reassigned to someone else after the consumer disconnects. However, if an Internet service provider retains the relevant data, it is able to correlate the IP address at a specific date and time to a particular service subscriber.

An IP address is not in and of itself information about an identifiable individual. But it can provide some information about the geographic location and the means by which that individual accesses the Internet. It is the potential for how the IP address can be combined with other information (or could be reasonably combined with other information) that has privacy advocates concerned. If you can combine enough of this online and offline information, you might have enough data to make a high-probability guess about who was doing what and where. For instance, in the 2012 scandal that enveloped CIA director General David Petraeus, the FBI was able to backtrack the anonymous sender of a series of threatening e-mails to the business center of a hotel that his mistress turned out to be staying at.

The information gathered about identity is not the same as proof of identity. Relying on the IP address would be like relying on license plates to identify drivers. A sophisticated user can easily hide or disguise her IP address by routing her activities through another point on the Internet, making it appear that that node was responsible for the original traffic. There are, however, many other types of data that can be collected that are harder to hide. Even the patterns of how individual users browse and click through a website can be used to identify them.

This question of how *can* we identify and authenticate online activities is a different question from how *should* we. You may not have wanted your Social Security number to be revealed at a party. Or that dog might have preferred its identity remain secret, at least until the two of you had gone out on a few more online dates.

For the purposes of cybersecurity, the bottom line is that digital identity is a balance between protecting and sharing information. Limiting acquired information is not only good for privacy, it can prevent others from gaining information for more sophisticated authentication fraud. At the same time, each system has incentives to maximize the amount of data it collects, as well as use that data for its own goals.

What Do We Mean by "Security" Anyway?

There's an old joke in the security industry about how to secure any computer: Just unplug it.

The problem is not only that the joke is becoming outdated in an era of wireless and rechargeable devices, but once a machine is plugged in, there are practically an infinite number of ways its use might deviate from its intended purpose. This deviation is a malfunction. When the difference between the expected behavior and actual behavior is caused by an adversary (as opposed to simple error or accident), then the malfunction is a "security" problem.

Security isn't just the notion of being free from danger, as it is commonly conceived, but is associated with the presence of an adversary. In that way, it's a lot like war or sex; you need at least two sides to make it real. Things may break and mistakes may be made, but a cyber problem only becomes a cybersecurity issue if an adversary seeks to gain something from the activity, whether to obtain private information, undermine the system, or prevent its legitimate use.

To illustrate, in 2011 the Federal Aviation Administration ordered nearly half of US airspace shut down and more than 600 planes grounded. It seemed like a repeat of how American airspace was shut down after the 9/11 attacks. But this incident wasn't a security issue, as there was no one behind it. The cause was a software glitch in a single computer at the Atlanta headquarters building. Take the same situation and change the glitch to a hack: that's a security issue.

The canonical goals of security in an information environment result from this notion of a threat. Traditionally, there are three goals: Confidentiality, Integrity, Availability, sometimes called the "CIA triad."

Confidentiality refers to keeping data private. Privacy is not just some social or political goal. In a digital world, information has value. Protecting that information is thus of paramount importance. Not only must internal secrets and sensitive personal data be safeguarded, but transactional data can reveal important details about the relationships of firms or individuals. Confidentiality is supported by technical tools such as encryption and access control as well as legal protections.

Integrity is the most subtle but maybe the most important part of the classic information security triumvirate. Integrity means that the system and the data in it have not been improperly altered or changed without authorization. It is not just a matter of trust. There must be confidence that the system will be both available and behave as expected.

Integrity's subtlety is what makes it a frequent target for the most sophisticated attackers. They will often first subvert the mechanisms that try to detect attacks, in the same way that complex diseases like HIV-AIDS go after the human body's natural defenses. For instance, the Stuxnet attack (which we explore later in Part II) was so jarring because the compromised computers were telling their Iranian operators that they were functioning normally, even as the Stuxnet virus was sabotaging them. How can we know whether a system is functioning normally if we depend on that system to tell us about its current function?

Availability means being able to use the system as anticipated. Here again, it's not merely the system going down that makes availability a security concern; software errors and "blue screens of death" happen to our computers all the time. It becomes a security issue when and if someone tries to exploit the lack of availability in some way. An attacker could do this either by depriving users of a system that they depend on (such as how the loss of GPS would hamper military units in a conflict) or by merely threatening the loss of a system, known as a "ransomware" attack. Examples of such ransoms range from small-scale hacks on individual bank accounts all the way to global blackmail attempts against gambling websites before major sporting events like the World Cup and Super Bowl.

Beyond this classic CIA triangle of security, we believe it is important to add another property: resilience. Resilience is what allows a system to endure security threats instead of critically failing. A key to resilience is accepting the inevitability of threats and even limited failures in your defenses. It is about remaining operational with the understanding that attacks and incidents happen on a continuous basis. Here again, there is a parallel to the human body. Your body still figures out a way to continue functioning even if your external layer of defense—your skin—is penetrated by a cut or even bypassed by an attack like a viral infection. Just as in the body, in the event of a cyber incident, the objective should be to prioritize resources and operations, protect key assets and systems from attacks, and ultimately restore normal operations.

All of these aspects of security are not just technical issues: they are organizational, legal, economic, and social as well. But most importantly, when we think of security we need to recognize its limits. Any gain in security always involves some sort of trade-off. Security costs money, but it also costs time, convenience, capabilities, liberties, and so on. Similarly, as we explore later on, the different threats to confidentiality, availability, integrity, and resiliency each require different responses. Short of pulling the plug, there's no such thing as absolute security.

What Are the Threats?

It sounds odd that reporters took a passenger jet to Idaho just to watch a cyberattack, but that's exactly what happened in 2011.

Worried that the public did not understand the magnitude of growing cyberthreats, the Department of Homeland Security flew journalists from around the country to the Idaho National Laboratory. Only four years earlier, the INL, an incredibly secure and secretive facility that houses a Department of Energy's nuclear research facility, had conducted a top-secret test to destroy a large generator via cyberattack. In 2011, in an effort to raise awareness about cyberthreats, government experts not only declassified a video of the 2007 test, but held a public exercise for journalists to "watch" a faked cyberattack on a mock chemical plant. The government wanted to show that even their own experts couldn't prevent a team of hired hackers (known as a "red team") from overwhelming the defenses of a critical facility.

This episode is a good illustration of how those who professionally think and talk about cybersecurity worry that their discussions of threats are ignored or downplayed. Frustrated, the result is that they resort to turning the volume up to the proverbial 11 à la *Spinal Tap*, conducting outlandish exercises and only talking about the matter in the most extreme ways that then echo out into the media and public. Indeed, following a series of warnings by US government officials, by 2013 there were over half a million online references in the media to "cyber Pearl Harbor" and another quarter million to a feared "cyber 9/11."

The complacency these experts worry about stems in part from our political system's reluctance to address difficult, complex problems in general, and cybersecurity in particular. But this kind of tenor also feeds into a misunderstanding of the threats. For example, three US senators sponsored a large cybersecurity bill in the summer of 2011, and so wrote an op-ed in the *Washington Post* urging support for their legislation. They cited a series of recent, high-profile attacks, including those against the Citigroup and RSA companies and the Stuxnet worm's attack on Iranian nuclear research. The problem is that these three cases reflected wildly different threats. The Citigroup attack was about financial fraud. The RSA attack was industrial theft, and Stuxnet was a new form of warfare. They had little in common other than they involved computers.

When discussing cyber incidents or fears of potential incidents, it is important to separate the idea of vulnerability from threat. An unlocked door is a vulnerability but not a threat if no one wants to enter. Conversely, one vulnerability can lead to many threats: that unlocked door could lead to terrorists sneaking in a bomb, competitors walking out with trade secrets, thieves purloining valuable goods, local hooligans vandalizing property, or even cats wandering in and distracting your staff by playing on the keyboards. The defining aspects of threats are the actor and the consequence.

The acknowledgment of an actor forces us to think strategically about threats. The adversary can pick and choose which vulnerability to exploit for any given goal. This implies that we must not only address a range of vulnerabilities with respect to any given threat, but also understand that the threat may evolve in response to our defensive actions.

There are many kinds of bad actors, but it is too easy to get lulled into using media clichés like "hackers" to lump them all together. An actor's objective is a good place to start when parceling them out. In the variety of attacks cited by the senators above, the Citigroup attackers wanted account details about bank customers with an ultimate goal of financial theft. In the attack on RSA, the attackers wanted key business secrets in order to spy on other companies. For Stuxnet (a case we'll explore further in Part II), the attackers wanted to disrupt industrial control processes involved in uranium enrichment, so as to sabotage the Iranian nuclear program.

Finally, it is useful to acknowledge when the danger comes from one of your own. As cases like Bradley Manning and WikiLeaks or Edward Snowden and the NSA scandal illustrate, the "insider threat" is particularly tough because the actor can search for vulnerabilities from within systems designed only to be used by trusted actors. Insiders can have much better perspectives on what is valuable and how best to leverage that value, whether they are trying to steal secrets or sabotage an operation.

It is also important to consider whether the threat actor wants to attack *you*, or just wants to attack. Some attacks target specific actors for particular reasons, while other adversaries go after a certain objective regardless of who may control it. Untargeted malicious code could, for example, infect a machine via e-mail, search for stored credit card details of anyone, and relay those details back to its master without any human involvement. The key difference in these automated attacks is one of cost, both from the attacker's and the defender's perspective. For the attacker, automation hugely reduces cost, as they don't have to invest in all the tasks needed, from selecting the victim to identifying the asset to coordinating the attack. Their attack costs roughly the same no matter how many victims they get. A targeted attack, on the other hand, can quickly scale up in costs as the number of victims rises. These same dynamics shape the expected returns. To be willing to invest in targeted attacks, an attacker must have a higher expected return value with each victim. By contrast, automated attacks can have much lower profit margins.

The good news is that there are only three things you can do to a computer: steal its data, misuse credentials, and hijack resources. Unfortunately, our dependence on information systems means that a skilled actor could wreak a lot of damage by doing any one of those. Stolen data can reveal the strategic plans of a country or undermine the competitiveness of an entire industry. Stolen credentials can give the ability to change or destroy code and data, changing payrolls or opening up dams, as well as the ability to cover tracks. Hijacking resources can prevent a company from reaching customers or deny an army the ability to communicate.

In the end, there are many things that can happen, but they have to be caused by someone. Threats should be assessed by understanding potential bad actors, what they are trying to do, and why.

And you shouldn't need to fly all the way to Idaho to learn that.

One Phish, Two Phish, Red Phish, Cyber Phish: What Are Vulnerabilities?

In 2011, London police confronted a mysterious and unusual spike in car thefts. The odd thing wasn't just that so many cars were being stolen, over 300 in all, but that the cars were all of a particular brand, new BMWs. And, second, the thieves were somehow stealing hundreds of cars equipped with some of the most advanced car security systems in the world, without activating the alarms.

What the police soon figured out by watching hidden security camera footage of the thieves in action was that the robbers had figured out how to use the car's advanced technology against itself. First, they used radio frequency jammers to block the signal of a car's electronic key. Instead of the car owner locking the doors as they walked away, the doors would remain unlocked. Once in the car, the thief would then plug into the OBD-II connector (the electronic port that mechanics use to diagnose your car's problems) and then use that to obtain the car's unique key fob digital ID. Next, the thief would reprogram a blank electronic key to correspond with the car's ID. Then they simply drove away, with the owner of the advanced luxury car none the wiser. It all took only a few minutes. These vulnerabilities led to so many thefts that police resorted to leaving paper leaflets on all BMWs parked in London warning them of the danger.

The case of the lost luxury cars is a good illustration of how building a complex system can create new openings and hidden vulnerabilities that bad guys can try to exploit. Different vulnerabilities allow an attacker to achieve different goals. In some cases, it might be the ability to read confidential data. Or the goal could be the ultimate prize—compromise of the entire system. When the attacker has such "root access," the ability to execute any command, the victim is completely vulnerable, or what hackers call "pwned" (An apocryphal story is that a hacker meant to type that a target was now "owned." But he typed too fast, mistakenly hit the *p* key right next to the *o*, and a cool term was born.)

Often the easiest way to gain control of the system is simply to ask. A time-honored tradition for breaking into systems from hacking's early days is to call up a low-level employee, claim to be from technical support, and ask for the person's password. This falls into the category of what is known as "social engineering," manipulating people into revealing confidential information and thereby helping the attacker. The manipulation can take many forms, often with the attacker trying to set up a scenario designed to encourage cooperation through psychological mechanisms. Fear is a powerful motivator. When a user's computer displays a message threatening to expose activities on a pornographic website, fear of exposure can motivate payment. More often, however, users just follow social cues. In our daily lives, we regularly encounter problems that need fixing, like a program that won't close until you just "click here," or people who need our help, like your Aunt Suzy who somehow got robbed in Iceland and needs you to wire her money via Bangkok.

A particularly common form of social engineering is the "phishing" attack. Phishing e-mails look like official e-mails from the victim's bank, employer, or some other trusted entity. They claim to require some action by the victim, perhaps to correct an account error or see a message on Facebook, and fool victims into visiting a web page where they are asked to enter their credentials. If the victim enters his or her account details, the attacker can now do anything with that information, from transfer money to read confidential e-mails. The phony credentials web page may have a URL that looks similar to the authentic one. If you don't look closely, maybe www.paypai.com looks like www.paypal.com. In sophisticated phishing attacks, the fake page may also actually log the user into the real website to minimize the chance of detection.

One of the most challenging subsets of these "phishing" attacks is known as "spear phishing." These target not just networks but key individuals inside those networks. It's the difference between you, along with scores of others people, receiving an e-mail from that kind Nigerian prince who just needs your bank account information, versus receiving an e-mail that looks exactly like it's from your mother. This is a good illustration of the difference between the automated and targeted threats you read about in the last section. Such specialized attacks require prior intelligence gathering to figure out how to trick a particular person and are mostly reserved for prime targets.

Attackers also prey on systems that have ignored basic precautions, such as products that have default login names and passwords, which users often forget to change. Most home wireless routers have default passwords that a shocking number of users leave in place. Find the right one and it is easy to steal a neighbor's Wi-Fi and eavesdrop on their conversations. This kind of vulnerability can also be created by product manufacturers that don't prioritize security enough or fail to factor in the likely human errors and even laziness of their customers. For instance, Microsoft's database product MS-SQL 2005 shipped without an administrator password, so that any user could control the entire database until an admin password was set. Other situations involve systems that have features that may be convenient but represent real security vulnerabilities, like that of the BMW remote access keys.

Applications can also create vulnerabilities if they are misconfigured. In one study, researchers at Dartmouth searched peer-to-peer file-sharing services, where users share specific files from their own computers with others, usually entertainment files like movies or TV shows. Because of misconfigured settings, in addition to users sharing episodes of *Game of Thrones*, a large number also had unintentionally shared personal bank statements and tax documents. A similar study found that large financial institutions were unintentionally leaking highly sensitive internal documents through misconfigured applications.

Another vector is mistakes in the systems themselves—software vulnerabilities—that are exploited by more advanced attackers. It is practically impossible to build a modern IT system without some hidden vulnerabilities waiting to be discovered. Modern operating systems have millions of lines of code and have hundreds of sub-components that interact. An attacker's goal is to find some chink in the armor of this code, where the system does not behave precisely as designed and exploit that weakness. An attack that exploits a pre-viously unknown vulnerability is known as a "zero day." The term comes from the notion that the attacks take places on the zeroth day of the awareness that the rest of the world has of these vulnerability and thus before a patch to fix it can be implemented.

There are different types of vulnerabilities with different ways of exploiting them, but a common approach is to find some way of tricking the victim's computer into executing the attacker's com-mands rather than the intended program's. A key is that most com-puter systems treat data as both information to be processed and commands to be executed. This principle is foundational to the very idea of the modern computer, but also a major source of insecurity. A good illustration is a SQL (pronounced "sequel") injection, one of the most common ways a website is attacked. Many web appli-cations are built on Structured Query Language (SQL), a type of programming language used to manage data. It's a highly effective system that dates back to the 1970s. But an attacker, instead of enter-ing a name and address as requested, can enter specifically crafted commands that the database will read and interpret as program code, rather than just data to be stored. These commands can be used to learn about the database, read data, and create new accounts. In some cases, access can be used to discover and change security set-tings on the server, allowing the attacker to control the entire web system. As we explore later in the Part II section on hactivists, the Anonymous group used this kind of attack to penetrate the security firm HB Gary and share its embarrassing secrets with the world.

Beyond attacking applications, attackers can also exploit vulner-abilities in code at the system level. A common vulnerability is the buffer overflow. Computers use memory to store data and instructions. If a program can be tricked into writing inputted data that is larger than expected, it can spill over the allocated "buffer," or storage area, and overwrite the space where the computer stores the next instruction to be executed. If that newly written memory space is then read and interpreted by the computer, the program can break or follow the attacker's instructions. Once the program executes arbitrary instructions, the attacker can effectively gain control of the system. In essence, it follows the same principle as the SQL attack, where the computer interprets data as instructions, but now it takes place at the system memory level.

Designing these types of attacks requires a great deal of skill and experience, but once the vulnerability has been exploited it is relatively easy to package. This "exploit" is a piece of software or set of commands that can take advantage of the vulnerability. And that is where cyber risk takes on a whole new level of concern, as it allows other, less sophisticated attackers in on the action. It's as if the master thief now writes a book about safecracking that comes with a handy-dandy set of tools.

Malicious software, or "malware," is a prepackaged exploitation of a vulnerability. There is often a "payload" of instructions detailing what the system should do after it has been compromised. Some types of malware contain instructions for reproduction, in order to spread the attack. "Worms" spread themselves automatically over the network. In some cases, this can be sufficient to cause drastic harm: many of the worms that attacked Microsoft Windows in the late 1990s and early 2000s had no direct malicious effect but still overwhelmed corporate networks because they tried to send out an exponentially large number of copies. One worm even sought to patch vulnerable computers, a "good worm," but still managed to cripple networks. Other vulnerabilities have been exploited to allow the attacker to capture valuable personal data or, in an anarchistic turn, just destroy data on the victim's computer.

Malware can also be spread over the Web via "drive-by" attacks, where the victim's only mistake is visiting the wrong website. Such attacks exploit vulnerabilities in the web browser or in the many components and add-ons that web browsers use to take advantage of sophisticated websites. The attacker first compromises the web server and then simply attempts to exploit vulnerabilities in any browser that requests files from that website. Drive-by attackers often target groups by going after websites used by specific communities, a so-called "watering hole" attack (taken from the ideas that smart lions don't chase after their prey across the African savannah, but rather just wait for them all to come to the watering hole). For example, a group out to steal secrets from a US defense company indirectly targeted it by compromising the website of a popular aerospace magazine that many employees read. In one case, a watering hole attack infected five hundred accounts in a single day.

More recently, malware has been used not only to take control of a computer system but to keep control of that computer, in order to exploit its computational and network resources. By capturing victims' systems and coordinating their behavior, attackers can assemble armies of "zombie" computers. Millions of machines can be controlled by a single actor through a range of different command and control mechanisms. These are referred to as "botnets," and most computer users will never know if they are part of one.

Botnets are powerful resources for a host of nefarious activities. Regular access to the victims' machines allows monitoring to capture valuable data. Botnet controllers can also leverage the network connections of their victims' systems to send spam, host websites to sell illegal products, or defraud online advertisers. Perhaps most insidiously, botnets can launch a "distributed denial of service" (DDoS) attack.

DDoS attacks target the subsystems that handle connections to the Internet, such as web servers. Their vulnerabilities are based on the principle that responding to an incoming query consumes computational and bandwidth resources. If someone were to call your phone incessantly, you would first lose the ability to concentrate and then lose the ability to use your phone for any other purpose. Similarly, in the cyber world, if the attacker can overwhelm the connection link, the system is effectively removed from the Internet. It is fairly easy to defend against a single attacker from a fixed source: one just has to block the sender, just like blocking an annoying caller's number (but never your mother's. Never.). In a distributed denial-of-service attack, the attacker uses a botnet of thousands or even millions to overwhelm the victim. It's the equivalent of having thousands or even millions of people trying to call your phone. Not only would you get nothing done, but the calls you actually want to receive wouldn't easily get through.

This kind of power, and the fact that such attacks are fairly overt and obvious, means that DDoS attacks are often linked to some other goals. Criminal gangs may go to a website and threaten to take it offline unless they pay for "protection." ("That's a nice website you've got there. It'd be a real shame if anything were to...happen.") Or they may also be used as a diversion, to overwhelm the attention and defenses of the victim while going after data elsewhere. They are also increasingly common as a form of political protest or even suppression. During the initial stages of the crisis in Syria in 2011, supporters of the Syrian regime shared DDoS tools to attack critics of the government and news organizations that covered the growing violence.

The bottom line is that vulnerabilities exist on every type of information system in cyberspace. Despite how scary they sound, many of them are not new. For instance, the common buffer overflow attack was first developed in the 1970s and almost brought down the adolescent Internet in the 1980s. By 1996, a detailed how-to guide appeared in a hacker's magazine.

As threats evolve, so too must our responses to them. Some can be mitigated with small changes in behavior or tweaks in code, while whole classes of vulnerabilities can be prevented only by developing and implementing new technologies. Other vulnerabilities are simply a structural consequence of how we use systems. As we explore in Part III, how we navigate these challenges comes down to accepting that bad guys are out to exploit these vulnerabilities and then developing the best possible responses that allow us to keep benefiting from the good parts of the cyber age.

Or you could opt out, sell your advanced luxury car and ride the bus instead. Just make sure you don't check the bus schedule online.

How Do We Trust in Cyberspace?

There is perhaps no more important duty for a citizen than to vote, and no part of the voting process is more important than preserving the integrity of that vote. And yet the Founding Fathers of American democracy didn't imagine a world of computerized voting machines, nor one in which Pac-Man might chomp his way into an election.

The incident started out as one of those fun projects that hackers like to undertake, spending a few afternoons playing around with an old piece of computer equipment. The difference here was the hardware in question was an AVC Edge electronic voting machine used in the 2008 elections. Such systems are supposed to be tamper-proof or at least reveal if anyone tries to doctor them. Yet the two young researchers from the University of Michigan and Princeton were able to reprogram the machine without leaving any sign on the tamper-resistant seals. While they chose to reprogram the voting machine to innocuously play Pac-Man, the beloved 1980s video game, they made it clear that the supposedly tamper-proof machine was vulnerable to far more insidious attacks.

As the incident shows, our dependence on digital systems means that increasingly we face the question of how we can trust them. For cybersecurity, the users must trust the systems, and the systems must know how to trust the users. Not every machine is going to have a unwanted Pac-Man on the screen to tell us something is wrong. How do we know that the computer is behaving as we expect it to or that an e-mail from our colleague is actually from that colleague? And, just as importantly, how do computers know if we're supposed to be and are behaving the way we're supposed to?

Online trust is built on cryptography—the practice of secure communications that goes all the way back to the first codes that Julius Caesar and his generals used to keep their enemies from understanding their secret messages. We often think of cryptography as a means of keeping information confidential, but it also plays an equally important role in integrity, or the ability to detect any tampering.

A key building block in cryptography is the "hash." A hash function takes any piece of data and maps it to a smaller, set-length output, with two specific properties. First, the function is one-way, which makes it very difficult to determine the original data from the output. Second, and even more important, it is incredibly hard to find two input pieces of data that generate the same output hash. This lets us use the hash function to "fingerprint" a document or an e-mail. This fingerprint can then verify the integrity of a document. If a trusted fingerprint of a document does not match the fingerprint that you generate yourself using the same method, then you have a different document.

Cryptographic integrity checks are useful, but for them to apply to trust, we need some means to introduce identity. Trust is both a noun and a transitive verb, after all; it requires someone or something to trust. Cryptographic digital signatures provide that trust by using "asymmetric" encryption. This explanation is starting to get complex, so it might be useful to take a brief diversion into understanding a few basic points of cryptography.

Modern cryptosystems rely on "keys" as the secret way of coding or decoding information on which trust is built. "Symmetric encryption" relies on sharing the same key with other trusted parties. I encrypt data with the same key that you use to decrypt it. It is like us both sharing the same key for a bank lockbox.

But what if we have never met each other? How will we exchange these secret keys securely? "Asymmetric cryptography" solves this problem. The idea is to separate a secret key into a public key, which is shared with everyone, and a private key that remains secret. The two keys are generated such that something that is encrypted with a public key is decrypted with the corresponding private key, and vice versa. Figure 1.2 illustrates how public key cryptography works to protect both the confidentiality and the integrity of a message. Suppose Alice and Bob—the classic alphabetical protagonists of cryptographic examples—want to communicate. They each have a pair of keys, and can access each other's public keys. If Alice wants to send Bob a message, she encrypts the message with Bob's public key. Then the only person who can decrypt it must have access to Bob's private key.

A digital signature of a message ties together the notion of a digital fingerprint with public key cryptography. Returning to our friends above, Alice takes the fingerprint of the document and signs it with her private key and passes it to Bob, along with the unencrypted document. Bob verifies the signature using Alice's public key and compares it with a fingerprint he can generate of the unencrypted document. If they do not match, then someone has changed the document in between. These digital signatures can provide integrity for any type of data and can be chained to allow for transitive trust.

But where does the trust come from in the first place? For example, I can verify that software I have downloaded from a company is valid by checking it against the company's public key, but how do I know that the key actually belongs to that company? Remember,

---

How public key encryption works

---

1 Meet Alice and Bob. They would like to talk to each other securely.

2 Alice and Bob each have a pair of mathematically linked keys, sharing one and keeping one private.

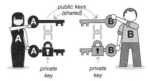

3 To send a message, Alice encrypts the message with Bob's public key, and signs with her private key.

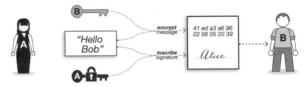

4 Bob receives the message. He then decrypts the message with his private key, and uses Alices's public key to verify her signature.

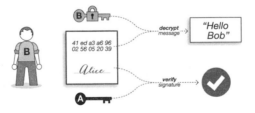

Encryption protects the confidentiality of the message, while the digital signature preserves integrity by preventing modification.

Figure 1.2

a signature only implies access to the private key that corresponds with the public key, not the validity of that public key. Asymmetric cryptography requires some means of trusting the public keys. In most modern systems we rely on a "trusted third party." These are organizations that produce signed digital "certificates" that explicitly tie an entity to a public key. Known as certificate authorities

(CAs), they sign the certificates, and their public keys are known widely enough so that they cannot be spoofed. If you trust the CA, then you can trust the public key signed by the CA.

Every person online uses this system on a daily basis, even if we do not realize it. When we visit HTTPS web addresses and get the little lock icon to verify the secure connection, we are visiting a secure website and are trusting the certificate authorities. Our web browsers ask the secure domain for its public key and a certificate signed by a CA, tying the public key explicitly to the Internet domain. In addition to verifying that the server our browser is talking to belongs to the organization it claims to belong to, this also enables trusted communication by exchanging encryption keys. Such trust serves as the basis for almost all secure communication on the Internet between unaffiliated parties.

As the source of trust, certificate authorities occupy a critical role in the cyberspace ecosystem, perhaps too important. If someone can steal a CA's signing key, then the thief (or whoever they pass the key on to) could intercept "secure" traffic without the victim noticing. It is hard to pull off, but it has been done. In 2011, someone (later leaks fingered the NSA) stole a Dutch CA's keys and used them to intercept Iranian users' access to Google's Gmail. Some have complained that there are too many CAs around the world, many in countries with less than savory histories in security and privacy. As attacks evolve, the roots of trust will be even more at risk.

If one side of trust online is about the user feeling confident about the system and other users, the other side is how systems should trust the users. After identification and authentication, a system must authorize the user to use the system. Most systems use some kind of "access control" to determine who can do what. At its simplest, access control provides the ability to read, write, or execute code in an operating environment.

The core of any system is the access control policy, a matrix of subjects and objects that defines who can do what to whom. This can be simple (employees can read any document in their small work group, while managers can access any document in their larger division) or much more complicated (a doctor may read any patient's file, as long as that patient has one symptom that meets a prespecified list, but may only write to that file after the billing system can verify eligibility for payment). Good access control policies require a clear understanding of both organizational roles and the architecture of the information system as well as the ability to anticipate future needs. For large organizations, whose users make extensive use of data, defining this policy perfectly is incredibly difficult. Many believe it may even be impossible.

Failures of access control have been behind some of the more spectacular cyber-related scandals in recent years, like the case of Bradley Manning and WikiLeaks in 2010, which we explore next, and the 2013 Edward Snowden case (where a low-level contractor working as a systems administrator at the NSA had access to a trove of controversial and top-secret programs, which he leaked to the press). These cases illustrate poor access control in all its glory, from low-level individuals being granted default access to anything and everything they wanted, to poor efforts to log and audit access (for several months after Edward Snowden went public with leaked documents about its various monitoring programs, the NSA still didn't know how many more documents he had taken, but hadn't yet released).

Whether the organization is the NSA or a cupcake store, the questions about how data is compartmentalized are essential. Unfortunately, most organizations either greatly overprovision or underprovision access, rather than trying to find a good medium. Overentitlements grant too much access to too many without a clear stake in the enterprise, leading to potentially catastrophic WikiLeaks-type breaches. In many business fields, such as finance and health care, this kind of overaccess even runs the risk of violating "conflict of interest" laws that are supposed to prevent individuals from having access to certain types of information. Finally, and most relevant to cybersecurity, if access control is poor, organizations can even lose protection of their intellectual property under trade secret law.

At the other extreme, underentitlement has its own risks. In business, one department may inadvertently undermine another if it doesn't have access to the same data. In a hospital, it can literally be a matter of life and death if doctors cannot easily find out information they need to know in an emergency. Former intelligence officials have implied that the stakes are even higher in their world, where a lack of information sharing can leave crucial dots unconnected and terrorist plots like 9/11 missed.

What this all illustrates is that even amid a discussion of technology, hashes, and access control, trust always comes back to human psychology and the decisions used to make explicit risk calculations. Pac-Man isn't an actual man, but the system that allowed him to enter a voting machine, and the consequences of that access, are all too human.

Focus: What Happened in WikiLeaks?

bradass87:   hypothetical question: if you had free reign [*sic*] over classified networks for long periods of time…say, 8–9 months…and you saw incredible things, awful things…things that belonged in the public domain, and not on some server stored in a dark room in Washington DC…what would you do?…

(12:21:24 PM) bradass87:   say…a database of half a million events during the iraq war…from 2004 to 2009…with reports, date time groups, lat-lon locations, casualty figures…? or 260,000 state department cables from embassies and consulates all over the world, explaining how the first world exploits the third, in detail, from an internal perspective?…

(12:26:09 PM) bradass87:   lets just say *someone* i know intimately well, has been penetrating US classified networks, mining data like the ones described…and been transferring that data from the classified networks over the "air gap" onto a commercial network computer…sorting the data, compressing it, encrypting it, and uploading it to a crazy white haired aussie who can't seem to stay in one country very long =L…

(12:31:43 PM) bradass87:   crazy white haired dude = Julian Assange

(12:33:05 PM) bradass87:   in other words…ive made a huge mess.

This exchange on AOL Instant Messenger launched one of the biggest incidents in cyber history. WikiLeaks not only changed the way the world thinks about diplomatic secrets, but also became a focal point for understanding how radically cyberspace has changed our relationship with data and access.

In 2006, the website WikiLeaks was launched with the goal of "exposing corruption and abuse around the world." With an agenda that scholars call "radical transparency," the concept was to reform powerful actors' behavior by exposing documented evidence of their wrongdoing online. Led by the now-iconic "crazy white haired dude," Australian Julian Assange, it used the Wikipedia model of an "open-source, democratic intelligence agency," where activists from around the world could upload information and share it through a central but communally archived repository.

The group quickly gained a reputation for "releasing information relating to a range of very different countries, and to potential corruption, malfeasance, or ineptitude." Early projects exposed alleged wrongdoings by Kenyan politicians, Church of Scientology lawyers, and international trade negotiators. It soon won accolades from anticensorship and human rights organizations.

In turn, the dangers of radical transparency quickly became apparent to organizations that depended on secrecy. In a 2008 report, the Pentagon noted, "WikiLeaks.org represents a potential force protection, counterintelligence, OPSEC and INFOSEC threat to the U.S. Army." (Ironically, we only know about this classified assessment because WikiLeaks itself published it in 2010.)

The Pentagon's prescience was remarkable, as the website was poised to publish a massive cache of documents that ranged from diplomatic cables to memos and videos directly related to the US military's war efforts in Iraq and Afghanistan. This story's beginning goes back to "bradass87," the online handle of Bradley Manning, born in 1987.

Bradley Manning was a private first class in the US Army, and not a terribly happy one. As he described in instant messages sent to another hacker turned journalist, "im an army intelligence analyst, deployed to eastern baghdad, pending discharge for 'adjustment disorder' in lieu of 'gender identity disorder.' "

Later investigations found that Manning fit in poorly with other soldiers and that he had already been reprimanded for disclosing too much information in video messages to his friends and family that he posted to YouTube. In fact, he almost wasn't deployed to Iraq because his superiors had described him as a "risk to himself and possibly others." But the need for intelligence workers in the field was too great, and he was sent to the war zone.

While Manning was trained to handle classified information, he was not an analyst. Instead, his job was "to make sure that other intelligence analysts in his group had access to everything that they were entitled to see." His position thus gave him access to a huge range of data streams from across the government's computer networks.

After growing increasingly distraught about the war, a reaction likely compounded by his personal troubles, Manning decided that "Information has to be free." While the Department of Defense had banned USB storage devices for fear of malware and had tried to "air gap" the secure networks from the Internet, they did not close off writable CD drives. Manning would bring in CDs with music on them and then overwrite the music with file upon file of classified data. As he wrote, "I listened and lip-synced to Lady Gaga's Telephone while exfiltratrating [sic] possibly the largest data spillage in american history."

In April 2010, WikiLeaks published a provocatively titled video, "Collateral Murder," depicting an edited, annotated video from a US Army Apache attack helicopter firing on civilians in Iraq, including two Reuters reporters. WikiLeaks followed this up in July and October 2010 by releasing immense troves of classified documents relating to the wars in Afghanistan and Iraq.

While Manning had originally wanted to remain anonymous, as was the WikiLeaks model, his facilitator, Assange, instead sought to achieve maximum publicity. The video was first displayed at a news conference at the National Press Club in Washington, DC. For the classified documents, Assange worked with the *New York Times*, the *Guardian*, and *Der Spiegel* to verify, analyze, and present the documents to the public. Unsurprisingly, US officials condemned the release of these documents in strong language and began to hunt down the source of the leaks.

Just a few months later, WikiLeaks dropped another virtual bomb. In what became known as "Cablegate," Manning had also passed on 251,287 State Department cables written by 271 American embassies and consulates in 180 countries, dating from December 1966 to February 2010. Much of the communication was boring stuff, but there were also a number of embarrassing secrets, from what American ambassadors really thought about their counterparts to the fact that the United States had secretly eavesdropped on the UN Secretary General in the lead up to the Iraq war. Amusingly, the US government then ordered federal employees and contractors not to read the secret State Department documents posted online, which the *New York Times* described as "a classic case of shutting the barn door after the horse has left."

Originally, WikiLeaks relied on media sources like the *Guardian, El País*, and *Le Monde* to publish the cables, which they did at a relative trickle. The media focused on what they thought was most newsworthy and edited the content wherever it might endanger someone inadvertently revealed in the cables, such as a secret informant. Only a hundred or so were released at a time, a tiny fraction of the stolen documents. A few months later, however, the password to the full data set was "accidentally" released (reporters from the *Guardian* and Assange each blame the other). With the site now accessible, WikiLeaks decided to publish the whole treasure trove of secret information, unredacted.

The leaking of documents was roundly condemned, and WikiLeaks was accused of putting people at risk, and not just American officials. In China, for instance, nationalist groups began an "online witch hunt," threatening violence against any Chinese dissident listed in the cables as meeting with the US embassy.

At this point, WikiLeaks became more than just a nuisance to those in power. According to the US Director of National Intelligence, the leaks risked "major impacts on our national security," and a senator called for Assange to be tried for espionage. Others sought to downplay the impact. As then Secretary of Defense Gates put it, "Is this embarrassing? Yes. Is it awkward? Yes. Consequences for U.S. foreign policy? I think fairly modest."

In either case, the heat was turned up on the organization and its key players. Assange's personal Swiss bank account was closed on the grounds that he had falsely claimed to live in Geneva upon opening the account. Even more damaging, Swedish prosecutors issued a warrant for Assange for sexual assault. After fighting and losing a legal battle for extradition, Assange sought asylum at the Ecuadorian embassy in London, where he remains at the time of this book's publication.

In another illustration of how the cyber world intersects with the real world, the online group was also pressured via the online financial front. PayPal announced that it would no longer allow individuals to send money to WikiLeaks's account, citing a letter from the US government declaring WikiLeaks's engagement in illegal behavior.

MasterCard and Visa followed suit, making it much harder for sympathizers around the world to contribute to the legal and technical defense of the website.

Despite this pressure, the WikiLeaks organization survived. The leaked documents are still available around the Web on dozens of mirror websites to anyone who wants to see them (aside from federal employees), while the group has popped up in subsequent scandals from the NSA domestic spying revelations to the Syria Files, a release of over two million e-mails from the Syrian regime, including personal e-mails from Bashar al-Assad. More importantly, WikiLeaks's model has proved powerful, inspiring copycat attempts like Local Leaks, a website associated with Anonymous. Local Leaks came to prominence in 2012, when it posted evidence of a brutal sexual assault by prominent high school football players in an Ohio town.

As for Manning, his role was revealed by the very same person he shared his supposedly secret Internet chat with. A hacker named Adrian Lamo had told Manning, "I'm a journalist and a minister. You can pick either, and treat this as a confession or an interview (never to be published) & enjoy a modicum of legal protection." Instead, Lamo turned Manning in to the FBI. Manning was subsequently court martialed for data theft and espionage and sentenced to thirty-five years in military prison.

In the end, those who wished to set information free are themselves no longer free. Others may be deterred by what has happened to this episode's main characters, or heartened by their enduring impact.

What Is an Advanced Persistent Threat (APT)?

We were at a meeting of Washington, DC, government officials and business leaders. A so-called consultant in cybersecurity (at least that's what his website said, and who are we to question the Internet?) spent half his presentation talking up the massive boogeyman of cyber danger that loomed for us all, repeatedly mentioning the new specter of "APTs." But fortunately, he spent the second half of his talk explaining how all that was needed to deter such threats was to be "good enough." He made a joke that it was like the two friends chased by a bear. As one told the other, "I don't have to outrun the bear, just you." As long as you made sure your defenses were slightly better than the next guy's, he explained, the cyberattackers would give up and quickly move on. And, lo and behold, his firm had a generic package for sale that would satisfy all our cybersecurity needs. The presentation was slick, effective...and wrong.

APTs are "advanced persistent threats," a phenomenon that has gained more and more notoriety in recent years (Google reports the term as being used some 10 million times by 2013) but is still poorly understood. It illustrates the challenge in the policy world of calling attention to very real emerging challenges in cyberspace but also avoiding overreaction, hype, and hysteria.

If cybersecurity threats were movies, an advanced persistent threat would be the *Ocean's 11* of the field. It's not that APTs star handsome actors like George Clooney or Brad Pitt; indeed, they are more likely to be run by their polar opposites, clad in T-shirts instead of Armani suits. Like the high-profile heists in the movie, however, APTs have a level of planning that sets them apart from other cyberthreats. They are the work of a team that combines organization, intelligence, complexity, and patience. And as with the movie, they are quickly followed by sequels. No one knows how many APTs are out there in the world, but one cybersecurity firm CEO told us how, "Five years ago, I would get very excited, and very proud, if we found signs of an APT inside a client's networks. It was something that might happen once every few months. Now, we're finding them once a day."

An APT starts with a specific target. The team knows what it wants and who it is going after to get it. APT targets have ranged from military jet designs to oil company trade secrets. So while many of us would like to think that we are important enough to be targeted by an APT, the reality is that most of us don't rise to that level. But if you do, well, watch out; locking your windows like everyone else in the neighborhood probably isn't going to be enough. The bear in the sales guy's story actually doesn't care how fast your friend runs; it just wants to take a bite out of you.

The hallmark of an APT is its coordinated team of specialized experts, who each take on different roles. Much like a robber "casing" a bank or a spy observing a military base, a surveillance team engages in what is known as "target development," learning everything it can about the person or organization it is going after along with key vulnerabilities. In this effort, online search tools and social networking have been a godsend to the attackers. Want to steal a widget and therefore need to know who the vice president of product development is? In the past, you might have sent James Bond to seduce the receptionist in human resources and then sneak into her files while she was sleeping off a night of shaken martinis and sex. Now, it's more boring. Just type the name into an Internet search engine and you can get everything from that executive's resume to the name of her daughter's pet iguana. As cybersecurity expert Gary McGraw notes, "The most impressive tool in the attackers' arsenal is Google."

It is this phase that also differentiates the attacks as "persistent." The reconnaissance and preparations can take months. The teams are not just trying to understand the organization of the target but also its key concerns and even tendencies. One APT, for example, was casing a major technology firm headquartered in Minnesota. Team members eventually figured out that the best way to crack the system was to wait until a major blizzard. Then they sent a fake e-mail about the firm changing its snow day policy; in Minnesota, this was something that everyone from the CEO on down cared about. Another effort, which American national security officials have blamed on Chinese intelligence and military units, gathered details not only on targets' key friends and associates but even what farewell they typically used to sign off their e-mails (e.g., "All the best" vs. "Best regards" vs. "Keep on Trucking") to mimic it for a spear phishing attack vector.

With the target understood, an "intrusion team" will then work to breach the system. What's notable here, though, is that the initial target is frequently not the main prize. An effective way into a network is via trusted outsiders, who often have lower levels of defense, or by targeting people in the network who have some access permissions to open the gates wider. For example, a series of American think tanks (including our place of work) were targeted in 2011 and again in 2012 by an APT that sought access to the accounts of scholars who worked on Asian security issues (they were interested not just in their files, but also their address books, which had the contact information for senior government leaders). But the APT initially went after other employees who had administrative rights and access to passwords.

These attackers frequently use spear phishing and faked e-mails, with some exploit hidden inside triggering a download of malware. In "Operation Shady RAT" (an APT we talk about later on in Part II), when the counterfeit e-mail attachment was opened, malware was implanted. This then created a backdoor communication channel to another outside web server that had, in turn, been compromised with hidden instructions in the web page's code, an effort by the attackers to cover their tracks.

The malware used in these attachments is often quite sophisticated. The emphasis is on stealth, so the authors will not only try to hide from traditional antivirus defenses, but burrow deep into networks and operating systems to avoid discovery, attempting to impersonate legitimate network traffic. Like other businesses, APT groups often conduct dry runs and even "quality assurance" tests to minimize the number of antivirus programs that can detect them. But e-mail is not the only way in. Other APTs have, for example, used networks like Facebook to find friends of individuals with a high level of privilege inside a targeted network. Then they compromise these friends' instant messaging chats to sneak in. Perhaps the most interesting example of this use of social networking tools saw senior British officers and defense officials tricked into accepting "friend requests" from a faked Facebook account that claimed to be Admiral James Stavridis, the commander of NATO. Who wouldn't want an admiral as a friend; imagine their disappointment when it turned out to be a hacker!

Once the team is in, they branch out like a viral infection, often with more personnel joining the effort. They jump from the initial footholds, compromising additional machines inside the network that can run the malware and be used to enter and leave. This often involves installing keystroke-logging software that tracks what people are typing and a "command and control" program that can direct the malicious code to seek out sensitive information.

At this point, the target is "pwned." Now at the mercy of the attackers, an "exfiltration team" works to retrieve the information the APT was targeting all along. Here is another APT hallmark: Instead of the usual criminal ethic of "Grab what you can get," they go after very specific files. Frequently, the attackers don't even open the files, suggesting that their reconnaissance was so thorough that they didn't need to review what they were targeting. Instead, someone draws up a specific list of collection requirements and the team is disciplined enough to stick to it.

Not all APTs just copy and exit with the data. Some add technology to allow them to steal new secrets beyond what was inside the network or even gain control. French officials, for example, have accused APTs linked to Chinese intelligence of gaining access to the computers of several high-level French political and business leaders and then activating microphones and web cameras so that they could eavesdrop on conversations. Even more nefarious are those that don't simply steal data but also alter files, which as we explore later can have major consequences. This ultimately shifts the APT from an act of crime or espionage to an act of sabotage or even war.

The exfiltration phase, when massive amounts of data leave the network (such as when an entire e-mail file exits), is actually when many successful APTs are detected. This "phone home" phase makes for an anomaly in network traffic that is hard to mask.

Exfiltration teams therefore use all sorts of tricks to sneak the information out and then hide their tracks. One common tactic involves routing data through way stations in multiple countries, akin to a money launderer running stolen funds through banks all over the world. This not only makes it more difficult to track them down, but also routes the APT's activities through different countries and legal jurisdictions, ultimately complicating prosecution.

What makes APTs even more of a challenge is that when a target finally realizes it has been attacked, the pain is not over. Finding which machines inside the system have been infected can take months. Even worse, if the effort is truly persistent—say if the target has some sort of ongoing value to the attacker—there might be an additional unit in the APT whose very job it is to maintain an electronic foothold in the network. Rather than focusing on what information to steal, this unit will monitor internal e-mails to learn how the defenders are trying to get them out. In one case, an American company hired a Pentagon-qualified computer security firm to clean its infected network after being targeted by an APT. Despite this, a few months later, a thermostat and printer in its building were caught sending messages to a server located in China. With their e-communication compromised, the defenders' response is often to go old-school. They will literally yank hard drives out of their computers and post handwritten signs in the hallways about password policy changes.

APTs are a nightmare scenario for any organization. Most don't know they've been targeted until it is too late. And even if they do find out, it is often impossible to prove who's behind it. Indeed, that's why APTs may be the most controversial of all the threat vectors. Except in cases where the attackers are sloppy (our favorite example being when a high-ranking Chinese military officer employed the same server to communicate with his mistress and coordinate an APT), there is little actual proof that would stand up in a court of law or sway a country's position. What we are often left with instead are suspicions and finger-pointing, which makes APTs so poisonous for diplomatic relations, as we've seen over the last few years between the United States and China.

How Do We Keep the Bad Guys Out? The Basics of Computer Defense

It is by far the world's largest zoo. In 2013, it held more than 110 million different species painstakingly collected from "the wild." And yet it is a strange sort of zoo, where you can't actually see the animals. The reason is that they only exist in the virtual world.

The McAfee "malware zoo" is what the computer security firm calls its collection of the various types of malicious or malevolent software (known as "malware") designed to wreak havoc on Internet users. Its growth illustrates the seemingly insurmountable scale of the problem. In 2010, McAfee thought it impressive that it was discovering a new specimen of malware every fifteen minutes. In 2013, it was discovering one every single second!

If we think of each type of malware as a unique threat, these numbers are overwhelming. Instead, we must understand why there are so many "unique" threats. The answer reflects the cat-and-mouse game that attackers and defenders play. Since the early Internet, attackers have tried to exploit vulnerabilities, and the defenders have sought to deny them. The adversaries, in turn, adapted and altered their patterns of attack, changing it into an evolutionary game.

The advantage of defending a computer system is that once you know what might attack you, you can just tell the computer what to watch for and how to avoid it. Traditional antivirus software relies on detecting these "signatures." The programs scan all files on the system as well as incoming traffic against a dictionary of known malware, looking for anything that matches these signatures of malice.

This classic approach has a few glaring flaws. As the number of attacks grows over time, these definition files and the time it takes to search them also grow. Most of these old signatures don't represent current threats, and as the threats proliferate, it becomes a losing game. One study found that only 0.34 percent of signatures in common antivirus programs were needed to detect all the malware found in all incoming e-mail. And yet prudence dictates that we still must look for the 99.66 percent of the old malware, just in case the attacker gets sneaky and goes back to them.

The bigger problem is evolution. Authors of malware have fought back against the traditional antivirus approach by taking a page from biology. Just as some viruses such as HIV and the flu change their protein coatings to avoid detection by the human immune system, malware creators change the outward appearance of their attacking programs. The very same attack can be made into very different signatures, disguised by programs that automatically generate new features. This gives rise to enormous numbers, like those reflected in the "zoo" statistics cited above and renders the old approach of detection by signature less useful. One analysis found that, over an eight-day period, while over one hundred thousand new signatures of new known malware were added by a major antivirus vendor into the list of what to scan for, only twelve new detections resulted. Twelve detections for processing one hundred thousand signatures may seem paltry, but this reflects the camouflage techniques used by malware authors more than ineptitude on the part of antivirus companies. Inflating the number of signatures may make the malware problem seem bigger than it is, but it would be equally wrong to conclude that malware is not a problem at all.

Security vendors have thus had to change how they detect malicious code. Modern antivirus don't just screen, they use "heuristic" detections to identify suspicious computer code behavior based on rules and logical analysis. Static analysis breaks apart the computer code and looks for patterns associated with the behavior of an attacker. Virtual machines and other sophisticated defenses dynamically simulate the code operation to determine whether the file examined will misbehave without putting the actual system at risk. Just as police bomb squads test suspicious packages, virtual "detonation chambers" can cause an incoming piece of malware to mistakenly think it is inside the machine and detonate prematurely.

If securing a modern operating system is difficult, an alternate approach tries to prevent the bad stuff from reaching the computer over the network. The simplest form of network defense is a "firewall." Taken from the concept of barriers built into cars or buildings to prevent fires from spreading, computer firewalls are like filters that reject traffic based on specific rules. Firewalls can prevent external computers from connecting to the firewalled machines except under preset circumstances or prevent certain applications on the computer from opening network connections.

Firewalls are filters that only permit valid activity on the network; the next layer of defense is a set of sensors that look for invalid behavior. "Intrusion detection systems" exist at the computer level or on the network. They detect attack signatures and identify anomalous behavior ("That's funny, the janitor's computer doesn't usually open an encrypted connection with Moldova at 2 in the morning"). These systems alert administrators to potential attacks and keep logs for detailed forensic analysis. Most detection systems now have some intrusion prevention capacity as well, which closes suspicious network connections and throws away anonymous traffic. Like antivirus software, these systems come with a price; in addition to typically costing more money, they cost time and performance resources inside the machine, especially if a system must evaluate all incoming traffic on a large network in real time.

While you heard earlier about a "zero day" that goes after a newly found vulnerability, most attacks attempt to exploit vulnerabilities that the vendor has already discovered and attempted to ameliorate via a code update or "software patch." The presence of a patch indicates that the vendor has found a vulnerability, identified a threat mitigation, and perhaps most importantly, built a fix into the existing code.

The problem is that many users don't always pay attention to these security updates and leave the vulnerabilities unpatched. This why we have seen an evolution from the makers sending out simple notifications of new updates, which puts the burden of action on the user's part, to automatic downloads and even installation of the patch. But other costs have come along with this shift. Modern software is very complex, and fixing one small vulnerability could affect countless other processes in the program. Horror stories describe patches turning brand-new smartphones into rather snazzy paperweights or breaking entire enterprise networks. Since every large organization runs different software and has different configurations, patch management is an important part of any IT support.

Just as your body's defenses aren't just skin-level, serious threats are countered not only by keeping them out. There are measures to protect what's valuable even if threats get in. In the case of cyber espionage, for example, if you cannot prevent attackers from accessing the data, you can limit their ability to understand the data through encryption.

The last line of defense is akin to the strategy that nuns use to police Catholic school dances. The nuns often stuff balloons between teenagers dancing too closely, creating an "air gap" to ensure nothing sneaky happens. In cybersecurity terms, an air gap is a physical separation between the network and critical systems. Such practice is common with critical infrastructure, such as with power companies, and was even attempted by the Iranians to protect their nuclear research from cyberattack.

The problem with air gaps, much like the abstinence that the nuns try to enforce, is that it often doesn't work in practice. Giving up control of operational infrastructure involves sacrifices in efficiency and effectiveness. Power companies that don't link up, for instance, may be less vulnerable, but they can't run "smart" power grids that save both money and the environment.

Similarly, maintaining an air gap is often unrealistic, as the Iranians discovered when their supposedly air-gapped systems still got infected by the Stuxnet virus. At some point, old data needs to come out, and new instructions need to go in. Systems need to be patched, updated, and maintained. Indeed, the National Cybersecurity and Communications Integration Center has conducted literally hundreds of vulnerability assessments of private American business air-gapping attempts. Not once did it find an operations network successfully separated from the firm's other computer enterprise networks.

Finally, some advocate the old slogan that the "Best defense is a good offense." In the cyber world, this is known as "hackback," and a number of firms have emerged to go after the attackers' own computer networks. Like vigilantism, it both feels good and may teach the original attacker a lesson.

But the hackback business has two major problems. The first is that the question of who has the "right" to carry out cyberattacks is unclear, which means that "cyber Blackwater" firms are "skating on thin ice" legally, says Nate Fick, CEO of the cybersecurity firm Endgame. The second is that it's not yet clear that hackback is even that effective over the long term. Alex Harvey, a security strategist for Fortinet, explains that "Breaking in and shutting them down isn't hard, but a new one will just pop up. You'll get a couple of minutes of peace and quiet."

The bottom line in cyber defense is that it is a hard task, with various options that are far from perfect. But the only other option is to close the zoo and let the malware animals run free.

Who Is the Weakest Link? Human Factors

In 2008, a US soldier was walking through a parking lot outside of a US military base in the Middle East when he spotted an unwrapped candy bar lying on the ground. Without knowing who had left it or how long the candy had been on the ground, he decided to take the bar inside the base and eat it for lunch.

Sounds absurd and even a bit disgusting, right? Well, substitute a USB flash drive for that candy bar, and you have the story of what started Buckshot Yankee, one of the largest cyber breaches in US military history. In 2008, a foreign intelligence agency left flash drives in the parking lot outside a US base, a tactic known as a "candy drop." A soldier saw one of the drives in the dirt, picked it up and thought it a good idea to plug the drive into a computer on the US military's Central Command network. The drive uploaded a worm named agent.btz that scanned computers for their data, created backdoors, and linked to command and control servers. The Pentagon spent the following fourteen months cleaning the worm out, all because one soldier didn't have the common sense to apply the "five-second rule" to how he treated his computer.

The real battle in cybersecurity is not just about high technology. It is also driven by the human factor, the fight over our behavior. To use a metaphor from the wars of old, the walls protecting a network don't always have to be knocked down or tunneled under by an attacker. Sometimes, as in ancient Troy, oblivious defenders simply open up the gates without recognizing the attacker's deception. While there are varied advanced threats in cybersecurity, many of the most successful take advantage of good old-fashioned human error. Examples range from the executive at an IT company who found a malware-ridden CD in the men's bathroom and popped it into his computer to see what was on it (again, think of the comparisons: would you pick up a comb you found beside the urinal? A sandwich?) to the employee at a defense company, who used his business network to file-share music. Besides sharing proprietary rock songs online, he also unintentionally shared designs for the electronics of the US presidential helicopter with Iranian hackers.

It is for this reason that many IT experts believe that if a network has any kind of sensitive information in it, all users need to be regularly certified in cybersecurity basics. This means everyone, from junior staff all the way up the leadership. This is not just about enforcing the five-second rule for things you plug into your computer. Clever attackers take advantage of our innate trust to convince us to click links, open attachments, or give out our passwords to strangers over the phone. Since 99 percent of the time our phone calls and e-mails are not malicious, it is hard to be constantly vigilant.

Even experts can and will be fooled. Professor John Savage founded the Computer Science department at Brown University in 1979 and has devoted much of his distinguished career to studying information security, including a stint advising the Department of State. Yet while teaching a class on computer security, one of his students successfully tricked him into clicking a link in an e-mail and entering his password. (We subsequently hired that very enterprising student as a research assistant for this book.)

We will go more into this in Part III, but the goal is to recognize the key part that human behavior plays in enabling threats, and then build constant awareness, reinforcing it with new training. If users fail to learn the lessons of proper caution, then their access privileges should be revoked. Indeed, some companies like Lockheed Martin even have "red team" programs that every so often try to trick their own employees. If the employee opens a link in a suspicious e-mail, for example, it links the offender to a refresher course on cybersecurity. Better we learn our lesson this way than download real malware, Trojan Horses, or any other Greek-borne cyber gifts.

Part II

WHY IT MATTERS

What Is the Meaning of Cyberattack? The Importance of Terms and Frameworks

It had taken a long time to bring the two groups together, but finally the senior American and Chinese officials were gathered around the same table. The important issues on the two great powers' agenda ranged from trade and finance matters to emerging cybersecurity concerns. But when the discussion finally started, the Chinese were baffled. The US representatives spoke about the importance of the "engagement." The Chinese translator wasn't sure whether the Americans were making a "marriage proposal" or discussing an "exchange of fire," neither of which seemed appropriate for a meeting of diplomats.

Trying to talk about a new issue can be a bit like traveling to a foreign land. New discussions require entire new vocabularies and frameworks just to understand what is happening. It can get even more complex in the realm of cyber issues, as the topics mix highly technical matters with broad concepts in which even the most basic terms can be loaded with meaning. For instance, when the United States and the USSR negotiated arms control treaties during the Cold War, they may have argued over things like the definition of a cruise missile, but there was no dispute as to whether the cruise missile was a weapon, nor that using a weapon like that against the other would be construed as an attack.

The same cannot be said of the cyber realm, especially when it comes to what constitutes an "attack" in cyberspace. This term has been used to describe everything from online protests to the stealing of Internet secrets to cyber sabotage of nuclear research to battlefield acts of war. And people fall prey to this confusion all the time. As we saw in Part I, in 2011, a group of top US senators talked about a $3 million case of credit card fraud at Citigroup and the Stuxnet worm, specially designed to cripple Iranian nuclear research, as if they were one and the same problem. Likewise, Chinese Foreign Ministry officials have talked about the spreading of rumors via social networks like Facebook as an "attack" in the same vein as hacking into power plants.

Even experts in the field can fall prey to this problem or sometimes take advantage of others' confusion on the topic. In 2010, the lead US general for the military's Cyber Command testified to Congress that "Every day, America's armed forces face millions of cyber attacks." To get those numbers, though, he was combining everything from probes and address scans that never entered US networks to actual data theft. But none of these attacks was what most of his listeners in Congress thought he meant by an "attack," the feared "digital Pearl Harbor" or "cyber 9/11" that his boss, the Secretary of Defense, had been warning them about in a simultaneous series of speeches, testimony, and interviews with the mainstream media.

Essentially, what people too often do when discussing "cyberattacks" is bundle together a variety of like and unlike activities, simply because they involve Internet-related technology. The parallel would be treating the actions of a prankster with fireworks, a bank robber with a revolver, an insurgent with a roadside bomb, and a state military with a cruise missile as if they were all the same phenomenon simply because their tools all involved the same chemistry of gunpowder.

When the US government convened the National Research Council to study cyberattacks in 2009, it defined them as "deliberate actions to alter, disrupt, deceive, degrade, or destroy computer systems or networks or the information and/or programs resident in or transiting these systems or networks."

It's a good summary, but if you really want to know what a cyberattack is, you first have to distinguish it from traditional attacks. To begin, cyberattacks employ different means. Instead of using kinetic force (a fist, a sword, a bomb, etc.), they use digital means, a computer action of some sort. This is significant: a cyberattack is not constrained by the usual physics of traditional attacks. In cyber-space, an attack can literally move at the speed of light, unlimited by geography and the political boundaries. Being delinked from phys-ics also means it can be in multiple places at the same time, meaning the same attack can hit multiple targets at once.

The second way a cyberattack differs is in the target. Instead of causing direct physical damage, a cyberattack always first targets another computer and the information within it. The intended results of the attack may be to damage something physical, but that damage always first results from an incident in the digital realm.

Stemming from these two fundamental differences are all the other ways that a cyberattack seems different from a physical attack. For instance, cyberattacks are often more difficult to attribute to a particular actor, at least compared to a clear "smoking gun" of a literally smoking gun. Of course, snipers sometimes shoot rifles spe-cifically designed to thwart detection, while some cyberattackers sign their name into their malware to make sure they get credit for an attack. Similarly, the effect of a physical attack is usually, but not always, easier to predict. You can drop a laser-guided bomb through a window and project with near certainty the explosion's damage radius. With a computer virus, you can't always know whose com-puter it might end up on. Of course there are exceptions: that bomb might also unintentionally collapse the building or explode a gas line that no one knew was inside, while, in turn, some viruses like Stuxnet are specially designed only for a specific set of targets.

Moreover, the costs to conduct a physical attack are likely in the purchase of actual weapons and their materials, while in cyberat-tacks the costs are more on the research and development side. That said, the experience of the Manhattan Project and the atomic bomb shows the exception to this rule. Bottom line: the only hard and fast difference between cyberattacks and other attacks is in their digital means and digital targets.

But how then can we distinguish among cyberattacks them-selves? As we've seen, they involve everything from "denial of ser-vice," where the targeted system is simply flooded with too many requests from other networks, to Stuxnet, where the malware caused physical equipment in an Iranian nuclear lab to malfunction and spin out of control. It's like categorizing everything from a band of neighborhood kids ringing your doorbell and running away to the

Norwegian resistance's sabotage of Nazi nuclear research in World War II.

In Part I, we discussed the classic "CIA triad," the three fundamental goals that make up information security: Confidentiality, Integrity, and Availability. Unsurprisingly, the best way to categorize attacks is by which of these three goals is being threatened.

Availability attacks are those that try to prevent access to a network, whether by overwhelming it with visits, a denial of service, or even taking it offline to shut down the physical or virtual processes that depend on it. As Dmitri Alperovitch, a leading cybersecurity expert, notes, "Scale and impact are absolutely key" in trying to weigh these attacks. A one-hour denial-of-service attack on a video-gaming website might seem a big deal to the gamers, but it isn't a strategic matter. By comparison, "A prolonged denial of service attack that is not easily mitigated and which shuts down critical parts of the nation's infrastructure may very well be strategic and something we want to try to deter."

Confidentiality attacks are efforts to gain entry into computer networks in order to monitor activities and extract information on the systems and on users' data. Weighing this kind of attack depends on both the information extracted and the scale of the effort. A criminal stealing your credit card and a spy agency stealing a jet fighter design are both conducting confidentiality attacks, but the consequences of financial fraud versus espionage are obviously different. As we explored with APTs, the real challenge occurs when these attacks extract information in a massive, organized way. Entities that have suffered such confidentially attacks range from consumer goods companies that have seen their designs replicated without payment, to oil companies that have had their bidding strategy and drilling secrets taken, to aerospace companies that have seen designs of combat aircraft stolen. Over time these can add up to a huge loss, which is why confidentiality attacks on intellectual property have become a strategic matter in US-Chinese relations. Indeed, while the focus of US debate is more frequently on fears of a so-called "digital Pearl Harbor," the more serious problem may actually be a long-term economic "death by a thousand cuts."

Finally, integrity attacks involve entering the system to change rather than extract information. They manipulate data in the virtual world as well as the systems and people who depend on that data in the real world. Most often, these attacks intend to either change the user's perception or situational awareness or cause sabotage or subversion of physical devices and processes that are guided or operated by information systems. Such integrity attacks can be particularly insidious, since we rely on computer systems to understand what's going on inside these same systems.

Here, too, the goals and consequences of an integrity attack vary widely. The effect could be mere vandalism for political purposes, such as a defaced public-facing website of a government agency. An attack might be aiding or executing some sort of illegal endeavor, such as by changing access or identities to allow criminals through security barriers. Or it might seek to cause major harm of a strategic nature, such as damaging another country's ability to implement official decisions, to defend itself, or to provide services to its citizens (via delivery of electric power, health care, etc.). The data that is being changed, therefore, is what determines an integrity attack's importance. For instance, a hacker changing the software code for the White House website's welcoming picture of the president and a hacker changing the president's code for nuclear weapons commands are each conducting an integrity attack. But they will have vastly different results, and call for vastly different responses.

The difficult challenge is often not so much classifying these kinds of attacks as it is distinguishing them from each other, especially when they happen in real time. A confidentiality attack and an integrity attack both exploit vulnerabilities to gain entry to a system. They can use the same approaches and technical specs to get inside, but it's what the attackers do once there that makes the difference. Do they observe and steal data, change data, or add new data, depositing what is known in weapons terms as a "payload?" Often the victim won't be able to tell until the act plays out. To continue with our White House example, when the Secret Service notices a man sneaking over the fence, they don't wait to see whether he wants to peek at papers on the President's desk or plant a bomb there. The difference in the cyber realm, however, is that such drama can play out in a matter of nanoseconds.

To go back to our original "engagement" problem, defining these terms is only the start. Next is crossing the huge gulf between how different nations conceive them. Take the notion of "information," which is the target of all these types of attacks whether the intent is to disrupt, steal, or change it. But information and its flow across the Internet can be interpreted in vastly different ways. The provision of online news and connections across geographic borders via social networking tools has been described by American leaders as an essential human right. By contrast, the very same free flow has been described by leaders in Russia and China not as a human right but as an "information attack" designed to undermine state stability. As a result, in international exchanges US officials have talked about cyberattacks in terms of "assaults on and intrusion of cyber systems and critical infrastructure," while their counterparts, from places like Russia, have discussed them as part of a Western "information war" to undermine regimes "in the name of democratic reform."

Figuring all this out is going to take a very long "engagement," indeed.

Whodunit? The Problem of Attribution

The name came from either a mash-up of the domain name "trafficconverter.biz" or a play on the German swear word for "fucker."

In either case, "Conficker" wasn't so much innovative as it was nasty, combining several types of malware to enter into unprotected computers, hide under a random file name in the root directory, and use the compromised computer to connect out and build a botnet. It first surfaced in late 2008 when a vulnerability was discovered in Microsoft Windows programs. The company rushed to release a patch to the public, but as many as 30 percent of users did not apply the protection. Soon after, security experts in different parts of the IT industry detected the first moves of what became known as "Conficker," a computer worm. Within a few months of Conficker's appearance, some seven million computers had been compromised into one of the biggest botnets in the world. Computers in networks ranging from the French navy to Southwest Airlines were all pulled into what one security expert called "the Holy Grail of a botnet."

Spooked by its scale, a diverse group of investigators representing security firms, consumer software companies, ISPs, and universities assembled to battle Conficker. Still, no one could figure out the worm's exact purpose or origin. Someone was building a massive botnet, but who was doing it and why? Then the team found a tantalizing hint—an early version of the malware checked the targeted computer's keyboard layout. If it was set to the Ukrainian language, the attack aborted. But what did this mean? Was it a sign that it was authored in Ukraine (not Russia or China, as some had originally thought) and the authors wanted to avoid infecting their compatriots and avoid committing a crime in their own local jurisdiction? Or was it a clever bit of misdirection, designed to make it seem like whoever designed it was Ukrainian? Years later, the who and why of Conficker still remain a mystery.

As this episode illustrates, beyond the issue of terminology, there are other dimensions that make the cyber arena so challenging to secure and therefore need to be explored further. Perhaps the most difficult problem is that of attribution.

Many forms of malware take control of the victims' computers and form a botnet that links unrelated computers and enables the controller to leverage their combined computing and communications capabilities. The resulting network of secretly linked devices can easily grow to extraordinary dimensions. For example, in 2010 three not so terribly sophisticated Spaniards created a global botnet that included over 12 million computers using a program they bought on the black market. In other cases, a controller may seek to capture and leverage only a small number of computers. Controllers use this tactic when concealing their identity is a priority.

Three key features of this capability to capture and utilize other computers are particularly important. First, there are no geographical limits. For example, someone in Brazil can compromise computers in South Africa to launch attacks on systems in China, which might be controlled by computers physically located in the United States. Second, the owner of a captured computer often has no idea that it is being used by a remote actor for pernicious purposes. Of the computers that attacked Estonia in the cyber incidents of 2007, 25 percent were US-based, even though the attack was originally Russian sourced, as we describe later. And third, when some pernicious activity is perpetrated, sophisticated analysis can typically, at best, identify the computer being used to launch the attack. It is far more difficult to determine whether that computer is being operated remotely and, if so, by whom.

Even if a computer is not being remotely accessed, in many situations (such as with a computer at a university or an Internet café) it is difficult to determine the identity of those sitting behind the computer, their nationality, or what organization they represent. Such information would be crucial in a crisis but is rarely available in a timely manner, and attempts to gather it raise huge privacy concerns.

It does not take much imagination to see how damaging these problems can be. Take how cybersecurity concerns have increasingly poisoned US-Chinese relations (which we personally witnessed as part of exchanges with US and Chinese cyber experts and officials). Since many in the United States assume that the Chinese government has significant control over its citizens, it is easy to assume that the government is behind most insidious activities launched by computers located within China. But, of course, this also means that bad actors elsewhere may be incentivized to target Chinese computers for capture and use in their activities, to misdirect suspicions. This very same logic, though, also enables Chinese actors to deny responsibility. They consistently argue that activities actually launched from China are being perpetrated by others who want to take advantage of the widespread suspicions of China, pointing to the large number of vulnerable, unpatched computers in their country. And the same type of misdirection can be carried out using computers physically located inside the United States. Essentially, you get a lot of finger-pointing and not much certainty.

The issue is that establishing attribution is not the same as establishing complicity. It is sometimes possible to track an actor's efforts to a certain geographic locale, but it is more difficult to establish any formal government role, whether as perpetrator or sanctioner of the operation. As we explore later, "patriotic hacker" communities and other nonstate groups, including student and even cybercriminal groups, have been mobilized by their governments for such purposes. They offer deniable, but directed, attack. Ronald Deibert is a leading Canadian expert who has tracked various cyber espionage networks like GhostNet, which stole information from over 1,200 computers in 103 countries. He explains, "Attacks can be 'crowd sourced' by governments . . . or arise from acts of spontaneous participation, or both. In such an environment, it complicates the task of assigning blame to a state and forming an appropriate response. This is potentially destabilizing to the global order."

Attribution is further complicated by the fact that in some kinds of attacks, it is difficult to initially determine if what is going on is "hostile." A shift in routing information at an Internet access point, for example, might be a normal update or it could be a malicious attempt to reroute Internet traffic. A stream of unusual traffic that hits a system's firewall could just be a misconfigured application somewhere in the world, or it could be a probe of defenses. Packets are not like ICBMs, where radar can quickly detect the missile for what it is.

On top of this, once malware enters a system, it does not always bear any telltale sign of its origin or intent. Unlike bullets or even atomic bombs (each nuclear reactor has a distinctive "signature" to which a bomb's fissionable material can typically be traced), when malware is uncovered it often does not point to a particular culprit.

What this means is that "proving" attribution is a crucial but excruciatingly difficult task. In TV shows like *Law & Order* or *Perry Mason*, the prosecutors tell juries to focus on three aspects of a crime to determine a culprit's guilt: means, motive, and opportunity. The same is true in cyber sleuthing, where investigators must often painstakingly connect the dots. For instance, Ron Deibert's team of researchers confirmed that a group of Chinese hackers conducted a series of cyber intrusions (known as the "Byzantine Hades" attacks) aimed at Tibetan groups, including the office of the exiled Dalai Lama. They did so by tracking communications from the infected computers back to control servers that had previously gone after Tibetan targets during the 2008 Olympics in Beijing.

But this is also where TV has it wrong. Contrary to what the lawyers say in those dramatic shows, a real court can't convict just on the mere presence of those three elements. There has to be compelling proof that the means were used and that the motivated defendant being charged actually acted upon the opportunity. Often in these cyber situations, one can point a finger, but not with the needed precision. The investigators of Byzantine Hades, for example, could confirm it was a team of hackers located in China, yet as Deibert explained, "We could not pinpoint the attacks to the Chinese government itself, but they certainly would benefit by the information that was stolen from compromised victims."

In cybersecurity, we are instead usually left with an attribution dilemma. One has to weigh the potential gains versus losses of pointing the finger at the group or person you think is behind a cyberattack. In deciding this, your real-world goals then matter more than what took place in the cyber realm. Are you trying to figure out who harmed you as a prelude to justifying your own counterattack? Or are you simply trying to communicate that you know which people are behind an attack, in order to "out" them, blow their cover, and maybe cause some kind of public shaming that will force them to stop? Different goals and different actions require different standards. The US government's 2011 counterintelligence report is a good example. It was willing to point a finger at China's general direction for cyber theft, in the hope of causing some shaming effect, but it repeatedly indicated at the very same time that it lacked "absolute certainty" that would have forced matters further.

Two years later, the *New York Times* went one step further when Chinese hackers were caught trying to penetrate its networks. Working with the Mandiant computer security company, it tracked the activities to a specific set of IP addresses assigned to a neighborhood in Shanghai that was home to a specific unit of the Chinese military. The *Times* published a front-page article with a picture of the unit's headquarters. The reporters then tracked down individual hackers using clues mistakenly left on social media, including the hackers' personal mobile phone numbers and even that one was apparently a "keen Harry Potter fan" but not a great speller (all his security questions and passwords revolved around "Harry Pota"). Yet the Chinese government continues to deny the allegations, and few people think we'll see a TV-style dramatic courtroom confession.

The takeaway here is twofold. First, attribution has an inverse relationship to scale. The more people involved, the bigger their operations (and likely impact), but also the more likely that someone will make mistakes that allow them to be tracked down. But, secondly, the context and goals of this backtracking matter greatly. You might use far different standards if you were trying to prosecute in a court of law than in a court of public opinion. Simply put, lawyers may want evidence "beyond a reasonable doubt," but this is not always possible in cybersecurity.

What Is Hactivism?

In October 1989, administrators at the Department of Energy and NASA sat down to their computers to find that they had been "WANKed." Instead of letting them log in, their screens blasted a message from "WANK: Worms Against Nuclear Killers" that said, "You Talk of Peace for All, and Then Prepare for War."

The WANK worm had actually been placed by young hackers from Australia (explaining both the double entendre of the name—to "wank" is Aussie slang for masturbating—and the origin of the message, which were lyrics from the Australian anti-nuclear band Midnight Oil). The youth wanted to protest a new program of nuclear energy research, but rather than travel to the United States to stand with other protesters holding posters outside the Kennedy Space Center, they spread their message from within their target's computers. As it was early in the age of networked computers, the worm they built now seems fairly simple. It targeted accounts that had the same password as their username (remember these good old days?) and was easily cleared from the system. But WANK is still significant. A few young hackers WANKing off had carried out one of the first examples of "hacktivism."

Hacktivism is a term often credited to the Cult of the Dead Cow, a hacker group founded in a former Lubbock, Texas, slaughterhouse. They were among the first to argue that access to online information was a universal human right (among their early efforts was an effort to hack Chinese government agencies and Western companies cooperating with them) and so organized Hactivismo, a project to fight Internet censorship and provide technical help to those living under oppressive governments. The idea is exactly what the mash-up of the words "hacker" and "activism" might suggest: the idea of promoting or resisting some kind of political or societal change through nonviolent but often legally questionable cyber means of protest. Just as Martin Luther once harnessed the revolutionary power of the printing press to spread his message, and Martin Luther King, Jr. similarly used the new venue of television, hacktivists are simply tapping into the latest technology to aid their own civil disobedience, agitation, and protest. But unlike in the past, this technology offers the ability to operate instantaneously, transnationally, and anonymously.

Much like other actors in cyberspace, hacktivists can range from single individuals to loose coalitions like Anonymous, which come together around a common target, to tightly organized groups. As a result, the scale of action includes small protests against a single target that barely make a ripple in cyberspace to what the *New York Times* somewhat erroneously called "World Wide Web War I" in 2001. After a US Navy P-3 surveillance plane and Chinese fighter jet collided, anger in China skyrocketed and some one hundred thousand Chinese hackers worked together to knock the White House website offline with a denial-of-service attack, plant viruses in the Justice Department's network, and even deface the home pages of some Ohio high schools. Groups of American hackers then responded by changing various Chinese websites to display American flags and messages like "Slouching Tiger, Hidden Dragon."

One of the big misconceptions about hacktivists is that they are all bona fide hackers with a real understanding of their actions. Actually, the vast majority are what are known as "script kiddies." That is, they use "scripts," or programs made by others, that allow them to download attack software from a website and then join in with the click of a button, no expertise required. Expert hackers tend to look down on them, hence the notion of a "kid" or juvenile. As a report for the US Defense Department explained, script kiddies are the "more immature but unfortunately often just as dangerous exploiter of security lapses on the Internet. The typical script kiddy uses existing and frequently well known and easy-to-find techniques and programs or scripts to search for and exploit weaknesses in other computers on the Internet—often randomly and with little regard or even understanding of the potentially harmful consequences."

These politically motivated "hactions" therefore usually aren't as complex or even sophisticated as many other types of cyberthreats. Typical incidents involve defacing websites, such as changing the front page of a company or government agency's website into something embarrassing, and "Virtual Sit-ins." Much like the sit-ins at college campuses in the 1960s, the idea is to use the power of the crowd to block traffic and hinder work. Now it is Internet traffic rather than long-haired hippies that block the corridors of power. One of the first of these occurred in 1997. The Electronic Disturbance Theater, a group that crossed hacktivists with performance artists, organized a virtual sit-in that flooded Pentagon and Mexican government websites with messages to try to bring attention to the Chiapas conflict. Recent sit-ins have targeted physical location, such as a specific government building, by trying to overwhelm the networks and devices at that site with large geotagged files, such as YouTube videos.

More sophisticated hactions tend to involve efforts along the lines of cyber espionage. They penetrate a network, find valuable information, and then extract it. In this case, though, they usually target information that is more embarrassing than valuable and then display it to the world. Examples range from the hacking of former US vice presidential candidate Sarah Palin's Yahoo e-mail account to WikiLeaks' posting of internal memos from the Stratfor private intelligence firm, which showed that a firm charging others for supposedly super-sophisticated strategic analysis was actually fairly clueless. When an attack focuses on an individual's personal information, it's referred to as "doxing," as in revealing personal documents publicly. Often, doxing requires minimal network penetration, relying more on careful research to link public but hidden personal or embarrassing data to the victim. The Chinese expression *Rénròu Sōusuǒ* describes this practice and translates as "human flesh search engine."

The most complex operations, however, are those that ironically circle back into the real world, combining both new hactivism and old-school civil disobedience. For example, in 2004 an undercover video showed a variety of acts of animal cruelty at the Huntingdon Life Sciences testing lab, including employees punching beagle puppies in the face. So a hacktivist group called Stop Huntingdon Animal Cruelty (SHAC) organized a campaign. They gained access to the company's networks, and through them, the firm's entire life cycle, including the names and home addresses of all its employees, shareholders, customers, and business partners. They published all these names and addresses online, even those of the firm's caterers and cleaners. Many of these individuals and companies were subsequently targeted in a strategy to undermine "every critical relationship of a company necessary to thrive." Neighbors were told embarrassing facts about employees. Investors who thought themselves anonymous were sent letters at home, while an entire New York yacht club was covered in red paint after it was revealed many of its members traded shares in the beagle-punching firm. These actions extended to more violent attacks, such as when the firm's marketing director opened his front door only to be sprayed in the eyes with a stinging chemical (the activists claimed to be simulating what was done to test animals). The campaign proved somewhat successful; so many investors and partners were spooked that the company ended up being delisted from the New York Stock Exchange. But, in turn, several of the SHAC hactivists were convicted for various crimes, including Internet stalking and using their websites to incite violence.

But no one should think that hactivism is solely antibusiness. Recently, private firms have grown more involved in various hacktivist endeavors. For example, during the 2011 "Arab Spring" popular uprisings, firms like Google, Twitter, and Skype provided technical support to protesters and various workarounds to the government Internet censorship. When the Egyptian government tried to shut down Internet access during the mass protests, the firms provided a service called "Speak to Tweet," whereby voicemail messages left by phone were converted to text tweets and downloadable audio files, so that news could still get out.

An interesting issue for hacktivism moving forward, however, turns the notion of Internet freedom of expression on its head. Many see hactivism as a new form of civil disobedience that echoes back to past generations of activists, whether it be Thoreau's essays in the 1840s or the Chicago Eight's use of TV in 1968, just now on a new medium. Others note that the tactics, like denial of service or altered websites, involve some attack on the other party's use of the Internet, effectively undermining their freedom of speech. Moreover, as the SHAC example illustrates, the anonymous nature of hactivism and the frequent posting of private information can inspire or provide cover for more nefarious, even violent actions. Thus, hactivism faces the same constant question as traditional activism: Do the ends justify the new cyber means?

Focus: Who Is Anonymous?

Aaron Barr made a terrible mistake.

On February 5, 2011, the CEO of the computer security firm HB Gary Federal announced that his company had infiltrated the Anonymous hacktivist group and would reveal its findings to the media at a major conference in San Francisco. It wasn't to be. As

Wired magazine reported, instead of the acclaim and profits he expected, Barr and his firm walked into "a world of hurt."

HG Gary Federal's website was quickly compromised by Anonymous, which posted its own message on the firm's very own site: "Your recent claims of 'infiltrating' Anonymous amuse us, and so do your attempts at using Anonymous as a means to get press attention for yourself.... What you have failed to realize is that, just because you have the title and general appearance of a 'security' company, you're nothing compared to Anonymous. You have little to no security knowledge.... You're a pathetic gathering of media-whoring money-grabbing sycophants who want to reel in business for your equally pathetic company. Let us teach you a lesson you'll never forget: you don't mess with Anonymous."

The group then made a complete mockery of the firm's claims to offer its clients security. Besides taking over the website, it also seized control of HB Gary's e-mail system and dumped more than 68,000 private messages and memos onto the public Internet. All sorts of embarrassing laundry were aired, from the company's offer to clients to target journalists and donors to the WikiLeaks organization (a business proposal that many considered not just a bad idea, but potentially illegal), to the CEO's discussion of logging onto teen chat rooms and posing as a sexy sixteen-year-old girl with the handle of "Naughty Vicky." Anonymous also carried out doxing attacks, taking control of Barr's personal Twitter account and then using it to post his Social Security number and home address.

HB Gary's reputation as a security firm was destroyed in what *Wired* magazine described as an electronic version of a "beatdown." By the end of the month, a congressional committee was investigating inappropriate contracts by the firm, and Barr had resigned in disgrace. As Anonymous concluded its message on HB Gary's website, "It would seem the security experts are not expertly secured. We are Anonymous. We are Legion. We do not forgive. We do not forget. Expect us."

With exploits like this and its signature use of Guy Fawkes masks (in honor of the 1605 Gunpowder Plot, popularized as an antigovernment symbol in the movie *V for Vendetta*), Anonymous may be the most noted of the hactivist groups. Ironically, its notoriety is due to its anonymity. It is not a single, easily identifiable organization.

Instead, the best words to describe the soup reflect the Internet itself, "decentralized" but "coordinated."

Anonymous is essentially composed of unidentified users from various Internet forums who gather to conduct organized protests and other actions using cyber means. As one member explained, "Anyone who wants to can be Anonymous and work toward a set of goals.... We have this agenda that we all agree on and we all coordinate and act, but all act independently toward it, without any want for recognition. We just want to get something that we feel is important done."

With no single leader or central control authority, the group visualizes itself not as a democracy or a bureaucracy, but as a "do-ocracy." Members communicate via various forums and Internet Relay Chat (IRC) networks to debate potential causes to support and identify targets and actions to carry out. If enough of a collective is on board for action, a date will be selected and plan put into action; one member described it as "ultra-coordinated moth-erfuckery." The members then use various media such as Twitter, Facebook, and YouTube to distribute "attack posters" to announce the plans, further coordinate steps, and draw new volunteers from around the world into the attacks, building up the ranks of an "Anonymous" army of hactivists. The paradox is that for such a supposedly secretive group, most of Anonymous's planning and action takes place in the open.

There is no exact date linked to the founding of Anonymous, but most accounts credit its formation to the mid-2000s, merging early hacker communities dating back to the 1980s with a new genera-tion of hactivists, who congregated around online bulletin boards like 4chan. For the next few years, the group would rarely pop up outside of the computer security world media. One of the first men-tions came in 2007, when Canadian news reported the arrest of a fifty-three-year-old child predator who had been tracked down and turned into the police by a "self-described Internet vigilante group called Anonymous." This was notable not just because of the revela-tion of the group, but also because it was the first time a suspected online predator was arrested by the police as a result of "Internet vigilantism."

Soon the group made bigger news with "Project Chanology" in 2008. As with all great world events, this started with a Tom Cruise video. A somewhat embarrassing interview of the actor gushing about Scientology (including claims that Scientologists are the only people who can help after a car accident) leaked onto YouTube. The Church of Scientology then threatened the online video-sharing site with legal action if it didn't take the video down. Members of Anonymous were angered by what they viewed as a heavy-handed attempt at controlling online information. So they organized a systematic effort instead to knock Scientology websites offline, with members assembling to launch a wave of denial-of-service attacks, akin to building a voluntary botnet.

In 2010, the group made more serious waves when an active node called AnonOps undertook a series of actions with names like "Operation Payback (is a Bitch)," "Operation Avenge Assange," and "Operation Tunisia." The first started as a battle over Internet copyright issues, with Anonymous targeting various organizations the hactivists saw as being too stringent or abusive in trying to restrict Internet piracy. Groups like the Motion Picture Association of America, the Recording Industry Association of America, copyright law firms, and even Gene Simmons, the lead singer of the band KISS (targeted because he had threatened to "sue everybody" who had downloaded his music without permission and "take their homes"), saw their websites knocked offline repeatedly and/or had their files opened to the world.

Eventually, this effort to battle what Anonymous saw as growing restrictions on Internet freedom connected to broader political issues. Companies like PayPal, Bank of America, MasterCard, and Visa were targeted because they stopped processing payments to the whistle-blowing website WikiLeaks, following its controversial publication of US diplomatic cables. The Zimbabwe government's websites were targeted after its president's wife sued a newspaper for US$15 million for publishing a WikiLeaks cable that linked her to the blood diamond trade. The Tunisian government was targeted for censoring the WikiLeaks documents as well as news about uprisings in the country (in a poignant twist, a noted local blogger, Slim Amamou, who had supported Anonymous in the effort, was arrested by the old regime and then became a minister in the new regime that the effort helped put into power). The British government was threatened with similar attacks if it extradited WikiLeaks founder Julian Assange.

As Anonymous went after bigger and more powerful targets, the group garnered more and more attention. This notoriety, however, has ironically rendered Anonymous less anonymous, bringing real costs in the process. Law enforcement agencies became motivated to identify and arrest members involved in the operations, especially any that connected to government agencies. Police raids sent members in places like the United States, the UK, and the Netherlands to jail. By 2011, the challenge grew more complex, when dangerous foes emerged outside of traditional states. As a US Army War College report explored, "Two clandestine non-state groups—a hacktivist collective and a Mexican drug cartel—stared each other down in the digital domain, with potentially fatal real world consequences for both sides."

The episode started when the Los Zetas, a drug cartel founded by former Mexican army commandos, kidnapped a member of Anonymous. The hacktivists then threatened to post an extensive array of information about Los Zetas and its partners online unless their member was released. This "doxing," however, wouldn't just be embarrassing to the Zetas, but deadly, as the revelations would open them up to arrest and likely assassination by their rivals. In response, the cartel hired experts to help it "reverse hack" Anonymous, seeking to uncover some of its members, and threaten them with death. Ultimately, they came to a shaky ceasefire. The kidnap victim was released but with an accompanying online threat from the Zetas that they would kill ten people for every name Anonymous publicized.

The ultimate question for Anonymous, as well as for other hactivists, is the same as for earlier generations of activists and agitators: can the power of the crowd actually have a lasting impact? Some argue that the group is "all bark, no bite," a new form of a "noisy political demonstration." Others argue that such critique misses the point: a handful of anonymous computer hackers have garnered worldwide attention for their personal causes, simply by putting forward a new model for mobilization on a global scale. As Electronic Frontier Foundation cofounder John Perry Barlow described, it may well be the new "shot heard round the world—this is Lexington."

The Crimes of Tomorrow, Today: What Is Cybercrime?

When we were kids, you could visit a strange, wonderful place known as a "library." There you could check out an encyclopedia (for you youngsters, imagine a paper Wikipedia) entitled the *World of Tomorrow*. As this guidebook to the future was published in 1981, "Tomorrow" was, of course, the far-off land of the twenty-first century. It was a wonderful world, but one of the chapters in the book did warn children that the future might not be perfect. Alongside the picture of a shady man, who is obviously guilty of something heinous (because he is wearing a Members Only jacket), the book explained:

> There is one kind of crime which may exist in the future—computer crime. Instead of mugging people in the streets or robbing houses, tomorrow's criminal may try to steal money from banks and other organizations by using a computer. The computer criminal works from home, using his own computer to gain access to the memories of the computers used by the banks and companies. The criminal tries to interfere with the computers in order to get them to transfer money to his computer without the bank or company knowing that it has been robbed.

It's a scary future we now live in.

Cybercrime, as we now think of computer crime, is most often defined as the use of digital tools by criminals to steal or otherwise carry out illegal activities. As information technology grows more pervasive, however, it becomes harder to find crimes that *don't* have a digital component. The European Commission, for instance, has tried to sharpen the definition in its laws by distinguishing between traditional crimes that may use cyber tools and cybercrimes as being unique to electronic networks in both the ends and means.

The most pervasive type of cybercrime is "credential fraud," or the misuse of account details to defraud financial and payment systems. Such systems include credit cards, ATM accounts, and online banking accounts. In order to access these accounts, criminals can obtain security credentials like passwords and other data wholesale by attacking computers that store account details for the merchants, banks, and processors in charge of the whole system. Or they go directly after the individual account owner by tricking him or taking over his computer. A common tool is the "phishing" e-mail, which poses as a communication from a financial institution and presents a link where the victim is prompted to enter his credentials.

In the end, a credential's worth depends on the criminal's ability to extract value. A credit card number, for instance, is only useful if the attacker can turn it into desired goods and services. This might be easy to do with one stolen credit card, but what about ten thousand? In the case of online banking fraud, a thief can't just transfer money to her personal account since the banks can easily track that. The result is that effective credential fraud requires a large organizational infrastructure of sellers, resellers, patsies, and "money mules," who act as intermediate steps in the transfer of money or goods. It's similar to more traditional money laundering, but in reverse. Rather than washing criminal profits into a wider legitimate pool, the goal is to create a series of seemingly legitimate transactions to get the money into the hands of criminals.

Another kind of cybercrime attacks intermediaries more directly, by identifying sources of value in the advertising mechanisms that drive the free Web we know and love. When advertisers pay by the click, scammers develop automated click-fraud to drive up the profits of hosting advertisements (and cost to the marketer). Criminals take advantage of advertising revenue by registering web domains just a few letters different from popular websites, or "typosquatting," and collect ad revenue from the page visits by those with clumsy fingers. Enterprising scammers even take advantage of "trending" topics on the Web by quickly registering websites in the hopes of being seen by users searching for newly popular stories, again extracting advertising revenue. These attacks reduce the efficacy of online advertising, which is the lifeblood of freely available content. This technique isn't easy, however, and requires infrastructure and an understanding of the internal mechanics of advertising financing.

Internet scammers employ trickery of a different sort. Their goal is to persuade the victim to deliver his or her money willingly. These efforts target our most basic human emotions: greed, fear, and love. An example from the greed category is the notorious "Letter from

Nigeria" scam, which offers the victim huge potential wealth for just a token deposit.

Scams built around fear often hype threats and then target the supposedly security-conscious. While we explore the policy side of this later in the section on the "cyber industrial complex," at the individual level these scams often involve fake antivirus software. Sometimes appearing as fake pop-up "warnings" on websites, the victim thinks he is gaining added protection from the scary online world, but he is really downloading malware. And once their genuine antivirus software is disabled, the victim is repeatedly prompted for payments to update the fake software. One study estimated that this is a $100 million business.

Finally, online cons also prey on the love we have for one another, whether for someone we know or for the wider world. In the "Stranded Traveler" scam, criminals take over a victim's e-mail, social network account, or both, and issue a plaintive call for help, claiming to be stuck in a remote location without their wallet or passport. The victim's friends and family are encouraged to send money to help the (safe at home) victim. Broader efforts include fake charity websites, which pop up after natural disasters and sadly siphon off money from those truly in need.

What makes scams so hard to combat systematically is that, unlike credential fraud, the victims are willing participants, at least until they learn of the scam. Related to this is another type of crime, fraud. The Internet has enabled the widespread sale of counterfeit or illegitimate goods, whether knock-off luxury handbags or Hollywood blockbusters. Here, even when they're aware, many users are still eager to participate, as they see the true victims as being someone else.

As anyone who has waded through an inbox full of erectile dysfunction drug ads can attest, fake pharmaceuticals are also particularly popular. Contrary to popular belief, many criminals make good on their illegal offers, delivering real drugs from offshore pharmaceutical plants. These organizations use an affiliate program to coordinate advertising, product sourcing, payments, and the technical infrastructure of botnets to coordinate their activity. Interestingly, the reasons there are more erectile dysfunction and diet ads is that such programs tend to eschew offering drugs that might attract particular attention from law enforcement, such as opiate painkillers.

All of these illegitimate offerings violate intellectual property controls as well as laws governing medical safety and supervision. Harm can occur through unscrupulous manufacturing or tainted products, especially when it comes to pharmaceuticals. Most losses, however, are indirect, through missed sales and diluted brand value for the companies that followed the rules.

Many cybercrimes target businesses more directly. We explore one particularly widespread type, trade secret and intellectual property theft, later. But companies can also be harmed directly through extortion attacks. This is the category that uses the type of ransomware attacks we read about earlier. The victim has to weigh the potential cost of fighting a well-organized attack versus paying off the potential attacker. Websites with time-dependent business models, such as seasonal sales, are particularly vulnerable. One study reported that, "In 2008, online casinos were threatened with just such an [extortion] attack, timed to disrupt their accepting wagers for the Super Bowl unless the attackers were paid 40,000 dollars."

Of course, gambling itself is illegal in many jurisdictions, making it just one of many illicit activities that have extended into cyberspace. What makes these activities relevant to cybersecurity is their virtualization challenges territorial definitions. Some activities, such as the distribution of pedophilic images, are widely condemned around the world whether in a physical magazine or a website. Other behaviors, such as gambling, enjoy the legal protection of some jurisdictions in both the physical and the online worlds. The extended scope of online wagering may have even contributed to the 2013 football match-fixing scandal in Asia, in which gangsters were accused of "reverse-engineering the safeguards of online betting houses." Another sticky area is hate speech. The EU's resolve to condemn "incitement to racial hatred" online in European criminal codes is contrary to American free speech protections, both on- and offline.

So how big is cyber crime? These varying attack types illustrate how it is difficult to put any single exact, meaningful figure on the size of the problem. There's also a scarcity of reliable data; criminals don't tend to share their information or statistics with academics. As Cambridge University's Ross Anderson lays out, "There are over one hundred different sources of data on cybercrime, yet the available statistics are still insufficient and fragmented; they suffer from under- and over-reporting, depending on who collected them, and the errors may be both intentional (e.g., vendors and security agencies playing up threats) and unintentional (e.g., response effects or sampling bias)."

Even if data were available, defining the costs of cybercrime isn't that simple. Direct costs fall not only on the direct victims but also on intermediaries like banks and ISPs that have to handle spam volume. These indirect costs can really add up. By 2013, an average firm of 1,000 employees or more was spending roughly $9 million a year on cybersecurity, whether it was a bank or paint maker. One can think of these costs as a collective tax we all pay, resulting from the infrastructure that supports criminal enterprises, like the costs of cleaning up botnets, and the ancillary harms of an untrustworthy cyberspace, including the reduced use of money-saving online services. This is in addition to the money, time, and effort spent mounting a defense, from technical defenses at the organizational level to the cost of law enforcement, all of which could be put toward more useful endeavors. When viewed holistically, cybercrime imposes a substantial cost across society, and defending against it requires an appreciation of modern cybercriminals' true sophistication.

A different way of looking at cybercrime is not the costs, but the size of its business. One approach is to examine cybercriminal income, but here too it gets complex, setting aside few report their incomes. The money can certainly be good. According to prominent cybersecurity expert Jim Lewis, "Cybercrime pays well. One pair of cybercriminals made $2 million in one year from click fraud on Facebook. Another pair created those bogus malware warnings that flash on computer screens—the FBI says those cybercriminals made $72 million from people paying to have the phony threats 'removed.' A gang in Russia extracted $9.8 million from a U.S. bank over Labor Day weekend in 2008. . . . Million-dollar crimes probably happen every month, but are rarely reported."

Other attempts do a great deal of harm but yield little reward for the criminal. Rogelio Hacket Jr. was convicted in 2011 of stealing credit cards linked to $36 million in fraud. Although his crimes spanned seven years, this criminal mastermind was not about to retire on his ill-gotten gains. According to court filings detailing his nefarious deeds, "In all, the defendant personally received over $100,000 from his credit card fraud scheme."

The point is that most types of cybercrime require organization for execution as well as profitability. Each successful fraud requires many different steps that are often individually worth relatively little.

So the scale of cybercriminal activity is another way to approach cybercrime. Investigators and researchers have had the opportunity to study the organization of cybercrime by infiltrating digital "black markets," where criminals trade the necessary components of their schemes. Forum sellers post offers for spam, credit card numbers, malware, and even usability tools. When we started writing this book, a twenty-four-hour denial-of-service attack was listed on a major black market for only $80, while a mere $200 would pay for "large projects."

In any market, even black markets, customer relationships are important. As one criminal posted, "Price for a million of delivered mails is starting at $100, and drop real fast, practically to $10, for regular clients. Selection of countries is free." These independent brokers don't represent the entire threat, though. More enterprising criminals vertically integrate; that is, they control the entire process from top to bottom. Security expert Eugene Spafford describes this as the far more daunting cybercriminal threat: "It is well-funded and pursued by mature individuals and groups of professionals with deep financial and technical resources, often with local government (or other countries') toleration if not support."

As in weighing cybercrime's costs, scale also matters more in indirect ways. In the same way that a drug den opening up in a neighborhood will drive away customers from other local businesses, a growth in these cybercrime organizations and black markets can undermine trust in the broader digital systems that make all business more efficient. If we come to believe that every e-mail claiming to be from our bank is a phishing attempt, for instance, then our banks can no longer effectively communicate via e-mail.

The ultimate risk is that the ever-growing scale of cybercrime will undermine the broader system. If banks decide that the fraud rate from stolen banking credentials is greater than the cost savings and customer service benefits of online banking, they may just turn it off.

Yet this is where cybercriminals differ from more traditional crooks; they, too, have a stake in the system. The vast majority of cybercriminals are parasites, interested in leaching off as much value as they can rather than destroying the system. And that may be the fundamental difference between cybercrime and other types of online harm we explore later, like espionage, war, and terrorism.

Fortunately, this "world of tomorrow" playing out today is not all bad news. The old books about the future may have predicted "computer crime," but they also depicted how we would solve it. The scary future criminals would be chased down by futuristic policemen armed with ray guns.

"Nevertheless, a computer criminal may succeed now and then and the detectives of the future will have to be highly skilled computer operators. There will probably be police computer-fraud squads, specially trained to deal with computer crime. Here you can see a squad arriving at the home of a computer criminal and arresting him as he makes a dash for it. He is clutching a computer cassette that contains details of his computer crimes, and the police will need this as evidence to prove that he is guilty."

We'll get to this in Part III, where we explore the path to a more secure cyberspace, which fortunately doesn't require ray guns.

Shady RATs and Cyberspies: What Is Cyber Espionage?

In 2011, Dmitri Alperovitch and a team of threat researchers at the cybersecurity firm McAfee cracked the logs of a command-and-control server that they suspected had been part of a series of cyberattacks. The attacks were like many other APTs. They went after specific targets, often using spear-phishing e-mails aimed at particular individuals with the right level of access inside an organization. Once downloaded, malware communicated back to a command-and-control server. Live intruders then remotely jumped onto the infected machine and used their new access to move across the network, implanting even more malware and exfiltrating key data. So, in many ways, "Operation Shady RAT," as it came to be called (after the notion of a Remote Administration Tool), was rather unremarkable.

But as it began to analyze the logs, the McAfee team pieced together that something much bigger was going on. This wasn't a case of hacktivists seeking attention or cybercriminals pursuing monetary gain. The attackers, as Alperovitch described, had bigger things in mind; they seemed motivated by "a massive hunger for secrets." This one group had spent five years targeting files everywhere from governmental national security agencies to solar energy companies. One major US news organization saw its New York headquarters and Hong Kong bureau compromised for over twenty-one months, while the World Anti-Doping Agency's internal files were cracked right before the 2008 Beijing Olympics.

And the logs showed the attackers had been hugely successful, ultimately penetrating seventy-two major targets around the world. The data they made off with included national security secrets, product design schematics, and negotiation plans. As he added up the scale of what "had fallen off the truck" in terms of overall national and economic security value, Alperovitch realized he had just watched one of the biggest thefts in history unfold in slow motion on his computer screen. While he declines to explicitly identify the attackers, preferring to speak only on known specifics, Alperovitch does say the effort had all the hallmarks of a state-related campaign, given the range of secrets targeted, and that the state likely behind the efforts certainly had a strong interest in Asia. If this was a Harry Potter novel, China was Voldemort, the large Asian cyber power that "shall not be named."

Shady RAT illustrates an important change in the art of stealing secrets. Before the computer came along, governments and other actors would keep their secrets in locked file cabinets, behind a locked door, in a locked building, and behind high walls. Today, though, if that information is to be useful in any way, it's stored in a digital form on a computer that is connected to a network. Even in organizations as secretive as the CIA, analysts must use computers (invisible ink has gone the way of the shoe phone) to send and receive classified information across offices and agencies, especially if they ever want to do something like connect the dots needed to stop a terrorist attack.

The problem, as we explored earlier, is that many of these networks are not as secure as their users may think. And so while computer networks are allowing groups to work more efficiently and effectively than ever before, they are making it easier to steal secrets. We have entered what one security organization calls the "golden age" of intelligence. As one report notes, "Nations don't need expensive ground stations, satellites, airplanes or ships to spy. Global intelligence capabilities now just need a few laptops and a high-speed connection."

Cyber espionage is the use and targeting of computers to obtain a secret of some sort. Much like other forms of espionage, it is clandestine (i.e., not using open means) and usually involves a government agency. This digital form of intelligence gathering dates at least to 1982, when Soviet KGB spies reputedly stole a Canadian firm's software that had been laced with a logic bomb secretly planted by the CIA. It is in the twenty-first century, however, that digital espionage has truly taken off. Every intelligence agency in the world operates in this realm, and every country has been targeted. As an example, in 2009 researchers uncovered a network of 1,295 infected host systems in 103 countries. This "GhostNet" had targeted foreign affairs ministries, embassies, and multilateral organizations in places from Iran and Germany to the Tibetan government in exile. While the origin of the operation was never confirmed, researchers pointed out that the servers utilized were all located on Hainan Island in China. But before we point too many fingers at China for operating in this realm, remember that the United States is just as active; indeed, large parts of its intelligence apparatus, like the aforementioned CIA and NSA, are dedicated to this same mission; the 2013 Snowden leaks showed 213 of these operations in 2011 alone.

One of the big changes from past espionage, though, is not just the global scale of cyber operations but their increasingly economic quality. In many circumstances, the advantage a state gains from stealing such secrets is fairly direct and obvious. Examples range from the theft of several Western governments' preparatory documents for the G-20 summit in 2011, which would have given the other sides an edge in international negotiations, to a spate of attacks targeting the F-35 fighter jet's design and manufacturing process. Intended as the West's next-generation, highly computerized, stealthy plane, the F-35 program's computer networks have instead been penetrated at least three times. In one instance, intruders compromised the plane's onboard systems responsible for diagnosing mid-air maintenance problems. The attackers gained access as the plane was literally in the midst of a test flight!

And as with Shady RAT, these losses affect both national and economic security. The data taken from the F-35 program, for instance, has to be weighed both in terms of the billions of dollars of research that the attacker gained for next to nothing as well as of the informational edge it might have on a future battlefield. Jason Healey, a retired US Air Force officer, was a "plankholder" (founding member) of the Joint Task Force–Computer Network Defense, the world's first joint cyberwar-fighting unit. He compares the strategic impact of this kind of theft to cancer. "You can't see it, but it will kill a lot of us as we get older."

But many see a broader espionage campaign that is not just about traditional security per se, but economic competitiveness. Today's modern economy is driven by innovation, while cyber theft provides a low-cost shortcut. As Greg Garcia, assistant secretary for cybersecurity at the US Department of Homeland Security, puts it, "Any country that wants to support and develop an indigenous industry may very well use cyber espionage to help do that." Indeed, Dmitri Alperovitch believes the scale of such theft is even more significant than the large but lone Shady RAT operation he uncovered. "I am convinced that every company in every conceivable industry with significant size and valuable intellectual property and trade secrets has been compromised (or will be shortly), with the great majority of the victims rarely discovering the intrusion or its impact. In fact, I divide the entire set of Fortune Global 2000 firms into two categories: those that know they've been compromised and those that don't yet know."

This cross between digital espionage of a political and business nature is why fingers typically get pointed at China. A key concern in Beijing, which has more state-run and state-affiliated corporations than its trading partners, is how to keep China's economy growing at its incredibly fast pace. But its challenge is not just a matter of continued growth, but of capturing more of that growth's value. Over the last generation, China's economy primarily produced goods using foreign intellectual property. It worked to jump-start the Chinese economic boom, but it is not the most attractive approach in the long term; the Chinese factory that made early model iPhones, for example, earned only about $15 per phone for assembling a $630 iPhone.

As it tries to become the world's largest economy, experts argue that the Chinese government is increasingly turning to cyber espionage to maintain its expansion. "They've identified innovation as crucial to future economic growth—but they're not sure they can do it," says Jim Lewis, an expert at the Center for Strategic and International Studies. "The easiest way to innovate is to plagiarize."

Accusers cite disconnected sales of high-tech computer software (China is oddly the world's second-largest market for computer hardware sales but is only the eighth-largest for software sales) to more mundane illustrations, such as the manufacture of a certain type of furniture in China, shortly after the cyber theft of its design.

Unsurprisingly, Chinese writers and officials have reacted angrily to direct and veiled accusations, describing them as "groundless." But the reality is that of some thirty successful prosecutions of economic espionage tied to a foreign actor, eighteen have direct ties to China. Indeed, a study by Verizon's Data Breach Investigations team found that "96 percent of recorded, state-affiliated attacks targeting businesses' trade secrets and other intellectual property in 2012 could be traced back to Chinese hackers."

The outcome is a cyber irony. Cyber espionage is turning into a major political problem more due to the accusations of intellectual property (IP) theft than political secret theft. While there is an expectation that all governments have and will continue to try to steal each other's state secrets, the IP theft issue is creating global tensions in two major ways. First, it reinforces a sense that not everyone in the world marketplace is playing by the same set of rules. While many hold to the theory of free markets, this new practice privileges not those who innovate new business ideas but those who steal them. This, then, further exacerbates tensions that normally arise when democracies and authoritarian systems interact. Cyber theft has been described in the *New York Times* as "the No. 1 problem" that the United States has with China's rise. In turn, those in China describe these accusations as evidence that the United States is still "locked in a Cold War mentality."

Second, this theft threatens nations' long-term economic security. Cyber espionage creates both strategic winners and losers. Dmitri Alperovitch, for example, is careful not to call what goes on mere theft, but a "historically unprecedented transfer of wealth." As business plans, trade secrets, product designs, and so on move from one country to another, one side is strengthened and the other weakened. The target loses future potential economic growth derived from that secret in addition to forfeited development investment. Many worry that this "transfer" can ultimately have a hollowing-out effect on an entire economy. Each loss from cyber espionage is too small to be fatal on its own, but their accumulation might prove crippling. As one US official put it, "We should not forget that it was China where 'death by a thousand cuts' originated."

As for Dmitri Alperovitch, he grew tired of simply watching secrets get stolen without consequences. A year later, he helped found a cybersecurity company called CrowdStrike, which aims not only to identify hackers stealing information but strike back using the same cyber skill sets. He explains, "If I tackle you on the street, that's assault and battery. But if a few minutes prior you had taken my wallet, it's completely legal, I'm defending my property rights." This has a certain direct logic, but as we'll see, this kind of cyber retaliation is not nearly as simple in execution.

How Afraid Should We Be of Cyberterrorism?

Thirty-one thousand three hundred. That's roughly the number of magazine and journal articles written so far that discuss the phenomenon of cyberterrorism.

Zero. That's the number of people who had been physically hurt or killed by cyberterrorism at the time this book went to press.

The FBI defines cyberterrorism as a "premeditated, politically motivated attack against information, computer systems, computer programs, and data which results in violence against non-combatant targets by sub-national groups or clandestine agents." But in many ways, cyberterrorism is like Discovery Channel's "Shark Week" (wherein we obsess about sharks despite the fact that you are roughly 15,000 times more likely to be hurt or killed in an accident involving a toilet). As with so many of the other issues in cybersecurity, what's real and what's feared often get conflated.

This is not to say that terrorist groups are uninterested in using the cyber technology to carry out acts of violence. For example, in 2001, al-Qaeda computers seized in Afghanistan showed models of a dam and engineering software that simulated catastrophic failure of controls. Similarly, in 2006, terrorist websites promoted cyberattacks against the US financial industry in retaliation for abuses at Guantánamo Bay. But fortunately, what terrorists have actually accomplished online so far doesn't come close to their unfulfilled dreams, our broader fears, or, more importantly, the scale of destruction they've wrought through more traditional means. Despite plenty of speculation and foiled potential plots, there have been no actual successes.

As one congressional staffer put it, the way we use a "term like cyberterrorism has as much clarity as cybersecurity, that is none at all." Indeed, the only publicly documented case of an actual al-Qaeda attempt at a cyberattack doesn't even meet the FBI definition. A detainee at Guantánamo Bay, Mohmedou Ould Slahi, confessed to trying to knock the Israeli prime minister's public-facing website offline. Beyond this there have been various unsubstantiated claims, such as that of September 2012, when the "Izz ad-Din al-Qassam Cyber Fighters" claimed responsibility for a series of denial-of-service attacks on five US banking firms. While many believe they stole credit for cybercriminals' work, the effects of the attacks were negligible, shutting down customer access to the sites for a few hours. Most customers didn't even know there had been an attack. Take out the word "cyber" and we wouldn't even call such a nuisance "terrorism."

Let us be crystal clear: the worries over vulnerabilities in critical infrastructure to cyberattack have real validity. From 2011 to 2013, probes and intrusions into the computer networks of critical infrastructure in the United States went up by 1700 percent. And the worries of cyberterrorists harming this infrastructure are certainly a real concern. For instance, in 2011 a water provider in California hired a team of computer hackers to probe the vulnerabilities of its computer networks, and the simulated attackers got into the system in less than a week. Policymakers must be aware that real versions of such terror attacks could expand beyond single targets and have a wider ripple effect, knocking out the national power grid or shutting down a city or even region's water supply.

But just as our fears inspired all sorts of potential new terror attack scenarios in the immediate aftermath of 9/11, the key is distinguishing between our nightmarish visions of what *might* happen from the actual uses of the Internet by terrorist groups. As one cyber expert put it to us, "There are threats out there, but there are no threats that threaten our fundamental way of life."

This is because cyberattacks of a massive scale are fairly difficult to pull off, especially compared to more traditional terrorist activities. In 2011, then US Deputy Defense Secretary William Lynn, the Pentagon's second highest civilian leader, spoke to the RSA conference in San Francisco, a gathering of the top experts in cybersecurity, about the dangers of cyberterrorism. "It is possible for a terrorist group to develop cyberattack tools on their own or to buy them on the black market," Lynn warned. "A couple dozen talented programmers wearing flip-flops and drinking Red Bull can do a lot of damage."

But here again, he was conflating a fear and a reality, not just about what such Red Bull–drinking programmers are actually hired to do but also what is needed to accomplish a truly violent cyberattack of major scale. It goes well beyond finding top cyber experts. Taking down hydroelectric generators or designing malware like Stuxnet that causes nuclear centrifuges to spin out of sequence doesn't just require the skills and means to get into a computer system. It requires knowing what to do once you're there.

To cause true damage entails an understanding of the devices themselves: how they run, their engineering, and their underlying physics. Stuxnet, for example, involved cyber experts as well as experts in nuclear physics and engineers familiar with a specific kind of Siemens-brand industrial equipment. On top of the required expertise, expensive software tests had to be conducted on working versions of the target hardware. As a professor at the US Naval Academy explains, "the threat of cyber terrorism, in particular, has been vastly overblown," because conducting a truly mass-scale act of terrorism using cyber means "simply outstrips the intellectual, organizational, and personnel capacities of even the most well-funded and well-organized terrorist organization, as well as those of even the most sophisticated international criminal enterprises. To be blunt: neither the 14-year old hacker in your next-door neighbor's upstairs bedroom, nor the two or three person al Qaeda cell holed up in some apartment in Hamburg are going to bring down the Glen Canyon and Hoover Dams." By comparison, the entire 9/11 plot cost less than $250,000 in travel and organizational costs and used simple box-cutters.

There is another cautionary note that puts the impact of such potential attacks into perspective. The 2007 cyberattacks on Estonia were allegedly assisted by the Russian government and hence were well beyond the capacity of most terror organizations. And yet, while they were able to interfere with public-facing government websites for several days, they had little impact on the daily life of the average Estonian and certainly no long-term effect. Compare that with the impact of a plane crashing into the center of the US financial system. Indeed, even when you move into the "what if" side of the largest-scale potential terror attacks, a successful cyberterror event still pales compared to other types of attacks. The disruption of the electric power grid for a few days or even months would most definitely be catastrophic. But the explosion of just one nuclear bomb, even a jury-rigged radiological "dirty bomb," would irradiate a city for centuries and set off an earthquake in global politics. Similarly, while a computer virus could wreak havoc in the economy, a biological weapon could change our very patterns of life forever.

As Mike McConnell, former Director of National Intelligence, put it when talking about cyberterrorism, we need to weigh the balance of what is real and what is potential. "Terrorist groups today are ranked near the bottom of cyberwar capability." But just because no one has pulled off an attack thus far doesn't mean one shouldn't be mindful of the threats. "Sooner or later [they] will achieve cyber-sophistication."

So How Do Terrorists Actually Use the Web?

That cyberterrorism may not be as likely or scary as the media and some government leaders portray doesn't mean that terrorists are Luddites who never use technology. Far from it. The Internet offers the means to connect with vast groups of people, overcoming traditional geographic constraints. It links people of similar interests and beliefs who otherwise wouldn't normally meet while allowing voices to be magnified and reach more people. So, just as the Internet has been used by everyone from companies looking to recruit new workers to Christian singles looking to mingle, so too has it been a boon to terrorist groups.

Indeed, if you want to understand terrorists' use of cyber technology, just look at how others use it to engage in less nefarious acts. For terrorists, and the rest of us, cyberspace is a medium mostly for communication and information sharing. Al-Qaeda, for example, rarely used the Internet during its formative years in the early 1990s. Osama bin Laden's messaging was spread through the distribution of audio- and then videotapes, usually passed surreptitiously between vetted followers. Indeed, the very name "al-Qaeda," or "the base," is thought to have originated after the name of the first terrorist training camps in the mountains of Afghanistan (anyone who had gone through the camps was already known, trained, and trusted). But in the 2000s, two key changes occurred. After 9/11, the US military's operations in Afghanistan eliminated a physical safe haven for training and organization, while simultaneously cyber technology became more commonplace and usable.

The result was a group, guided by medieval ideals, embracing twenty-first-century technology. Al-Qaeda didn't use cyberspace to conduct cyberterrorism as it is usually defined, but to conduct information operations, harnessing the power of the Internet to reach the wider world in a way never before possible for such a small group. Bin Laden's speeches and musings could be delivered alone in a hideout yet uploaded onto the Internet and seen by millions.

Notably, these messages were often distributed not just to the media but also within Internet chat rooms, where individuals who reacted positively could then be targeted for recruitment. Here, too, technological change was crucial. At the time of the 9/11 attacks, downloading such a propaganda video would have taken so long that few would have even been able to watch it, let alone find out about it. Now, video clips can be uploaded and downloaded in seconds.

As the cyber world has evolved, so too has terrorist groups' use of it, especially in information operations. Just as in other parts of cyberspace, the more attention-grabbing the content, the more likely it is to be watched, thus rewarding aberrant and abhorrent attitudes and behavior with more web clicks (this is what terrorists and the Kardashians have in common). It has allowed fringe groups to reach the mainstream, often to the disadvantage of more moderate and representative voices. For example, searches for generic terms like "Islam" on YouTube will yield speeches by radical imams with fringe followings, like the one that inspired the 2013 Boston Marathon bombers, who often get higher page counts than those by reputable Muslim scholars. Accordingly, groups have begun to tailor their activities to recruit adherents who can operate inside the West, especially as borders become harder to cross for would-be terrorists. The al-Anser Forum, for instance, is a jihadi site published mainly in English.

The Internet revolution has allowed terrorist groups to obscure their operations in new ways that complicate the old ways of thinking about threats. Terror groups, eerily like the rest of us, value the Internet for its reliable service, easy terms, and virtual anonymity. The Taliban, for example, ran a propaganda website for over a year that kept a running tally of suicide bombings and other attacks against US troops in Afghanistan. And yet the host for the website was a Texas company called ThePlanet that rented out websites for $70 a month, payable by credit card. With some 16 million accounts, the company wasn't aware of the Taliban site's existence and took it down once notified by authorities.

And even when these sites are discovered and taken down, what we know and love about the Internet's structure works to these groups' advantage. Osama bin Laden's very last video before his death was simultaneously uploaded onto five different sites. And while counterterrorism agencies rushed to take them down, within one hour the video had been captured and uploaded by over 600 sites. Within a day, the number of sites hosting the video had doubled once again.

For terror groups, Internet communication does more than just create new connections and spread viral ideas; it also maintains old ones much in the same way that the rest of us use social networking to keep in touch with high school friends. Here, too, the relative anonymity and shrinking of distance that cyberspace allows are valuable advantages. Anarchist groups in the 1800s, the progenitors of many of the terror groups today, sent secretly coded messages by post and had to wait months for a reply. Today, a group can link members continents away instantaneously. All of the 9/11 attackers, for example, had Hotmail accounts, and they were thought to have coordinated through notes left in the guestbook section of a website run by the brother-in-law of one of Osama bin Laden's lieutenants.

Where cyberspace has had perhaps the greatest impact is in the sharing of knowledge in new and innovative ways. Some organizations take advantage of this for the positive, like the Khan Academy, which has allowed children around the world to learn math and science via online tutorials. But terrorists have also spread their peculiar type of knowledge, or what security experts call "TTPs" (short for tactics, techniques, and procedures), in ways not possible before. The recipes for explosives are readily available on the Internet, as are terrorist-provided designs for IEDs for use across conflict zones from Iraq to Afghanistan. This diffusion of terror teachings has been hugely important as these groups have found fewer and fewer training spaces free from global drone strikes.

The transfer of knowledge is not just about the "how" of a terror attack, but also the "who" and the "where" on the targeting side. Groups use cyberspace as a low-cost, low-risk venue to gather intelligence in ways they could only dream about a generation ago. For example, no terrorist group has the financial resources to afford a spy satellite to scope out targets with pinpoint precision, let alone the capability to build and launch one into space. Yet Google Earth worked just as effectively for Lashkar-e-Taiba, a Pakistan-based terror group, when it was planning the 2008 Mumbai attacks.

As in other areas of cybersecurity, we have to be aware of our own habits and uses of the Internet and how such bad actors might take advantage. In 2007, US soldiers took smartphone photos of a group of new US Army helicopters parked at a base in Iraq and then uploaded them to the Internet. The helicopters weren't classified and the photos showed no seemingly useful information to the enemy. But the soldiers didn't realize the photos also included "geotags," which revealed where the photographers had been standing. Insurgents then used these geotags to pinpoint and destroy four of the helicopters in a mortar attack. Experts now use this example to warn people to be more careful about what they share when engaged in an important activity. "Is a badge on Foursquare worth your life?" asked Brittany Brown, social media manager at Fort Benning, Georgia.

A growing worry is that groups may fully exploit social networking to locate better targeting information, and not just for geographic targets, but human ones. After the bin Laden raid in 2011, an American cybersecurity analyst was curious as to what he could find out about the supposedly super-secret unit that carried it out. He told us how he was able to find twelve current or former members' names, their families' names, and home addresses. This was not a matter of leaks to the press but rather through a series of social networking tricks. He identified one member of the raid team from a website photo of his SEAL training class, and another after he located an online image of a person wearing a SEAL team T-shirt with a group of friends and then tracked down those friends.

Using these same tactics, he also found the names of FBI undercover agents and, in another case, two married senior US government officials who were participating in a swinger site (and thus vulnerable to blackmail).

The analyst carried out the exercise to warn these targets to beware that there was more about them on the Internet than they thought, a useful reminder for us all.

What about Cyber Counterterrorism?

"It seems that someone is using my account and is somehow sending messages with my name...The dangerous thing in the matter is that they [those replying to what they thought was a genuine e-mail] say that I had sent them a message including a link for download, which they downloaded."

We can all empathize with this fellow. Many of us have received similar warnings from friends or family that someone has hacked their account and to beware of suspicious messages. The difference is that the individual complaining about being hacked in this case was "Yaman Mukhadab," a prominent poster inside Shumukh, a supposedly elite, password-protected forum for radicals. Before he sent out his warning to the forum, the group's agenda had included assembling a "wish list" of American security industry leaders, defense officials, and other public figures for terrorists to target and kill.

Mukhadab's cyber hardships illustrate that technology is a double-edged sword, even in the cyber realm that otherwise seems to be perfect for terrorists. Consider how much better and faster the Internet is today for terrorists wanting to communicate versus the experience of their 1800s forebears, who had to use snail mail to plan bombings. Yet, just as the mail of the past proved a liability for nineteenth-century anarchists once police learned to track them down by searching their correspondence, so too can today's terrorists' online activities shift from an advantage to a vulnerability.

A new debate has emerged in recent years, with some arguing that in lieu of playing a never-ending game of whack-a-mole, trying to track and then shut down all terrorist use of the Internet, it might be better to let the groups stay. "You can learn a lot from the enemy by watching them chat online," said Martin Libicki, a senior policy analyst at the RAND Corporation, a nonprofit research organization.

The point is that the advantages of cyberspace for terrorism can be equally useful for counterterrorism. The Web has aided terrorist groups by acting as both a Rolodex and playbook. But those on the other side of the fight have access to the same Rolodex and playbooks.

The networking effects of cyberspace, for instance, allow terrorists to link as never before, but they also allow intelligence analysts to map out social networks in unprecedented ways, providing clues about the leadership and structure of terrorist groups that would otherwise be impossible to gain. The world learned just how powerful some of these tools can be from documents leaked by NSA contractor Edward Snowden in 2013, detailing how US intelligence agencies and their allies engaged in online surveillance of an unprecedented scale. The approach was to monitor as much Internet traffic as possible, with a particular goal of collecting what is known as "metadata."

Essentially data about the data itself, metadata is information that describes the nature of communication, rather than the content. In traditional telephone surveillance, for example, this would simply be a record of what phone number called another phone number at what time, as opposed to what was said on the call. In the cyber era, metadata is far more complicated and thus far more useful. It includes information about geographic location, time, e-mail addresses, and other technical details about the data being created or sent. When this data is gathered together from sources around the world, sophisticated algorithms can be used to connect dots and reveal new patterns, as well as track individual devices, even when the user is trying to hide her identity. The effort was designed to help find links between terrorists. But the NSA programs controversially entailed collecting such information on the online activities of millions of non-terrorists. Think of it as trying to find a needle in a haystack, by collecting the entire haystack.

Online efforts can even be used as a means to pinpoint those not yet linked into terror networks, such as those pondering joining extremist groups or engaging in the sort of "lone wolf" attacks that have become more prominent in recent years. For instance, in 2008 and 2009 US intelligence agencies reportedly tried to attack and shut down the top terrorist propaganda websites on the anniversary of

9/11, in order to delay the release of an Osama bin Laden video celebrating the attacks. In 2010, however, they took a different tack. As *Wired* magazine reported, "The user account for al-Qaida's al-Fajr media distribution network was hacked and used to encourage forum members to sign up for Ekhlaas, a forum which had closed a year before and mysteriously resurfaced." The new forum turned out to be a fake, an online spiderweb entangling would-be terrorists and their fans. Similarly, while the Internet might spread potential terrorist tactics, defenders can also gain crucial insight into which tactics are taking hold and need to be defended against.

And, of course, one doesn't have to just watch but can also engage in cyberattacks against the terrorists. One known example (we only want to talk about the cases the terrorists already know about!) is using the terrorists' own computers to spy on them. This is what happened to Yaman Mukhadab and to the Global Islamic Media Front (GIMF), a network for producing and distributing radical propaganda online. In 2011, it had to warn its members that the group's own encryption program, "Mujahideen Secrets 2.0," actually shouldn't be downloaded because it had been compromised.

Just as cyberattacks don't always just seek to breach a network to gain information, cyber counterterrorism can change information inside a terrorist's networks. This might include playing a cheeky game of propaganda. In 2010, the terror group Al-Qaeda in the Arabian Peninsula (AQAP) issued "Inspire," an English-language online magazine designed to draw in recruits and spread terror tactics. Their first issue was reportedly hacked by British intelligence agencies, who replaced the terrorist "how to" pages with a cupcake recipe. Or the corruption of information might flip the idea of cyberterrorism on its very head. In one case, online bomb-making instructions were changed so that the attacker would instead blow himself up during the construction of the device.

What's notable about these online counterterror efforts is that, as with the rest of cybersecurity, governments are not the only players. Nonstate "hacktivism" has even played an important role in policing the Web. Jon Messner, for instance, is a private citizen from Maryland, who took down al-Neda, an al-Qaeda site. Fighting terrorism online is a hobby for Messner, though. His day job is running an Internet pornography business, being perhaps best known for originating the "housewife next-door" genre. It's yet another illustration of how the Internet isn't ungoverned, but rather is self-governed in strange and fascinating ways.

Security Risk or Human Right? Foreign Policy and the Internet

Cloud computing, the concept of delivering computing resources remotely over a network, is both a multibillion-dollar industry and a growing field that many believe is key to the future of the online world (as we'll explore later on). But for three days in 2011, the Dutch government threatened to undermine the new era of cloud computing, all in the name of human rights.

Taking issue with American laws that gave the US government access to any data stored on computers controlled by American companies, the Dutch Minister of Safety and Justice threatened to deny any American firm the ability to offer cloud-computing services to the Dutch government in 2011. Yet if no country was willing to let its data be held by a foreign company for fear of government surveillance, the transformative power of cloud computing to store and distribute data globally would be severely undermined. The Dutch ultimately backed down, but these calls have been echoed even more sharply around the world following the disclosure of certain NSA surveillance practices in 2013. Such episodes highlight a key tension: How do we balance the need for security with the importance of privacy and free expression?

Often couched in the language of human rights, the term "Internet freedom" centers on the idea of online free expression and the right to access the Internet as a means of connecting to others around the world. This idea builds on political rights granted well before the cyber age, like those in the 1948 Universal Declaration of Human Rights and the 1966 International Covenant on Civil and Political Rights "that guarantee the right to seek, receive and impart information and ideas through any media and regardless of frontier."

As the world moved into the digital age, democratic states argued that the online world wasn't just structured with a democratic ethic in mind, such as through the governance models we discussed in Part I; it also had to respect rights in the same spirit. This became a major part of former US Secretary of State Hillary Clinton's agenda, when she argued that our basic human rights must include cyberspace, since "people are as likely to come together to pursue common interests online as in a church or a labor hall."

The battle over Internet freedom is not simply a matter of access (such as whether Chinese or Iranian citizens should have access to online news reports). It has evolved to be more pointed and relevant to cybersecurity issues, as the Internet has become viewed as a means to change regimes themselves.

A number of nations, including the United States and the UK, as well as advocacy groups, have reached out to dissident groups operating under repressive regimes in ways that complicate cybersecurity. This effort has gone beyond traditional diplomacy, providing not just cyber training for the groups, but also the development and distribution of new technologies, like Tor, that aid users in evading government surveillance and censorship. It seems simple enough, but the problems are manifold. By enabling behavior on the Internet outside control or observation of the local government, regimes have often seen the technologies and those behind them as a security threat. For instance, in China, the government views its censorship not as a violation of human rights but as a tool for stability. Thus, these technologies have been categorized by China and its allies in international forums as tools of cyberattacks.

Freedom of speech is not only viewed differently among authoritarian and democratic states, but also across cultural and historic lines. In Thailand, it is illegal to defame the monarch; in Britain, it's a popular hobby. Controversial laws limit behavior online in the West, too. France successfully sued Yahoo! to ban the sale of Nazi memorabilia, something legal in the United States. Indeed, at the very moment the US State Department was pushing an online freedom agenda, other parts of the Obama administration and the US Congress were considering the Stop Online Piracy Act, which would have forced American ISPs to prevent access to foreign websites that illegally offer copyrighted material. An online protest movement, including a blackout of Wikipedia, forced the administration and Congress to back down.

The conflict between rights and security is not just a matter of political expression but also tests how issues of cybersecurity might be resolved. The debate about Internet governance has spilled into the security space. Those opposing American dominance in the multistakeholder process of setting Internet standards (discussed in

Part I) point to the revelations of NSA surveillance and the build up of Pentagon cyberwar capabilities as evidence for why a shift is needed. Defenders of the ICANN model, in turn, observe that many of those nations pushing for more government control just happen to be the most active at restricting speech within their own countries.

Ultimately, these questions turn on basic political questions of who should and who does have the power to decide whether something is a security risk or a human right. It is a matter that has vexed everyone from ancient Greek philosophers to the Founding Fathers, and it continues with us today.

Focus: What Is Tor and Why Does Peeling Back the Onion Matter?

It has received financial backing from the US Department of Defense as part of a Naval Research Lab program to keep digital secrets secret, but in turn, Edward Snowden revealed that any use of it is grounds for surveillance by the NSA. It has been described by *The Economist* as a "dark corner of the Internet," while it also won the 2010 Award for Projects of Social Benefit for enabling "36 million people around the world to experience freedom of access and expression on the Internet." Tor is one complex character.

Suppose you want to communicate with another computer user and not have anyone know. You could use encryption, but that would only prevent any eavesdropper from knowing what you were saying. Sometimes it's also important to keep private who you are communicating with. This type of privacy is important for a wide variety of online players: intelligence agencies communicating with undercover sources, companies exploring the competition's public website without their IP address showing up in the server logs, and especially for political activists inside authoritarian states, who don't want their governments to identify other dissidents whom they're working with.

A simple approach is a single-hop proxy, where you send your traffic to a computer that then passes it along to the final destination. This can be effective for an adversary watching an endpoint, but now you have to trust the intermediary. Who controls it? Do they keep records? What legal jurisdiction do they operate under?

Many users are rightly hesitant to use anonymity infrastructure that they do not control. However, on an open network such as the

Internet, running one's own system won't work. A system that carries traffic for only one organization will not hide the traffic entering and leaving that organization. Nodes must carry traffic from others to provide cover.

The solution is a system called Tor, short for "The Onion Router." Tor is an "overlay network" that provides online protection against surveillance and traffic analysis. An overlay network sits on top of the Internet but provides its own virtual structure of nodes and links. The network is formed by volunteers who offer their machines as nodes. Internet traffic is broken up into chunks, much like the underlying Internet packets, and encrypted to provide confidentiality. Communication then takes a multiple-hop path through the network, forcing any surveillance regime to watch every node in the network if they want to trace communication between the endpoints. Communication between each hop is separately encrypted so that an eavesdropper cannot learn as much from watching any single node. In short, Tor uses a network of intermediates to disguise both the source and endpoint of a conversation.

While it offers complex protection, Tor engineers have worked hard to make the network easy to use. You can download a whole web browser with Tor built in. Individuals with access can then e-mail, surf the Web, and share content online without anyone knowing who or where they are.

The positive social side of Tor is that it provides anonymity that supports free expression on the Internet by circumventing censorship. Tor originated in 2004 but rose to greater prominence a few years later during the 2009 "Green Revolution" protests in Iran and the 2011 "Arab Spring" as a means for dissident movements to collaborate but remain hidden in plain view.

Yet that same advantage also means that it provides anonymity for criminals seeking to avoid law enforcement's online surveillance. Tor has been used in cases involving child pornography (an FBI agent told us about one forum where anonymous users exchanged information on the best way to drug children), bank fraud, malware distribution, and an online anonymous black market called "Silk Road," where Internet users buy and sell controlled substances, guns, and narcotics.

The result has been a mixed attitude toward the technology and its uses. Despite the fact that it originally funded Tor, parts of the US military have described it as a threat, not least because of its use in several whistleblower cases like WikiLeaks. Meanwhile, because it has proved to be a thorn in the side of authoritarian governments, the US Congress and State Department have been supportive, describing it as an enabler of online freedom.

Tor's future rests on how this battle over Internet freedom is resolved, not just on the policy side but also technologically. Increasingly, regimes like China are employing new Internet censorship technology to fight a cat-and-mouse game with Tor developers. As the censors seek to find ways to block access to the network, Tor tries to circumvent each new technique. For instance, one innovative effort to keep Tor open for users behind the "Great Firewall of China" piggybacks Tor traffic inside a Skype video conference connection. This technique is innovative not only because it successfully hides Tor traffic within another protocol, but also because if the Chinese authorities were to shut it down, they would be forced to shut down all Skype traffic in the country, an impossible task given Skype's importance to multinational firms communicating with branch offices. Censorship then comes with a real monetary cost.

Tor illustrates the tension that can emerge between cyber freedom and security. The onion router has given extra layers of security to those who want to stay secret online, but secrecy can be scary to the established order.

Who Are Patriotic Hackers?

When Estonia's websites were attacked in the "Estonian Cyberwar" of 2007, Urmas Paet, the tiny nation's foreign minister, was quick to point his finger at neighboring Russia. He angrily accused the Kremlin of trying to paralyze his nation's economy and government through a massive denial–of–service attack. "Russia is attacking Estonia.... The attacks are virtual, psychological and real." But the Russian parliamentary leader Sergei Markov suggested the accusers look elsewhere than the Russian government: "About the cyberattack on Estonia...Don't worry, that attack was carried out by my assistant."

It sounds odd, but Markov's version of the story actually has an element of truth in it. Far from denying his role in what many thought of as an illegal action, Markov's young assistant openly

acknowledged it. He was a leader in Nashi ("Ours"), a movement of some 120,000 Russians between the ages of seventeen and
twenty-five. While not officially part of the Russian government,
the group was organized by pro-Putin regime supporters to take
on "anti-Fatherland" forces. Modeled in some ways after the Young
Soviet Kosomol, its activities ranged from running summer camps
to beating up antiregime protesters in street rallies. It also engaged
in cyber activities against what it saw as the twin perils of "Nazism
and liberalism." In this case, Estonia had moved the Bronze Soldier
of Tallin, a Russian grave marker from World War II. It was an act
that Russian nationalists like members of Nashi believed deserved
retribution, including by cyber means.

What Nashi was involved in is often called "patriotic hacking," an
action that involves citizens or groups within a state joining together
to carry out cyberattacks on perceived enemies of that country.

While those executing the attacks are private citizens and groups,
one of the hallmarks of patriotic hacking is the subtle role that a
government often plays in orchestrating the action to make it effective. One lone Russian youth trying to carry out a denial-of-service
attack would meet with little success. But in the Estonian case, tools
and instruction kits detailing how to carry out the DDoS attack were
posted in Russian forums, mobilizing vast numbers of individual
hackers to give it a state-sized scale. In an even better example, cyberattacks against Georgia only a year later during the Russian-Georgia
War were not only timed to coincide with Russian military operations but even utilized, in the words of one study, "vetted target
lists of Georgian government websites," thought to be provided by
Russian intelligence.

The advantage of using patriotic hackers is that a government can
utilize the synchronization and large-scale effort it wants without
being officially involved, giving it just enough cover to claim plausible deniability. Without cross-border police cooperation (which
the Russians refused to provide—another hallmark of the phenomenon), it was impossible to determine exactly who was behind all
the computer accounts involved in the Estonia attacks (besides parliamentary leaders ratting out their assistants). Thus, in an ironic
twist, governments that orchestrate such attacks can act aggrieved
whenever accused of involvement. Ultimately, while attacks against
Russia's foes occurred in cyberspace and a parliamentary leader

spoke of his office's own role in it, a Russian ambassador could retort, "If you are implying [the attacks] came from Russia or the Russian government, it's a serious allegation that has to be substantiated. Cyber-space is everywhere."

Patriotic hackers, though, aren't limited to youth groups. An interesting nexus actually exists with criminal organizations. They usually operate for their own profit motives but can also be mobilized by a state for political purposes. Many of the very same tools, platforms, and tactics used in the 2008 Georgia attacks, for instance, were also utilized by the Russian Business Network, one of the larger cybercriminal organizations. This leads many to believe that agreements have occasionally been struck in the patriotic hacker world. Criminal groups are given some freedom to operate in exchange for demonstrating their patriotism when governments ask for aid. Think of it as the cyber equivalent of the deal struck between the FBI and Mafia during World War II, when the Feds agreed to lay off their investigations in exchange for the mobsters watching the docks for Nazi spies and aiding military intelligence operations in Italy. Similarly, Russia was fairly active in cracking down on cybercrime rings before the cyberattacks of the late 2000s, but it has been far more lax in its law enforcement since. Indeed, it's notable that while nearly any publication that the Russian government considers objectionable has been prosecuted and harassed into prohibition in recent years, the hacker magazine *Xaker: Computer Hooligan* remains in broad circulation.

Sometimes, these activities are more explicitly condoned. In 2011, a hacker collective calling itself the Syrian Electronic Army defaced or disabled news websites that were critical of the Syrian regime's behavior in the widening civil war. Syrian president Assad praised these activities, calling the group "an electronic army which has been a real army in virtual reality." This led to "patriotic hacker" versus "hacktivist" drama as Anonymous entered the fray against the Syrian regime, and the SEA retaliated by targeting Anonymous-affiliated sites.

Another advantage is that patriotic hackers allow governments to tap into expertise and resources that lie beyond the state. Some governments even appear to be working in concert with patriotic hacker groups in order to scout new talent and create a "B-team" of cyber reserves. In 2005, the Chinese military reportedly organized a series of regional hacker competitions to identify talented civilians. As a result, the founding member of the influential hacker group Javaphile (hugely active in Chinese patriotic hacker attacks on the United States in the early 2000s, including the defacement of the White House website) joined the Shanghai Public Security Bureau as a consultant.

However, this comes with a price. While patriotic hackers have proved able to hamper state foes in cyberspace while maintaining plausible deniability, they may not have the level of control that governments, especially authoritarian ones, desire. Once set loose in cyberspace, hackers can go off message or engage in unwanted activities. In an embarrassing episode, the winner of China's 2005 regional competition was later arrested for attacking rival hacker groups' websites. And when the Chinese government only wanted positive news to surround the 2008 Beijing Olympics, Chinese patriotic hacker forums made negative news by providing tutorials on how to launch a DDoS attack against the CNN website (they were upset by its reporting on riots in Tibet). Things proved especially escalatory in 2010 when patriotic hackers from Iran and China, two ostensible allies in the real world, got into an escalating series of retaliatory attacks after baidu.com (the Chinese version of Google) was hit by the "Iranian Cyber Army."

Thus, governments are sometimes forced to crack down on the very patriotic hackers they once relied on. For instance, in 2010, the Chinese government ordered the Black Hawk Safety Net site shut. Previously, the site had been a hub for patriotic hacker tools and lessons, with some 170,000 members.

Some governments, however, then embrace these groups, bringing them into the fold through "cyber militias." Many trace this trend back to the 2001 Hainan Island incident, during which a Chinese J-8 fighter pilot veered too close to an American Navy P-3 surveillance plane and the two aircraft collided in midair. The smaller Chinese plane spun to earth and its hotdogging pilot was killed, while the American plane had to make an emergency landing at a Chinese airfield on Hainan. As the two governments angrily accused the other of causing the collision, the Communist Party encouraged computer-savvy citizens in China to deface American websites to show their collective displeasure. As we discussed earlier, Chinese teens organized online by the thousands and gleefully joined in the cyber vandalism, targeting everything from public libraries in Minnesota to the aforementioned White House website.

After an eleven-day standoff, the recently elected Bush administration agreed to send a "letter of sorrow" and pay China $34,000 for the detained crew's "food and lodging," after which the American crew was released. And with that, the Chinese government declared an end to the episode and sought to normalize relations with the United States. The only problem was that, once loosed, the young patriotic hackers were stoked with nationalism and proved difficult to rein in. Several were ultimately arrested when they wouldn't stop unauthorized hacks. As a result, the Party organized the once informal recreational groups into more formal, controllable organizations.

A first step in this direction took place in 2003 in the Guangshou Military Region, where part of China's IT economy is clustered. People's Liberation Army officers conducted a survey to identify "those with advanced degrees, who studied overseas, conducted major scientific research, [and] those considered computer network experts." Unpaid, volunteer (as much as that means in such an environment) units were organized around these individuals, who then operated out of computer labs and commercial firms rather than military bases. This gave the militia the combination of "politically reliability," educated staff, modern commercial infrastructure, and advanced software design capabilities. It's now estimated that these units have well over 200,000 members.

Mobilizing the skills and scale of civilian hackers while maintaining greater government control may be how patriotic hacking evolves globally in the future. This alignment, however, also makes it harder for many states to use patriotic hackers, because they forfeit plausible deniability. As we'll see, striking the right balance often comes down to more than how the groups are organized; the ways they operate are also important.

Focus: What Was Stuxnet?

Ralph Langner is a jovial fellow with a quick wit, whose sense of whimsy is perhaps best illustrated by the fact that he wears cowboy boots. Wearing cowboy boots shouldn't be all that notable, until one realizes that Ralph is not from Texas, but Germany, and is not a cowboy, but a computer specialist. Langner is also incredibly inquisitive.

It was this combination that led him to play a role in the discovery of one of the most notable weapons in history; and not just cyber history, but history overall.

Since 1988, Ralph and his team of security experts had been advising on the safety of large-scale installations. Their special focus was industrial control systems, the computer systems like SCADA (short for "supervisory control and data acquisition") that monitor and run industrial processes. SCADA is used in everything from the management and operation of power plants to the manufacture of candy wrappers.

In 2010, like many other industrial control experts, Ralph grew concerned about a cyber "worm" of unknown origin that was spreading across the world and embedding itself in these control systems. Thousands of computers in places like India and the United States had been infected. But the bulk of the infections (roughly 60 percent) were in Iran. This led many experts to infer that either Iran had particularly poor cyber defenses for its SCADA-related programs, which made it more vulnerable, or a virus had initially targeted some site in Iran and, as one report put it, "subsequently failed in its primary purpose and run amok, spreading uncontrollably to unintended targets all over the world, and thus demonstrating how indiscriminate and destructive cyber weapons were likely to be."

Both turned out to be far from the case. Curious, Ralph began to dissect the code of "Stuxnet," as it became known. The more he and his team explored it, the more interested they became. It was a wonderfully complex piece of malware like none the world had ever seen. It had at least four new "zero days" (previously unknown vulnerabilities), utilized digital signatures with the private keys of two certificates stolen from separate well-known companies, and worked on all Windows operating systems down to the decade-old Windows 95 edition. The number of new zero days particularly stood out. Hackers prize zero days and don't like to reveal them when they don't have to. To use four at once was unprecedented and almost illogical given that one new open door is enough. It was a pretty good sign that Stuxnet's makers had enormous resources and wanted to be absolutely certain they would penetrate their target.

Stuxnet also slipped by the Windows' defenses using the equivalent of a stolen passport. To gain access to the "kernel," or operating system's control system, Stuxnet had to install a component that could talk to the kernel. The authors chose a "device driver," a common tool that allows hardware devices to interact with the operating system. Windows uses a scheme of digital signatures to allow trusted hardware manufacturers to write device drivers that are trusted by the operating system. Unsigned drivers raise an alert for the user, while signed drivers do not. The drivers in Stuxnet were signed by two real companies in Taiwan, indicating that the authors had access to the secret signing keys—most likely stolen. Again, this is a rare style of attack: stolen signing keys are incredibly powerful, would have been well protected, and would be very valuable in any illicit market.

The malware's DNA revealed something even more interesting: Rather than being truly infectious, Stuxnet was hunting for something in particular. As Langner delved deeper, he discovered that Stuxnet was not going after computers or even Windows software in general, but a specific type of program used in Siemens's WinCC/PCS 7 SCADA control software. Indeed, if this software wasn't present, the worm had built-in controls to become inert. In addition, rather than trying to spread as widely as possible, as was the goal with past worms, Stuxnet only allowed each infected computer to spread the worm to no more than three others. It even came with a final safeguard; a self-destruct mechanism caused it to erase itself in 2012. Ralph realized that whoever made Stuxnet not only had a specific target in mind, but didn't want the code lingering in the wild forever. This was a very different worm, indeed.

But what was the target? This was the true mystery. Here Langner's background in working with industrial firms proved particularly useful. He figured out that Stuxnet was only going after a specific industrial controller, manufactured by Siemens, configured to run a series of nuclear centrifuges—but not just any old nuclear centrifuges you might have lying around the house, only a "cascade" of centrifuges of a certain size and number (984) linked together. Not so coincidentally, this was the exact setup at the Natanz nuclear facility, a suspected site in Iran's illicit nuclear weapons program.

Things got especially tricky once Stuxnet found its way into this target (it was later revealed that the delivery mechanism was infiltration through Iranian nuclear scientists' own laptops and memory sticks). Langner discovered that the cyberattack didn't shut down the centrifuges in any obvious manner. Instead, it ran a series of subroutines. One, known as a "man in the middle," caused tiny adjustments in pressure inside the centrifuges. Another manipulated the speed of the centrifuges' spinning rotors, causing them to alternately slow down and then speed back up, throwing the rotors out of whack and ruining their work. On top of this, every so often the malware would push the centrifuge speeds past the designed maximum. So the centrifuges weren't just failing to produce refined uranium fuel, they were frequently breaking down and grinding to a halt from the damaging vibrations that the various random surges caused. At other times, the machines were literally spinning out of control and exploding.

The effect, Langner wrote, was "as good as using explosives" against the facility. In fact, it was better. The victim had "no clue of being under a cyber attack." For over a year, Stuxnet had been inside Iranian networks, but the nuclear scientists initially thought their facility was just suffering from a series of random breakdowns. The scientists just kept replacing the broken centrifuges with new ones, which would then get infected and break again. Soon, though, they wondered whether they were being sold faulty parts or were suffering from some kind of hardware sabotage. But the machines checked out perfectly every time, except for the fact that nothing was working the way it should.

This was perhaps the most insidious part of Stuxnet: it was an integrity attack par excellence. Stuxnet didn't just corrupt the process, it hid its effects from the operators and exploited their trust that the computer systems would accurately and honestly describe what was taking place. Iranian engineers didn't even suspect a cyberattack; their systems were air-gapped from the Web, and up to this point worms and viruses had always had an obvious effect on the computer, not the hardware. Eventually, the Iranian scientists suffered low morale, under the impression that they couldn't do anything right; seventy years earlier a bunch of Americans had built an atomic bomb using slide rulers, and they couldn't even get their modern-day centrifuges to work. Overall, Langner likened the Stuxnet effect to the cyber version of "Chinese water torture."

When Ralph Langer revealed his findings on his blog, the little-known German researcher quickly became an international celebrity. First, he had exposed a top-secret campaign of sabotage (later leaked to have been a collaborative effort between US and

Israeli intelligence agencies, known as "Olympic Games"), and second, it was a find of global importance. A new kind of weapon long speculated about but never seen, a specially designed cyber weapon, had finally been used.

What Is the Hidden Lesson of Stuxnet? The Ethics of Cyberweapons

"The musket of cyberwarfare. What will be its rifle? Its AK-47? Its atomic bomb?"

Judith Donath of Harvard University described Stuxnet as a demonstration of a new kind of weapon that could only get better. But others worried that these better weapons would promote a new kind of escalation and global risk. "Stuxnet was the absolute game changer," wrote cyber thinker Mikko Hypponen. "We are entering an arms race where countries start stocking weapons, only it isn't planes and nuclear reactors they're stocking, but it's cyberweapons." And still others worry that not enough people took notice of this "opening shot in a war we will all lose," says Leslie Harris of the Center for Democracy and Technology.

Stuxnet was all of these things, perhaps, but it was also notable for another reason. This nasty little worm was a superb illustration of how ethics can be applied to cyberwar.

There is the notion that all is fair in love and war, but the reality is that there are actually a series of strict guidelines that are supposed to shape behavior in war—what seventeenth-century legal thinker Hugo Grotius called *jus in bello* ("Laws in War"). The two biggest laws are proportionality and discrimination. The law of proportionality states that the suffering and devastation that you cause, especially collateral damage to unintended targets, can't outweigh whatever harm prompted the conflict. If the other side stole your cow, you can't justifiably nuke their city. The law of discrimination maintains that the sides must distinguish legitimate targets from those that shouldn't be targeted (be they civilians or wounded) and do their utmost only to cause harm to the intended, legitimate targets.

Stuxnet stood out as a new kind of weapon in that it was designed to cause physical damage via cyber means. Its makers wanted it to break things in the real world, but through action only on digital networks. But what really stands out compared to traditional weapons is how small its physical impact was, especially compared to the intense stakes. The target was a nuclear bomb-making program, one that had already been targeted by diplomatic efforts and economic sanctions. While it's certainly arguable whether preemptive action against the Iranian program is justifiable, this is when the question of proportionality becomes relevant. Stuxnet broke nothing other than the nuclear centrifuges that had been illegally obtained by Iran to conduct illicit research. Moreover, it neither hurt nor killed anyone. By comparison, when Israel attempted to obstruct Iraqi nuclear research in 1981, its forces dropped sixteen 2,000-pound bombs on a research site during "Operation Opera," leveling it and killing eleven soldiers and civilians.

But discrimination also matters when judging the ethics of these attacks. At face value, Stuxnet would seem to have been incredibly indiscriminant. While limited in its promiscuity compared to prior malware, this was a worm that still got around. It infected not just targets in Iran but thousands of computers across the world that had nothing to do with Iran or nuclear research. Many lawyers see this facet of cyber weapons as proof of their inherent violation of "prevailing codes of international laws of conflict, as they go beyond just the original target and deliberately target civilian personnel and infrastructure."

While Stuxnet lacked discretion under the old way of thinking, its very design prevented harm to anyone and anything beyond the intended target. This kind of discrimination was something never previously possible in a weapon. As George Lucas, a philosopher at the US Naval Academy, wrote in an assessment of Stuxnet's ethics, "Unless you happen to be running a large array of exactly 984 Siemens centrifuges simultaneously, you have nothing to fear from this worm."

In effect, judging the ethics of Stuxnet and cyber weapons more generally turns on which part of the story you care about most. Do you focus on the fact that this new kind of weapon permitted a preemptive attack and in so doing touched thousands of people and computers who had nothing to do with Iran or nuclear research? Or do you focus on the fact that the cyber strike caused far less damage than any previous comparable attack and that the weapon was so discriminating it essentially gave new meaning to the term? Are you a cyber weapon half full or half empty kind of guy?

History may render the ultimate judgment of Stuxnet, however. As Ralph Langner put it, the fascinating new weapon he discovered "could be considered a textbook example of a 'just war' approach. It didn't kill anyone. That's a good thing. But I am afraid this is only a short-term view. In the long run it has opened Pandora's box."

"Cyberwar, Ugh, What Are Zeros and Ones Good For?": Defining Cyberwar

"Be it resolved by the Senate and House of Representatives of the United States of America in Congress assembled, that the state of war between the United States and the Government of Bulgaria, which has thus been thrust upon the United States, is hereby formally declared."

This June 5, 1942, text describes the last time the United States actually declared war. The declaration covered the minor Axis powers, who were feeling left out after the first post–Pearl Harbor vote to go to war against Nazi Germany, Japan, and Italy. In the years since, America has sent troops to Korea and Iraq and launched airstrikes into places like Yugoslavia, Cambodia, and Pakistan, but the United States has not formally declared war on another state. Wars have been declared on various other things, however: President Johnson's 1964 "Nationwide War on the Sources of Poverty"; Nixon's 1969 "War on Drugs"; and what some conservative leaders more recently claim is a secret "War on Christmas."

The disconnect between an actual state of war and the far more frequent uses and misuses of the concept of "war" is important to keep in mind when discussing a term like "cyberwar." War is used to describe an enormously diverse set of conditions and behaviors, from a state of armed conflict between nations (World War II) to symbolic contestations (New York City's "war on sugar"). As for "cyberwar," the term has been used to describe everything from a campaign of cyber vandalism and disruption (the "Russian Estonian cyberwar," as it is too often called) to an actual state of warfare utilizing cyber means. Indeed, in 2010 *The Economist* ran a cover story on cyberwar that portrayed it as everything from military conflict to credit card fraud.

Defining cyberwar need not be so complicated. The key elements of war in cyberspace all have their parallels and connections to warfare in other domains (the real kind, not the symbolic "war between the sexes" kind). Whether it be war on land, at sea, or in the air, or now in cyberspace, war always has a political goal and mode (which distinguishes it from crime) and always has an element of violence. Currently, the US government's position is that to meet this definition of the use of force, a cyberattack would have to "proximately result in death, injury or significant destruction." That is, even if conducted through cyber means, the effect must be physical damage or destruction. To provide a parallel, a plane dropping bombs is engaged in air warfare; a plane dropping leaflets, not so much.

Knowing when cyberwar begins or ends, however, might be more challenging than defining it. Most wars don't actually have the clear start and negotiated ends that World War II had. Instead, their starts and ends blur. For instance, the United States may not have formally declared war on North Korea in 1950, but it's hard to argue that a conflict in which 5.3 million perished was just a "police action," as President Truman called it at the time. In turn, while the Korean War, as the history books record it, has never formally ended with a peace treaty, the actual fighting ceased in 1953.

Cyberwar's lines can be just as fuzzy. "We in the US tend to think of war and peace as an on-off toggle switch—either at full-scale war or enjoying peace," says Joel Brenner, former head of counterintelligence under the US Director of National Intelligence. "The reality is different. We are now in a constant state of conflict among nations that rarely gets to open warfare. . . . What we have to get used to is that even countries like China, with which we are certainly not at war, are in intensive cyberconflict with us."

This may be where cyberwar has more in common with more informal concepts of conflict like the Cold War, during which constant conflict didn't actually result in direct, open violence. Indeed, the editor of *Foreign Policy* magazine, David Rothkopf, has argued we may be entering the era of the "cool war," not only because of the remote nature of the attacks but because "it can be conducted indefinitely—permanently, even—without triggering a shooting war. At least, that is the theory."

A War by Any Other Name? The Legal Side of Cyber Conflict

"The Parties agree that an armed attack against one or more of them in Europe or North America shall be considered an attack against them all."

This sentence opens Article 5 of the Washington Treaty, which in 1949 established the North Atlantic Treaty Organization, or NATO. It is one of the most important passages ever written in international politics. These simple words outlined the concept of "collective defense," which created the most successful alliance in history. This "All for one, one for all" approach to sharing risk and response allowed the United States and its allies to stand together, taking them from the start of the Cold War to the fall of the Berlin Wall and beyond, including their collective response to the 9/11 attacks on the United States and subsequent deployment half a world away to Afghanistan.

But in April 2007, NATO and its collective defense ideals faced a twenty-first-century test. A new alliance member, Estonia, was one of Europe's most wired states. The majority of its citizens conducted everything from their banking to their voting online. Suddenly, Estonian banks, media web pages, and government websites were hit with a large-scale denial of service attack. While the attack resulted from a series of botnets that had captured over a million computers in seventy-five countries, as we read about earlier, Estonia quickly pointed the finger at its neighbor Russia, with whom it was embroiled in a political dispute over the move of a statue honoring Russian soldiers from World War II. Estonia's foreign minister called for help, believing that the massive cyberattack threatened its security and hence the alliance's as a whole. It argued that under the Washington Treaty NATO was obliged to defend against this start of a new "cyberwar."

While they were concerned about the attacks, however, the other members of NATO didn't think Article 5 applied. Estonia was being bullied in cyberspace, but no one was dead or hurt and no property was actually destroyed or damaged. It didn't look like the start of a war, at least as NATO understood it, and certainly wasn't worth the alliance risking an actual war with Russia. Instead, the defense ministers of NATO waited a few weeks to issue a joint statement deploring the cyberattacks and sent technical experts to aid Estonia in unblocking its networks. Amusingly, while NATO's political leaders judged that the cyberattacks were not an act of war, NATO's Department of Public Diplomacy later created a short film about the episode entitled *War in Cyberspace.*

The Estonia case is instructive because it shows the back and forth that takes place between old laws and new technologies, especially when it comes to the question of what constitutes an act of war in the cyber realm. Much of today's thinking on the laws and state-craft of war dates to the post–World War II 1945 UN Charter and 1949 Geneva Conventions. The challenge is that concepts developed back when computers used punch cards don't necessarily apply as clearly to the cyber realm.

In international law, for instance, an "aggression" that would jus-tify going to war is described by the UN Charter as a "use of force against the territorial integrity . . . of a state." The problem is that this assumes only a physical world of clearly demarcated borders. This was perfectly acceptable back in 1945 but not in the contemporary world; cyberattacks don't use physical force, take place in a geo-graphic realm, nor necessarily involve only states.

That old laws are growing more challenging to apply doesn't mean, however, that the cyber world is the Wild West. There are nascent efforts to either update the old codes or create new ones. For example, after the confusion over the Estonia incident, the NATO Cooperative Cyber Defence Centre of Excellence commis-sioned twenty law professors to formally examine how the known laws of war apply to cyberspace, in a document entitled the "Tallinn Manual on the International Law Applicable to Cyber Warfare." The manual laid out their ideas on everything from what self-defense might mean in the cyber world to a controversial (but logical) argu-ment that any civilian fighting in a cyberwar loses legal protections as a civilian. While an important effort, it has no legal standing, and obviously a number of nations outside of NATO, such as Russia, were less than enthusiastic about the manual's findings. Even more, certain NATO members like the United States were not quick to embrace the manual they had sponsored.

The reality is that the "process of formalizing rules for cyber-space will likely take decades given the differing priorities among various governments," reports *Foreign Policy* magazine. This seems to leave a massive vacuum in the interim. So until the old treaties are updated or new ones are accepted for the cyber world, there is a third option: apply existing laws' basic principles and values to cyberspace. Charles Dunlap, a military lawyer who retired as a US Air Force major general and now teaches at Duke University Law School, notes, "A cyber attack is governed by basically the same rules as any other kind of attack."

The primary way to determine when a cyberattack constitutes the kind of "use of force" that legally justifies war is to weigh its effects. What did the act do to the real world, regardless of the fact that it happened via cyber means? Look to the amount of damage, caused or intended, and establish parallels.

Focusing on impact is important because it recognizes that not all attacks have to involve traditional armed violence. Indeed, in international law an enemy that uses unarmed means to intentionally divert a river to flood a neighboring state or set fires to burn wildly across the border would still be committing an armed act of aggression equivalent to the use of guns for the same effect.

The same logic applies in reverse. You wouldn't go to war if someone defaced your posters in the street, so neither should a government if an enemy defaces its websites. By comparison, when the action causes death and destruction, the discussion moves into the realm of war. If your power plant explodes in a fiery blast that kills thousands, whether the cause was an actual bomb or logic bomb is not a major distinguishing factor.

The real challenge is the gray area in the middle, incidents between destruction and disruption, such as a denial-of-service attack. When it was under attack, Estonia wanted NATO to declare that its sovereignty had been violated, which would have triggered the collective self-defense article of the NATO treaty. In the virtual world perhaps it had been, but not in the physical world. Here again, even these seemingly new forms of attack have parallels to guide us. While they may not have imagined cyberspace, the 1940s-era statesmen who wrote the UN Charter did imagine things like the interruption of "postal, telegraphic, radio, and other means of communications." Such interruptions were certainly frowned upon, but they did not constitute war. Professor James Hendler, former chief scientist at the Pentagon's Defense Advanced Research Projects Agency (DARPA), says that in the case of Estonia, the attacks were "more like a cyber riot than a military attack." It was disruptive, but it wasn't war.

Another example in Estonia's neighborhood serves as illustration. In 2008, the nation of Georgia also got in a dispute with its larger neighbor. Just as in Estonia, Georgian websites suffered denial-of-service attacks, as we saw earlier, thought to have been coordinated by Russian sources. The attacks crippled the websites' operations for several days and limited the Georgian government's ability to communicate with its people and the outside world. At the same time, several brigades of Russian tanks crossed into Georgia, and Russian bombers and missiles pummeled the country, causing over 1,300 casualties. The difference in impact was stark. The cyberattacks alone were not war, but a war was clearly taking place.

The severity of the attack is not the only thing to keep in mind. There are all sorts of actions that could ultimately spark a chain of events that cause the same death and destruction as real war. A young boy drops a banana, upon which a diplomat slips. The diplomat goes to the hospital instead of peace talks. The peace talks consequently fail and war breaks out. We can conceptualize how the boy's action helped lead to war, but was his dropping the banana an act of war? Of course not; the invasion was the action that mattered when looking to judge how the war actually started. Cause is not the same as effect.

This points to the second key determinant of when a cyberattack becomes an act of war: directness and measurability. There must be some fairly direct and intended link between cause and effect. This factor is often applied to distinguish acts of espionage from acts of war. The theft of government secrets could certainly lead to soldiers losing their lives one day by revealing to the enemy, for instance, how a plane operates or the location of a secret base. But it is only if and when the war starts that this theft could ever have that impact. This indirectness is why nations have traditionally not gone to war over acts of espionage, be they physical or increasingly now virtual. No one likes to be the victim of espionage, to be sure. But spying is cast more as part of the rough game of statecraft that nations play rather than the all-out breaking of international rules that starts real wars.

An important part of these discussions, however, is often forgotten. While we'd like to think that law is the guide to our behavior, clearly delineating when a cyberattack escalates into war is not just an issue of law or just for the lawyers to decide. As the great philosopher of war Carl von Clausewitz wrote, "War is not an independent phenomenon, but the continuation of politics by different means." War is political. And by being political, it is also always interactive. That is, there are sides to the war, each with their own goals, actions, and responses, each trying to bend the other to its will.

This fundamentally political nature of war means that all of these questions on when a cyberattack reaches the realm of war will come down to making tough political decisions, in what Clausewitz would see as a digital version of his famous "fog of war," the messy, fast-moving, unclear circumstances that always accompany war. Ultimately, cyberwar is what we in the real world believe it to be. "At the end of the day, it's the President who gets to decide if this is war or something else," explains Jim Lewis, a senior fellow at the Center for Strategic and International Studies. "The standard is ambiguous. Deciding when something is an act of war is not automatic. It's always a judgment."

What Might a "Cyberwar" Actually Look Like?
Computer Network Operations

Like so many stories in the world of cybersecurity, Operation Orchard began with simple human carelessness. In 2006, a senior official in the Syrian government left his laptop computer in his hotel room while visiting London. When he went out, agents from Mossad, the Israeli intelligence agency, snuck into his room and installed a Trojan horse onto the laptop to allow them to monitor his communications. That was bad enough for the Syrians.

But one man's poor computer security turned out to have more significant consequences when the Israelis began to examine the files that the official had stored on the laptop's hard drive, including pictures. One photo in particular caught the Israelis' attention. It showed an Asian man in a blue tracksuit standing next to an Arab man in the middle of the Syrian desert. It could have been innocuous, but then Mossad identified the two men as Chon Chibu, a leader of the North Korean nuclear program, and Ibrahim Othman, director of the Syrian Atomic Energy Commission. Combined with other documents lifted from the hard drive, such as construction plans and photos of a type of pipe used for work on fissile materiel, the Israelis realized the laptop was an atomic alarm bell. The Syrians were secretly constructing a facility at al Kibar to process plutonium, a key step in the assembly of a nuclear bomb, with aid from North Korea (an International Atomic Energy Agency investigation would later confirm the Israeli suspicions).

This news led to Operation Orchard, the next key part of the cyber story. Just after midnight on September 6, 2007, seven Israeli F-15I fighter jets crossed into Syrian airspace. They flew deep into the Syrian interior and dropped several bombs, leveling the Kibar complex depicted in the photos. The whole time the planes were in Syrian airspace, the air defense network never fired a shot.

Reportedly, the Syrian defense didn't even detect the jets, meaning they didn't even know they were under attack until the bombs started to go off. Yet Syrian radar officers hadn't all turned traitor that night. Rather, their technology had. If initially planting the Trojan horse into the Syrian officials laptop had been about finding secret information via cyber means, this was its cousin, a cyber operation with a military outcome. The Israelis had successfully penetrated the Syrian military's computer networks, allowing them to see what the Syrians were doing as well as direct their own data streams into the air defense network. This caused the Syrian radar operators to see a false image of what was really happening as the Israeli jets flew across the border. By effectively turning off the Syrian air defenses for the night, the Israelis not only got to their target without any losses, but they also did so with a much smaller force.

Orchard is a great illustration of the concepts behind "computer network operations," as such military cyberattack operations are dubbed. While much is shrouded in secrecy about the rise of such operations, one of the first known US military exercises in this space was "Eligible Receiver," a test of computer network operations in 1997. In many ways it was akin to the Fleet Problems of the 1920s, when the US Navy first experimented with aircraft carriers, or the Louisiana Maneuvers of 1940, when the US Army evaluated mechanized tank forces. After a small "red team" of computer experts gained access to the computers at the US Pacific Command's headquarters as well as the 911 emergency phone systems in nine US cities, the Pentagon decided that, just as with the airplane or the tank, the time had arrived for computers to play a part in military operations. Indeed, the naysayers were hushed the very next year when hackers compromised over five hundred Pentagon computers in an incident that became known as "Solar Sunrise."

Today, the vast majority of the world's militaries have some sort of planning or organization in place for cyber warfare. These plans can be thought of as the "Five D's plus One." The US Air Force describes cyberwar as the ability "to destroy, deny, degrade, disrupt, [and] deceive," while at the same time "defending" against the enemy's use of cyberspace for the very same purpose.

Such military programs range from focused infiltrations and raids like Israel's Operation Orchard to broader efforts like the US military's "Plan X," a $110 million program designed to "help warplanners assemble and launch online strikes in a hurry and make cyber attacks a more routine part of U.S. military operations." But across the world, what the *New York Times* called "a new type of warfare" actually has much in common with war as it has always been conducted. The computer used as a military weapon is just a tool. Just as with the spear, the airplane, or the tank, it simply aids in achieving the goals that are part of any military operation.

Before battle begins, a smart commander engages in what is known as "intelligence preparation of the battlefield." Much as Allied efforts to crack Axis radio codes proved crucial to victory in World War II, intercepted digital communications can be just as critical today. As the Israelis did in Orchard, this part of cyber warfare is about deploying one's digital weapons even before the battle has begun, infiltrating networks, gathering information, and potentially even laying the groundwork for more aggressive action. For example, some of the information inside US military computers suspected to have been targeted by Chinese military hackers includes unit deployment schedules, resupply rates, materiel movement schedules, readiness assessments, maritime prepositioning plans, air tasking for aerial refueling, and "the logistics status of American bases in Western Pacific theater." This kind of data might prove useful if war ever broke out. And, as the 2013 Snowden leaks showed, US cyber warriors are gathering the same information about their potential adversaries in China and elsewhere.

But the difference between current cyber efforts and past intelligence collection programs is how computer network operations also allow aggressive actions inside the enemy's communications once the shooting has begun. It's the difference between reading the enemy's radio signals and being able to seize control of the radio itself.

The modern military is what some folks call "network-centric," utilizing computers bound together in a "system of systems" to coordinate across great distances with digital speed. But these advantages can create vulnerabilities. If you can compromise an enemy's networked communications, you move from knowing what they're doing, which is advantage enough, to potentially changing what they're doing.

Inside a foe's communications networks, one can disrupt or even disable command and control, keeping commanders from sending out orders, units from talking to each other, or even individual weapons systems from sharing needed information. In one example, over one hundred American defense systems, from aircraft carriers to individual missiles, rely on the Global Positioning System (GPS) to locate themselves during operations. In 2010, an accidental software glitch knocked 10,000 of the military's GPS receivers offline for over two weeks, including the US Navy's X-47 prototype robotic fighter jet. Cyber warfare would, in effect, make such software glitches deliberate.

Alternatively, the attack might not try to disable or jam these communications but instead attack the information within them, feeding the enemy false reports via its own devices. "Information warfare" is how the military has traditionally described operations that try get inside the enemy's mind and influence decision-making. Now the idea is to use modern information technologies to the same ends. The objectives might be highly strategic, such as false commands from top leaders, to more tactical insertions along the lines of what the Israelis did in Orchard, compromising individual weapons systems and their sensors.

One of the more interesting potential effects of such attacks is how success might be multiplied by the impact on the minds of the users of the networks under attack. Only a relatively small percentage of attacks would have to be successful in order to plant seeds of doubt in any information coming from a computer. Users' doubt would lead them to question and double-check everything from their orders to directions. This illustrates again the notion of trust, which was so important in Part I. The impact could even go beyond the initial disruption. It could erode the trust in the very networks needed by modern military units to work together effectively;

it could even lead some militaries to abandon networked computers for anything important and set their capacity back decades.

Such technological abstinence sounds extreme, especially when computers have proven so useful in modern war. But imagine if you had a memo that you needed to get to your boss with absolutely no mistakes, at the risk of losing your job. Would you e-mail it if there were a 50 percent risk of it somehow being lost or changed en route? Or would you just hand-deliver it? What about if the risk were 10 percent? How about just 1 percent, but still at the risk of losing your job? Then apply the same risk tolerances when it's your life in battle rather than your job. How do your risk numbers change?

Computer network operations, though, won't just be limited to targeting command and control with indirect effects. As more and more unmanned systems are introduced into warfare (the US military has over 8,000 "drones" like the famous Predator and Reaper, while over eighty countries now have military robotics programs), targeting command-and-control networks opens up even more direct avenues of attack. These robotic weapons systems all link into computer networks, providing everything from GPS location to remotely controlled operations. Here again, the very same networking that allows drones to strike targets with precision thousands of miles away also opens up new possibilities of disruption and even co-option. What we enter is an era of "battles of persuasion."

One could never co-opt the flight of a bullet, steering it away from where the gunner shot it. Nor has anyone proven able to brainwash a bomber pilot in midair and shift his allegiance. But if the computers on robotic weapons systems are compromised, they could be "persuaded" to do the opposite of what their owners intended. This creates a whole new type of combat, where the goal may not be merely to destroy the enemy's tanks but to hack into his computer networks and make his tanks drive around in circles or even attack each other.

And, of course, cyberwar might see computers used in the same way that other weapons have been used to cause destruction and loss of life among enemy forces. As opposed to traditional kinetic attacks (a blade, a bullet, an explosion), these would involve more destruction through indirect means. Many military systems like ship engines operate under SCADA programs, meaning that they can be targeted in much the same way that the Stuxnet virus caused Iranian centrifuges to spin out of control. In 2009, for instance, an employee at the Shushenskaya dam in Siberia accidentally turned on an unused turbine with a few mistaken keystrokes, leading to the release of a massive "water hammer" that destroyed the plant and killed seventy-five people. This is the computer software version of how allied planes in World War II and Korea dropped bombs on dams, using the ensuing wave to destroy enemy targets in the flood's path.

As in traditional war, though, what sounds easy in description can prove hard in execution. This is not just due to the complexity of target systems and the operations needed to exploit them, but because every war, even in cyberspace, has at least two sides. Every potential operation meant to attack and defeat a foe would be met by the opponent's efforts to keep the enemy out or threats of an equivalent attack to make the aggressor think twice about conducting it.

These difficulties drive adversaries to instead go after "soft targets," as has long been the case in traditional modes of war. In theory, war is only a contest among warriors. In reality, well over 90 percent of the casualties in the last decades of war have been civilians. Unfortunately, one can expect the same dynamic in cyberwar.

The more conventional type of civilian targeting in computer network operations would attack civilian networks and operators viewed as directly or indirectly supporting the military enterprise. These range from civilian contractors, who provide much of the supply and logistics support to modern militaries (about half of the American force in places like Afghanistan and Iraq were actually private contractors), to the infrastructure that the military relies on for its operation, such as ports and railroads. Of note, the computer networks that these civilian forces rely upon often don't have the same levels of security as military networks because they lack similar resources, standards, and incentives. The result is they make particularly choice targets. In one 2012 Pentagon-sponsored war game we participated in, a simulated enemy force hacked the contractor company supplying the logistics of a US force, with the simple purpose of transposing the barcodes on shipping containers. It seems a minor change with little impact. But had it been a real attack, US troops in the field would have opened up a shipping pallet expecting to find ammunition and instead only found toilet paper.

The history of warfare shows that it's not just those who directly support the military who might cross the cyber firing line. When new technologies like the airplane expanded forces' reach beyond the front lines, militaries gradually expanded who they defined as a legitimate target. First, it was only those working directly for the military. Then it was those engaged in the war effort, such as workers at a tank factory. Then it was the workers' houses. And by the end of World War II, all the sides had engaged in strategic bombing against the broader populace, arguing that the best way to end the war was to drive home its costs to all civilians. Given civilians' greater vulnerability to cyberattacks, we should expect nothing less as part of any cyberwar. Thanks to the modern military's dependence on civilian networks, they might even make up a new center of gravity to target.

As scary as this all sounds, it's important to note two key differences between war in the cyber realm and other past modes of conflict. First, unlike previous transitions in warfare, cyber is unlikely to immediately multiply the level of destructive power in ways that previous technological innovations did. Because of its reliance on indirect effects, cyber's effects will have less long-term destructive impact. That is, attacks that change GPS codes or shut down the energy grid would be quite devastating. But they would be nowhere near the destruction visited by explosive-filled bombs and incendiaries upon Dresden or the permanent irradiation of Hiroshima.

Second, the weapons and operations in cyberwar will be far less predictable than traditional means, leading to greater suspicion of them among military commanders. For instance, the blast radius of a bomb can be projected to exacting standards; not so the radius of most malware. Most cyberattacks rely on the second- and even third-order effects that might result, and while these widen the impact, they can also have unexpected outcomes. During the Iraq war, for instance, US military officers were very excited by the prospects of taking down an enemy computer network facilitating suicide bombings. But the operation accidentally took down over 300 other servers in the wider Middle East, Europe, and the United States, opening a whole new can of worms. Similarly, Stuxnet was specifically tailored to target just a few Iranian centrifuges and yet ended up spreading to well over 25,000 other computers around the world.

In the end, we are still at the early stages of conceptualizing what cyberwar will look like. Predicting the future of computer network operations now is akin to those who laid out their visions of air war in the early days of "flying machines" at the turn of the last century. Some of their predictions proved right, like the idea that planes would bomb cities, while others proved woefully wrong, like the prediction that airplanes would render all other forms of war obsolete.

The same is likely to happen with cyberwar. It will prove to be fantastically game-changing, introducing real-world capabilities and operations that once seemed science fiction. But even in a world with digital weaponry, war will still be a chaotic domain. This means that war, even cyber-style, will still remain a waste of resources and efforts better spent elsewhere.

Focus: What Is the US Military Approach to Cyberwar?

Do you know what "9ec4c12949a4f31474f299058ce2b22a" means? If so, the US military may have a job for you.

The answer is actually a wonderful summary of where the US military stands in its approach to cybersecurity. This code appears in the logo of the US military's Cyber Command, a revolutionary new military organization formed in 2010. In cryptography, a hash is a one-way function that creates a unique "fingerprint" of a file. The MD5 (Message-Digest algorithm 5) hash was a widely used way to add security by detecting tampering in files. The code above is the MD5 hash of Cyber Command's mission statement, which reads: "USCYBERCOM plans, coordinates, integrates, synchronizes and conducts activities to: direct the operations and defense of specified Department of Defense information networks; and prepare to, and when directed, conduct full spectrum military cyberspace operations in order to enable actions in all domains, ensure US/Allied freedom of action in cyberspace and deny the same to our adversaries." There is an irony, however. The same year Cyber Command put the code on its logo, the US Department of Homeland Security announced that it was moving the US government away from the MD5 hash for its computer systems. The once sophisticated code was now too easy to break.

Cyber Command brings together all components of the US military that work on cyber issues, from the Army's Ninth Signal Command to the Navy's Tenth Fleet (the Fleet Cyber Command). All told, the organization boasts a cyber warrior force of just under 60,000 personnel, with headquarters located at Fort Meade, Maryland. Its location was deliberate, placing CYBERCOM, as it is known, next door to the National Security Agency, the spy agency that focuses on signals and information intelligence and protection. This allows the two agencies to share resources at the field level, such as the hundreds of PhDs in mathematics, computer science, engineering, and other fields who work there, all the way up to the top. Currently, the director of the NSA and the commander of CYBERCOM is the same person. General Keith Alexander was named the head of both organizations simultaneously, or "double-hatted" in military parlance.

While some see this pairing as natural, given the two entities' close responsibilities, many worry about blurring the lines between a military command and a civilian spy agency. There is a question as to which mentality will prevail: the spy's inclination to watch and learn or the warrior's inclination to act? There is also a worry about one person trying to take on too many different roles at once.

In contrast, others worry that CYBERCOM is not distinct enough, not merely from the NSA but from the military services that source it. Much as the Air Corps was once part of the Army before evolving into its own service (the Air Force) in 1947, some feel that Cyber Command, too, needs to become its own military branch. Two US Army officers have observed that the current military services are "properly positioned to fight kinetic wars, and they value skills such as marksmanship, physical strength, the ability to leap out of airplanes and lead combat units under enemy fire. Unfortunately, these skills are irrelevant in cyber warfare. Technical expertise isn't highly valued in the three services. Just look at military uniforms: no decorations or badges honoring technical expertise."

Regardless, CYBERCOM is growing rapidly in both size and perceived importance inside the US military. Indeed, the Pentagon's 2013 budget plan mentioned "cyber" 53 times. Just a year later, the 2014 budget plan discussed "cyber" 147 times, with spending on CYBERCOM's headquarters alone set to effectively double (all the more notable as the rest of the US military budget was being cut).

The strategy that guides CYBERCOM draws from the overall idea that cyberspace is a new domain of both possibilities and risks, and the US military had better do its utmost to protect its ability to use this domain (its traditional "freedom of maneuver") as well as preserve the initiative, and prevent others from using it to their full potential (establishing "dominance"). As Lieutenant General Jon Davis, the deputy commander of CYBERCOM, describes, the US military is treating cyber issues with a whole new level of seriousness. "This is now commander's business; this is no longer admin tech business."

The current plan runs over twelve pages in its unclassified version and thirty pages in the classified form. In sum, CYBERCOM focuses on five objectives: treat cyberspace as an "operational domain" as the rest of the military does the ground, air, or sea; implement new security concepts to succeed there; partner with other agencies and private sector; build relationships with international partners; and develop new talent to spur new innovation in how the military might fight and win in this space. As part of this mission, CYBERCOM is to create and lead three types of cyber forces: "cyber protection forces" that will defend the military's own computer networks, regionally aligned "combat mission forces" that will support the mission of troops in the field, and "national mission forces" that will aid in the protection of important infrastructure.

While turning these ideas into an actual working military doctrine, three key concerns have bedeviled CYBERCOM planners. The first is the long-standing question over mission areas and responsibilities. The wider cybersecurity roles that CYBERCOM has taken on have pushed it closer and closer to the civilian sphere, creating a twofold problem. Not only is CYBERCOM continually operating on civilian and government computer networks that it must now seemingly defend, but these responsibilities are frequently competing with others who have a duty to monitor the same networks, including the private sector and other government agencies like the civilian Department of Homeland Security. To make a parallel to the expanded role of "national mission forces," when banks are moving physical money, it isn't the Pentagon that defends the cash, but rather a combination of hired security and the police. But when the cash is virtualized, CYBERCOM has now joined into the discussion.

The second big concern is how far can and should the US military go to maintain the freedom of maneuver it so desires in cyberspace. When the command was first formed, defense leaders like then Deputy Secretary of Defense William Lynn publicly talked about how CYBERCOM would simply busy itself with the "day-to-day defense and protection of all DOD networks." Within four years, the new roles and strategy pushed well beyond that. As one CYBERCOM official put it, "We need the capabilities to do things offensively in cyber...everybody acknowledges that, but how we specifically employ that in an operational context is classified." Or, as a former National Security Agency watch officer put it, the goal is to ensure that US capabilities remain more advanced than those of potential adversaries. "Whatever the Chinese can do to us, we can do better."

Another strategic question is whether the United States can manage the way threats shift between the cyber domain and the real world and still maintain deterrence in both. It sees the concept of "equivalence" as key to addressing this question. As one report described, "If a cyber attack produces the death, damage, destruction or high-level disruption that a traditional military attack would cause, then it would be a candidate for a 'use of force' consideration, which could merit retaliation."

The idea is to send a message to adversaries that the US military plans to fight and win in cyberspace, but it reserves the right to play a different game if it doesn't like the outcome. Or, as one US military official put it more bluntly, "If you shut down our power grid, maybe we will put a missile down one of your smokestacks."

The central problems this strategy faces are whether cyberspace dominance is achievable and whether deterrence in cyberspace is workable in execution. Such posture requires knowing who your adversaries are, which is exceedingly difficult in cyberspace. As a study on American cyberattack policy and ethics concluded, "Absolute, unambiguous technical proof could be lacking, which forces more reliance on non-technical info than policy makers like."

Additionally, deterrence is not as effective against nonstate groups, which, of course, are major players in cyberspace. Not all are rational actors, and even those that are rational weigh costs and benefits very differently than governments with broad territories and populaces to defend. Nonstate groups frequently don't have fixed locales to target, and many of them would even welcome counterattacks. A response from the United States would provide the recognition that so many nonstate groups crave while possibly even generating public sympathy. There is also a deep concern that the strategy of equivalence could be escalatory, cascading an attack in cyberspace into a much bigger conflict.

Perhaps the biggest issue cyber experts raise about US strategy, though, is whether it places too much emphasis on the offense. Indeed, budget plans in 2014 show the US Air Force spending 2.4 times as much on cyber offense research as on cyber defense. The concern goes beyond the traditional view that offense is the more destabilizing side (the worry that it encourages an attack mentality) and that defense is typically stabilizing (good defenses reduce the likely gains of any attack, discouraging offensive attacks in general). Rather, experts worry about the inherently seductive nature of cyber offense and the impact it might have on the military. As one report put it, offensive concepts like "cyber war, software exploit, digital catastrophe and shadowy cyber warriors" are much more glamorous than the defensive, like "security engineering, proper coding, protecting supply chains." Yet defense is where the United States should be putting more of its efforts, not just because of how it aids stability and deterrence, but as a senior US military official said bluntly, "We're already very good at offense, but we're just as bad at defense."

Regardless of where CYBERCOM and the broader US military come down on these issues in the years ahead, it's critical that the civilian side of the national security apparatus and civilian government leaders start to understand and contribute to them. Important plans and strategies for a powerful new technology are being made, but the broader civilian political system and populace has largely remained apart from the discussion. For example, the United States' strategic policy laying out its budding offensive cyber posture, is designed to "offer unique and unconventional capabilities to advance US national objectives around the world with little or no warning to the adversary or target and with potential effects ranging from subtle to severely damaging." But it only emerged in public discourse via leaks to newspapers, months after it had been decided.

It would be a mistake to draw a historic parallel between the destructive power of cyber weapons and nuclear bombs, as some civilian leaders have recently done (the head of the US Senate Armed Services Committee amusingly described a cyber weapon as just "like a WMD"). Yet there is a worrisome parallel in how civilian leaders nowadays, as in the past, might be caught off guard by how operational plans actually make use of these new weapons. For instance, when General Curtis LeMay headed the new Strategic Air Command in the 1950s, he surprised civilian leaders when they finally got around to asking what he planned for American nuclear bomber forces, if there ever were a crisis with the Soviets. LeMay explained that he was not too concerned, because he'd just order a preemptive nuclear attack. "I'm going to knock the s**t out of them before they take off the ground." It's a good thing they asked and shut down such plans before the Cuban Missile Crisis just a few years later. Today's leaders might want to ask if there are any cyber equivalents.

Focus: What Is the Chinese Approach to Cyberwar?

"The most threatening actor in cyberspace."

So who won this not-so-prized description? Not al-Qaeda. Not the US military's Cyber Command. Not Facebook's privacy policy. Not even "RickRolling," the Internet meme wherein victims are tricked into watching a horribly addictive music video by 1980s singer Rick Astley. Rather, this is how the US Congress described China in a major report.

Time and again, China has been described as the bane of the cybersecurity world, whether in government reports like those issued by Congress (another one by the US executive branch specifically named China as the "most active and persistent" perpetrator of cyber intrusions in the United States) or Western media articles (a typical headline: "China: No. 1 Cyber Threat"). Behind these pointed fingers are real concerns. While it did not specify an individual nation, the Pentagon's 2011 *Strategy for Operating in Cyberspace*, designed to guide Cyber Command, clearly placed China among the most important threats in this realm. Indeed, many are now framing the US-Chinese relationship in cyberspace as a digital echo of that between the United States and USSR during the Cold War. Former presidential national security adviser Brent Scowcroft, for instance, describes the situation as "eerily similar," while journalist David Ignatius summed up his meetings with top Pentagon officials in an article titled "Cold War Feeling on Cybersecurity."

Unsurprisingly, Chinese writers and officials have reacted angrily to direct and veiled accusations, describing them as "groundless and reflecting Cold War mentality." Moreover, they assert that it's China that is the aggrieved party and the one more frequently under attack. And in one way they're right. By the raw numbers, China suffers the largest number of cyberattacks in the world. The Chinese Ministry of Public Security has reported that the number of cyberattacks on Chinese computers and websites has soared by more than 80 percent annually, while some 10 to 19 million or more Chinese computers are estimated to be part of botnets controlled by foreign computer hackers.

But the story isn't that simple. The reason for China's heavy malware infection rate is that as much as 95 percent of the software that Chinese computers use is pirated, meaning that it doesn't get the same security upgrades and patches that legal license holders do, leaving them vulnerable to basic threats. As computer security expert James Mulvenon explains, "Therefore, China is right when it says that it is a victim of hacking, but the main culprit is its own disregard for intellectual property, not state-sponsored espionage."

Regardless of the structural causes, Chinese analysts are quick to push back the country's reputation as an abusive cyber power. "China is accused time and again for launching cyberattacks abroad but there is never any solid proof. Actually, China has become a victim of such repeated claims," summarizes Su Hao, an expert on international security at the China Foreign Affairs University. Moreover, Chinese officials and writers assert that most of the increasing attacks on Chinese computers originate in the United States. Government officials claimed in 2011 that China was the target of some 34,000 cyberattacks from the United States, while in 2012 the numbers escalated to the point that Chinese military sites alone were targeted by American sources almost 90,000 times.

While the numbers are arguable (they turn on the same varied meaning of "attack" that we saw US officials abuse as well), it is undeniable that a large amount of malicious Internet activity emanates from or at least moves through the United States. For example, security researchers at HostExploit have found that twenty of the top fifty crime-spewing ISPs in the world are American. Moreover, US government agencies like the NSA and Cyber Command are clearly active and expert in cyber operations. When documents leaked by

Edward Snowden in 2013 showed that the NSA had hacked the prestigious Tsinghua University in Beijing—home to one of six "network backbones" that route all of mainland China's Internet traffic—as well as the Hong Kong headquarters of Pacnet, which operates one of the Asia-Pacific region's largest fiber-optic networks, Chinese state media had a field day. "The United States, which has long been trying to play innocent as a victim of cyber attacks, has turned out to be the biggest villain in our age."

Finally, Chinese cyber experts often express frustration at being painted as the main villain in a world they had little hand in creating. Many feel that the United States enjoys too highly privileged a position in the global cyber community, a legacy of its role in developing the Internet. They note, for example, that of the thirteen root servers that are essential to the functioning of the entire Internet, ten were originally located in the United States (and include US government operators like the US Army Research Lab and NASA), and the other three are in US allies (Japan, the Netherlands, and Sweden). Similarly, ICANN, which manages the protocol addresses essential to preserving the stability and smooth operation of the global Internet, started as a US government entity.

The result is that, far from taking the blame for cyber insecurity, China has increasingly taken the position that it must also equip itself for future cyberthreats and conflicts. As we read earlier, in 2011, the Communist Party–controlled *China Youth Daily* newspaper published an article by two scholars at the Chinese Academy of Military Sciences. In direct terms it described how the Chinese military establishment viewed developments in cyberspace, from the creation of the US military's Cyber Command to the revelation of Stuxnet. "Of late, an Internet tornado has swept across the world...massively impacting and shocking the globe. Behind all this lies the shadow of America. Faced with this warm-up for an Internet war, every nation and military can't be passive but is making preparations to fight the Internet war."

In real terms, this has translated into a buildup of the People's Liberation Army's (PLA) cyber capabilities at just as rapid a pace as the building out of Cyber Command and the NSA over the same period. According to government sources, Chinese spending on cyber warfare became a "top funding priority," and a host of new units were created with the responsibility of "preparing attacks on enemy computer networks."

While the Chinese military organization responsible for cyber operations is not as open about its structure as the United States military's (no online password-guessing games like at Cyber Command), many think it falls under the PLA General Staff Department's Third Department. This entity, based in Beijing, is very similar to the NSA, with a focus on signals intelligence and code-breaking, making it a natural fit for cyber activities. The department has some 130,000 personnel reportedly assigned to it. A key part is the Beijing North Computer Center (also known as the General Staff Department 418th Research Institute or the PLA's 61539 Unit), which some believe to be the Chinese equivalent of Cyber Command. It has at least ten subdivisions involved in "the design and development of computer network defense, attack, and exploitation systems." There are at least twelve additional training facilities located around the country. Of special note is a unit located in Zhurihe that is permanently designated to serve as an "informationized Blue Team." That is, the unit simulates how the US military and its allies use cyberspace and provide targets for Chinese units to hone their skills on in war games.

A particular hub that has drawn unwanted attention is the Second Bureau of the Third Army, Unit 61398, also known in cybersecurity circles as the "Comment Crew" or "Shanghai Group." This is a key unit tasked with gathering political, economic, and military-related intelligence on the United States through cyber means. In 2013, it was caught stealing employee passwords to break into the *New York Times'* computer networks. Proving that the old saying "Never argue with a man who buys his ink by the barrel" still holds true in the cyber age, the *Times* then got its revenge by publishing a series of embarrassing exposés. The paper revealed that the once-secret Chinese unit was behind some 141 APT attacks across 20 different industries and governments, targeting everyone from Coca-Cola to the Pentagon and the United Nations. It even suffered the indignity of having a picture of its no-longer-secret headquarters, located on Datong Road in Shanghai, splashed across the newspaper's front page.

The 61398 unit is far from alone; some estimates point to as many as 40 other APT operations of a similar scale. While its 12-story office building is next door to a massage parlor and wine importer, a number of the other PLA cyber programs are colocated with engineering schools and technology firms. For instance, the 61539 center is next to Beijing University and the Central Communist Party School in the city's northwestern Jiaoziying suburbs.

Just as many US military cyber facilities are colocated with the NSA and civilian research programs, the PLA also draws from the wider cyber expertise resident in its eight-million-strong people's militia, supplementing official forces with a "patriotic hacker" program. These universities also make prime recruiting grounds, although sometimes in ways that later hinder attempts to keep the units secret. When Unit 61398 started to garner attention, researchers were found that its digital tracks hadn't been cleaned up. The Zhejiang University website even had a public notice that "Unit 61398 of China's People's Liberation Army (located in Pudong District, Shanghai) seeks to recruit 2003-class computer science graduate students."

Guiding this buildup is the concept of "informatization," a hallmark in the Chinese military's approach to cyber operations. As one key Chinese military report put it, modern forces, and especially the American military, are so highly reliant on information that whoever dominates the battle of cyberwar will occupy the "new strategic high ground." Gaining the "upper hand of the enemy" will be determined by "whether or not we are capable of using various means to obtain information and of ensuring the effective circulation of information; whether or not we are capable of making full use of the permeability, sharable property, and connection of information to realize the organic merging of materials, energy, and information to form a combined fighting strength; [and] whether or not we are capable of applying effective means to weaken the enemy side's information superiority and lower the operational efficiency of enemy information equipment."

In execution, the Chinese plan for informationized war would most likely focus on defending PLA networks and, in turn, targeting the adversary's key nodes of communication, command, and coordination. The idea is to degrade an enemy's decision-making, slow down its operations, and even weaken its morale. Most importantly, they believe that the side that controls the flow of information can create "blind spots" that can be exploited, windows of opportunity to attack undetected or with a reduced risk of counterattack.

By focusing on an adversary's information systems, China advances the idea that cyberattacks turn technical advantage into a liability. In a controversial 1999 volume, two PLA officers wrote, rather pugnaciously, "Who now dares state with certainty that in future wars this heavy spending will not result in an electronic Maginot line that is weak because of its excessive dependence on a single technology?" The basic thinking is that any foreign power that might threaten China (i.e., the United States) would depend on well-coordinated technical systems. Infiltrating and disrupting these systems is thus a natural "defensive" posture. Unfortunately, to those on the opposite end of the cyber gun barrel, the emphasis on infiltrating and disrupting communications and command systems looks aggressive.

This amount of military activity and planning in the cyber realm is certainly worrisome to other nations watching China's historic rise over the last few years in economic, political, and now military power. But, for all the concern, no one should confuse ambition with full capability. In fact, Chinese military officers echo many of the same complaints that American officers have about their own cyber problems. Chen Weizhan, head of the Military Training and Service Arms Department of the Guangzhou Military Region, has talked about how "many generations of weapons and equipment exist at the same time... incompatible software systems, unmatched hardware interfaces, and non-unified data formats." He concluded that "there are considerable gaps in the fundamental conditions of the units, and the level of informationization is not high."

Despite these problems, China's growth in military cyber power still has two major implications, each of which parallel America's own growing military cyber power. Just as in the United States, there is concern whether the Chinese civilian political leadership is involved in and understands enough about their military's own plans. This may be even more of a concern for China, though, as the current Chinese political system gives the PLA an immense amount of leeway. Indeed, there is no equivalent to America's civilian-led and staffed National Security Council or Department of Defense. The risk, therefore, is that Chinese military cyber capabilities and operations could outpace civilian leaders' understanding of them, perhaps crossing "red lines" in a crisis that could have been avoided.

The other problem is what such rapid efforts to militarize cyberspace might do to the Internet. China isn't just a looming superpower, it's also home to the world's largest number of Internet users. As it follows in the United States' steps, it continues a dark trend. A uniquely democratic space created for communication and sharing is instead being transformed into a future battleground. "Winning IT-based warfare" (former Chinese president Hu Jintao) and "Fighting and winning wars in cyberspace" (General Keith Alexander, the first head of the US military's Cyber Command) are certainly important new military responsibilities in the twenty-first century. But that doesn't make them positive developments for the wonderful World Wide Web that so defines modern life.

Fear of a militarized cyberspace, however, may well lead us to avoid the very cyber conflicts we are all gearing up for. At a meeting with US officials, a high-ranking Chinese military officer explained how his views of cybersecurity have evolved as each side has built up its cyber powers and raised the stakes in a potential conflict: "The United States has big stones in its hands but also has a plate-glass window. China has big stones in its hands but also a plate-glass window. Perhaps because of this, there are things we can agree on."

What about Deterrence in an Era of Cyberwar?

"Cyber offense may provide the means to respond in-kind. The protected conventional capability should provide credible and observable kinetic effects globally. Forces supporting this capability are isolated and segmented from general-purpose forces to maintain the highest level of cyber resiliency at an affordable cost. Nuclear weapons would remain the ultimate response and anchor the deterrence ladder."

These lines come from a 2013 US Defense Science Board report, one of the highest-level official advisory groups to the Secretary of Defense. While the text reads like typical Pentagonese, what these lines translate into is a proposal to create a new US military force specially designed to retaliate against a cyber strike. Of note, it wouldn't just be able to respond with counter cyber weapons, but also would include "Global selective strike systems e.g. penetrating bomber, submarines with long range cruise missiles, and Conventional

Prompt Global Strike [a ballistic missile]." *Foreign Policy* magazine's reaction to the news perhaps sums it up the best: "Wow."

When we think about deterrence, what most often comes to mind is the Cold War model of MAD, mutually assured destruction. Any attack would be met with an overwhelming counterstrike that would destroy the aggressor as well as most life on the planet, making any first strike literally mad.

Yet rather than just getting MAD, deterrence really is about the ability to alter an adversary's actions by changing its cost-benefit calculations. It reflects subjective, psychological assessments, a "state of mind," as the US Department of Defense says, "brought about by the existence of a credible threat of unacceptable counteraction." In addition to massive retaliation, the adversary's decisions can also be affected by defenses, in what has been called "deterrence by denial." If you can't get what you want by attacking, then you won't attack in the first place.

Theorists and strategists have worked for decades to fully understand how deterrence works, but one of the key differences in the cyber realm, as we have explored, is the problem of "who" to deter or retaliate against. Specifically, this is the issue of attribution we explored earlier.

The effect of this on real-world politics is driven by the fact that the question of "who" in cyberspace is far more difficult than ever could have been imagined by the original thinkers on deterrence theory back in the 1950s. Tanks and missile launches are hard to disguise, while networks of compromised machines or tools like Tor make anonymity easy. The threat of counterstrike requires knowing who launched the initial attack, a difficult thing to prove in cyberspace, especially in a fast-moving crisis. Computer code does not have a return address, and sophisticated attackers have grown adept at hiding their tracks. So painstaking forensic research is required, and, as we saw, it's rarely definitive.

Moreover, for the purposes of deterrence, it's not enough to trace an attack back to a computer or find out who was operating a specific computer. Strategically, we must know what political actor was responsible, in order to change their calculations.

This problem has made improving attribution (or at least making people think you have improved attribution) a key strategic priority for nations that believe themselves at risk of cyberattack. So, in addition to considering the massive retaliatory forces outlined by the Defense Science Board, the United States has grown its messaging efforts on this front. In 2012, for example, then Secretary of Defense Panetta laid down a public marker that "Potential aggressors should be aware that the United States has the capacity to locate them and to hold them accountable for their actions that may try to harm America." In turn, these potential aggressors must now weigh whether it was bluster or real.

The "who" of deterrence is not just about identification but also context. The United States has approached deterrence very differently when facing terrorists, rogue nations, and major powers. While the theory often lays out a series of set actions and counteractions, the reality is that different actors can dictate very different responses. Imagine, for example, what the Bush administration's reaction might have been if the groups attacking the United States' NATO partner Estonia in 2007 had been linked to Tehran instead of Moscow.

If the actor is known, the next component in deterrence is the commitment to retaliate, a decision whether to match or escalate the use of force. Unlike when the United States and the Soviet Union pointed nuclear weapons at each other's territory, the players and stakes in the cyber realm are far more amorphous. Some even argue that if one wants to change an adversary's "state of mind," the "credible threat" against cyberattack needs to go beyond the cyber realm.

This is the essence of the Pentagon's plan for a mixed cyber- and real-world retaliatory force, which has also been proposed even in situations of espionage. But going back to the issue of context, the challenge of intellectual property theft is that an in-kind response would not be effective; the very fact that your secrets are being stolen is a pretty good indicator that the enemy doesn't have anything worth stealing back. Likewise, the traditional deterrence and retaliation model in espionage (they arrest your spies, you arrest theirs or deport some embassy staff) doesn't translate well when the spy is thousands of miles away and likely outside of the government. Thus, some have argued that alternative means have to be found to influence an enemy's calculations. Dmitri Alperovitch, who watched the massive Shady RAT attacks play out, argues that we should try to "raise the economic costs on the adversary through the use of such tools as sanctions, trade tariffs, and multilateral diplomatic pressure to impact their cost benefit analysis of these operations."

Timing also plays a more complicated role in cyber deterrence. In the nuclear age, speed was key to MAD. It was crucial to show that you could get your retaliatory missiles and bombers off the ground before the other side's first strike. In the cyber age, however, there is simultaneously no time and all the time in the world to respond. The first strike might play out in nanoseconds, but there are many compelling reasons to delay a counterstrike, such as to gain better attribution or better plan a response.

Similarly, how much of a guarantee of reprisal is needed? In the nuclear realm, the game theory that guided American Cold War planners put a mandate on having comparable "survivable" counterstrike forces that would make sure the other guy got nuked even if he tried a sneak attack. In a cyber era, it's unclear what a "survivable" counterforce would look like, hence the US plan to establish a nuclear equivalent.

The same lack of clarity extends to the signals that the two sides send each other, so key to the game of deterrence. If you fire back with a missile, the other side knows you have retaliated. But fire back with malware, and the effect is not always so evident, especially as its impact can sometimes play out just like a normal systems failure. This means that different types of cyber weapons will be needed for different purposes in deterrence. When you want to signal, "noisy" cyber weapons with obvious effects may be better, while stealthy weapons might be more key to offensive operations. The result, though, is something that would be familiar to those wrestling with past deterrence strategies: in the effort to head off war, new weapons will be in constant development, driving forward an arms race.

In short, the growing capacity to carry out multiple types of cyberattack is further complicating the already complex field of deterrence. Without a clear understanding or real reservoir of test cases to study for what works, countries may have to lean more heavily on deterrence by denial than during the nuclear age.

Ultimately, while the technologies may be shifting, the goals of deterrence remain the same: to reshape what an enemy thinks. Cyber deterrence may play out on computer networks, but it's all about a state of mind.

Why Is Threat Assessment So Hard in Cyberspace?

In the 1960s there was a heated argument in the Pentagon between Alain Enthoven, a civilian strategist, and an air force general about the number of nuclear weapons that the United States would need if the Cold War ever turned hot. Angry that this nerdy civilian didn't see the threat the same way, the general told Enthoven that his opinion was not wanted. Enthoven then famously responded, "General, I have fought just as many nuclear wars as you have."

This anecdote is useful when thinking about cybersecurity and all the potential ripple effects it will have for arms races, wars, and other conflicts. A "threat assessment" is the process of weighing the risks that any entity faces, be it a nation, a business, or even an individual. Herbert Lin is Chief Scientist for computer science at the National Academies and one of the leading thinkers in the field of cybersecurity. As he has explained, to do a proper threat assessment, one essentially evaluates three basic factors: "The feasibility of adversaries being able to identify and exploit your vulnerabilities, the effect that would happen if they were able to take advantage of these vulnerabilities, and, finally, the likelihood that they will, in fact, be willing to do so."

Threat assessments are notoriously hard. There are usually layers upon layers of uncertainty, not just in evaluating your own vulnerabilities but also gauging the enemy's capabilities and likely intentions. And because it's about weighing risks, there is a natural human and organizational inclination toward "threat inflation." When you don't know what the exact risks are, many will play it safe and assume a worst-case scenario. You may get it wrong, but you also don't get caught with your pants down. It sounds sensible enough, except you can then waste immense time and energy worrying about risks that aren't real. A good example of this occurred during the Cold War. In 1967, the United States deployed new advanced spy satellites that could monitor Soviet missile sites at a whole new level of detail. It was only then that President Lyndon B. Johnson realized that the US counts of Soviet missiles had been way off. Rather than the previous threat assessment pointing to a "missile gap" that had driven US strategy for the last decade, "We were doing things that we didn't need to do. We were building things that we didn't need to build. We were harboring fears that we didn't need to have."

The scary realization waiting for us in the twenty-first century may be that these twentieth-century strategists had it easy. Threat assessments in cyberspace may be even more difficult.

The nature of vulnerabilities in cyberspace makes assessing them extremely difficult. While it's easy to look at a map of your country and figure out likely approaches of attack (for instance, "My enemy is more likely to attack across this open plain than through these rugged mountains"), the very term "zero day" illustrates the problem in cyberspace. The vulnerabilities that are most often targeted are the ones that no one but the attacker knows about.

Similarly, a key element of any threat assessment is the capability of the adversary and its weapons. While you may not always have perfect information about an enemy's current or next generation of weapons, there have traditionally been at least some bounds that could be placed around any assessment. At the bare minimum, you could at least "ballpark" estimate a threat based on what the last generation of weapons could do, your own experience with similar weapons, and perhaps most of all, the basic laws of physics. An enemy might surprise you with a new tank, but it wouldn't drive 1,000 miles per hour faster than a current version.

Cyber weapons, by comparison, are not bound by the same laws of physics. Each new piece of malware can be designed in very different ways to do very different things. That is, their nonphysical nature means that they can be produced and stored in a manner and number that makes the already tough task of threat assessment an order of magnitude more difficult. During the Cold War, the United States could watch Soviet tank, ship, or missile factories to see what was going in and then leaving the assembly line. They would then watch Red Army bases to see how many weapons were stored and the rough order of battle they were organized into, and then track movements to and from these bases to see where units and their weapons were headed. We may have frequently gotten the count wrong, as LBJ explained, but at least there were "things" to count. With malware, there are no factories, no storage yards, and of course, no things.

This nonphysical nature of cyberthreats becomes even more important when trying to assess a potential adversary's actions and intent. With physical weaponry, there are sometimes tea leaves that can be read as telltale signs that trouble might be coming, whether it's an enemy fleet headed out to sea or reservists reporting to duty. The cyber realm doesn't have this, and the waters are made even murkier by the problem of attribution; pinpointing an adversary is difficult in a world filled with so many different potential state and nonstate players. And, even if you know that you're being targeted and by whom, determining the adversary's actual intent can be tremendously difficult. Someone could be targeting your systems, but the goal might be to gather intelligence, steal information, shut down your operations, or just show off the hacker's capability. Threat assessment is about predicting the likely risks. But in cyberspace, many of these risks will remain undiscovered until after an attack takes place.

Given all this uncertainty, the main lesson for threat assessment in cyberspace goes back to the problem that Enthoven and the general faced in the early days of nuclear weapons. Instead of claiming any kind of perfect knowledge in the midst of any cyber crisis, we should instead recognize our inherent limitations and uncertainties and act accordingly. As one former Justice Department cybersecurity official put it, "I have seen too many situations where government officials claimed a high degree of confidence as to the source, intent, and scope of an attack, and it turned out they were wrong on every aspect of it. That is, they were often wrong, but never in doubt."

Does the Cybersecurity World Favor the Weak or the Strong?

In 2009, American soldiers captured an insurgent leader in Iraq. As they went through the files on his laptop computer, they made a remarkable discovery: he'd been watching them watch him.

A key part of the US military effort was the fleet of unmanned systems ("drones") that flew overhead, gathering intelligence on the insurgent force, tracking their movements and beaming back video to US Air Force pilots on the ground. But inside the captured leader's laptop were "days and days and hours and hours of proof" that the digital feeds were being intercepted and shared among the various insurgent groups. The insurgents had evidently figured out how to hack and watch the drones' feed, like a robber listening in on a police radio scanner. Even more disturbing to the US soldiers was how the insurgents had pulled it off. It turned out they were using commercially available software originally designed by college kids to illegally download satellite-streamed movies. Skygrabber, as it was known, cost as little as $25.95 on a Russian website.

Examples like this lead many to believe that cyberspace is one of those strange places where the weak have an advantage over the strong. On one hand, the barriers to entry to developing cyberattack capabilities are relatively low, especially compared to building up more traditional military capabilities. For instance, it cost the United States roughly $45 million for the unmanned plane system and several billion dollars for the space satellite network that its feed traveled over. The $25.95 spent on illegal software to undermine those systems was a pretty good bargain. As the head of Israeli military intelligence has explained, "Cyberspace grants small countries and individuals a power that was heretofore the preserve of great states."

However, the real worry for states like the United States is not just that others can now build up cyberthreats but that traditional strengths are proving cyber vulnerabilities. As director of national intelligence from 2007 to 2009, Mike McConnell oversaw a surge of US cyberwar capabilities, funded by tens of billions of dollars, that culminated in the development of weapons like Stuxnet. But instead of feeling more confident about where the United States stood in cybersecurity after this effort, McConnell testified to the Senate, "If the nation went to war today, in a cyberwar, we would lose. We're the most vulnerable. We're the most connected. We have the most to lose."

Unlike many of its potential adversaries in this space, the United States and especially the US military is highly reliant on computer networks for everything from communications to electricity (the vast majority of electrical power used by US military bases, for instance, comes from commercial utilities using a fairly vulnerable power grid). So cyberattacks of equivalent strength would have far more devastating consequences on the United States than on potential adversaries like China, whose military is still less networked, let alone a cyber pygmy like North Korea, whose economy never entered the information age. As former NSA official Charlie Miller explains, "One of North Korea's biggest advantages is that it has hardly any Internet-connected infrastructure to target. On the other hand, the United States has tons of vulnerabilities a country like North Korea could exploit."

This creates the strange irony of cyberwar. The more wired a nation, the more it can take advantage of the Internet. But the more wired a nation, the more it can potentially be harmed by those using the Internet maliciously. To think of it another way, the nations most skilled at throwing rocks live in the biggest glass houses.

That nations like the United States are feeling increasingly vulnerable is not, however, a sign that the strong are toothless in the cyber realm or even that the weak are now at an advantage. As Joseph Nye, a former Pentagon official and dean of the Harvard Kennedy School, writes, "Power diffusion is not the same as power equalization."

Nonstate groups and weaker states can certainly now play in a game that was once out of their reach. But that doesn't mean they have the same resources to bring to bear in it. The most strategic cyberattacks, as opposed to ones that prove a nuisance or merely have a disruptive effect, combine sophisticated new weapons with vast economic and human resources, sometimes outside the cyber realm. What made Stuxnet so effective was that it combined multiple new exploits built into the weapon's design and that it was specifically targeted to hit a precise configuration of centrifuges that painstaking intelligence had identified at an Iranian facility. It had even been tested on an expensive dummy set of centrifuges built just for the effort. Low-end actors can now carry out copycat attacks, but the cyber powers that will break new ground or have the most lasting and sustained effects are still likely to be the major powers. The configuration of power has something old and something new: "Governments are still top dogs on the Internet," as Nye puts it, "but smaller dogs bite."

The true advantage for the strong in these cyber conflicts and arms races may come, however, from their powers outside the cyber realm. While the small groups and weak states are now able to create more cyberthreats, the powerful still retain what is known as "escalation dominance." As we saw in the earlier discussion of US cyber deterrence strategy, if things go poorly in the cyber realm, the United States "reserves the right" to take the matter outside cyberspace, where it might have a clearer advantage.

Being powerful means you have the choice. Being weak means you don't. The insurgents in Iraq would rather have had the drones than just their pirated video feed. That's why it still pays to be the stronger in battle, even on a cyber battlefield.

Who Has the Advantage, the Offense or the Defense?

"Whatever the question, to attack was always the answer."

Attaque à outrance, or "Attack to excess," was a concept that took hold in European military circles at the turn of the last century. The idea was that new technologies like the railroad and telegraph gave an advantage at the strategic level to whichever nation could mobilize first and go on the offensive, while new technologies like the fast-firing cannon, machine guns, and rifles meant that the troops who showed the greatest offensive élan (a concept that combined both willpower and dash) would always carry the day on the battlefield. The philosophy gained huge popularity. In Germany, it drove the adoption of the Schlieffen Plan (which envisioned a rapid mobilization of Germany's army to first knock out France to its west with a lightning offensive and then swing to face Russia to the east), while in France it was actually written into military law in 1913 that the French army "henceforth admits no law but the offensive."

There were only two problems with *Attaque à outrance*, an idea that historians now call the "cult of the offensive." The first was that it drove the European powers into greater and greater competition and ultimately war. When crisis loomed after the assassination of Archduke Franz Ferdinand in 1914, few thought it worth going to war. But soon the sides feared that they were losing a tight window of opportunity during which to mobilize to their advantage, or even worse, that they would be caught helpless. Fear of being on the defensive prompted the powers to move to the offensive, launching their long-planned attacks as part of a war most didn't want.

The second problem was even worse. These new technologies didn't actually give the offense the advantage. Once the war started, it became clear that "attacking to excess" against fast-firing artillery, rifles, and machines guns was not the way to quick victory, but rather to a quick death. A bloody stalemate of trench warfare instead resulted.

This question of whether a new technology favors the offense or the defense is a critical one for cybersecurity, as it might similarly shape everything from the likelihood of war to how governments and even businesses should organize themselves. For the most part, there is a general assumption that cyberattack has the advantage against cyber defense. As one Pentagon-funded report concluded in 2010, "The cyber competition will be offense-dominant for the foreseeable future."

This assumption is what has helped drive the larger spending on cyber offense by militaries around the world. Their basic thinking behind the offense's advantage is that "It will be cheaper and easier to attack information systems than it will be to detect and defend against attacks." Compared to traditional military capabilities, those needed to put together a cyberattack are relatively cheap. More importantly, the attackers have the initiative, the advantage of being able to choose the time and place of their attack, whereas the defender has to be everywhere.

This is true with any weapon, but in cyberspace a few other factors kick in. While in the physical world territory is relatively fixed, the amount of "ground" that the defender has to protect is almost always growing in the cyber world, and growing exponentially. The number of users on computer networks over time is an almost constant upward curve, while the number of lines of code in security software, measured in the thousands two decades ago, is now well over 10 million. By comparison, malware has stayed relatively short and simple (some is as succinct as just 125 lines of code), and the attacker only has to get in through one node at just one time to potentially compromise all the defensive efforts. As the director of the Defense Advanced Research Project Agency (DARPA), put it, "Cyber defenses have grown exponentially in effort and complexity, but they continue to be defeated by offenses that require far less investment by the attacker."

Just as before World War I, however, the story of the offense's inherent advantage is not so simple. The cyberattacks that are truly dangerous require a great deal of expertise to put together. And while they might play out in terms of microseconds, they often take long periods of planning and intelligence gathering to lay the groundwork. Neither Rome nor Stuxnet was built in a day, so to speak. This means that crippling attacks out of the blue, the ultimate threat from the offense's advantage, are not as easy to pull off in the cyber world as is often depicted.

Another challenge for the offense is that the outcome of a cyberattack can be highly uncertain. You may be able to get inside a system or even shut it down, but that is only part of the story of what makes a good offense. The actual effect on your target is hard to predict, and any damage assessment can be difficult to estimate.

Nor is the defender so helpless in cybersecurity. The attackers may have the luxury of choosing the time and place of their attack, but they have to make their way through a "cyber kill chain" of multiple steps if they actually want to achieve their objectives. Charles Croom is a retired US Air Force lieutenant general, who once led the Defense Information Systems Agency (DISA), the agency that services the IT needs of the entire US military, and now is Lockheed's vice president for cybersecurity solutions. As he explains, "The attacker has to take a number of steps: reconnaissance, build a weapon, deliver that weapon, pull information out of the network. Each step creates a vulnerability, and all have to be completed. But a defender can stop the attack at any step."

And, as we saw earlier, defenders who are losing in the cyber realm don't have to restrict the game to just that domain. They can try to impose some other costs on the attacker, whether they be some kind of economic or diplomatic costs, traditional military action, or even a cyber counterattack. Rather than just sitting there defenseless, they can take action either to deter the attack or reduce the benefits from it.

The most important lesson we have learned in traditional offense-defense balances, and now in cybersecurity, is that the best defense actually is a good defense. Regardless of which side has the advantage, any steps that raise the capabilities of the defense make life harder on the offense and limit the incentives for attacks in the first place. In cybersecurity, these include any and all measures that tighten network security and aid in forensics to track back attackers.

Beyond the best practices we'll explore in Part III that weigh risks and make individuals and important infrastructure more secure, there is also the potential for new technology that can continue to function even if compromised. The idea is to build systems where the parallel for measuring offense and defense isn't war, but biology. When it comes to the number of bacteria and viruses in our bodies, our human cells are actually outnumbered by as much as 10 to 1. But the body has built up a capacity of both resistance and resilience, fighting off what is most dangerous and, as Vint Cerf puts it, figuring out how to "fight through the intrusion." No computer network will mimic the human body perfectly, but DARPA and other groups are working on "intelligent" computer security networks that learn and adapt to resist cyberattacks. The defense would start to outsmart an adversary and turn the tables on them. Just the mere existence of such a system would always sow doubt in the offense that the attack is going to work.

The final question, though, is whether an offensive advantage (if it is even possible) actually does have to doom a system to instability and risk. Some are now arguing that the real problem in cyber is not that the offense may have an advantage, but that it isn't talked about enough, which fails to warn all sides of the risks if ever used. "We've got to step up the game; we've got to talk about our offensive capabilities and train to them; to make them credible so that people know there's a penalty to this," said James Cartwright, the four-star Marine Corps general who led much of the initial US strategy in cyber issues until his retirement in 2011. "You can't have something that's a secret be a deterrent. Because if you don't know it's there, it doesn't scare you." (Two years later, this quote took on far greater resonance, when General Cartwright was reported to have been the alleged source of leaks to the media that revealed the US role in building Stuxnet, the first true use of a cyberweapon.)

A New Kind of Arms Race: What Are the Dangers of Cyber Proliferation?

In 280 BC, King Pyrrhus of Epirus invaded Italy with an army of 25,000 men, horses, and war elephants. In the battle of Asculum, his force soundly defeated the Romans, but at the loss of a large portion of his force. When one of his officers congratulated him on the win, a despondent Pyrrhus supposedly responded, "One more such victory and we shall be utterly ruined."

This idea of a "Pyrrhic victory" has come to describe accomplishments that seem to offer great benefit but ultimately sow the seeds of defeat. Many now describe Stuxnet in a similar way. The development and use of a cyber weapon seriously damaged Iran's nuclear program in a way that avoided direct military confrontation for several years. But by proving that it could be done, the episode also perhaps opened the page to a new kind of arms race.

Over the last decade, the idea of building and using cyber weapons moved from science fiction to concept, and now to reality. Much of the work is naturally shrouded in secrecy, but most estimates are that this new arms race is quite global. As one report put it, "By one estimate, more than one hundred nations are now amassing cybermilitary capabilities. This doesn't just mean erecting electronic defenses. It also means developing 'offensive' weapons."

The capabilities of these nations, though, greatly differ. Just as in traditional military clout, Burundi's cyber power pales compared to that of the United States or China. McAfee, a Santa Clara, California, computer security firm, for instance, estimates that there are only around twenty countries that actually have "advanced cyberwar programs" that could build something comparable to a new Stuxnet-like weapon.

Michael Nacht, the former US Assistant Secretary of Defense for Global Strategic Affairs, told us how all this work impacts global politics: "An arms race is already going on in cyberspace and it is very intense." The irony is that, just as in past arms races where nations rushed to construct everything from battleships to nuclear weapons, the more states compete to build up their capabilities, the less safe they feel. As we saw, the United States and China are perhaps the two most important players in this game, but both are deeply on edge about the threat they see from the other. This is perhaps the true hallmark of an arms race.

What sets this twenty-first-century cyber arms race apart from the past is that it is not just a game of states. As we've explored again and again, what makes cyberspace so simultaneously positive and problematic from a policy standpoint is that it is populated by both public and private actors. So when it comes to arms races within it, there are new wrinkles of decentralization and scale.

While the impact of individuals is often overstated in cybersecurity (the best types of malware often require the cooperation of multiple experts, skilled in a variety of areas, rather than the popular trope of a single teenaged hacker in his parents' basement), the cyber realm is one in which small groups can potentially generate enormous consequences. In software programming, businesses like Google and Apple have found that the productivity difference between a good and an elite programmer can be several orders of magnitude. The same goes for those who program malware. Nonstate actors all the way down to individuals are now key players in a major arms race, something that hasn't happened before.

Ralph Langner, the cybersecurity expert who discovered Stuxnet, for example, discussed with us how he would rather have ten experts of his own choosing versus all the resources of the US Cyber Command at his disposal. While Ralph was slightly exaggerating to make a point, the fact is that small groups or organizations can be meaningful in a manner unimaginable in earlier times. New malware can be extremely harmful on a global scale and yet can be developed and deployed by only a few people.

The key is not just these groups' power but their ability to share it, what arms control experts call proliferation. Unlike with battleships or atomic bombs, those same groups or individuals can, if they wish, almost instantaneously communicate knowledge of how to create any new capability to millions of others. For example, it may have taken the combined efforts of a team of experts almost a year to build Stuxnet, but within weeks of its discovery an Egyptian blogger had posted an online how-to guide to building this new cyber weapon.

This new kind of cyber proliferation can take two paths. One is just to try to use the new capability "as is" by making a direct copy. This wouldn't seem like such a big problem, as good defenses would plug any gap identified and exploited by the use of a new weapon like Stuxnet. Except many pieces of malware turn out to be more than one-time-only weapons because their potential targets are irresponsible, and fail to adapt their defenses. Part of Langner's original motivation to go public about Stuxnet was to encourage adoption of the vendor patches needed to prevent future exploitation among potential targets in the West. Yet a full year after Stuxnet was first revealed to the world, Langner and other security experts were lamenting that that a number of major public infrastructure companies had still not plugged the vulnerabilities that Stuxnet attacked.

The more problematic proliferation path, however, is via inspiration. Each construction and use of a new type of cyber weapon lowers the bar for the rest of the crowd. Stuxnet had a complex infection package that included new zero-day attacks, as well as a novel payload that attacked SCADA controllers, but its beauty (and the lesson for others) was in how the different parts of this complex attack worked together. Some of the copycats were fairly simple. Duqu, for example, was a worm that was discovered in the wild soon after Stuxnet using very similar Microsoft Windows–exploiting code. Many took to calling it "son of Stuxnet," with the idea that it must be the next version designed by the same team. However, while there are key similarities, experts also have noticed key differences and thus now believe that it was more a case of inspiration than evolution. As Ralph Langner describes this new kind of proliferation problem:

> Son of Stuxnet is a misnomer. What's really worrying are the concepts that Stuxnet gives hackers. The big problem we have right now is that Stuxnet has enabled hundreds of wannabe attackers to do essentially the same thing. Before, a Stuxnet-type attack could have been created by maybe five people. Now it's more like 500 who could do this. The skill set that's out there right now, and the level required to make this kind of thing, has dropped considerably simply because you can copy so much from Stuxnet.

The booming underground black market of creating and distributing malware, in which transnational criminal groups buy and sell specialized cyber capabilities, makes this proliferation even smoother and more worrisome.

This combination is what makes the cyber realm so different when it comes to arms races. It's not just that the ideas behind the weapons spread globally in mere microseconds, but that the required tools to turn a blueprint into action do not require the kind of large-scale human, financial, or physical resources one used to need. To make a historic comparison, building Stuxnet the first time may have required an advanced team that was the cyber equivalent to the Manhattan Project. But once it was used, it was like the Americans didn't just drop this new kind of bomb on Hiroshima, but also kindly dropped leaflets with the design plan so anyone else could also build it, with no nuclear reactor required.

Are There Lessons from Past Arms Races?

"We are here to make a choice between the quick and the dead....If we fail, then we have damned every man to be the slave of fear. Let us not deceive ourselves; we must elect world peace or world destruction."

In June 1946, Bernard Baruch, the personal representative of President Truman, made this speech to the United Nations as part of an amazing offer that history little remembers. Despite the fact that the United States was the only nation with nuclear weapons at the time, it offered to turn over all its nuclear bombs to the United Nations. Baruch's condition was that all other nations also agree not to build them and open themselves up to inspection. It seemed a noble gesture, but the Soviets (who wouldn't be able to figure out how to build nuclear bombs for another three years) balked. They demanded that the United States instead first give up its weapons and only afterward should the world develop a system of controls. They were also deeply suspicious of the UN, feeling that it was too US-dominated to be trusted (how things have changed!). With the two superpowers at loggerheads, the Baruch plan fell apart. Instead, a nuclear arms race would shape the next 50 years of global politics, a time in which over one hundred thousand atomic bombs would be built and the world would almost be destroyed several times over, as during close calls like the Cuban Missile Crisis.

While today's emerging cyber arms races are far from identical to the Cold War, there are still lessons that can be learned from it. Or, to paraphrase Mark Twain, while history may not always repeat itself, "It does rhyme."

One of the most instructive lessons is that the initial periods of a burgeoning arms race are often the most dangerous. These early days have a dark combination. The possessors of the new technology see themselves as having a unique advantage but one that is fleeting, creating a "use it or lose it" mentality. It is also the period in which the technology and its consequences are least understood, especially by senior leaders. In the Cold War, for example, probably the scariest time was not the Cuban Missile Crisis, but the late 1940s and 1950s when the real-world versions of *Dr. Strangelove* were taken seriously, arguing that nuclear war was something that was not only survivable but winnable. This was a period that saw everything from General Douglas Macarthur's 1951 demand to be given sole discretion to drop atomic bombs on mainland China to perhaps one of the most outrageous nuclear concepts of all, Project A-119. When the Soviets launched the Sputnik satellite into space in 1957, the US Air Force proposed a nuclear missile be shot at the moon, just to demonstrate that the United States could also do exciting things in space.

In the cyber world, there is justifiable concern that at least some elements of this combination are also present today. The National Academy of Sciences has reported that emerging technologies "greatly expand the range of options available to US policy makers as well as the policy makers of other nations," which makes leaders often very itchy to take action. And yet, as the report continued, "Today's policy and legal framework for guiding and regulating the use of cyberattack is ill-formed, undeveloped, and highly uncertain." Or, as James Mulvenon, president of the Cyber Conflict Studies Association, puts it: "Here's the problem—it's 1946 in cyber. So we have these potent new weapons, but we don't have all the conceptual and doctrinal thinking that supports those weapons or any kind of deterrence. Worse, it's not just the United States and Soviets that have the weapons—it's millions and millions of people around the world that have these weapons."

What this means is that, akin to the Cold War, any great strategic advantages a nation is able to seize in a cyber arms race will be fleeting. The United States only had a window of four years before the Soviets were able to build their own bomb. That seemed incredibly quick at the time. By comparison, the proliferation of cyber weapons happens at Internet speed, so any window that first users had with weapons like Stuxnet has already closed.

This raises the question of whether some kind of stability like that during the Cold War will then set in. While the nuclear arms race put humanity on the precipice of disaster for almost a half century, once the two sides both had nuclear weapons, the balance of terror known as MAD took hold, and the great powers shied away from directly fighting each other. The problem is that, unlike in the Cold War, there is no simple bipolar arrangement, since, as we saw, the weapons are proliferating far more widely. Even more, there are no cyber equivalents to the clear and obvious tracing mechanism of a missile's smoky exhaust plume heading your way, since the attacks can be networked, globalized, and of course, hidden. Nuclear explosions also present their own, rather irrefutable evidence that atomic weapons have been used, while a successful covert cyber operation could remain undetected for months or years.

Instead of trying to get MAD, the better lesson from arms races past may be that "Talk is cheap(er)," as defense analyst Rebekka Bonner has said. Arms races are relatively expensive. Indeed, she found that the United States alone spent almost $9 trillion on the Cold War arms race "that resulted in a net decline in national security." While early efforts like the Baruch plan didn't work, it doesn't mean that efforts at arms control were not worthy. The whole time that nuclear weapons were building up during the Cold War, there were off-and-on attempts to build them down. These started with bold offers like the Baruch Plan and continued into everything from the Pugwash dialogues between nuclear scientists to the SALT and START arms control talks between world leaders. Not all met with success, but they were relatively costless. More importantly, they helped dampen tensions and ultimately set the table for the Cold War to end.

As we'll explore soon in Part III, the comparison to today highlights the glaring need for similar efforts. It is unlikely (and unverifiable) that the various players in this cyber arms race will just give up their capabilities in some new form of the Baruch Plan. But the basic choice is much like that back in the 1940s. One path is to be a "slave to fear," solely to focus on the threats, and race to build up a capability to counter them, even if it likely won't deliver much security in the end. The other is to recognize the mutual risks that all the participants in cyberspace face from this new arms race and explore how we can be responsible stakeholders. The direction we take won't just shape this new twenty-first-century arms race, but also will shape the future of the Internet itself.

Behind the Scenes: Is There a Cyber-Industrial Complex?

"Unlike most wars, the Cyber War will have no end, as the Internet along with the continued globalization of industries central to the development of a middle class, will create new battlefields to protect. The investment required to protect corporate America and the US Government will grow at almost exponential rates, public and private partnerships will have to flourish, more and more existing defense companies will have to pivot, and the Merger & Acquisitions and investment opportunities will increase. If you wish to invest in the Cyber Arms Race, then this is the conference for you."

This is from an invitation that we received to a conference in 2013. Where some see threats, others see opportunities. And maybe that should worry us all.

The rise of cybersecurity as an issue has gone hand in hand with a boom in the number of companies trying to make money from it. And there is a lot of money to be made. Indeed, the 2013 cybersecurity market in the United States alone was estimated to be $65 billion and projected to grow at a 6 percent to 9 percent rate per year for at least the next five years. In only ten years, cybersecurity could be a $165 billion market. Other estimates already place the global scale of the cyber-industrial complex at "somewhere between $80 billion and $150 billion annually."

What is notable is that this growth is happening at the same time that traditional defense budgets are going down. "In a barren global defence market the cyber security domain has provided a rare oasis" is how a leading defense industry magazine described the world of cybersecurity. And, like much else in cybersecurity, the boom is not just an American phenomenon. For instance, even in an environment of austerity and dramatic cuts across the UK government, the 2010 Strategic Defence and Security review recommended an increase in cybersecurity funding of $1.7 billion. As Professor Peter Sommer of the London School of Economics wrote, "In terms of the involvement of the big military companies, you have to realize that they are finding it extremely difficult to sell big, heavy equipment of the sort they are used to because the type of wars that we're involved in tend to be against insurgents. And so they are desperately looking for new product areas—and the obvious product area, they think, is cyber warfare."

With these trends in play, traditional defense firms have taken three primary approaches to getting on board what they see as a cyber gravy train. Or, as we were told in the conference invitation, they are seizing the "wealth of opportunity" that awaits in "the migration from traditional 'warfare' to "cyber war."

The first strategy has been to expand their own internal cyber operations. Companies like Lockheed Martin and Boeing may be better known for making jet fighters, but now they also run cybersecurity centers for defense ministries and other government agencies. Second, there has been a buying spree of the smaller cyber firms. Indeed, since 2010, 15 percent of all mergers and acquisitions transactions completed by defense companies involved a cybersecurity target. Sometimes these have been military-oriented firms, while at others it has been military firms bringing in niche skills from other domains. BAE may be known for building Typhoon fighter jets and *Queen Elizabeth* class aircraft carriers, but it also paid almost $300 million in 2011 to become the proud owner of Norkom, a cyber fraud and anti-money-laundering specialist. Its competitor Boeing has spent over $1 billion buying up smaller cybersecurity firms in the last five years. Finally, there have been a series of corporate alliances. Boeing, for instance, doesn't just sell F-15 fighter jets to Japan, but also in 2012 inked a partnership with Sojitz, a leading Japanese conglomerate, in which the two megafirms agreed to help protect critical Japanese government, civil, and commercial IT infrastructures. As one report described, the outcome is that "Companies with cyber security relevant capabilities have seen financial worth increase almost on dot-com levels witnessed in the late 1990s."

But with this growth comes some concern, especially in the role such firms seek in influencing public policy. In 2001, only four firms were lobbying Congress on cybersecurity issues. By 2012, it had risen to 1489 companies. The *Washington Post* even gave an article on the phenomenon the title "Good News for Lobbyists: Cyber Dollars."

As Ronald Deibert, a cybersecurity expert who helped found the Information Warfare Monitor project, worries, "This not only creates a kind of feeding frenzy among defense contractors, but also propels the development of more refined techniques of monitoring, exploitation, and attack. This new cybersecurity market brings to mind Dwight Eisenhower's warnings of a looming 'military-industrial complex.' When you have a major defense budget served by the private sector, a constituency is created that has enormous influence over policy, perceptions of threats, and strategic interests."

This potential cyber-industrial complex now has vested interests in developing newer and better modes of both cyber defense and attack, which, of course, must go hand in hand, driving up the levels of threats and tensions in this space. Perhaps the more worrisome aspect has been the manner in which very real risks and threats in cybersecurity have sometimes been mischaracterized. In a study called "Loving the Cyber Bomb" (a play on the old Cold War movie *Dr. Strangelove or How I Learned to Stop Worrying and Love the Bomb*), cyber experts at George Mason University found extensive evidence of threat inflation in Washington, DC, cyber discussions, most frequently by those with political or profit incentives to hype the threats.

As we've seen, such hype inflation ranges from the mischaracterization of unsophisticated attacks as war to full-blown falsehoods. A repeatedly cited example is the "cyber Pearl Harbor" attack carried out on the Brazilian power grid. This supposed episode was even featured in a 2009 episode of *60 Minutes*, with pundits positing that a series of power blackouts in Brazil had been caused by cyber blackmail. It turns out the blackouts were actually just non-cyber-related failures at a single power supplier.

The point here is not that cyberthreats are all just the work of a vast conspiracy or that "cyberwarfare is a meaningless buzzword coined by rapacious defense contractors," as writer Cory Doctorow once put it. As we have explored, there are very real and very dangerous things going on in cyberspace, and, indeed, that is why we wrote this book. But these threats have to be put in their proper context and understanding. And part of that understanding requires us all to realize that there is now a lot of money to be made in the field. With that money comes the risk of bias and even hype.

The most important takeaway, then, is that we must avoid letting our fears get the better of us, or even worse, let others stoke our fears and thus drive us into making bad decisions. How we respond to this world of growing cyberthreats will shape everything from our personal privacy and the future of the Internet to the likelihood of regional crises and even global wars. So we better try to get it right. And that is what Part III is all about.

Part III

WHAT CAN WE DO?

Don't Get Fooled: Why Can't We Just Build a New, More Secure Internet?

The proposal started out as an April Fool's joke, but many people still took it seriously.

Steve Bellovin, a computer network and security researcher, can claim to have literally written the book on firewalls, being one of the earliest researchers on how to repel what he called "the wily hacker." On April 1, 2003, he issued a new proposal for an Internet-wide standard to ensure network security. Noting that the problem in cybersecurity was really just one of separating the bad traffic from good traffic, he proposed that each packet come with a new flag on it, a one-digit signifier that could be 1 or 0. "If the bit is set to 1, the packet has evil intent. Secure systems SHOULD try to defend themselves against such packets."

Of course, the Internet's very structure has no way of enforcing "evil bit" settings, and there is no reason why an evildoer would set such a flag. That was the essence of the joke. Nonetheless, it is easy to look at all of today's problems with Internet security and wonder if there is a way to just start over.

Some argue that the threats the cyber age has brought are so "terrifying" that, as *Washington Post* columnist Robert Samuelson wrote, we should just "repeal the Internet. It is the technological marvel of the age, but it is not—as most people imagine—a symbol of progress. Just the opposite. We would be better off without it."

To put it bluntly, such an idea is a nonstarter. Setting aside that a technology is not a law—it can't be "repealed" or uninvented—the notion of going back to the world right before the Internet makes as much sense as rebooting *Beverly Hills 90210*. The world has changed. We are now dependent on the Internet in everything from commerce to communications to, yes, even conflicts, while the modes and expectations of cyberspace have become woven into an entire generation's very worldview.

If we can't roll back time, others argue for something seemingly more modest, building a more secure section of cyberspace: a new region of peace and predictability set inside the supposed lawless Wild West of the Internet. This approach advocates creating trusted networks inside the Internet, which would solve the problems of anonymity and inability to limit access. The model might be applied only to the most critical infrastructure systems, such as power plants, or more the more frequent online targets, such as consumer banks.

A number of senior government leaders have pushed this ".secure" model. The concept has been described in different manners, but essentially argues that the current Internet and network architecture were not designed with enough security to meet today's threats, and a new part of the Internet should be created with just this in mind. General Keith Alexander, head of both the NSA and US Cyber Command, argued for a "secure, protected zone." Similarly, the FBI's former Assistant Director Shawn Henry argued for a "new, highly secure alternative Internet."

Many in the private sector have watched these discussions of separating out the Internet or making it anew and started to explore their associated business opportunities. In 2012, the security company Artemis declared its intention to buy a new domain of .secure and create a "neighborhood on the Internet where security is required, and users know that." Rather than focus on any network aspects, the .secure domain would be a brand of sorts. Any website wishing to use the .secure appendage would have to meet Artemis's security standards, including no hosted malware, fully implemented top-of-the-line protections, and rapid vulnerability patching.

Will these approaches work? It depends on two features. The first is what kind of security is actually offered. The commercial .secure domain offers no protection from malicious actors on the network or on your computer. Instead, it will only secure the websites themselves. Your bank's website won't attack you, but you would still be vulnerable to having your bank account credentials stolen.

Similarly, the government's secure Internet could take one of several forms of added security. The least amount of reengineering and effort would simply be to build a model of opting in at the network level, allowing more government analysis of network traffic to detect threats. This would offer benefits, to be sure, but would hardly create the kind of "more secure Internet" that people talk about as the needed alternative. More rigorous proposals require individual authentication at the network level to support connectivity. Even if we could engineer a mechanism to convey real authentication at the network level (as opposed to the application level), a vulnerable computer could still allow credential theft and undermine security.

The second feature to solve is scale. Network security is generally inversely correlated with size, while network utility is positively correlated. To put it another way, the bigger the network, the more security problems, but the smaller the network, the less useful it is. If the network spans a large set of organizations and risks, its security becomes less and less certain, depending on more and more people not making mistakes. But if the inner circle of protection doesn't extend that far, then it's not all that useful for solving the problems these advocates cite. For example, will the government approach include smaller organizations, a rural power plant for instance, that are clearly vulnerable? But how will those less able organizations live up to the supposedly newly high security standards set for the extremely critical infrastructure? Moreover, how would we treat a large organization with critical functionality? Does the payroll department also have to conform to the new super-duper security standards for the new secure Internet? If not, how do we enforce segregation between those systems that everyone uses and the critical systems that only some people use some of the time? As we've seen, separating secure and insecure systems by "air gapping" them is very difficult in practice, and hasn't been a guarantee of safety. If it was so simple, the Pentagon's Secure Internet (SIPRINET) wouldn't have been repeatedly compromised by relatively unsophisticated cyberattacks, nor would Stuxnet have been a problem to the Iranians.

These same kinds of problems strike the private side, just with added layers. Suppose your mother hears about all these new fangled cyberthreats and decides only to trust websites with the .secure domain. Now any company that wants to reach her must join this group. This seems a positive step for the market, shaping it toward more security. The problem is that the bigger the market gets, the more it increases the number of websites (and all the people behind them) that could deviate from the security goals. What's more, when her grandson comes and surfs the Web on her computer or phone, not always using .secure, she'll lose her protection, and when it no longer works the way she was sold, she will see little reason to continue following the brand.

In practice, too many of the concepts of building an entirely new Internet end up a lot like the idea of relying on Bellovin's joked "evil bit." This isn't to say that the goal of a less risky Internet isn't worth pursuing. But starting anew just isn't the easy option that is oft portrayed. Instead, the task is to analyze carefully the changes proposed, and compare their costs with their potential to affect specific security goals.

Rethink Security: What Is Resilience, and Why Is It Important?

"Hundreds of Thousands May Lose Internet."

Articles with this headline not so ironically hit the Internet in the summer of 2012. The story started when the FBI caught the group behind the DNS Changer virus. This cybercriminal ring based out of Estonia had been able to infect more than 570,000 computers worldwide, reprogramming the victim's machines to use DNS servers run by the criminals. They would then steer the computers to fraudulent websites, where the hackers would profit (to the tune of over $14 million) from websites that the victims were tricked into visiting. But when the FBI got ready to shut down the ring, said Tom Grasso, an FBI supervisory special agent, "We started to realize that we might have a little bit of a problem on our hands because.... If we just pulled the plug on their criminal infrastructure and threw everybody in jail, the victims were going to be without Internet service. The average user would open up

Internet Explorer and get 'page not found' and think the Internet is broken."

Faced with this problem, the FBI entered the Internet server provider business. With the help of the Internet Systems Consortium, on the night of the arrests the agency installed two of its own Internet servers to take over the operations run by rogue servers that the victims' computers had been using, which by then were sitting impounded in an FBI evidence locker. For the next nine months, the FBI tried to let victims know that their computers had been infected and how to fix the problem. But after running its own servers at a cost of $87,000, the FBI said it had to pull the plug on its safety net, hence the media warnings of mass Internet loss. Fortunately, the "Internet Doomsday" that Fox News described was avoided; it turned out many of the systems were no longer used, while other ISPs set up various technical solutions to steer people to assistance.

In a world that depends so much on the Internet, the fear of losing access to it is very real. It's not just the lost social connections on venues like Facebook or Twitter, or the emptiness of a day without online cat videos, but the impact it can have on things like politics and economics. As a result, the need to build "resilience" against such shocks has become one of the magic words of cybersecurity.

Resilience is another one of those concepts that is both overused and underexplored. A study by the Homeland Defense Institute identified 119 different definitions of the term. The general idea behind resilience is to adapt to adverse conditions and recover. It is a wonderful concept, but the problem is that it can apply to everything from computer systems to our own love life. Indeed, there have been over 3,000 books written with "the word 'resilience'" in their title, most of them in the "self-help" section!

In cybersecurity, we should think about resilience in terms of systems and organizations. Resilient systems and organizations are prepared for attacks and can maintain some functionality and control while under attack. "Intrusion tolerance" is how security expert Dan Geer frames it. "We must assume that intrusions have happened and will happen. We must maximize the probability that we can tolerate the direct effect of those intrusions, and that whatever damage is done by the intruder, the system can continue to do its job to the extent possible."

There are three elements behind the concept. One is the importance of building in "the intentional capacity to work under degraded conditions." Beyond that, resilient systems must also recover quickly, and, finally, learn lessons to deal better with future threats.

For decades, most major corporations have had business continuity plans for fires or natural disasters, while the electronics industry has measured what it thinks of as fault tolerance, and the communications industry has talked about reliability and redundancy in its operations. All of these fit into the idea of resilience, but most assume some natural disaster, accident, failure, or crisis rather than deliberate attack. This is where cybersecurity must go in a very different direction: if you are only thinking in terms of reliability, a network can be made resilient merely by creating redundancies. To be resilient against a hurricane just requires backups located elsewhere, ready to just flip on if there is flooding at your main computer center. But in cybersecurity, an attacker who understands a network can go after the key nodes that connect all these redundancies, shutting the whole thing down.

Resilience in cybersecurity starts with the primary goal of preserving the functions of the organization. As a result, the actions that are needed to be resilient vary. Preparedness and continuity might depend on the ability to quickly lock down valuable information or dynamically turn on otherwise onerous defenses. Outward-facing Internet services could be shut down, with some alternative process in place for a less efficient but more secure alternate. In other situations, resilience might depend on mitigation or the ability to "fail gracefully." One example is having mechanisms that keep attacks on web servers from gaining access to internal servers. It's the difference between your picture on the company website being defaced with a funny mustache, and sensitive data being compromised.

This notion of multiple modes of planned failure is important to resilience planning: systems and organizations should not fail critically from a single attack but should have enough distributed control to continue operations. Another key aspect is that failure must be evident. If the system allows "silent failures," its operators can't adapt in a timely fashion.

Still, it's not terribly useful for a policymaker or senior manager to send off planners with the dictums to "Be resilient" and

"Expect the unexpected." We need metrics to support organizational decision-making, influence system design, and guide technical investment. There are dependability metrics that measure, for instance, how critical any component is to the overall system. Similarly, understanding the means and timing of a system's recovery from the accidents or non-attack-related failures that normally happen can inform resilience against targeted attacks. Particularly useful are exercises that test security, such as having an outside "red team" test potential vulnerabilities and the recovery from them, before an actual foe makes a real attack.

Resiliency cannot be separated from the human component, though. Adaptability and recovery cannot happen without individuals, processes, and practices that can quickly assess the situation, handle dynamic environments, and learn from their experiences. As the famous World War II British poster advises, the most resilient response is not to freak out that the Internet sky is falling, but rather to "Keep Calm and Carry On."

The biggest challenge perhaps is that the structural aspects of resiliency are frequently at odds with other goals. The media that writes headlines warning of an "Internet Doomsday" want to draw in readers, not supply answers. The same government bureaucracies that should be building an ethic of public resilience benefit from public fears that drive up their budgets and powers. And even in private firms, the incentives for efficiency can drive in opposite directions. Redundancy is intuitively wasteful. Meeting day-to-day goals requires looking away from the big picture. And the kind of employee who is best at adapting to changing conditions may not be as good at doing the same thing again and again, which many firms want instead. Indeed, when the World Economic Forum tried to sell its corporate members on the importance of building cyber-resilient organizations, its business case mostly relied on public goodwill, which is nice, but less than compelling to companies focused on the bottom line.

There are, however, incentives to adopt a more holistic approach to resilience. Media that continually warn the sky is falling end up losing the trust and attention of their intended audience. Government leaders who can only talk in terms of threats become discounted. And organizational theorists have noticed that businesses that have the greatest apparent efficiency actually are too lean, and suffer from an inability to adapt or innovate. They lack "organizational slack" that drives a positive culture and enables future growth. The same organizational features that create resiliency enable this organizational slack. Similarly, being better at self-assessment and cultivating employees who understand the broader goals of the organization are other areas that help both resiliency and a broader mission.

There is no single definition, path, or strategy for resilience. We need to avoid treating it like a magical buzzword that has no real meaning, whether as a falsely claimed property of every new product or as a black box inserted into organizational planning documents. Instead, resiliency is about understanding how the different pieces fit together and then how they can be kept together or brought back together when under attack. Like all the other cybersecurity solutions, it's not only a matter or architecture and organization, it's about people and processes.

Reframe the Problem (and the Solution): What Can We Learn from Public Health?

In 1947, the seven staff members of what was then known as the Office of Malaria Control in War Areas took up a collection to raise $10. They needed the money to buy fifteen acres of land in DeKalb County, Georgia, where they planned one day to build their new headquarters. Over the next six decades, the organization widened its focus beyond malaria, changed its name, and the $10 investment in real estate more than paid off. Today, the acreage just outside Atlanta houses the Centers for Disease Control (CDC), a program with 15,000 staff members that is considered one of the most successful government agencies in history. The CDC serves as a bulwark of the modern American public health system, having ended the scourge of killers like smallpox and now standing guard against new disease outbreaks like pandemic flu.

While the Cold War is by far the most frequent analogy used in policy discussions of cybersecurity, this historic parallel is actually not so apt. The Cold War was a competition between two superpowers with political leadership and decision-making clearly located in Washington and Moscow, each hubbing a network of allied treaties and client states and competing over the so-called Third World. By contrast, the Internet isn't a network of governments but the digital activities of billions of public and private users, traveling across an infrastructure that is in the hands of some 5,000-plus Internet service providers (ISP) and carrier networks owned by an array of businesses. The Cold War was also a war of ideas between two competing political ideologies. The ideas at play on the Internet sometimes touch on serious ideology, including free speech and human rights, but they also include the 800,000 hours of videos of keyboard-playing cats and pop song parodies uploaded onto YouTube each day.

It is this diversity that leads many experts to argue that agencies like the CDC are a more apt comparison for the needed future of cybersecurity. It's not just that there are many similarities between the spread of malware and the spread of communicable disease (even the terminology is the same—"viruses," "infection," etc.). It's that the broader public health approach might be a useful guide to how cyber policy overall could be more effectively reimagined.

Organizations like the CDC play a key role in public health by serving as research organizations, trying to understand emerging threats, as well as trusted clearing houses, transparently sharing information to anyone and everyone who needs it. The CDC's success has made it a one-stop shop for reliable reporting on everything from how to protect yourself from the common cold to the latest genetic analysis of bird flu.

Given the similar problem with information that clouds effective responses to cyberthreats, there may now be the need for an equivalent "Cyber CDC." The concept is to form an agency much like the CDC, linked to a relevant department like Homeland Security, but independent enough to focus on its core mission of research and information sharing, which also differentiates it from both organizations like CYBERCOM and private firms with their own profit interests. Indeed, cybersecurity research firms' incentives to hoard information parallel the incentives of drug companies, which, while not happy to see diseases break out, do prefer to be the one with the patent on the cure.

As one study explained, the cyber CDC equivalent's "functions might include threat and incident watch, data dissemination, threat analysis, intervention recommendations, and coordination of preventive actions." It would be structured in a similar way, with leadership appointed by the government but with staff recruited across a wide range of specialties. Just as the CDC now has offices beyond Atlanta to allow it to research and track disease outbreaks of various types and locales across the nation (hence the name "Centers"), so too would the Cyber CDC equivalent distribute itself physically and virtually in order to cast a wider net around emergent threats on the World Wide Web. It would also be able to navigate privacy concerns in much the same way that CDC research on disease outbreaks focuses on trends rather than individual case identities. As one blog joked, "Essentially, take everything the CDC already does and slap a cyber in front of it."

One of the pillars of modern public health is the sharing of responsibility for action across the system. Thus, the cyber version of the CDC would not stand alone but simply serve as a hub for cooperation with all the various other state and international agencies as well as nonstate actors that matter in cyberspace, just as the CDC works collectively with groups like the World Health Organization (WHO) all the way down to local hospitals, universities, and research centers. (There is an argument to be made for a WHO equivalent at the international level for cyber, but that level of international cooperation may be a bridge too far at this time).

Framing cybersecurity as like a public health problem may not just be more effective, but also have huge policy and political implications. Importantly, while the rethinking still allows for the problem of deliberate attacks (public health must defend against biological weapons attacks, for instance), it shifts the focus away from a meme of just cyberattack-counterattack and toward the needed goal of cooperation, among individuals, companies, states, and nations. As opposed to the current trend of leaders calling for a "cyber Manhattan Project to build weapons," looking at the matter through a health lens would aid coalitions of governments and network organizers to collaborate around solutions and go after many of the core, shared problems of cybersecurity. Indeed, by even just focusing on research and information, such an agency might serve as a key intermediary in heated political environments, just as the health version of the CDC does. (The international battle to stop smallpox was actually first introduced by a Soviet deputy health minister, allowing the CDC to serve as an alternative track of cooperation between Cold War enemies.)

Like the eradication of most diseases, the cyber equivalent to public health would be to focus both on the causal factors and vectors of spread. For instance, botnets create a huge amount of infection across the Internet by spewing out spam, but they also make it hard to track down the more directed, malicious actors conducting more advanced cyberattacks. In much the same way that the CDC targeted malaria, dedicated efforts could be made to "drain the Internet swamp" of botnets through efforts to take infected computers offline, to collect and share information about which ISPs (and which owners of IP addresses) are the originators or relay points for the most malicious traffic, and to improve cooperation across network providers by developing "white lists" of firms that follow best practices. (One survey found that 27 percent of network providers "do not attempt to detect outbound or cross-bound attacks, and of those that do, nearly half take no actions to mitigate such attacks.")

As in public health, this kind of cooperation would ideally extend all the way to the individual level. For instance, the CDC has led efforts to bolster the average American citizen's awareness and education on basic steps to take to keep themselves safe, as well as prevent dangerous diseases from spreading. The underlying concept to emerge from the CDC's research is that Ben Franklin's saying, "An ounce of prevention is worth a pound of cure," really is true. In studies of everything from malaria to HIV, the CDC found that disease prevention was the best pathway to control and, in turn, that effective prevention required building an ethic of individual responsibility. We see the fruits of this work woven into our daily lives, from workplace reminders on how washing your hands can prevent the spread of the seasonal flu to TV and web advertisements on how abstinence and the use of condoms can prevent the spread of sexually communicable diseases.

The same kind of "cyber hygiene" and "cyber safe" ethics might be bolstered through similar efforts to convince users of cyberspace of their own responsibilities to help prevent the spread of threats and malware. As Scott Charney, Vice President of Trustworthy Computing at Microsoft explains, "Just as when an individual who is not vaccinated puts others' health at risk, computers that are not protected or have been compromised with a bot put others at risk and pose a greater threat to society."

Learn from History: What Can (Real) Pirates Teach Us about Cybersecurity?

In 1522, three Spanish galleons left Havana, Cuba, on their way to Seville, Spain. Loaded onto the ships were literally tons of gold, emeralds, jade, and pearls, all the riches of the Aztec empire gathered into one massive shipment. Hernando Cortés has just conquered Mexico and was sending its treasure as a tribute back to his king, Charles V. But once the fleet set out on its long journey, five more ships appeared on the horizon. The lumbering treasure-laden ships couldn't escape. A short fight ensued, and the Spanish lost to a squadron led by a French captain named Jean Fleury. By stealing the Aztec gold, Fleury had pulled the ultimate score. The episode would inspire generations to come and launch what is known as the "Golden Age of Piracy," a period romanticized in books like *Treasure Island* and movies like *Pirates of the Caribbean*.

In centuries past, the sea was a primary domain of commerce and communication over which no one actor could claim complete control, much like the Internet today. While most just used the sea for normal commerce and communication, there were also those who engaged in bad deeds, again much like the Internet today. They varied widely, from individual pirates to state militaries with a global presence. In between were state-sanctioned pirates, known as privateers. Parallel to today's "patriotic hackers" (or the private contractors working for government agencies like the NSA or Cyber Command), privateers were not formally part of the state but licensed to act on its behalf. They were used both to augment traditional military forces and to add challenges of identification (attribution in cyber parlance) for those defending far-flung maritime assets.

These pirates and privateers would engage in various activities with cyber equivalents, from theft and hijacking, to blockades of trade (akin to a "denial of service"), to actual assaults on economic infrastructure and military assets. During the War of 1812, for example, the American privateer fleet numbered more than 517 ships—compared to the US Navy's 23. Even though the British conquered and burned the American capital city, the private American fleet caused such damage to the British economy that they compelled negotiations. As in cyberspace today, one of the biggest challenges for major powers was that an attacker could quickly shift identity and locale, changing its flags and often taking advantage of third-party harbors with loose local laws.

Maritime piracy is still with us, but it's confined off the shores of failed states like Somalia and occurs on a miniscule scale compared to its golden age (only 0.01 percent of global shipping is taken by modern-day pirates). Privateering, the parallel to the most egregious attacks we have seen in the cyber realm, is completely taboo. Privateers may have helped the US against the British in the War of 1812, but by the time the American Civil War started in 1861 President Lincoln not only refused to recruit plunderers-for-hire, but also blasted the Confederates as immoral for opting to employ them.

The way this change came about provides an instructive parallel to explore for cybersecurity today. Much like the sea, cyberspace can be thought of as an ecosystem of actors with specific interests and capacities. Responsibility and accountability are not natural market outcomes, but incentives and frameworks can be created either to enable bad behavior or to support the greater public order.

To clamp down on piracy and privateering at sea, it took a two-pronged approach that went beyond just shoring up defenses or threatening massive attack (which are too often talked about in cybersecurity as the only options, again making false comparisons to the worst thinking of the Cold War). The first strategy was to go after the underlying havens, markets, and structures that put the profits into the practice and greased the wheels of bad behavior. Major markets for trading pirate booty were disrupted and shut down; pirate-friendly cities like Port Royal, Jamaica, were brought under heel, and blockades were launched on the potentates that harbored the corsairs of the southern Mediterranean and Southeast Asia.

Today, there are modern cyber equivalents to these pirate havens and markets. And much like the pirate friendly harbors of old, a substantial portion of those companies and states that give cybercrime a legal free pass are known. These range from known malware and other cyber black marketplaces to the fifty Internet service providers that account for around half of all infected machines worldwide. Without the support of these havens and networks, online criminal enterprises would find it harder to practice their illegal action, which not only would clean the cyber seas, but also make it easier to identify and defend against the more serious attacks on infrastructure and the like.

Melissa Hathaway, who led the White House's policy team on cyberspace issues, has talked about this as a strategy to " 'drain the swamp' of malicious cyber activity and tilt the playing field [back] in our favour." Much as with piracy at sea, some of the efforts might be taken as part of a cooperative global effort, while other actions could be taken on a unilateral basis, such as operations to disrupt or destroy the markets where hacker tools are traded, and tracking and targeting the assets of attackers themselves.

This links to the second strategy, the building of a network of treaties and norms, something explored in a following section. Fleury's attack launched a golden age of piracy that was great for the pirates but not everyone else, including the governments of the time. Pirates, who had been tolerated at the individual level, began to be seen as general threats to economic prosperity. In turn, privateers, who had been viewed as useful tools, turned into the bureaucratic rivals of the formal navies being built up in these states (here again, akin to how patriotic hackers lose their shine when states build out more of their own formal cyber military units). As Janice Thompson recounts in her seminal study of why the pirate trade ended, *Mercenaries, Pirates, and Sovereigns*, maritime hijackers (and their state-approved counterparts) became marginalized as nations' values changed and they saw the need to assert greater power and control.

Soon a webwork of agreements was established that set a general principle of open trade across the high seas. The agreements, some bilateral and others multilateral, also asserted that maritime sovereignty would only be respected when a nation took responsibility for any attacks that emanated from within its borders. Slowly, but surely, they paved the way toward a global code of conduct. By 1856, forty-two nations agreed to the Declaration of Paris, which abolished privateering and formally turned pirates from accepted actors into international pariahs to be pursued by all the world's major powers.

The cyber parallel today, again, is that all netizens have a shared global expectation of freedom of action on the Internet, particularly online trade, just as it is ensured on the open ocean. If you knowingly host or abet maritime pirates or privateers, their actions reflect back on you. The same should be true online. Building those norms will motivate both states and companies to keep a better check on individual hackers and criminals (the pirate equivalent). It will also weaken the value of outsourcing bad action to patriotic hackers (the latter-day privateers).

In addition to encouraging new accountability, this approach also offers opportunities for what are known as "confidence-building measures," where two states that don't get along can find ways to work together and build trust. After the War of 1812, for example, the British Royal Navy and nascent US Navy constantly prepared for hostilities against each other, which made sense since they had just fought two outright wars. But as the network of norms began to spread, they also began to cooperate in antipiracy and antislavery campaigns. That cooperation did more than underscore global norms: it built familiarity and trust between the two forces and helped mitigate the danger of military conflict during several crises. Similarly, today the United States and China are and will certainly continue to bolster their own cyber military capabilities. But like the Royal Navy and new American Navy back in the 1800s, this should not be a barrier to building cooperation. Both countries, for instance, could go after what the Chinese call "double crimes," those actions in cyberspace that both nations recognize as illegal.

The lesson here is that the world is a better place with commerce and communication made safe and freewheeling pirates and privateers brought under control. Indeed, the period was never all that good even for the pirates. Jean Fleury made away with all that Aztec gold, but he should have quit while he was ahead. Just five years after the ultimate pirate score, he was caught by the Spanish on another raiding expedition and hanged.

Protect World Wide Governance for the World Wide Web: What Is the Role of International Institutions?

In 1865, engineers from around the world gathered in Paris to discuss a dilemma. The invention of a new technology called a "telegraph" (taken from the Greek words for "far writing") had spread around the world rapidly, linking people in a way never thought possible. The only problem was that as messages were sent across national borders, each of the countries charged different tariffs, had different types of equipment, and used different codes for the messages. For example, American telegraphs communicated using the inventor Samuel Morse's concept of patterns of four basic keys representing letters of the alphabet, while the Germans communicated with a modified version invented by Frederich Gerke that just used two keys (what we now ironically call "Morse code").

At the meeting, representatives of the European powers (except Great Britain, which was not invited, as its telegraph networks were privately owned—a telling parallel to today's Internet problems) agreed on a set of standards that all the nations using telegraphy would follow. These agreements included uniform tariffs for international telegrams, the right of privacy for all correspondence, and the international use of Morse code (the German version). A new governmental body, an International Telegraph Union (ITU), was to be created to administer and monitor these efforts. It was to be led by a Swiss engineer, Louis Curchod, who had impressed the others at the Paris meeting with his wisdom and good cheer.

It was a landmark moment, both for international communication and cooperation, and news instantaneously spread around the world, by telegraph of course. There was one caveat, however, to this new concept of using an international organization to link people together; the ITU agreement included a clause that nations "also reserved the right to stop any transmission that they considered dangerous for state security, or in violation of national laws, public order or morals." The ITU helped ensure a new era of global communication, but it also made sure that the old governments would stay in control of it.

There is a notion that the Internet is a place without boundaries, where governments do not matter and therefore do not belong. John Barlow of the Electronic Frontier Foundation perhaps captured this sentiment best in his "Declaration of the Independence of Cyberspace." "Governments of the Industrial World, you weary giants of flesh and steel....I ask you of the past to leave us alone. You are not welcome among us. You have no sovereignty where we gather....Cyberspace does not lie within your borders....You claim there are problems among us that you need to solve. You use this claim as an excuse to invade our precincts. Many of these problems don't exist. Where there are real conflicts, where there are wrongs, we will identify them and address them by our means."

The problem with this thinking is twofold. First, governments have seen the Internet become crucial to global commerce and communication but even more so to their own national security and economic prosperity. And so, even if they're unwanted, they are involved, simultaneously solving and creating real problems in cyberspace. Second, as international relations expert Robert Axelrod writes, while there may be no actual physical territory or borders in cyberspace, these governments "have woken up to an interesting fact: every node of the network, every router, every switch is within the sovereign borders of a nation-state and therefore subject to its laws or travels on a submarine cable or satellite connection owned by a company that is incorporated in a sovereign nation-state and therefore subject to its laws. In other words, there is no non-sovereign, 'free' part of cyberspace."

The outcome of this is an important shift. Countries have long sought to control the Internet within their own borders, both legally and operationally. As a report from the Internet Governance Project described, "That's why Bradley Manning is in jail and WikiLeaks is persecuted; that's why China constructed the Great Firewall; that's why South Korea censors Internet access to North Korea and vice versa; that's why France prosecuted Yahoo for displaying Nazi memorabilia."

What has recently emerged is a push for regime change at the international level of cyberspace. The ostensible reason is cybersecurity. Much as with the origin of the ITU, there is a need to foster better technical coordination in the use and misuse of this cross-border technology. In reality, there is also an underlying issue of control, driven by many governments' discomfort with the mostly nongovernmental structures behind Internet governance.

Fred Tipson is a Special Adviser to the Center for Science, Technology and Peacebuilding at the US Institute of Peace, who has also worked at the United Nations and Microsoft. As he explains, the basic problem is that "Many governments view the unrestricted, un-channeled, uncontrolled dimensions of the Internet to be an aberration to be contained or even undone, not a wave of the future." As an illustration, *China Youth Daily*, a major newspaper owned by the Chinese Communist Party that often acts as a voice for the regime, has noted the need for China to "express to the world its principled stance of maintaining an 'Internet border' and protecting its

'Internet sovereignty,' unite all advanced forces to dive into the raging torrent of the age of peaceful use of the Internet, and return to the Internet world a healthy, orderly environment."

Because they see the problem as an international matter between states, the mechanism for much of this push for governmental control over the Internet has come at international institutions of states. And here is where the ITU, still functioning a century and a half after its formation, comes back into the story. In the time since its creation, the ITU moved from regulating telegrams sent over wires, to telephones, to messages sent wirelessly over radio, to now what it calls "Information and Communication Technologies," and so renamed itself the International Telecommunications Union.

This issue came to a head at the December 2012 meeting of the ITU. The nations of the world gathered in Dubai to renegotiate the International Telecommunication Regulations, ITU agreements that had governed telecommunications between nations. At the meeting, nations like Russia, China, Sudan, and others pushed for the Internet to be included in the ITU's responsibilities, giving countries the right to manage how the Internet was structured. Cybersecurity was at the center of their rationale, with these countries arguing that it was a step in the natural evolution of the ITU (from telegrams to radio to telephones, etc.) to help manage the Internet in its continued mission in order to build "confidence and security in the use of international communications technologies."

This proposed expansion, though, was a big deal. It would change the nature of Internet governance, in essence giving governments sweeping powers. Governments (not the community of nonstate, nonprofit organizations that you read about in Part I, which had previously managed the Internet) "would be ultimately responsible for making sure that people trying to reach a given website actually get there." Or, more worrisome, given the track record of the autocratic nations pushing the proposal, they could also ensure that people trying to reach a given website didn't get there. The fear was that, much as with telegraphs, governments could control not just access within their nations but also across borders.

The result is that the usually placid ITU has instead become a tense battleground of what the *Economist* magazine called "a digital version of the Cold War." Notably, the two sides were actually the same primary nations that had been divided by the Iron Curtain.

The United States, Europe, and other allies like Australia and Japan worried that cybersecurity fears were being misused to restrict freedom. They argued that the ITU should not even mention the word "Internet" and just stick to regulating traditional telecommunications such as international phone calls.

ITU agreements had a tradition of being decided by consensus, even during the height of the Cold War. But so far, cyberspace at the ITU has proven anything but consensus oriented. When the 2012 summit vote broke with tradition and was decided by majority vote instead of consensus, the bloc of allies angrily walked out of the meeting (yes, it was ironic the democratic countries were upset by a vote). So the proposal to have the ITU expand its role into cybersecurity issues passed, but with only half the world's nations on board and few of these being major Internet powers, most notably missing the very nation that had invented it. This uninspiring collection didn't stop the new ITU from issuing a press release claiming, "New global telecoms treaty agreed in Dubai."

The questions of what roles old international organizations should play when it comes to the Internet will remain with us for years to come. At the time of this book's writing, the new treaty still needs to be ratified by a number of the signatory states to become binding (a process that can take years), and it is unclear how it could be globally enforced with so many important states in opposition. The ITU also looks to be worse off for the episode, which is a shame. Not only has the nearly 150-year-old organization been a valuable player in global cooperation, but lost in the imbroglio were a number of positive steps that all could agree on, because of their benefit to all, such as agreements to spread fiber-optic networks to expand and speed Internet access. This points to the need to return the ITU to its more traditional mode of decision-making and focus on areas of consensus.

The bigger, longer-term issue is whether that will be possible. The world is dividing into very different visions of the Internet and its governance. One, coming largely from more authoritarian countries, wants "to turn back the clock and regain sovereignty over their own national bits of the Internet." The alternative vision, coming largely from democratic states, sees the very openness of the Internet as the key to its success, allowing it to evolve to meet its users' virtual wants and needs, regardless of their physical location in the world.

The interplay between these two global visions is what makes understanding the true issues and problems of cybersecurity so crucial. As one report on the future of Internet concluded, "Just as an appeal to patriotism was once described as the 'last refuge of a scoundrel,' all kinds of scoundrelly proposals to stifle free expression, invade privacy, abolish anonymity, restrict new businesses, and elevate state power invoke cybersecurity as the rationale. At the same time, who can oppose efforts to improve the security and privacy of digital services and the Internet infrastructure? Thus, discussions of cybersecurity must be careful and measured in their approach. They should be grounded in an awareness that there is a legitimate need for action, but mindful of the abuses and manipulations that can masquerade under the banner of security."

"Graft" the Rule of Law: Do We Need a Cyberspace Treaty?

"The rules of aerial warfare apply to all aircraft, whether lighter or heavier than air, irrespective of whether they are, or are not, capable of floating on the water."

This is how the 1923 Hague Rules on Aerial Warfare begins. The treaty was written just a decade after the strange new invention of flying machines were introduced to war, but today it still serves as "the basis of all current regulation of air warfare."

The use of the Internet is now well past the time it took for the use of the air to lead to the Hague Rules, leading many to argue that cyberspace is in need of an equivalent international treaty, or what some call a kind of Internet version of the Hague Rules, or a "cyber Geneva Convention," as some call it. "We have reached a tipping point on cybersecurity," says Neil Fisher, Vice President of Global Security Solutions at Unisys in London. "It is now a significant threat to a lot of economies. So getting an international agreement on what constitutes normal behaviour is now badly needed." Or, as one US government official writes, "With the risk of discovery almost nil, a disputed legal status, and little in the way of unified international law enforcement collaboration, the cyber domain is today's equivalent of the untamed American West during the 1800's."

To be clear, not everyone is pushing equally hard for such a treaty. As Rex Hughes, an adviser to NATO, explains, when one asks the United States and its allies whether they want a cyber treaty, "The official response is yes, we want there to be rules of the road and to apply the law of armed conflict. But unofficially the answer is no—countries that have advanced capabilities want to preserve that."

There are two main reasons for this reticence. The first is a fear among the more advanced cyber powers like the United States that they will be tying their own hands, while others will then catch up, or even worse, just ignore the new laws. For instance, back in 2009 Russia floated the idea at the United Nations that the use of any cyber weapon by a state be preemptively banned, essentially trying to apply the model of arms control to cyberspace. Setting aside how exactly one would monitor a cyber weapons treaty violation (you can't count malware like you can count ICBMs), there was also a slight problem of bias built into the proposal. Russia has used nonstate "patriotic hacker" networks to conduct cyberattacks and would likely benefit rather than suffer from such an agreement that only limited the state side.

The second reason is the very different priorities leading states have in cyberspace. The United States, for example, views the Wild West behavior as akin to problems in the original American West, as theft and bad guys running amuck with no consequences. They would very much want any treaty to limit espionage that targets intellectual property and guards against attacks that go after more vulnerable civilian infrastructure. States like China and Russia, by contrast, view the Wild West behavior as the Western democracies trying to export their wild values.

Given these problems, advocates point to several parallels for how the international community might build a cyber treaty. Many have proposed the 1967 Outer Space Treaty as a model. Like cyberspace, outer space is a realm opened up by technology, used for all sorts of purposes, and no one nation can claim to own it. The treaty prohibits harmful interference of the peaceful exploration and use of outer space and bans the launch of nuclear weapons from space back onto Earth. A similar approach is the proposal to mimic the international community's regulation of the Antarctic, another realm not owned by any one state but previously at risk of being militarized. In the 1959 Antarctic treaty, governments agreed that no weapons are allowed below 60 degrees latitude south. A cyber treaty equivalent would similarly ban any nation from using weapons in this new global zone.

The challenge with such efforts is that for all the similarities, cyberspace is a different beast than space or the polar regions. Any treaty modeled after them would be difficult to agree to and almost impossible to enforce. While it's relatively easy to track who is doing what in outer space, cyberspace is accessible to all. Similarly, as a virtual world, there is no clear line on a map to delineate where cyber weapons can be used and where not, not to mention that identifying a weapon in cyberspace is quite different from the obvious violation of a battleship crossing the 60 degrees latitude line on a map.

While you can't just substitute the word "cyber" for "outer" or "polar" in these treaties and solve the problem, they still are useful models at a broader level. As Ron Deibert explains, "With those agreements, the aim is less about controlling certain classes of weapons, than it is about controlling expectations and developing a set of principles, rules and procedures, and norms about how states behave with respect to an entire domain."

The goal of any initial cyber treaty effort should be to establish the basic building blocks, the key rules and values that all responsible parties can and should agree to. While there are clearly deep disagreements, there are mutual interests. All share an interest in making sure the Internet runs smoothly and cybercrime is controlled. Reflecting this, efforts should be made to expand the 2001 Council of Europe's Convention on Cybercrime. This treaty was originally intended to harmonize European nations' approaches to cybercrime, but with the United States, Canada, Japan, and South Africa also signing on, it holds the potential to evolve into a broader framework.

The strategy underpinning all of this has been described by Martha Finnemore, one of the world's leading thinkers on international cooperation, as a "grafting." Rather than starting anew, adapt the horticulture technique of adding a new plant to the roots of an older plant. Build off of established frameworks and interests to increase your chances of success.

The idea is not merely to add new signatories to this one regional treaty but to expand the scope of international law and agreements. For instance, botnets are a scourge to all (even China, which is often reticent to join cyber agreements; as many as 70 percent of the world's infected computers are in China), and efforts could be made to make building such a system illegal in all countries. To enable this, a global network of the exciting and new national computer emergency response teams (CERTs) and cyber CDC equivalents could be created. This would aid in creating international standards and monitoring information on the health of the Internet and noting any emergent threats. The system would operate along the lines of how nuclear tests are globally monitored or how the International Civil Aviation Organization reduces risks for all fliers, by sharing information and setting common standards.

The plan, writes Jim Lewis of the Center for Strategic and International Studies, is slowly but surely "moving from the Wild West to the rule of law." The value, though, should not be just judged by how it deals with cybercrime, but also by its knock-on effect on more potent threats. Cybercrime is often "the laboratory where malicious payloads and exploits used in cyber warfare are developed, and refined." Expanding such treaties and agreements against cybercrime and other related behaviors would be good for everyone, all the way down to individual users of the Internet who would no longer pay that equivalent to a crime tax we talked about in Part II. But it also would have an added security effect against many of the more troublesome nonstate groups and feared cyberterrorists that are harder to deter, who rely on cybercrime as a lab, as they can't afford their own NSAs to build their own weapons.

Taking on the low-hanging fruit of cybercrime would also impact broader security, including even relations between states, by limiting one of the key aspects of offensive advantage, so destabilizing for global affairs. Those tasked with defending advanced networks (such as critical infrastructure operators, defense contractors, and government agencies) have noted that they spend vastly more time, effort, and money addressing generic problems like botnets, spam, and low-level worms that hit all users of the Internet than they do on the APTs that hold the potential for far greater harm.

These efforts are also valuable simply for their convening power. Discussions of seemingly intractable areas can deepen mutual understanding of the differing underlying assumptions and concerns that make them so difficult. They therefore increase the prospect for addressing some of these issues—or at least limit their negative effects—over time.

Grafting might also be the best strategy for tackling the challenge of where campaigns of cyber espionage have morphed into intellectual property theft on a massive scale, otherwise described in corporate circles as "the China problem." As we saw in Part II, massive value has been lost to China-based APTs that appear to be linked to both the Chinese military and state-owned enterprises.

Some have advocated such measures as criminal indictments, punishing trade sanctions, changing the terrorism code to allow the seizing the foreign assets of any companies that benefit from such secrets, or even licensing cyber "privateers" to hack back at such campaigns. The problem is that such concepts ignore the state-linked nature of these campaigns and the politics of what might happen next in the real world. Indicting Chinese generals, seizing Chinese government assets, and authorizing private cyber strikes could take an already poisoned US-Chinese relationship down an escalatory path. Even more, such proposals ignore a crucial dynamic. While most of the corporate victims certainly don't want to be stolen from, they also fear the escalations and worsened tensions these responses would cause more, greater valuing their access to the broader Chinese market.

Thus, while it certainly sounds appealing to call for "fighting fire with fire," in both firefighting and cybersecurity it is actually better to try to snuff out the flames. This is where grafting comes back in again. While espionage is not against international law, intellectual property theft is contrary to both broader international laws and, even more important, the rules of the World Trade Organization. The WTO was created in 1995 to help foster international free trade, and China's joining in 2001 was crucial to its own economic boom. This dependency is why US Defense Department expert James Farwell believes that the best response is to change the nature of the game, by targeting the commercial side of cyber espionage in cases under the Trade Related Aspects of Intellectual Property Rights (TRIPS) agreement. "An internationally-recognized ruling, handed down in legal proceedings that found China guilty of intellectual-property theft or infringement, could render it liable for billions of dollars in compensation, expose it to multinational economic sanctions and cause it to be branded a 'pirate state.'" Even more, Farwell writes, "As a nation whose strategic thinking focuses on playing for psychological advantage, China would find that result uncomfortable."

Grafting through an international venue, especially one that China values, would also provide a place for China to feel its own grievances can be aired. As we saw in Part II, China also feels it is under cyber siege. The *Global Times*, a regime mouthpiece newspaper, for instance, has argued that "China should confront the U.S. directly. China should gather, testify, and publish evidence of the U.S.' Internet intrusions." Well, use of proper forums like the WTO would give the Chinese a place to put these accusations to the test.

These kinds of efforts show how even in the most contentious issues, where there seems to be little basis for agreement on what to do, there are still areas that can yield results. Beyond grafting, another strategic approach is to focus initially on common terms and definitions. For example, there may be wide disagreement on what constitutes an "attack," but coming to agreement on the definition of certain types of attacks and targets could prove very useful. One study of the United States and China found that mutual agreement on what constitutes "critical infrastructure" might end up making it easier to protect such infrastructure. This is analogous to what happened in nuclear arms control discussions, during which the parties did not always agree, but found common interest in defining and then seeking to limit particular types of weapons that created an incentive to strike first or that destabilized relations, such as missiles with multiple warheads.

There is another important side-benefit to engaging in treaty- and law-building exercises, even at the level of noncommittal discussions. It can concentrate healthy attention on the issue *within* each government. It allows leaders to understand not just what the other side is thinking but also what their own agencies and communities might be doing and the potential consequences. This is something that most senior policymakers around the world are not sufficiently focused on at present. In the cyber realm, as in life, it is important not just to point a finger, but also to take a long look in the mirror.

As these efforts build over time, more thorny problems should be tackled. The cybercrime convention is certainly a valuable building block, but it really can't be extended to some of the more vexing issues of cyber warfare. For example, the lines of when and how a cyberattack becomes an act of war and who can and should be held responsible for it remain fuzzy. And this gray zone is certainly exploited by some states, such as in the Russian attacks on Estonia. Reaching any kind of international concord on these questions, even at the most basic levels, would reduce the risks of miscalculation and unintended crises.

Facing that issue would also open up a much-needed discussion on whether the existing laws of armed conflict need to be updated for cyberspace, something that nations like the United States, Russia, and China don't yet agree on. But here again, it's not so simple. If the old laws do need to be updated, then where should we start? One key problem to wrestle with is how the current laws assume a strong distinction between military and civilian facilities. For example, if you are flying a bomber plane you can target an enemy's military vehicles, but you are supposed to do your utmost to avoid hitting civilian vehicles and try doubly hard not to hit special vehicles like ambulances. But this distinction isn't so clear-cut in cyberspace, where a network can simultaneously be both civilian and military.

Here too, there might be some hope for at least limited agreement. Nations may not agree on all the various definitions of threats, but expanded treaties might focus on the aspects that are viewed as threats to all. For example, while Russia's proposal to prevent any state use of cyber weapons was a nonstarter, there is an argument to be made "to call Russia's bluff" on where these weapons might be used by states, writes Jordan Schneider, a student of the issue at Yale University. Going after certain targets in cyberspace in a way that threatens not just the intended foe, but could also prove destructive for the entire global community, might be added to prohibited activities. As an illustration, banks don't have an extra special immunity in the old laws of war the way hospitals do. But they may need to be treated as a special case in the virtual side of any new laws. The international financial system is so integrated right now that "All states, save perhaps North Korea, would suffer greatly from the instability which would befall world markets should numbers be shifted in bank accounts and data wiped from international financial servers."

There is an important concept behind all this. Simply writing the treaty will not mean everyone will automatically adhere to it. Indeed, there's never been a law written that someone didn't break. Murder is a crime and yet happens every day. Rather, the strategy is to begin to set common definitions and understandings that can then be used to create norms to shape behavior. Until you establish the baseline of what everyone is supposed to follow, you cannot create incentives and rewards for following them and, in turn, identify and punish those who violate them.

In the end, many of these norms can move forward even if formal treaties aren't actually signed by all. As coalitions of nations form (as in the regional cybercrime treaty) and practices become more and more commonplace (like sharing data on emergent botnets), expectations of what is "normal" and "abnormal" behavior build and these expectations begin to matter. People and businesses no longer pollute the way they did back in the 1960s not simply because it's now against the law, but also because of the dirty looks and loss of brand reputation that now come if you are viewed as antienvironment.

These kinds of informal rules can even be created in darker realms, where good intent or worries about reputation matter less. During the Cold War, for instance, the CIA and the KGB certainly did not trust each other and competed hard to steal each other's secrets. But even these two spy agencies were able to come to certain understandings on how to keep their rivalry from escalating into war (for instance, Russian secret agents couldn't assassinate Americans and vice versa, but it was oddly kosher to kill each other's proxies in places like Nicaragua or Vietnam). Experiences like that lead some to believe that similar "red lines" might be possible in the cyber espionage, such as the back and forth that has so poisoned US-Chinese relations in recent years. The two sides might not be happy with the other stealing its secrets, but "There may be ways to get understandings between and among adult nations," says Michael Hayden, the former director of the CIA.

A linchpin of this agenda of norm building, even in the absence of formal treaties, is to create a concept of greater responsibility for activities that emanate from a network. The idea is that if a universally respected and reliable body like a CERT or CDC informs a network that hostile packets or attacks are coming from it, that network must make an effort to stop the activity, even if the owner of a network didn't intend to send it or the identity of the attacker isn't known. The penalty in this arrangement is reciprocity. If the owner doesn't follow the norm, the other networks in the system no longer owe it the same kind of reciprocal exchanges that allow it to access the Internet smoothly. You violate the norm, you lose the privileges that come with it.

The parallel here is how nations over time were persuaded to take action against money laundering and terrorist financing. As international relations expert Robert Axelrod explains, "This is a market-based policy solution, not a solution requiring an enforcement body. Over time, as more and more backbone providers adopt the norm, it dries up the swamp of sanctuaries for bad behavior." Axelrod adds that it might be a particularly useful mechanism for dealing with the thorny US-Chinese cyber relationship, "since it means we can 'work with Beijing' to stop intrusions while not getting them on their hind legs by directly accusing them of the intrusions."

The appeal of this strategy is that, historically, even the actors that are initially loathe to sign onto any formal treaties or agreements become more and more engaged with the underlying norms over time. As the rules spread and nonsignatories can't help but engage in the process, countries start to internalize the logic of cooperation. That is, they begin to act like rules are there, even if there are no formal rules agreed upon.

As this potential system of written and unwritten rules builds out, it will face the final, real test. If we can get international treaties and norms to cover issues of cyberattacks and digital attribution, can we also get them to cover the truly important problems, like the people who currently post more than one hundred years worth of Rick Astley songs and cat videos onto the Internet each day?

Understand the Limits of the State in Cyberspace: Why Can't The Government Handle It?

Toward the end of the Middle Ages, a new technology changed the world by spreading knowledge and communication to the masses. But like the Internet today, the printing press back then also spread disorder, sparking the Reformation and then a series of long wars that left Europe devastated and over eight million dead. Through this period, the governing structures of the old world, such as empires, confederations, and dukedoms, found that they couldn't keep up. In a process that crystallized at the 1648 Peace of Westphalia, the modern bureaucratic nation-state took over. Each nation's sovereignty was embodied by a government that monopolized legitimate force within these its borders and ensured that the national economy ran smoothly, setting up everything from national currency to taxes.

The governments of today's world are largely creations of these centuries past. The challenge is that much like the dukedoms and empires of old, the state as we once knew it is having a hard time keeping up with new actors and new technologies. Whether it's the rise of transnational threats like terrorism, the global financial crisis, climate change, and now cybersecurity, states are finding it difficult to control what happens within their borders as well as solve the new generation of global issues, where what happens beyond their borders is far more important.

In cybersecurity matters, the very structure of the Internet can work against the state. The diffuse and virtualized makeup of cyberspace means that there are real limits to the power of the state, which is traditionally derived from its control of a certain piece of territory. The Pirate Bay, for example, is a website that posts links to BitTorrent files, which are used for peer-to-peer sharing of large data. The problem is that many (if not most) of these files are supposed to be protected by copyright laws, traditionally written by and enforced within individual states. The Pirate Bay does not host the content itself, but merely links to files hosted by users throughout the world. Still, the legitimate owners of the copyrighted materials have repeatedly gone after The Pirate Bay. In response, The Pirate Bay moved both its physical servers and its domain, staying one step ahead. Initially, it shifted to Sweden (and the address changed from .com to .se), since Sweden did not have legal provisions for seizing domain names. When matters got tense in Sweden, The Pirate Bay shifted to a dynamically distributed system around the world. This meant that no one government could seize the contents of the website or the structure behind it.

It is not that governments are powerless. Indeed, many of the people involved in The Pirate Bay project have been arrested, and four were sentenced to short jail sentences. But again, the structure and norms worked against the state in its goal of control. After the arrests, a growing group of international volunteers stepped in to continue to manage the site.

Sophisticated actors with resources can play a fairly long game of whack-a-mole with governments, even in the face of determined foes and international cooperation. Perhaps the WikiLeaks case best illustrates what governments can and can't do. As we saw in Part II, American politicians reacted with horror to the documents released by the transparency website. Vice President Joe Biden labeled WikiLeaks head Julian Assange a "high-tech terrorist," while others wanted him labeled an "enemy combatant," to be jailed in Guantánamo Bay prison without traditional due process. Likewise, under pressure from the US government and its allies, a number of private companies began to sever ties with WikiLeaks, hampering its ability to operate. Visa, MasterCard, and PayPal, for instance, suspended payments, preventing their customers from supporting the organization through the traditional channels.

These actions, though, again showed both the strength and the limits of state power. Assange was detained, but not by the United States, was not placed at Gitmo, and was not prosecuted for the supposed crimes the government was so angered by. Similarly, WikiLeaks quickly announced a new wikileaks.ch domain registered in Switzerland, resolving to an IP address in Sweden, which in turn redirected traffic to a server located in France but registered in Australia. The organization still exists and now accepts donations through a range of sources, including traditional credit card brands routed through the French advocacy organization Defense Fund Net Neutrality, which is less vulnerable to outside pressure, as it uses the very tools of the state against state blackmail (it routes donations through the French national banking system).

Ultimately, the power of the state is territorially linked, which means it is most effective where it can lash up to the physical side of the Internet. While determined, technically sophisticated organizations can often hide behind the jurisdictional ambiguity of the Internet, any that have a physical presence run the risk of playing on the state's home turf. It is through the physical and financial assets that can be seized, the offices that can be closed, and the individuals who can be harassed or imprisoned, that governments are able to exert their power. A good example of this is the series of Internet search companies that have agreed to remove references to the 1989 protests in Tiananmen Square, so that they could maintain business offices in China.

But territoriality is not the only issue that matters for states. Another key characteristic is how private actors control most of the cyberspace infrastructure. Since the privatization of the Internet backbone, the "pipes" through which data flow belong to private actors. These national and international connections are regulated, but many of them enjoy much more freedom than their telephonic ancestors. This dependence on private networks even includes traffic of the most critical national importance. Former US Director of National Intelligence Admiral Michael McConnell estimated that "98 percent of U.S. government communications, including classified communications, travel over civilian-owned-and-operated networks and systems."

While many countries have sought to control the gateways between their country and the global Internet, its very structure means that they cannot segregate civilian from military or government. As we saw, this is not only relevant in terms of the ethics of offensive cyber operations, but it also means that states have a very difficult time getting the system to mold to their preferences. For example, in the old days the government could prioritize which phone calls would get through in a time of crisis. Today, in a world of Internet packet-based communication, a president's e-mail gets no more priority than a video of a baby dancing to "Gangnam Style."

This arrangement creates a crucial ensuing dependency for cybersecurity. Governments depend on private industry for almost every component of their information infrastructure. But this also means that states rely on private industry to take on their shared responsibilities in securing this world.

For example, in Part I, we read about the failed hunt for the makers of the Conficker worm, who had created the world's largest botnet. All the powers of all the world's states could not run down the makers, even though they had penetrated networks that ranged from the British Parliament to the French Air Force. And yet equally compelling to the story of states being sidelined is the story of Conficker's mitigation. A global group composed representatives of private business as well as a range of volunteers, known as the Cabal, assembled to coordinate a countereffort. They ultimately were able to stymie the Conficker botnet by steering messages from the compromised computers in more than 160 countries into a safe "sinkhole."

While the dynamic nature of the Cabal is held up by some as a success, the lack of a government role at its center is telling. Indeed, in a lessons-learned report drawn up by the group, the government role was summed up as "Zero involvement, zero activity, zero knowledge."

And yet, is it all that surprising that neither the US military nor FBI was central to the mitigation of Conficker, given that it was really about identifying a vulnerability in a Windows operating system and then developing and distributing the patch? That's a job for Microsoft and its customers, not for the government.

There are some who believe that these very limitations and dependencies mean that the government's "zero involvement, zero activity, zero knowledge" role in the Conficker case is actually optimal. However, this ignores the reasons that we have governments in the first place, and, in turn, the responsibilities these governments owe to their citizens. The government must secure its own virtual systems in cyberspace that allow it to conduct its real-world operations of defense, communication, and so on. In turn, government can't simply ignore the security of the systems its citizens depend on, such as power generation, water treatment, hospitals, and other sectors. Indeed, even before the advent of the Internet, such sectors were more heavily monitored and regulated than the rest of the economy, reflecting their disproportionate social impact. The same should hold true today.

The challenge for governments is to understand how to foster information security without trying to fight the Internet's architecture and undermining the very benefits of cyberspace. States certainly shouldn't ignore their roles or responsibilities to their citizens, but they must also recognize the structural limitations of their power. Governments have valid concerns, but they no longer have direct control over most of the key sectors, as they are largely in private hands.

Cybersecurity is not a realm where the state can simply take over. Nor can it have "zero involvement" or "zero activity." In finding the right balance, the most important strategy is attacking the third problem, the mentality of "zero knowledge" about the basic issues and responsibilities of cyberspace that we too often see in both the public and the private sectors.

Rethink Government's Role: How Can We Better Organize for Cybersecurity?

The cyber world is a place of exponentials, from the continual growth of online information, literally multiplying upon itself year after year, to the equivalent growth of online threats. But there is one piece that doesn't work at exponential speed: the government. It moves at a glacial pace, if that.

In 2004, the Government Accountability Office identified a set of characteristics that the US executive branch needed in a national cybersecurity strategy (as American writers, we focus on the United States, but the lessons below apply to most every other country). It encompassed everything from allocating resources to defining policies and helping to ensure accountability. A full decade later, the GAO reported that the White House was essentially at the same point. "No overarching cybersecurity strategy has been developed that articulates priority actions, assigns responsibilities for performing them, and sets timeframes for their completion."

At the other end of Pennsylvania Avenue, the legislative branch was no further along. Congress was certainly interested in cybersecurity, holding as many as sixty hearings a year to talk about it. But it wasn't able to pass a single piece of major cybersecurity legislation between 2002 and the writing of this book more than a decade later.

It is not that the government isn't taking cybersecurity action. Indeed, time and again, major governmental programs have taken shape, from Cyber Command to Stuxnet. Rather, it is the government's pace that is different, which matters greatly when thinking about how it can better organize for cybersecurity.

One of the best examples of the US government acting quickly to reorganize itself for cybersecurity actually illustrates the complexities of policy change. The Federal Risk and Authorization Management Program, or FedRAMP certification, was a program launched in 2013 that allowed, for the first time, a government contractor to be cleared just once to provide services for the entire civilian US government. This was a huge step forward, as it replaced a structure that had each and every agency performing its own mandatory security examination.

The process was celebrated with some irony in the media, as it took "only six months" for the first provider to win approval, which is a lifetime in the cyber world. But when one looks at the structure required for FedRAMP, that six months seems blindingly fast for the federal government. The Office of Management and Budget has legal responsibility for ensuring each federal agency is secure, and it delegates enforcement to the General Services Administration, which oversees FedRAMP. In turn, the Department of Defense and the

Department of Homeland Security design the risk assessment process with technical support from the National Institute of Standards and Technology inside the Department of Commerce. Guidance and cross-agency coordination is provided by the government-wide CIO Council. So six months is, in fact, an impressively short amount of time, when you consider all the players and steps.

The outcome of this disconnect of time, problem, and organization is that government efforts in cybersecurity are a patchwork of agencies and projects, often with little clear strategy and mixed levels of control. As we explored in Part II, the defense and intelligence establishments have the largest footprint organizationally in the cyber domain, simply because they have focused on attacking other networks and defending their own for so long. Beyond securing themselves, their experts, particularly in the NSA, occasionally share that expertise with other agencies and sometimes with the private sector for issues of national interest. For instance, the NSA and DoD have worked together to share attack signatures with a group of critical defense contractors, while the NSA agreed to offer technical support to Google following attacks in 2010 and to the financial industry following a series of DDoS attacks in 2012.

Relying on intelligence organizations for on-call protection and outsourced expertise may be the default mode, but it raises a number of concerns. First, there is always the question of privacy and the legal safeguards that are supposed to prevent intelligence agencies like the NSA or CIA (which are supposed to be focused on foreign threats) from gathering information about their own citizens. This is a huge area of controversy; in a number of instances the NSA has gathered information on US citizens' Internet activity without a warrant, either through their communications with foreign citizens or via massive levels of data mining of everything from online bank transactions to travel records. Much of this remains in the classified realm, but the rough privacy protection mechanism requires that the information be generalized; pulling out specific information on an individual is supposed to require a warrant. However, a long trail of scandals and abuses that run from the NSA's Prism and Verizon scandal in 2013 (as revealed by the Edward Snowden leaks) to the 2005 controversy over warrantless surveillance programs ordered by the George W. Bush administration, to the CIA and NSA roles in the illegal domestic phone wiretaps under President Nixon, show why many do not trust the sort of protections that are supposed to be baked into such arrangements.

Second, the intelligence establishment has a strong focus on espionage and the ability to exploit other systems. Their mission also includes building in backdoors to communication networks and maintaining open exploits to attack other nations' systems, which, of course, can run counter to a solely defensive focus. You wouldn't always want to close all the open doors if you depended on them being open elsewhere. Finally, these agencies also operate with less oversight and transparency than normal agencies; their sources and methods must be kept secret for operational reasons, which can sometimes be a problem in cyber defense, in which information sharing is a paramount.

While the military and the intelligence community have much of the capital, both human and technical, the official lead for American cybersecurity policy falls to the Department of Homeland Security (DHS). Unfortunately, that leadership role has so far come with relatively little in the way of enforcement authority. DHS coordinates the security of the civilian government networks and is directed to work with the private sector. Yet legal analysis in 2012 found that with great responsibility has come little power. DHS provides support to both the government and critical infrastructure but cannot compel any specific action. In response to an attack, "even when existing [legal] authorities provide DHS with responsibility to intervene during a cyber incident, they may not fully support actions necessary to manage and coordinate cyber incident response."

The same story also holds in the comparative budget numbers. DHS spent $459 million on its various cybersecurity programs in 2012. The Pentagon spent roughly eight times as much, not even including the NSA's classified budget (roughly $10.5 billion according to the Snowden leaks).

Despite unclear authorities and a much smaller budget, DHS has become the central square in the American patchwork of cybersecurity policy. Its United States Computer Emergency Response Team (US-CERT) serves as a hub of technical expertise, collaboration, and security information dissemination. A similar organization exists for industrial control systems, such as those that run water treatment plants and the power grid. Where DHS has been perhaps most effective is as an advocate for new technical security measures, including the security of the domain name system. Instead of DHS, it is the government regulatory bodies in the United States that are the primary authority for the cybersecurity issues of their respective industries. They are often aided by the National Institute of Standards and Technology (NIST), which is located in the Department of Commerce. NIST is the federal agency that works with industry to develop and apply technology, measurements, and standards in everything from the weights used at grocery stores to the primary building blocks of information systems, such as hash functions. NIST experts have developed standards and frameworks for areas where industry has no clear consensus on new technologies such as cloud computing and digital identity. Occasionally, they will weigh in on security in specific applications, such as electronic voting or electronic medical records, but their primary focus has been to offer guidance on the technical components that apply to many different sectors. NIST expertise may take the form of formal, prescriptive standards developed with input from industry, but it can also come with a lighter touch, such as through published best practices and research reports.

Sometimes this organizational setup works well. For banks, the Federal Reserve sets policies on the transfer of money between banks. This includes consumer protection for unauthorized transfers: the consumer is only liable for a maximum of $50, regardless of what was stolen from the account, or how it was stolen. By clearly assigning responsibility for fraud, this policy has forced the banks to develop fraud detection practices themselves. And, as we've explored, the banks have incentives to take cybersecurity seriously since they both understand and more directly feel the costs if they don't.

The problem is when the incentives are not aligned or where government regulatory agencies are not so focused, set unclear standards, or have overlapping or gaps in authority. In contrast to the clear liability of credit card processors for fraudulent transactions, for instance, the electricity sector is a mess when it comes to cybersecurity organization. Generation, transmission, and distribution are governed by separate entities. This leads to both overlapping regulations and gaps in coverage. Both NIST and the North American Electricity Reliability Corporation

(NERC) are responsible for developing Smart Grid standards, but neither has an explicit responsibility to lead security initiatives. Furthermore, the distribution layer of the power grid is not covered by either entity, creating a situation where two agencies simultaneously have and do not have the ability to set security standards.

Absent a uniform strategy, the dominant approach has been for each regulatory agency to look after its own industry. But the result, as the CEO of one cybersecurity firm told us, is that "The 'most critical' of the critical infrastructure are the biggest laggers in cybersecurity." While much attention has been paid to securing areas like finance, where the incentives are more in alignment for regulation and investment, other areas of even more core importance and danger like water control, chemical industry, or the ports have almost none. In 2013, for instance, a study we helped guide of six major American ports found only one had any proper level of cybersecurity, due to the fact that the Coast Guard and Department of Transportation officials, who are in charge of regulating and protecting the ports, had literally no power or expertise in the area.

This is why many have called for more national standards, especially for critical infrastructure industries. This has been the target of recent attempts at legislation. However, the idea of dictating security requirements at a legal level raises the hackles of many. They argue that firms always know best and always have the best incentives to protect themselves (something we've seen the opposite of over the course of this book). Of course, the very same arguments were made against regulation of the shipping community prior to the *Titanic* and of the nuclear power industry pre-Three Mile Island. So, as of now, the bills to establish standards have failed and Congress has not empowered regulators with any further legal tools to foster information security in industry.

With no new laws, in 2013, the Obama White House directed its executive agencies to "use their existing authorities to provide better cybersecurity for the Nation." But what this meant in execution remains opaque. This returns us to the question of coordination and broad strategy. What is missing most is a clear delineation of authority and leadership across the board for cybersecurity, setting more consistent standards and approaches in what does exist. The present mix is the worst of both worlds. It leads to increased expenses, where firms either aren't held to standards or have to sort out what regulation must be complied with. It also dilutes the ability of any agency to effect meaningful change and can create dangerous gaps in regulation that bad guys can hide in.

Besides establishing more consistent standards and ideally an update to legislation, there are other levers that governments can use to shape cybersecurity policy. One is buying power. As the country's largest purchaser of just about everything, the government has the capacity to affect the market, not just as a regulator but as a client. As one policy report noted, "Security requirements set by U.S. government procurement policies have the potential to become standardized for inclusion by other consumers, giving the government the ability to guide and direct industry developments in ways that would not be possible through legislation or regulation." This blends the role of customer and policymaker by subtly selecting IT security solutions at large scales. There is a caveat: it is no longer 1960 and the government no longer is the main player in the world of computers. The head of IT lobbying organization TechAmerica testified in 2010, "The Department of Defense accounts for only slightly more than 0.1 percent of all information technology expenditures worldwide." The tool should be used, but no one should think it a silver bullet.

The government is still a large enough market—almost $100 billion each year—that it can drive some change. Even if it can't simply demand that the systems it buys are 100 percent secure, it can mandate some accountability for where those systems come from and how they are produced. This will help bring attention to the "supply chain problem," highlighting the risks of the hardware we use as the building blocks for just about everything. Since the supply chain for these parts spans countless countries and companies, attackers can introduce corrupt or malicious components upstream of the final vendor. Use of electronics is ubiquitous, so that, as one industry observer noted, "a $100 microchip might keep a $100 million helicopter on the ground." Not only do we have scant protection against this attack, but it's currently difficult for any vendor to know who was involved in the upstream production to certify their security.

The government can use its purchasing power, as well as its role as a convener, to bring both transparency and accountability to the supply chain. The overall policy idea is to set up a system, as our colleague at Brookings Darrell West suggests, of "developing agreed-upon standards, using independent evaluators, setting up systems for certification and accreditation, and having trusted delivery systems." NIST has brought together government and industry stakeholders to develop supply-chain risk management best practices that can apply to both federal agencies and private enterprises. Specialized agencies like DARPA have begun to tackle more serious aspects of supply chain risk, such as verifying that the astoundingly complex integrated circuits that drive modern computers do not have malicious components baked in.

The government can also play an important role in better organizing around its power of research, where it is best positioned to tackle cybersecurity questions that individual firms might not be incentivized to explore on their own but all would benefit from, much like the Internet itself. Government-funded researchers, for example, have produced much of what we know today about the structure of cybercrime organizations and are active participants in industry groups such as the Anti-Phishing Working Group. The challenge again is how to better organize and disseminate this research. This is the essence of reframing the approach to reflect the model of public health, as we discussed earlier.

Given the patchwork of authorities, it is clear that more clarification and structure are needed in the government's efforts in cybersecurity, most of all to try to help it catch up its pace. A world where the best-case illustration of government organization is one that takes six months is clearly not ideal. But we also need to recognize that organization can only go so far, without the right incentives and understanding underscoring it.

Shortly after he took office, President Obama called for "the development of a comprehensive approach to securing America's digital infrastructure." It was a powerful vision. The problem was this same goal has been set by every single new resident of the White House dating back to Bill Clinton in the 1990s and still remains unfulfilled. On the other hand, since the world of cybersecurity is not a unified one, why should we expect a single approach to solve all the problems that have emerged, or frankly even to be possible?

Approach It as a Public-Private Problem: How Do We Better Coordinate Defense?

For a few weeks, a single blogger was the savior of the Internet. But, as with all superheroes, he actually needed a little bit of help.

In 2008, *Washington Post* reporter Brian Krebs, who blogs at the Security Fix site, became curious about a single company that was poisoning the Internet and why everyone else was letting them get away with it. The company in question was McColo, a web hosting company physically based in California with a client list that, as Krebs wrote, "includes some of the most disreputable cyber-criminal gangs in business today."

After spending four months gathering data on the company and its clients, Krebs then reached out to the large commercial ISPs that provided McColo with their bandwidth to reach the Internet. He presented them with the evidence that McColo was up to no good. Within hours he heard back from several, such as Benny Ng, director of marketing for Hurricane Electric, a major Internet provider for McColo. "We looked into it a bit, saw the size and scope of the problem you were reporting and said 'Holy cow!' Within the hour we had terminated all of our connections to them." Following in Hurricane Electric's footsteps, most of the other major service providers cut off service to McColo over the next two days. McColo was an obvious case of bad action, and service providers wanted nothing to do with it. But then came something that not even Krebs had suspected. Spam levels around the entire world instantly dropped by almost *70 percent*.

The McColo case is a good illustration of both how defending against the diffuse global threats of cyberspace requires a coordinated response and how incentives matter greatly. These firms acted promptly after Krebs contacted them because they worried about what hosting a known bad actor would do to their brand. But up to the point when Krebs planned to publicize McColo's actions to the world, they hadn't cared. The bad-acting firm was just another good client generating massive traffic (and thus good business).

Just as we saw with the worst threats in cyberspace, the best defenses against them rely on coordination. While Krebs had started out on his own, he depended on the network of companies that provided Internet service to act, who in turn depended on him to provide the information and intelligence they needed to act on. It's not enough for single actors or organizations to try to build higher walls or better malware detection on their own. Attackers adapt. Moreover, attackers exploit boundaries of control and responsibility, setting up a collective action problem.

By bringing together the necessary actors and information, Brian Krebs was able to spur effective action, leveraging cooperation against the right fulcrum. While cyberspace seems diffuse and decentralized—simultaneously one of the key advantages and insecurities of the Internet—there are often bottlenecks of control, choke points where the defenders can concentrate resources to gain an advantage. The dependence on large ISPs is one that helped shut down the McColo problem. In turn, payment systems offer another such natural advantage, especially when the malicious action is linked to crime.

The incentives for coordination are the key part to pay attention to solving most any cybersecurity problem. In some areas, as when money changes hands, the incentives are straightforward. In the case of major credit card networks, for instance, they have a natural incentive to avoid interaction with any illegal activity, since it can introduce risks of fraud and disputed transactions that go beyond just regular concerns over brand protection. In 2002, the Visa credit card company set up a system to identify instances when its payment network was being used by questionable sites, such as those hosting child pornography. Visa began terminating their relationships with those networks while at the same time reporting illegal activities to government officials. Within twelve months, 80 percent of the websites they identified as child porn were either shut down or could no longer use Visa to process payments.

More illegal activity has thus shifted to alternate payment systems, many of which have been specifically set up to allow individuals to move money around more freely. Payment networks, like the popular PayPal or the now defunct Canada-based Alertpay, allow individuals who can't personally accept credit card payments to conduct commerce. While these firms' business model is built on offering their users ease and flexibility, they still do have an interest in avoiding bad actors that might damage their networks' reputation. For this reason, they often work with "acquiring banks" that process their customers' payments. PayPal has very strict rules and internal monitoring to detect whether its online payment system is used in nefarious schemes. Indeed, its methods of identifying and tracking down anomalous payments proved so effective that they were later adapted by the CIA and other US intelligence agencies via a firm called Palantir, which was founded by people who had first worked at PayPal. Alertpay, on the other hand, was repeatedly warned by its acquiring banks for dealing with online scams and child pornography sites before being shut down in 2011.

To evade the growing security and control of the payment networks, some bad actors turn to digital currencies. These are alternate currencies that can be traded just like other forms of money, provided that you can find someone in the online world to accept them. Examples range from Bitcoin to the Linden Dollar used in the online world *Second Life*. Proponents of these currencies often make the argument that they are more efficient ways to trade in a virtual world that doesn't have clear national boundaries. Especially compared to developing world currencies, they can be more stable than government-backed money, as well as offer the more than 2.5 billion people in the world who don't have access to traditional banks a way to connect and trade. The problem is that many other users rely on digital currencies to engage in criminal enterprise and launder money.

Here again, though, there are choke points. A key part of their system is the exchange, where users turn their digital bits into more widely accepted currency. Since the days when Al Capone was arrested for tax fraud rather than murder and racketeering, law enforcement has long used more mundane financial laws to go after criminals. When the FBI wanted to crack down on online gambling, it charged the largest website operators not with gambling offenses but with money laundering. With digital currencies, the exchange point operators that swap digital currencies for traditional currencies are where law enforcement has focused its efforts so far. While they may be dealing in online digital currencies, these operators still must engage with other financial institutions and have assets in the real world under jurisdictions with financial regulations. This exposure allowed American officials to charge the creators of the alternative currency egold with money laundering.

Defense doesn't just coordinate around natural choke points, but also in the natural and unnatural flows of traffic across the Internet, which is even more important to identifying malicious behavior.

Some malicious behavior is fairly simple to detect. In a distributed denial-of-service (DDoS) attack, the owner of the botnet directs each computer to launch a massive amount of traffic at the target. This traffic rarely looks like the regular patterns associated with browsing, streaming videos, and consumer Internet uses. The ISP can identify botnet behavior without compromising its customers' privacy. Alternatively, a botnet may use a customer computer as a web server to host anything from phishing websites to advertisements for products advertised by spam. This can create more subtle but still detectable patterns. Once a user's machine has been identified, the ISP can take a range of actions, from blocking that particular stream of traffic to quarantining the entire machine from the Internet to prevent further malicious activity.

The incentives for ISPs to act in these instances are what must be cultivated. As Melissa Hathaway and John Savage note, "Precedents are emerging around the world for ISPs to shoulder more responsibility for the stewardship of the Internet." In the United States, this has taken the form of an industry-developed Anti-Bot Code of Conduct. Announced in 2012, this code emphasizes education, detection, notification, and remediation. It is voluntary and will evolve but has the support of major American ISPs.

In this coordination, however, tension between law enforcement and threat abatement can warp these incentives. A bank may not care about criminal gangs as long as they are not targeting their customers' accounts. In this case the old joke holds true, they don't need to be able to outrun the bear, just to outrun the other guy. So their focus is mostly on avoiding or mitigating attacks. Law enforcement, on the other hand, is interested in catching the bear. This introduces intermediate goals that differ: capturing evidence and producing public records of the crime. Coordination falls apart when these goals impose a greater cost on the real or potential victim, whether it's preserving forensic evidence or generating bad publicity for its customers and shareholders.

Interestingly, this tension between the private sector and public interest neatly flips for attacks against critical infrastructure. Essential industries make the case that national defense is a public good, and therefore they should not have to bear the costs of defending against cyberattacks of a political nature, any more than they should have to provide their own antiaircraft guns to defend against an enemy's bomber planes. Meanwhile, the government has to worry that the public is dependent on infrastructure like power and water plants, where the owners see little incentive in paying real money to secure facilities against a risk that can't be stated at the bottom of a monthly business report. Several major American power companies have told Congress that they judge the known loss of revenue needed to take plants offline for just a few hours to upgrade their cyber systems is greater than any unknown cyber risks, which they are not sure they face or would even be defeating.

These situations illustrate how problems are often bigger than any one actor can manage, or is incentivized to manage, on its own. Traditionally, we turn to governments or government-sponsored collaborations for this type of challenge. The government pushes collective action for what no one private actor can solve for itself.

The other path of coordination is via security standards, where the government plays a central role in helping the public and private sectors understand what they need to be doing to secure themselves. Specifically, it brings into the process expertise that lies outside the marketplace. Even if private firms and smaller organizations fully appreciate the need to secure themselves, there is not abundant, trusted information on how to do so. They must deal with various vendors that eagerly offer their own products as the silver bullet solutions. Instead, government can be a lynchpin in coordination by providing the basic standards.

This doesn't always have to be in the form of legal requirements, but can take shape through agenda setting. Building on its technical experience securing national defense networks, the NSA partnered with the private security training company SANS to develop critical security controls. They built a consortium of representatives from the defense and law enforcement communities, information security companies, and even representatives from the UK government's information assurance agencies. This public-private partnership developed a set of 20 critical controls, which were then vetted by the larger information security community. These collectively built controls, which lay out the need for such measures as inventories of authorized devices and software, and proper maintenance and analysis of audit logs, give any and every individual organization a set of clear security goals to follow. Government endorsement of these principles, from the statements by the NSA to the widespread implementation of these controls at other government agency, has lent further weight to the spread of such best practices and coordination.

The weakness of such a process is that it is designed to address known attacks and falls apart when the standards start to create costs among industries that see less incentive to spend more on protection. While defense agencies and financial firms saw clear incentives, for too many infrastructure companies the known costs to implement best-practice models like SANS outweighed the unknown costs of a cyber incident. Many make the parallel to the nuclear power industry, which required the major incident at Three Mile Island to overhaul training and safety. It took a proven cost to provoke a response, partly from the private utilities but mainly from regulators to take added steps to reduce risk. In the cyber realm, the flaws of the present system, in which too few critical infrastructure firms follow voluntary standards, is leading many to call for a transition to a world where all are required to follow shared standards or face fines or criminal charges. In short, the new system would treat cybersecurity like other areas of required compliance organizations have to follow in the real world, such as fire safety or building codes.

The question of the government's role in such coordination and requirements has become one of the sticking points in cybersecurity legislation in the United States. While there is widespread agreement that *something* needs to be done, many in the private sector resent government's attempts to create and enforce standards for critical infrastructure. They see regulations as adding to their costs and even argue that they will only make matters worse. The US Chamber of Commerce, for instance, has argued that a bureaucratic government will shift "businesses' resources away from implementing robust and effective security measures and toward meeting government mandates." Again, though, the same argument was made about lifeboats and other safety measures on early ocean liners like the *Titanic*, fire codes for buildings, protections at nuclear power plants, seatbelts and air bags in cars, and so on. By working together to find standards that meet evolving needs but still allow firms to flourish, the public and private sectors can find a good balance.

The key point is that cybersecurity requires coordination and action outside of the immediate victims or even owners of the networks under attack. Brian Krebs didn't have the power of the government behind him, but his actions mattered because he mobilized a network that could target key choke points by malicious actors in cyberspace.

But some problems of scale or target move the matter from the easily resolved situations where private parties have incentives to come together, like the ISPs in the McColo case or banks in financial fraud, to situations where the incentives might not be sufficient or the threat touches on public security concerns. The problem then becomes a political one that must address the role of government. The critical question is, where is government engagement both appropriate and most effective? In some instances, it may be enough to provide expertise or coordination. In other instances, the government has to intervene more directly to alter behavior. Cybersecurity may seem a story of technology, but understanding and shaping human incentives matters the most in any effective defense.

Exercise Is Good for You: How Can We Better Prepare for Cyber Incidents?

Twice in six months sophisticated attackers were able to gain access to the production code that runs Facebook's website, used by over a billion people around the world. The first time, a Facebook engineer's computer was compromised by an unpatched, zero-day exploit. This enabled the attacker to "push" their own malicious computer code into the "live build" that runs the website. The second time, in early 2013, several engineers' computers were compromised after visiting a website that launched a zero-day exploit on its victims. But this time, the attacker was unable to get inside sensitive systems, and could cause no major damage.

The reason these two attacks caused such differing effects lies in their origin. The attackers in the first incident were actually part of a security training exercise in 2012, led by an independent "red team." This preparation meant that when real attackers tried to harm Facebook in the second incident just a few months later, they weren't able to do much at all.

The challenge of defending against cyberthreats is not just due to their varied and diffuse nature, but also because so much depends on how organizations react and respond when cyber push comes to cyber shove. Prussian general Helmuth Graf von Moltke's famous military adage should serve as warning: "No plan survives first contact with the enemy." It is one thing to develop a plan; it's quite another to understand how well that plan will hold up when tested. In the cyber world this holds even truer. Responses must be considered at every level, from national security strategy to enterprise risk management, down to the technical level, where engineers must make fast decisions about network incursions. It is not just about protection; the wrong response could be worse than the attack itself.

This is where the value of exercises and simulations come in. They don't just test defenses at the pointy end of the cyber spear but also help all better understand the effects of their plans and procedures.

At the technical level, controlled environments offer a semiscientific environment to study both attacks and defenses. "Test beds" are extensible simulations of systems, networks, and operational environments that can be attacked over and over again. This repetition allows researchers to simulate failures, test the interoperability of equipment and standards, and understand how attacks and defenses interact. And, of course, you can carry out actions in a test bed that you would never want to in the real world. One test bed created by the National Institute of Standards and Technology allows researchers to repeatedly crash a simulated version of the electrical power grid to observe its failure modes and resiliency—this would obviously be problematic with the actual power grid!

Controlled environments can be used to study the offensive side of cyber as well. A particular tactic used by security researchers are "honeypots," or isolated machines that are intentionally exposed to attacks. By observing how different types of malware attack these machines, we can identify new types of attacks and devise defenses. Entire test "honeynets" simulate complete networks or even regions of the whole Internet. During these tests, there is a cat-and-mouse game that plays out between researchers and attackers: sophisticated attackers try to determine whether they are in a honeynet, in which case they change their behavior to avoid disclosing their offensive tactics and tricks.

Meanwhile, the military offensive capacity can be refined in "cyber ranges." One of the challenges in developing cyber weapons is understanding how an attack will spread. If they are to be used as a precision weapon, it is imperative both to avoid detection and to minimize the collateral damage beyond the intended target. This precision becomes even more important if the attack is to interfere with physical processes. In the case of Stuxnet, for example, many believe that practice was needed to understand how the software would deploy and how altering the industrial controllers would impact the targeted process of uranium enrichment. Reportedly, the new cyberweapon was tested at Israel's secretive nuclear facility in Dimona. As one source told the *New York Times* about the test effort, "To check out the worm, you have to know the machines.... The reason the worm has been effective is that the Israelis tried it out."

On the defensive side, vulnerability tests and practice exercises are quite valuable for the actors in cyberspace that range from militaries to private companies. This can be as simple as penetration testing, or having a "red team" of outside security experts look for vulnerabilities to exploit. These experts understand how to attack live networks in a controlled fashion, and lay the foundation for what might be a more damaging attack without putting the actual operation at risk. More sophisticated exercises can be completely simulated like a traditional war game. Again, the notion of a "war game" is a bit of a misnomer in that such exercises can help any cyber defenders, be they a military unit, a university, or a private firm, better understand what threats they face, and where they are vulnerable. More important, they then help these defenders better understand their own likely and needed responses.

As an illustration, one company that went through a war game studied by the McKinsey consulting firm found that their entire security team was completely dependent on e-mail and instant messaging and did not have a backup communication plan to coordinate defense under a full-scale network-based attack. These exercises also underscore the importance of coordination between technical decisions and business mission. In another war game, McKinsey found that disconnecting the network to secure it hurt their customers more than remediating the issue while still online.

Exercises also help key leaders grasp what matters before a real crisis. Senior management, which too often dismisses cybersecurity concerns as either too technical or too unlikely, can get a hands-on understanding of the importance of planning. This exposure can prevent future panic and open the manager up to committing more resources toward defense, resiliency, and response. Indeed, raising awareness and securing management buy-in for cybersecurity is a key outcome of many a simulation. As one Estonian defense official explained, leaders have many priorities and interests, and so a health minister "who will be yawning through cybersecurity talk" might pay attention if the attack in an exercise involves something relevant to his department, such as a pension database.

There is a natural trade-off between the scale of the exercise and the level of detail in what can be learned, however. This has often been an issue in simulations at the national defense level, where too often the events emphasize the performative aspect of the exercise. The Bipartisan Policy Center's "Cyber ShockWave" of 2010 was an attempt at a war game featuring former senior government officials playing the roles of simulated government officials as the nation was hit by a series of crippling cyberattacks. This exercise was criticized by some as focusing more on appearances than on the substance, especially when fake news coverage of the game was later broadcast on CNN under the title "We were warned." Given the cost of these larger, more complex simulations, the designers must have a clear vision of the goals of the exercise and design the game appropriately. For example, finding vulnerabilities is a different task from discovering better modes for coordination, just as testing strategy is different from raising public awareness.

Exercises can also create useful opportunities to strengthen personal networks of cooperation between different agencies and even different governments. For instance, the European Network and Information Security Agency's "Cyber Europe" war game is based on a fairly simple scenario but really has a goal of inducing key officials from different European countries to interact more on cyber issues. The whole idea is that you don't want these people to talk for the first time in the midst of an actual cyber crisis.

Such exercises can even be used as a means to actually help diffuse tensions between nations seemingly at odds. Think tanks in Washington and Beijing, for instance, have cooperated to run a series of small-scale cyber simulations involving the United States and China. While these were not official collaborations between governments, representatives from the State Department and the Pentagon participated, along with their Chinese counterparts. The goal was to build a shared understanding of how cyber weapons can be used and how each side approached the problem. The hope is that in the long run such exchanges will help build trust and reduce the likelihood of miscommunication during a real crisis or under poor assumptions.

Exercises and simulations are useful but have some obstacles that limit effectiveness. Like any model, they are simplifications and face a balance between verisimilitude and generalizability. If they are too focused and realistic, there are fewer lessons that can be learned and applied and it is easier to "fight the scenario." On the other hand, if they are too general, it is unclear what will be learned. This balancing act also applies to the scenarios and the "red team" that is implementing them. When groups are testing themselves, there is a risk that they will go too easy to show off how good they already are or staff their "attackers" with people from their own organization, who think and act in the very same ways. However, if the goal is to explore other areas, such as cooperation, making the tests too hard can also be a problem. Former DHS official Stewart Baker highlighted this tension in scenario building: "If it's so one-sided the attackers win all the time... then the exercise is not actually teaching people anything."

This gets back to the purpose of an exercise. While unexpected lessons are a lucky outcome, it is important to have a stated goal of the exercise to inform the scenario creation and simulation parameters along with a plan for debriefing and implementing lessons learned.

One of the noteworthy features of cybersecurity is that it spans traditional boundaries, whether they are national or organizational. Responses require the interactions of numerous individuals with different responsibilities, management structures, and incentives, not to mention different professional paradigms. Here is where exercises and simulations may bring the most value. IT professionals, managers, lawyers, and public relations experts may all instinctively approach a cyber incident differently. Thus, engaging in simulations and exercises allows a more direct confrontation between those personal and organizational viewpoints and roles.

The Facebook team learned this from their own self-testing experience. They saw how an effective response required cooperation between teams that ranged from the development team for the Facebook commercial product to the internal information security team responsible for the company network. The prior testing didn't just help them plug vulnerabilities, it yielded lessons in cooperation that proved critical when the war game came to life in an actual attack. As the director of incident response Ryan McGeehan said, "We're very well prepared now and I attribute that to the drill."

Build Cybersecurity Incentives: Why Should I Do What You Want?

"If the partnership doesn't make tangible and demonstrable progress, other initiatives are going to take their place."

This is what DHS cybersecurity chief Amit Yoran told a gathering of security and technology executives. It was meant to be an ultimatum, threatening the private sector to get its act together soon on enhancing cybersecurity through voluntary, public-private partnerships, or face the alternative of involuntary massive regulation. The problem is that Yoran made this statement in 2003. Over a decade later, the situation remains essentially the same, showing the emptiness of these kinds of threats.

Cyberspace may be a realm of public concern, but many, if not most, of the decisions to secure it are and will continue to be made by private actors. Our security depends on so many variables: individuals deciding whether or not to click a link; the companies these individuals work for deciding whether or not to invest in security and how; technology vendors and the creators whom they buy from both owning up to vulnerabilities and issuing patches for what they have already put out there (and customers downloading the patches when available); and so on.

Unfortunately, we've seen how again and again the incentives to make good decisions are often misaligned. The average user doesn't bear the full consequence of ignoring basic computer hygiene. Managers often don't see any return on money thrown at security solutions. Software developers are compensated for speed and new features, not making their code more secure. Why does this market fail?

As we've repeatedly seen, the basic question is one of incentives. In the language of economics, security is an externality. Externalities are costs or benefits from an action that fall to someone other than that actor. Pollution is a classic negative externality, where the firm benefits from production, but those benefits are countered by the public harm of toxic chemicals in the environment.

The predicament of insecurity in cyber today is that it has many of the same characteristics of such negative externalities. The owner gets the benefits of using a system but doesn't bear a huge cost for the vulnerabilities it introduces. Sometimes, the owner is not even aware that their own system is causing harm to others, such as when it is part of a botnet. The FBI repeatedly has found cases where companies have been infiltrated for months or years and only learned of their insecurity from a federal investigation. If a small utility company can lower the costs of maintenance by controlling remote transformers over the Internet, and no one will blame it if an attack disrupts service, it is likely do so. It may not be the most responsible thing from a public cybersecurity perspective, but it is the most rational action from its own private profit-seeking perspective.

The problem is that individual bad security decisions make many others worse off. When you fail to update your personal computer's defenses, its compromised security could add it to a botnet that is attacking the wider Internet. When a company fails to come clean about an attack, it allows attackers to go free, the vulnerabilities they targeted to be exploited elsewhere, and the security of partners and clients that connect to that company's system to be endangered. And at a wider level, it harms the economy by limiting investors' information about company risk and liability.

Understanding incentives is not always intuitive. Banks spend a great deal of time and money trying to combat phishing websites that try to steal their customers' banking and financial credentials. This is rational since those banks will have to absorb much of the costs of fraud. However, the same banks ignore other parts of the problem. The thieves using banking credentials will have to extract the money through a network of "money mules." The attackers transfer the money through a network of accounts owned by the mules, until they can safely extract it out of the financial system without being traced. So these mule networks are a key part of the phishing network. And making them even more ripe for takedown, these mules are often recruited via public websites. But the financial industry is not as concerned with removing the websites that recruit money mules. The reason is that unlike the phishing sites, the mule networks do not have the banks' individual brand names on them.

In other situations, when there are too many players involved at different steps, the market structure simply does not have a natural equilibrium to assign incentives to one party. This can happen even when all the players want security solutions. Android is a mobile phone operating system developed and distributed for free by Google. Google writes the specified architecture of the system and the high-level code. However, different Android phones are produced by different manufacturers that use different hardware. The operating system, which instructs programs on how to use the hardware, is customized by each phone manufacturer, often for each phone. The phones are then sold to mobile carriers that sell them to consumers. New versions of the Android OS are released frequently by Google, on an average of about once a year.

None of these groups wants their systems to be cracked, but when a vulnerability is discovered in an operating system, it's often unclear who has the responsibility to inform the consumer and issue a patch. As a result, fewer patches are actually made and there is no mechanism to get security updates out to older phones. In 2012, a technical study estimated that over half of Android devices have unpatched vulnerabilities.

Occasionally, incentives actually make things worse. TRUSTe is a company that offers certifications to companies that offer a privacy policy and commit to following it. The idea is that consumers can see the TRUSTe seal on the website and feel more comfortable using that site. This, in turn, gives websites an incentive to pay TRUSTe for the certification process. Unfortunately, since TRUSTe gets paid for every seal, they have incentives to attest to the trustworthiness of websites even when they are less than pure. One study compared "certified" sites with the rest of the Web and found that sites with the TRUSTe seal were actually *more* likely to be rated as "untrustworthy" by an automated security tool.

It is possible, however, to get the incentives structure right. In the United States, consumer protection laws limit the liability of credit card customers to $50 for unauthorized transactions. These laws were passed in the 1970s just as the credit card industry was taking off. Liability for charges from a stolen credit card was then decided between the customer's bank and the merchant's bank for a variety of circumstances, and the merchant's bank often passed the responsibility to the merchant. For in-person transactions where the main risk of fraud was a stolen card, this aligned incentives. The merchant was in the best position to verify that the user of the card was the legitimate owner of the card. This process imposed some cost on the merchant in terms of efficiency and customer relations. The merchant balanced the risk of fraud with the costs of fraud prevention and could make a rational decision.

The arrival of web commerce dramatically increased the amount of fraud, since scammers could use stolen credit card numbers remotely. It also increased the number of legitimate transactions where the merchants did not have access to the card. To rebalance the risk assignment, card issuers added an extra secret to the card, the code verification value. This value was only to be printed on the back of the card itself, and known to the card-issuing bank, so it could be a shared secret to verify that the user of the card had access to that card. Merchants who ask for the CVV are not liable for fraudulent transactions, although there are severe penalties if they store these values.

Now the credit card-issuing bank needed to detect mass use of stolen credit card numbers without the CVV. This job fell to the credit card networks (such as Visa and American Express), which are in the best position since they manage the exchange of payment data. The final step was to safeguard the CVV data to minimize its theft and abuse. The credit card companies worked together developed the Payment Card Industry Data Security Standards, which enforce a set of security rules to minimize collection and leakage of data that can lead to fraud. The result wasn't a magic solution to all credit card fraud, but it did create a marketplace where a smart law properly aligned incentives to drive sensible security investments.

By contrast, in looking at the cyber realm more broadly today, one can see how the incentives are broken for the user, the enterprise, and the system developer, each presenting their own challenges and opportunities. The individual users may be much maligned for not caring about security, but they really are just trying to use the Internet to do their jobs, or at least watching videos of cute cats playing a keyboard when they are supposed to be doing their jobs. Users are also human, so they will usually follow the path of least resistance and seldom deviate from system defaults. Make it easy for them and they will follow. This has been proven in areas that range from retirement planning to organ donation (countries that have default organ donation have a participation rate almost five times higher than those with an opt-in model).

Businesses equally act rationally. To justify an investment in security, a profit-minded organization (or even nonprofits, which are resource-constrained) must see some justification. Every dollar or man-hour spent on security is not spent on the organization's actual goal. There are a number of models for calculating some return on investment, but all depend on having some value for the harms of a security incident and the reduced likelihood or smaller impact of an incident that a specific security tool might have. As we discussed above, for severe incidents such as the theft of competitive data, both the harms and the defense are poorly understood.

The drive for incentivizing these kind of investments will have to come from three likely sources. The first is internal. This is a maxim in business that "If you can't measure it, you can't manage it." The Department of Homeland Security has found that organizations that are able to aggregate and analyze cyber data end up changing how they understand their incentives. They begin to see "how investments in cyber health can reduce operating costs, improve business agility, or avoid extensive mitigation costs." The more leaders in organizations understand cybersecurity and its near and long-term benefits, the more likely they are to invest in it.

The second source is external. Companies and other organizations exist in a marketplace of competitors and consumers. If industry norms highlight cybersecurity investments as requisite, companies will fall into line, so as not to fall behind their competitors. In turn, DHS has found that the more customers understand about cybersecurity, "Such insights would likely strengthen consumer demand for healthy products and services and reduce risks to participants." Security can be a virtuous cycle, with awareness driving a market response that, in turn, drives more awareness.

Finally, there may be situations where the incentives have to come from a source beyond the market. As we explored earlier, government regulation is a stopgap that can often set standards and amend situations where the market just isn't able or willing to respond on its own. It isn't by any means a silver bullet solution, but examples like the aforementioned Top 20 Critical Security Controls (put together by a joint team of US government and private security experts, so both the private and public were represented) can establish a set of baseline best practices. Just like safe building or fire codes, the Top 20 Controls lay out minimal requirements that any government agency or entity operating in an important business area should follow. They range from conducting an inventory of all authorized and unauthorized devices to controlling the use of administrative privileges that act as keys to the kingdom for hackers. Rather than onerous regulations, these imposed incentives should be easy to adapt and easy to verify as they are often just measures that smart companies are already taking. That they are easy, though, doesn't mean that even the most minimal norms won't have a major impact. The Top 20 controls, for example, were found to stop 94 percent of security risks in one study.

With the three forces of organizations, markets, and nukes in play, then we can get creative to shape change further. For instance, incentives can be introduced to add security by creating new markets. Selling knowledge of "zero-day" vulnerabilities was once the domain of researchers, who tried to find holes and tell companies about them, before criminals could exploit them. As cybersecurity has taken off, these "vulnerabilities markets" have become a big business.

Such new markets must be carefully monitored though. With a looming cyber-industrial complex, the buyer side is also evolving to include many new actors other than the software manufacturers looking to figure out how to protect themselves and their customers. As one report from Watchguard found,

Vulnerability markets or auctions are a new trend in information security, allowing so-called "security" companies to sell zero day software vulnerabilities to the highest bidder. While they claim to "vet" their customers and only sell to NATO governments and legitimate companies, there are few safeguards in place to prevent nefarious entities to take advantage.

That is, the booming cybersecurity field may be realigning incentives for how vulnerabilities are bought and sold in a direction that is harmful to wider cybersecurity. Some security services firms want the advantage of being able to protect their customers against undisclosed vulnerabilities that they alone know about, while others are more like cyber arms brokers, buying up and then selling these zero days for use in offensive cyber weapons designs. Here again, just like in any other marketplace that starts to move from white- to black-market activity, be it drugs or cyber vulnerabilities, the government has to stay aware and be prepared to police it when any actions become socially destructive.

The market can be a powerful force for cybersecurity when it functions properly. An economic perspective also acknowledges that some attacks are not worth defending against if the price of defense is greater than the direct and indirect cost of the attack. This links us to the next important issue in crafting better responses on cybersecurity: information sharing and accountability mechanisms. They are what support such key cost-versus-benefit calculations and ultimately are what steer the incentives toward security.

Learn to Share: How Can We Better Collaborate on Information?

"It's always more fun"

"To share with everyone!"

In preschools and kindergartens across the United States, young children sing "The Sharing Song" to learn the importance of giving up something that you have in order to help someone else. Unfortunately, the lessons of cooperation and sharing aren't taken to heart by many key players in the world of cybersecurity.

One of the best illustrations of the sharing problem comes from the world of banking. Banks often hire firms to detect and remove phishing websites for their brand. The faster the spoofed financial websites are removed, the fewer the number of users who can be duped into surrendering their credentials and ultimately enabling fraud. However, one study compared the lists of websites detected for two different takedown companies and found something interesting: each had discovered websites for the other's clients but had no incentive to remove them. Had the firms shared, they could have saved their collective clientele an estimated $330 million.

Competition can create a market for cybersecurity, but security decisions depend on good information. Sharing this information greatly expands all parties' knowledge, situational awareness, and preparedness for cybersecurity. As the White House's 2009 Cyberspace Policy Review explained, "Information is key to preventing, detecting, and responding to cyber incidents. Network hardware and software providers, network operators, data owners, security service providers, and in some cases, law enforcement or intelligence organizations may each have information that can contribute to the detection and understanding of sophisticated intrusions or attacks. A full understanding and effective response may only be possible by bringing information from those various sources together for the benefit of all."

The key benefit of information sharing is that it allows a more complete view of emerging threats and patterns, arming actors with the lessons learned from others' experiences. Attacks and their consequences are often not immediately obvious and require information from multiple sources to build an understanding of the new dangers and mitigations. Beyond empowering decision-makers with more data, successful information-sharing regimes benefit individual actors by supporting the diffusion of experience and best practices of each organization.

Information sharing comes in various different forms. Some cybersecurity information can be very technical, such as passing on to others the digital signature of a newly identified piece of malware. Alternatively, it can be more context-specific, such as a new approach to spear phishing that is targeting a certain type of executive in a specific industry. It can be preemptive, such as the specifications for how to fix a newly discovered vulnerability. Or it can be responsive, such as sharing the details on a successful security breach. Information can be time sensitive and needed for rapid decisions, or only useful when aggregated over time, such as a small part of a data set that will someday produce a breakthrough after combination and analysis.

The approach to sharing must be related to the data. Sharing requires us to ask "With whom?" and "How?" Sharing can be decentralized, with organizations working together, or it can be centralized, with the government collecting data from across the public and private sector, then redistributing actionable intelligence. Some technical data, such as that gathered automatically by computers, should be shared automatically with a wide audience to bolster defenses. Other types of data are very sensitive and require careful analysis before they can be used effectively. For example, data about a successful attack that is shared too widely or with too much specificity could unintentionally reveal sensitive information about the victim. Alternatively, information about how an attempted attack was defeated could help an adversary adapt its tactics to win the next time around.

This connects the notion of sharing to that other value we learn as little kids, trust. The best defenses utilize a sharing regime based on trust and the human capacity to understand and act on the data. Antivirus companies, for example, have traditionally shared samples of newly detected malware but only inside a trusted group.

Unfortunately, this diversity of information types and sharing requirements has led to a fragmented approach so far in cybersecurity. There are a host of information-sharing organizations and models, each built around specific needs and demands. The need for a wide range of information-sharing solutions is particularly pronounced in the United States, whose large economy has little in the way of policy coordination for any issue, particularly those spanning industrial sectors. The largest established model of information sharing is the Information Sharing and Analysis Centers (ISACs). Created in 1998 by presidential directive, the ISACs are organized around specific sectors of the economy, such as financial services or healthcare, with each sector determining its organizational form and function.

While the initial directive was somewhat unique at the time in explicitly recognizing cyberthreats, the ISACs have had a mixed record of generating real impact. Most offer a digital library of relevant resources and help coordinate interested participants through mailing lists and events. Some have 24/7 operations centers or crisis management protocols. The Information Technology center (IT-ISAC) offers "secure Web portal, listservs, conference calls with member companies, and dedicated analysts that provide analytical support." The IT-ISAC finds itself in an interesting position, since a great deal of the nation's cybersecurity information comes from its members. Executive Director Scott Algeier describes how market conditions have shaped its mission. "Private companies tend to disclose vulnerabilities to their customer base first before sharing information with outside entities.... So the new model is looking at ways we can facilitate information sharing by our members about what attacks they're seeing." Jason Healey, director of the Cyber Statecraft Initiative, stresses the importance of this kind of sharing across the public-private boundary. One good approach is for industry and government groups to have their own meetings first: "Then they gather together immediately and compare notes and learning." There's also a social component. "Then they all go out and have dinner. It builds trust and relationships."

Another model is built around buying power. As it saw cyberthreats building, the Department of Defense helped stimulate the creation of an information-sharing program inside its vast network of contractors and vendors. The network works in both directions of information sharing. The Pentagon would provide its Defense Industrial Base of corporate suppliers with both classified and unclassified threat information as well as security advice. "DIB participants, in turn, report cyber incidents for analysis, coordinate on mitigation strategies, and participate in cyber intrusion damage assessments if information about DoD is compromised." The information itself is mostly kept anonymous, so that the companies can share it, without worrying that they are aiding their competitors.

There are also smaller organizations that support information sharing on a local scale. The FBI has organized Infragard, where each of its field offices reach out to local businesses and researchers to talk about cybersecurity issues. Some regional chapters are very active, with regular seminars and mailing lists; others are less so. There are also various regional organizations, such as the Boston area's Advanced Cyber Security Center, that serve as forums to bring together local tech companies and researchers. Member-funded but with an eye to federal grants, ACSC has bimonthly meetings with presentations from experts and developed a unique full-scale participation agreement to share sensitive cyber information while maintaining confidentiality.

The private sector has had its own successes in collaboration. Consortia of vendors and researchers have grown around specific topics, such as the Anti-Phishing Working Group. Standards organizations can serve as venues to standardize key aspects of security information. The Institute of Electrical and Electronics Engineer's Malware Working Group is focused on packed, or obfuscated, malware and standardizing how this malware is studied and defeated.

Notably, it is the attention and career benefits of presenting a new security finding at a major security conference that seems to encourage much of the public sharing in these venues. This applies not just to individual researchers but to security companies themselves, who too often think holding information back gives them an edge against competitors. In 2013, the security company Mandiant took a very public role in publicizing its findings about Chinese infiltration into American corporate networks, with the *New York Times* nearly quoting its reports word for word. This information sharing had an enormous impact on global cybersecurity policy, but Mandiant also got something out of the bargain. Security blogger Adam Shostack has explained how such firms that go public are "really not giving the data away. They're trading it for respect and credibility." Sharing of information doesn't just build their brand as a company but can also help educate the market about risks, fostering broader investment. Working with more customers can, in turn, generate more data for the firm to analyze.

Given all these different mechanisms for information sharing, is there enough? Many believe that there is not. The high-tech trade association TechAmerica has argued that "the inability to share information is one of the greatest challenges to collective efforts toward improving our cybersecurity." Security consultant Erik Bataller insists that "the public and private sectors need to share more information—more parties must be included and new platforms used," ideally to the point where we can have "real-time identification and response as threats occur." This vision, shared by many, is that instead of the current series of loose coalitions built around types of information or industry sectors, with varied levels of energy and activity, there would emerge a more universal kind of sensor network that could work across cyberspace to detect and respond to threats.

It's a powerful concept, but there are some large obstacles. The main challenge is sharing between the private sector and the government. Without further legal protection, firms worry that information they share may be used as evidence by the government or in litigation that might come back to bite them. It might not even be on cybersecurity matters. One study, for instance, found that an energy company was unwilling to share information about its cybersecurity threat experiences because it worried that the data might somehow be used to damage the company in matters that had nothing to do with cybersecurity. That is, it cared less about the risks of power loss to the mass populace than pesky lawyers from environmental rights groups also getting hold of any of its data.

Such fears severely reduce any incentive to share with the government. Industry groups have asked Congress to provide legal protection before they participate in widespread programs. Paul Rosenzweig explains that this public/private mistrust is mutual: "Government institutions like the NSA...with (perhaps) superior knowledge of threat signatures and new developments in the arsenal of cyber attackers are deeply reluctant to share their hard won knowledge with the private sector at the risk of compromising their own sources and methods."

It is important to stress that sharing is not a panacea. While many cybersecurity breaches would be prevented or preempted, a number still would occur even in a world where companies and governments play perfectly nice. The key is to recognize that while sharing won't stop most "zero days," it will prove critical in most "day afters." The success of information sharing, though, is highly dependent on the context and parties involved. Even among the IT professionals responsible for securing organizations, most people will not be able to use most of the information that might be shared with them.

This is where policy becomes key. Organizational support to validate, then distribute, then enable data's use should be the primary goal of any information-sharing policy. Once it is understood how that goal can be achieved, limiting obstacles like liability protection or incentives can be tackled. Focusing on the process and then the barriers can help find innovative approaches to cooperation, finding ways to pass on important information even under unusual circumstances.

Here again, we see how recognizing the incentives and then reshaping them is so important. In the bank phishing takedown case, the competing firms could better serve their clients if they shared information, but holding back good security data was also to their competitive advantage. There was an alternative, a mechanism of sharing that preserved their interests. The phishing takedown firms could still compete by trying to detect websites, but a fee-based privacy-preserving protocol would have allowed them to pass on information without revealing any competitive information outside the exchange.

If we look hard enough and build the right structures, there's always a way to share. As the kids' song continues,

> If you've just got one
> Here is something you can learn
> You can still share
> Just by taking turns.

Demand Disclosure: What Is the Role of Transparency?

When politics becomes personal, it's easier to pass laws. In 2001, newly elected California state assemblyman Joe Simitian wanted a privacy bill that would make a splash, but could still get through the legislature. At the suggestion of privacy expert Diedre Mulligan, the proposed bill included a clause that companies who lose their customer's data be required to report this to the data subjects. Simitian knew this would be unpopular among big business, but included it in the bill as a negotiating tactic. The clause was intended to be something he could then give up in the messy legislative battle every bill goes through. Despite this attempt, Simitian's proposed bill stalled.

A year later, the state database of over 200,000 California employees was compromised by hackers, including Social Security numbers and banking information. Among those were eighty members of the California assembly and forty members of the Senate. Now the notions that had been in Simitian's bill were no longer theoretical. The planned throwaway clause became the centerpiece of a new data breach notification law that the victimized legislature passed, requiring organizations that fail to secure personal information to notify the data subjects.

This policy has had an enormous impact. In 2004, there were three publicized data breaches for companies traded on American stock markets. In 2005, when the California law into effect, there were fifty-one. As of 2013, forty-six American states have related laws.

These kind of transparency laws can be thought of as mandatory information sharing. After all, if we can obtain some positive results from voluntary information sharing, why not demand even more? An alternate framing might be to view transparency as a laissez-faire accountability model that focuses on adverse outcomes.

Organizations make security decisions on their own, but then must own up if their decisions result in a security failure.

Threat and attack disclosure forces all organizations to understand their risks. Data breach notification laws like California's serve as an excellent case study. These laws are agnostic to technology: they apply equally to a hacker cracking a sophisticated database and an employee losing an old-school magnetic backup tape. Their value is in creating an atmosphere of transparency. They haven't stamped out data breaches, but have helped mitigate their impact. Disclosure creates accountability inside an organization by not just raising awareness but also by defining costs for managers to avoid in the form of notification expenses and adverse publicity. This, in turn, guides the risk decisions that management of businesses and agencies needs to make. And, finally, the transparency law turned out not to be antibusiness, but instead spurred an entire new industry that has grown up to help organizations prevent data breaches and respond appropriately if they occur.

Today greater efforts at mandatory disclosure in the cyber realm are needed. While broader policies have been proposed at the national level in the United States and various European capitals, there is still a long way to go. The proposed EU cybersecurity directive, for example, calls for critical infrastructure sectors to report security incidents that relate to their core services to a coordinating organization.

Such goals are modest, but they have met with resistance. Part of this stems from the feared industry backlash that stalled the original effort back in California almost a decade back. A 2011 industry study found that more than half of one thousand companies surveyed chose not to investigate a breach of security. Technology entrepreneur Christopher Schroeder explained this reluctance to disclose security incidents or vulnerabilities: "Many executives fear the cost of exposing a vulnerability to competition or consumers and believe the risks associated with sharing information are greater than the risks associated with a network security attack."

This short-term view goes against the interests of not only the wider public but also private shareholders in a company. In 2011, Senator Jay Rockefeller wrote to the Securities and Exchange Commission noting the prevalence of security incidents and the relative silence on these incidents in companies' public filings, which are supposed to detail "material" risks and incidents. So the SEC issued guidelines later that year to help clarify that cybersecurity risks should also be disclosed. This was the bare minimum, not a new regulation, but rather just a clarification that cybersecurity risk is no different from any other business practice. According to the SEC, "As with other operational and financial risks, registrants should review, on an ongoing basis, the adequacy of their disclosure relating to cybersecurity risks and cyber incidents."

The impact of these guidelines is still playing out, but we can glean some details. Before this change, the SEC did not see cybersecurity as terribly important, claiming, "We are not aware that investors have asked for more disclosure in this area." Ignorance is bliss was the essence of their argument. But making it an explicit part of SEC filings, former White House cybersecurity coordinator Melissa Hathaway counters, will "force executives to really understand what's going on within their corporations. I think it will create the demand curve for cybersecurity." Transparency will help shareholders take note and hold companies accountable for failing to properly understand and deal with their risks.

This is especially needed, as a 2012 study of corporate board members and senior managers illustrates. Despite the growing importance of the issue and the scale of risks, it found little evidence of widespread awareness or concern among these leaders about cybersecurity. Almost all boards studied had actively addressed traditional risk management issues (fires, natural disaster plans, etc.), but only a third indicated that information security had the attention of the board. The majority of boards did not receive regular reports on cybersecurity risks or breaches, potentially troubling in light of the recently enacted SEC guidelines. Indeed, despite the recent attention paid to critical infrastructure, respondents from the energy and utility sector tended to perform even worse than their peers in many, if not most, of the indicators for good cyber risk management. Perhaps the lesson from the California legislature remains true: change will happen when the decision-makers have something at stake.

Unfortunately, the social benefits of transparency can play poorly with accountability mechanisms. If the harm of a security incident is driven by the firm's disclosure, either through reputational harms or a decline in its stock price, then it has a strong incentive not to report. This deprives the larger community of valuable information that could help set policy and guide others' decisions. (As we talked about earlier, policymakers simply don't have good data on the theft of trade secrets from companies.) At the same time, if firms suffered no direct or indirect harm from disclosure, it would minimize any accountability. Disclosure of security incidents is exactly what is needed and not just for accountability. As Tyler Moore explains,

> If the remote login to a power station's controls is compromised and the utility keeps mum about what happened, then other power companies won't fully appreciate the likelihood of an attack. When banks don't disclose that several business customers have quickly lost millions of dollars due to the compromise of the company's online-banking credentials, the business customers that have not yet fallen victim remain ignorant to the need to take precautions.

In short, it may always be more fun to share, but sometimes various parties have to be convinced to play nice. Transparency provides a way to disclose when things go wrong, which in turn incentivizes the various players to get it right in the first place. This, in turn, sets the stage for how the government can foster accountability more directly.

Get "Vigorous" about Responsibility: How Can We Create Accountability for Security?

"It's not being enforced very vigorously." The former US government senior advisor on health information policy and noted IT expert Bill Braithwaite either had an unusual definition of "vigorous" or he was speaking with Monty Python-worthy understatement.

The Health Information Portability and Accountability Act, or The HIPAA, that he was summarizing was intended to create accountability on how medical information was to be protected, with the government empowered to levy fines for violations of the law. Yet, of the 19,420 complaints made to the government during 2003–2006 about poor protection of medical data, there was not a single case of a punishing fine. The head of the enforcement division, Winston Wilkinson, defended this record of not so vigorous nonenforcement, arguing, "So far it's worked out pretty well." Critics countered that it was exactly this record of lax enforcement that had led to poor compliance. A consultant summarized the response: "HHS really isn't doing anything, so why should I worry?"

The question is one of accountability. Every organization has priorities that are viewed as more important than securing their networks. Hospitals, for example, focus on saving lives; every dollar or man-hour spent on cybersecurity could be seen as taking away from this core mission. The challenge for public policy is to create mechanisms that reframe how this is understood.

This is not easy. Take the example of the so-called "low-hanging fruits." We know that a large portion of publicly reported incidents is caused by exploitation of widely known vulnerabilities, such as default passwords, unpatched systems, or databases that lack basic security protections. Fixing one easy security problem may be simple, but this simplicity doesn't scale when the number grow. Finding and fixing all these "low-hanging fruits"—when one alone may be sufficient to cause substantial damage—is a complex and expensive organizational challenge. What mechanisms will hold managers and organizations accountable for addressing all of them?

Traditionally, prescriptive regulation shifts priorities: the government establishes standards and practices and organizations comply. This model dictates industrial behavior in everything from finance to food safety, yet may not fit well with security. As Dmitri Alperovitch notes, "The problem you have is that safety and security are not the same thing." To think of it another way, certain chemicals are not safe for you, but they don't stay up all night trying to find new ways to give you cancer.

The adversarial nature of security implies constant evolution and adaptation. Regulations that dictate specific solutions can be a poor fit for cyberspace. Moreover, the private sector seems to take a default stand against almost all regulation. "Any document that even hints at government-backed standards can make companies nervous. Many see it as the tip of the spear for future regulation." This spirit led the US Chamber of Commerce to lead the successful charge against cybersecurity regulation in 2012.

Some cybersecurity standards and regulations already exist, particularly in regulated industries, but they often fail to deliver the needed security gains. In the power grid, for example, standards developed jointly between industry and regulators in 2008 proved to be inadequate just three years later. Michael Assente, an energy security expert who runs an organization for security auditors, explained, "The standards have not been implemented with a strong sense of risk in mind. The complexity of enacting a new regulatory regime has taken our collective eye off security and turned it toward administrative issues and compliance." This focus on compliance can turn security from an iterative, adaptive process to an organizational routine disconnected from the risks faced. Compliance replaces accountability, since organizations can avoid any decision that might improve security.

Some regulations are contractually imposed between private actors. The Payment Card Industry Data Security Standard (PCI-DSS) dictates how any company handling credit or debit card data must secure its systems. Anyone working with credit card data who is found out of compliance can be fined by the credit card associations. If noncompliance led to a breach, fines can be up to half a million dollars.

This private model of accountability can work well, particularly when a security incident imposes direct costs. Banks must cover the costs of any illegally transferred funds that cannot be recovered. Credit card companies must reissue new cards. After an attacker compromised the integrity of RSA's SecurID token, RSA had to replace the small authentication devices for its 40 million users. Security incidents can even be terminal. When Dutch certificate authority DigiNotar suffered a breach that allowed the intruder to impersonate Google, the subsequent loss of market trust led to DigiNotar's bankruptcy. Companies take notice of these costs and act to avoid them.

But what about when the losses don't directly accrue to the party responsible? In other realms of business, common-law countries such as the United States and the UK use liability to realign incentives and impose some accountability. We have not yet seen liability play an enormous role in cybersecurity because (fortunately) there have been relatively few security incidents with substantial third-party damages. If a security incident leads to the physical, tangible harms, can the victims sue? Many think so. In turn, there are growing calls from industry to preemptively limit the liability of the attacked party.

This notion of liability leads to the role that insurance can and should play in the cyber realm. The business of insurance first started as field-protecting investments in seventeenth-century shipping and then expanded to realms that range from home ownership to sports star's knees. For all but the largest firms, paying an annual premium is usually better than the risk of incurring a larger blow. Cyber insurance is a field that is growing in fits and starts, largely waiting for the policy and business sides we've been discussing to catch up. A conservative estimate of premiums in 2012 was $1 billion. Even that overstates its application to cybersecurity. "Privacy coverage is pretty clearly driving the market," commented one analyst, as firms cover the risks of a data breach. As more firms suffer breaches covered by the laws in the preceding section, the consultants and service providers have grown adept at handling the response and can offer a predictable price. This, in turn, allows the firm to know how much coverage it needs.

Insurance by itself simply transfers risk from the covered firm to the underwriter and then reshapes the incentives behind the standard approach to security. Former national counterintelligence executive Joel Brenner explains, "Insurers play an important role in raising standards because they tie premiums to good practices. Good automobile drivers, for example, pay less for car insurance." The insurers have a natural incentive to minimize the likelihood and cost of a security incident and will push the firm to invest in defenses. The underwriters can compete by identifying the most efficient protections to impose on their portfolio, lowering the costs of compliance while they also lower premiums. Over time, insurance companies will accrue lots of data on defenses and breaches, developing and propagating best practices. This is the theory, at least. So far though, we have a long way to go for the insurance market to align incentives for better security.

Finally, this links to an important point: the individual user cannot be left off the hook. We've repeatedly seen how human fallibility represents the largest single vulnerability in cyberspace. The problem is that it can be hard for an individual to understand the connection between a single wrong click today and the consequences of a subsequent attack that only came to light much later. Larry Clinton, the head of a cross-sector industry group in favor of market solutions for cybersecurity, observed, "Many consumers have a false sense of security due to their belief that most of the financial impact resulting from the loss of their personal data will be fully covered by corporate entities (such as the banks)." In reality, the cost of poor decisions is borne by all of us. As the 2009 Cyberspace Policy Review put it, "People cannot value security without first understanding how much is at risk. Therefore, the Federal government should initiate a national public awareness and education campaign." In 2010, the "STOP. THINK. CONNECT." campaign was launched by the Department of Homeland Security, but too few in the wider public noticed.

In sum, given the strong evidence for a market failure, a buildup of accountability mechanisms is needed to drive good security decisions, from the individual Internet user all the way up to the CEO of a utility company. If we don't want only a prescriptive regime of rules and standards, imposed from above, to define the architecture of information systems, then we must also incentivize an approach to risk management from below that emphasizes the importance of security. Sometimes the sunshine of transparency can be enough to drive more responsible security behavior. In other contexts, the threat of actual punishment may be needed.

This takes the story full circle. After their embarrassing disclosure of nonenforcement, the healthcare regulators mentioned at the beginning of this section began to put some teeth behind the data security standards. In 2012, for instance, a Harvard Medical School teaching hospital was fined $1.5 million after regulators found "a long-term, organizational disregard for the requirements of the security rule." That is the actual meaning of "rigorous enforcement," which hospitals took notice of and began to change their practices.

Find the IT Crowd: How Do We Solve the Cyber People Problem?

Richard "Dickie" George served at the National Security Agency for over three decades in roles that ranged from cryptology mathematics (code making and breaking) to Director for Information Assurance, where he was responsible for the security of its most secretive communications. One of his biggest concerns in cybersecurity, however, is not merely the advancing threats in cyberspace but how we are going to find the people to respond to them. For this reason, he has often served as a "talent scout" for the NSA, seeking out top young recruits everywhere from universities to the BlackHat hacker convention. The problem he explains, though, is that when it comes to top talent, "It's a small pool and there are a lot of people hiring from it.... We're all looking at the same resumes."

The scope of the problem that George talks about is best illustrated by numbers. While the highly classified NSA doesn't release its staffing details, the Department of Homeland Security does. In 2008, it had just forty people working on cybersecurity issues full-time. By the end of 2012, the force had grown to more than four hundred. Another 1,500 cyber contractors were also working for the agency. But even as the force has grown nearly fifty times over, it still was viewed as not enough; the agency plans to add another six hundred more in just the next year.

Take what is happening at DHS and multiply it across all the other government agencies, private corporations, nongovernmental organizations, and so on who have understandably become concerned about cybersecurity, and you quickly see an emerging policy problem. This cybersecurity issue is not a question of what or how, but who. As one industry consultant explained, "The cyberwarfare market has grown so fast that it outstripped available labor pools."

So how big is the gap? No one is exactly sure, but in a report entitled *A Human Capital Crisis in Cybersecurity*, the Center for Strategic and International Studies argued that the US government had only 3 to 10 percent of the cybersecurity professionals it actually needs. Interestingly, Jim Gloser, a fellow at Sandia National Lab and former director of the CIA Clandestine Information Technology Office, made a similar estimate arguing that the government still had a need for tens of thousands more cyber experts. If the federal government, even with its massive amounts of cyber spending, has such a gap, the same can be expected of various other global, national, state, and local government agencies, as well as corporations, organizations, and other institutions that also now see needs in this field. By one estimate, as many as one million or more new cybersecurity workers will be needed by 2017 and beyond.

The cyber people problem, however, is not just one of raw numbers. As Ralph Langner, our cybersecurity expert who unearthed Stuxnet, explains, "Right now the cyber arms race is about talent." Indeed, one survey of chief information security officers and IT hiring managers at government agencies found that only 40 percent were satisfied with the quality of applicants for cybersecurity jobs.

It's not just that cybersecurity needs are growing but that demand for the skill set is growing beyond the people who work directly on cybersecurity day to day. "Even the managers now need hands-on skills in order to manage the newly emerging technical people," explains Alan Palmer, research director for the SANS Institute, a leading Internet security training firm.

The classic answer to a labor crunch is to throw money at the problem, and the same has happened in cybersecurity. For those with the skills, it has been a very good time to be in the field. Salaries for IT security specialists have skyrocketed in recent years; a 2011 study found roughly half make $100,000 or more. This good news for the labor force, however, is bad news for the organizations paying them, which repeatedly find themselves bidding against each other for skills in short supply.

A particular problem for the government is that it often pays for the creation of talent that it then loses to the private sector. A typical US government salary for a starting specialist in cybersecurity was around $60,000 in 2013. But with five years of experience and training on the government side, that same person could leave to join a private contractor for double the salary, perhaps even triple or more if the person is a real pro with security clearances. The movement of the more experienced talent to the private sector also means that many of the "cool jobs" inside government agencies (like the "incident response" teams, which are like SWAT teams for cyber emergencies) go to outside contractors, further driving internal talent to exit.

There's also a cultural issue. Even with interesting problems, many talented young people will be turned off by the inflexibility and environment of the federal government or traditional corporate bureaucracy. Beyond a preference for cargo shorts and a T-shirt over khakis and a tie, the culture of a high-tech firm will always be more dynamic. Culture extends into politics. Much of cybersecurity work is classified, and there is a lack of trust between the intelligence and defense establishment and the hacker community (NSA leaker Edward Snowden has much higher approval numbers in your average computer science lab than in most government agencies).

There's no one silver bullet solution to these problems, so the approach has to come from multiple directions.

One step is to build better means for the private sector and the public sector to collaborate at the human level, as well as cover the seams between the two. After suffering from cyberattacks in the mid-2000s, in 2010, Estonia pioneered a new model of defense known as "Küberkaitseliit," the Cyber Defense League. In essence, it was a cyber militia, allowing private citizens to volunteer to aid public efforts. The group includes everything from IT specialists to lawyers, and they have been used in roles that range from providing backup in cyber emergencies to helping as a "red team" in important national efforts, such as electronic voting.

Notably, though, the group is not like a national guard, in that there are no physical standards, nor are the participants putting themselves under military law, liable to be deployed to Iraq or whatnot, or asking for military pay and benefits. Instead, joining the league is voluntary, and then applicants are vetted for expertise and trustworthiness, which builds cachet. Members of the league both enjoy the work and think it beneficial beyond the cool factor, building knowledge and connections useful to their day jobs.

Nor is the group like a patriotic hacker community, in that it is formalized and transparent to the world, as there is no desire to keep it secret. In fact, it's just the opposite; the nation is trying to show that its defense extends beyond its official resources. In many ways this is the opposite of the model of cyberwar that we saw in the Part II focus on the US and Chinese strategies. Rather than arms racing toward MAD, it's more akin to how nations like Switzerland or Sweden planned to weather the Cold War with a strategy of "total defense" that applied the wider range of a nation's people and resources to its defenses.

The next step is to better enable governments to compete with the private sector. Recent proposals at DHS, for instance, have sought to give the traditionally bureaucratic government more flexibility in its hiring, such as allowing the leadership to change pay scales rapidly or provide additional benefits or incentives for cyber talent, including paying for additional education for free. To help the revolving door swing back, there is also the concept of an Information Technology Exchange Program. This would allow industry and government to swap cyber professionals for short stints, akin to a student exchange or fellowship program.

The bigger payoff, though, may not come just from more effective competition over the existing pool of professionals. Instead, we should widen the pool and build a bigger pipeline to tap it. For the United States, many of the difficulties in sourcing effective cyber talent come from systemic problems in science and mathematics education. American high school students rank 23rd in science and 31st in math among wealthy nations, and 27th in college graduates with degrees in science and math. Indeed, the trends are getting worse even at the university level. In 2004, the number of American computer science majors was 60,000. In 2013, it had shrunk to 38,000. Notably, the number of computer science majors was only half the number of journalism majors, despite the field being far more vibrant for job prospects.

A worthy approach is to link broader efforts to reverse these tends to specific needs and opportunities in cybersecurity. One concept is to play NICE, short for the National Initiative for Cybersecurity Education. Designed to take a national-level approach to increasing the cyber talent pool, among some of the ideas are a fellowship program that targets "Emerging Leaders in Cybersecurity," to help steer them into cybersecurity degree programs, and the DHS's Secretary's Honors Program for Cybersecurity Professionals, which recruits college students into ten-week internships at one of its cybersecurity programs and then offers them a full-time job after graduation. A similar program in Israel provides such opportunities as early as the tenth-grade level, seeking to find and excite kids before they even get to college.

Many major companies are discovering that they also have to set up similar programs to keep pace with their growing needs. Northrop Grumman, for instance, set up an internal Cyber Academy that will train well over one thousand employees a year. Its competitor Lockheed has a similar-sized Cyber University. These numbers sound enormous until one recalls the fact that it's not just the cyber warriors or IT professionals who increasingly need these skills. At Lockheed, only about 25 percent of the people who get the cybersecurity training actually work directly in cybersecurity jobs.

Building out this pipeline also requires us to rethink who and where we recruit. Lynn Dungle, president of Raytheon's Intelligence and Information Systems, describes this as one of the major problems of securing cyberspace today. "We are looking for talent in all the wrong places. And the organizations and companies that most need this type of talent will be the least likely to attract it."

Not only is talent scarce, but it often doesn't fit the same mold. Despite cybersecurity's relative youth as a field, many organizations approach it in the same old ways, which Dungle describes as too often "overreliant on historical learning methods and processes and have a real prejudice toward people who work 9 to 5, are willing to contain their personal time off to three weeks, and to charge their time in 6-minute intervals." Her own firm, Raytheon, is one of the leading defense and aerospace firms in the world. Like many other businesses, it understandably is biased toward college grads who show up at job fairs in a suit and tie, intending to join the firm at a junior level and then make a career of it by gradually moving up the ranks. They've discovered, though, this isn't always the best way to get the top cybersecurity talent.

So, much like the NSA, they also now recruit in nontraditional places to find new cyber talent. One of their best new hires was a young man who didn't have a high school diploma. Before he joined the firm, he'd been working at a pharmaceutical plant by day, stuffing pills into bottles. By night, though, as *Aviation Week* magazine reported, he was a "stellar performer" on professional hacker websites. Companies can also sponsor contests, such as the CyberPatriot high school competition, using prizes and prestige to draw out top talent.

While these efforts are all important, it is possible that, over time, the human resources problem in cyber may solve itself. The more that the field takes off and job prospects grow, the less encouragement will be needed to get people interested in cyber careers. Instead, as Robert Brammer, Vice President for Advanced Technology at Northrop Grumman argues, one day the field will be viewed as a key stepping stone to success. "With the breadth of issues they have to address—not only technology, but economic and psychology— a career in cybersecurity can provide the broad base necessary to reach the top."

Do Your Part: How Can I Protect Myself (and the Internet)?

Mark Burnett is a security consultant who has spent decades examining how to harden computer systems against attack. In one study entitled "Perfect Passwords," he accumulated and analyzed over two million user passwords (assembled everywhere from hacker list dumps to Google). The most common, unfortunately, showed how far we have to go in our personal approach to cybersecurity. Yes, the most popular password used to protect our computers was "password." The second most popular? "123456."

The issues of responsibility in cybersecurity are, in many ways, much like other issues of public and private safety. The government has a role in providing standards and enforcing regulation, and the industry has a responsibility to meet them, but the chain of responsibility does not stop there. The individual citizen must also play their part. Take the example of seat belts. The government created a requirement that all cars have them; many car companies, in fact, go even further and try to separate themselves from competitors with their greater safety features. But, at the end of the day, the individual still has to buckle up.

When it comes to cybersecurity, most people are not being targeted by APTs, Stuxnet, or other high-end threats. We are, however, part of an ecosystem where we have responsibilities both to ourselves and to the broader community. As one cybersecurity expert put it, "Most of us are not dealing with serious national security type issues, but our failure to show good sense can create a lot of noise that bad guys can hide in." Indeed, even if there are bad guys directly after us, there are still simple measures that can be taken. The Australian Defence Signals Directorate (equivalent of the US National Security Agency) found in one study that just a few key actions—"whitelisting" (i.e., allowing only authorized software to run on a computer or network), very rapid patching of applications and of operating system vulnerabilities, and restricting the number of people with administrator access to a system—would prevent 85 percent of targeted intrusions from succeeding.

The biggest change we can make at the individual level, though, is to change our attitude toward security. The Internet is certainly not the scary, awful place it is often painted by too many cybersecurity reports. But nor is it an innocuous realm. Indeed, one study found that roughly two-thirds of cybercrime victims were simply unaware of the risks in the realm. As the cartoon character Pogo would put it, "We have met the enemy, and he is us."

A shift in attitude is important not just in our own personal roles but also in the roles we play inside any organizations we belong to, especially when in leadership positions. Steven Bucci, senior research fellow at the Heritage Foundation, illustrates this point with a story of a US Air Force base commander in the 2000s (a period before the military took cybersecurity seriously). The commander forced his IT people to give him a one-digit password for his classified system. He told them he was "too important" to be slowed down by having to type multiple digits. "In five minutes after that happened, everybody on the base knew two things: one, their boss was a complete idiot. Two, that security wasn't important."

Accepting that there are risks and threats doesn't mean there is nothing that we can do. Rather, it emphasizes the second fundamental attitude change, recognizing the need to educate ourselves and then protect ourselves. In many ways, this education is requisite for the twenty-first century and should be taking place within the schools (we teach kids on everything from basic hygiene to driver's education, why not also cyber hygiene to protect themselves?). As technologist Ben Hammersly has written, the general state of cyber education is "shameful," from the primary school level on up, and helps explain some of the ignorance displayed even at the highest levels of media and government. "How many policy debates have you heard, from security to copyright reform, that have been predicated on technical ignorance? This is a threat to national prosperity itself far more severe than any terrorist organization could ever be. It remains, in too many circles, a matter of pride not to be able to program the video recorder. That's pathetic."

In the absence of formal education, it is imperative on all of us to learn the basics and act appropriately. And, just as in other areas, this responsibility is both a personal one and a parental one. If your children are online (and they are!), they too need to know how to act appropriately, recognize risks, and protect themselves. Imparting an ethic of stewardship (that this is their way not only to look after themselves, but also to help keep the Internet safe for others) is a better strategy than trying to convince them through fear factors.

What follows is certainly not the exhaustive list of all that you can do to better your cybersecurity but simply some of the key steps—from entry to equipment to behavior—that any smart and responsible user should be thinking about. Or, as one retired army officer responded when asked what was the most important thing people could do for cybersecurity, "Stop being so damned stupid on computers."

Access and Passwords: Update passwords regularly and always use "strong" passwords that are both lengthy and mix numbers, letters, and signs. Never use common words and phrases.

As *Wired* magazine explained of the problem of using passwords like "12345" or "password," "If you use a dumb password like that, getting into your account is trivial. Free software tools with names like Cain and Abel or John the Ripper automate password-cracking to such an extent that, very literally, any idiot can do it. All you need is an Internet connection and a list of common passwords—which, not coincidentally, are readily available online, often in database-friendly formats."

Don't share these passwords and don't use the same passwords repeatedly across your various accounts (as then a hacker can "daisy chain" to connect across all your online personas). One study of hacked websites found that 49 percent of people had reused usernames and passwords between hacked sites. This is also why many organizations require you to change your password regularly. It not only minimizes risk, in case your password was already compromised, but it minimizes the likelihood that an irresponsible user has used his work password to, say, buy shoes, and now that password is compromised.

At the very least, your e-mail passwords should be strong and unique, since many web applications allow you to reset many account details by e-mail. You may also want to consider a "password manager." This application generates random, secure passwords for all the sites you need, and enters them automatically. Modern password manager applications work across platforms and devices, requiring you to only have to remember one password for the tool itself—just make sure that's a good one!

Given how many accounts also allow you to reset a password by answering some personal question, never use any personal information that could be found online to answer these questions. You may think that no one could guess your mother's maiden name or your first grade teacher, but often that is findable with a quick web search of you and your friends and family's social media accounts. So-called "socialing" was responsible for 37 percent of the total data stolen in one government study of cybercrime. Indeed, it was through public information that a rather unethical teenager was able to gain access to Sarah Palin's personal Yahoo! e-mail account. Many suggest using counterintuitive information to confuse a system. What's your mother's maiden name? Answer your first pet's name.

Even after following all this advice, passwords still only offer a single line of defense, vulnerable to a compromised server or a brute-force guessing attack. There is a growing effort to protect more valuable information and accounts with what is known as "multi-factor authentication."

Multifactor authentication operates under the idea that entry doesn't just have to be allowed because of something the user knows, like a password. Their identity can also be verified by something the user has (like a smart card), where the user is, and/or something the user is, such as a biometric characteristic like fingerprints. This seems an onerous requirement, but has actually become the way that banks control access to automated teller machines (ATMs). The bank card is the physical object the customer has, while the code is the second verifying information that the customer knows. Similarly, many e-mail programs like Gmail can restrict access to computers in certain physical locations or require secondary codes pushed out to users' mobile phones. The security here comes from multiple channels—even if your computer has been compromised, if your cell phone hasn't, then a text message serves as a second layer of security.

None of these are perfect. Even one of the top multifactor defenses used by the Pentagon was cracked when hackers broke into the company that manufactured the physical tokens that provided users a random, algorithmically determined secondary password. But that doesn't mean the effort is not worthwhile. The goal is to shift the password from being the first and last line of defense into part of a multilayered series of hoops and hurdles far more difficult for a hacker to go through.

Systems and Equipment: Cyberthreats are constantly evolving, but the reality is that many breaches do not happen through new zero days. The Conficker worm, one of the most successful pieces of malware in history, for example, spread to several million computers through a vulnerability in Windows that was widely known and for which patches were available online. Such threats are easily defeated by simply keeping operating systems, browsers, and other critical software constantly up to date. The fact that security updates and patches are freely available from major companies makes it all the easier.

Many of the more targeted cyberthreats utilize wireless access to gain entry, sometimes from with the same building, other times from nearby parking lots, or via crowds, and so on. Restricting unwarranted access is useful, but can only go so far. Indeed, some of the sneakier threats have even utilized remote operated helicopters to get inside buildings to tap their wireless networks. For this reason, it's also important to secure your wireless network with the best available protection, including encrypting the traffic from your device to the router. Note that many popular wireless encryption schemes have been broken, so be sure to use the most recent. If you are using an unencrypted wireless network in a public place, be careful what you're doing. Any activity that isn't encrypted through SSL (the little lock icon in your browser) is easily intercepted by anyone nearby, with free and easy-to-use software.

Finally, given the likely threats, it is important to back up any valuable information, whether it's your financial statements or those cute pictures of your toddler girl blowing bubbles. This should be done both in external networks, but ideally also in a physical hard drive set aside just for that kind of important information.

A good rule is that if you can't bear to lose it, then prepare to lose it.

Behavior: Most threats enter through some kind of vulnerability created by the users themselves. Like the three little pigs, don't open the door before checking. If your system has an option to automatically download attachments, turn it off and instead always use the highest privacy and security settings to limit the exposure of your systems. Never open links that come from users you don't know or who seem fishy (such as varying in spelling or domain), nor should you open attachments unless you can verify the source. And, just like with candy, never accept hardware from untrusted sources.

Wherever you can, operate in a mentality based on the multi-factor authentication. If you receive a message asking you to send important or personal information, verify the sender through other means, including that antique technique of picking up the phone and calling your mom to know exactly why she wants your bank account number. Even if the e-mail is not from her, she'll be glad you called, and you'll save yourself a lot of trouble.

This is even more important as mobile devices become more and more common. Links sent via texts are just as likely a threat as those in an e-mail. Even if you think you know the sender, it is not a good idea to click on unknown links. Similarly, apps should only be downloaded from trusted marketplaces. Social media further compound this threat, where we have become accustomed to shortened link services such as tinyurl.com. As we were preparing the final version of this manuscript, someone we didn't know commented on a Twitter exchange between the two of us, trying to steer us to a shortened link. Using a URL unshortener that checks the redirect for us, we discovered that the participant in our discussion was keen to share with us a very long string of obfuscated (almost certainly malicious) code. Common sense would also have worked: this Twitter account had zero followers and was not following anyone, but was sharing links with several other high-profile Twitter users with abandon. Bottom line, the best behavior is not to be afraid, but rather wary.

Just as wearing your seat belt doesn't mean you'll not be hurt when you enter a car, such steps are no guarantee to cybersecurity. They are, however, recognition that we can all contribute to the solution while better protecting ourselves and the Internet as a whole.

CONCLUSIONS

Where Is Cybersecurity Headed Next?

In 2008, the Roadrunner first ran online.

The world's first "petaflop" supercomputer, Roadrunner was able to perform one quadrillion (that's a million billion) floating point operations per second. At a cost of more than $120 million to build, it had 296 server racks that contained 122,400 processor cores. This meant it was huge in physical scale, covering over 560 square meters (6,000 square feet), or roughly the size of the Jumbotron video scoreboards at modern sports stadiums.

Built by IBM for the US Department of Energy, in 2008 Roadrunner's original purpose was to conduct incredibly complex simulations of how nuclear weapons age, in order to keep America's nuclear arsenal reliable but unused. It would go on to make calculations in many other fields, like aerospace and high finance. Notably, Roadrunner was not just the world's fastest computer but also the first hybrid designed supercomputer, using a mix of AMD Opteron dual-core processors and IBM PowerXCell 8i CPUs, essentially an enhanced version of the Sony PlayStation 3 video game processor.

But technology moves fast, even for supercomputers. As we sat down to write the conclusion to this book, news broke that Roadrunner's run was done. Once the world's fastest computer, it was no longer competitive a mere few years later. It wasn't just that research was reaching "exascale" speeds (1,000 times faster than Roadrunner's petaflop), but that the machine's once cutting-edge design was now incredibly inefficient. Roadrunner needed 2,345 kilowatts to operate, which meant it cost roughly several million dollars just to power and then cool the system. And so, just five years after it had been the world's most powerful computer, Roadrunner was dismantled. In a final indignity, the no-longer-supercomputer's parts were shredded. Because of the classified nature of the calculations that had once run on it, Roadrunner couldn't be trusted, even after death.

The sad fate of Roadrunner is something to keep in mind for weighing the broader lessons. Cyberspace, and the issues involved, will continue to evolve, including beyond the Roadrunner-like tour you have taken in this book through the world of cybersecurity and cyberwar. New technologies will emerge, and new social, business, criminal, and warfare models for using them will be developed that will create transformational change.

While none of us can know exactly what the future world is going to look like, we think it is important to pay attention to the key trends today that might shape that world. To use a metaphor, imagine a kettle filled with water on a stove. With all our science, we can put a robot rover on Mars that sends back pictures via Twitter, but even with supercomputers like Roadrunner we cannot reliably predict where any single molecule of water in that kettle will be next. We can, however, reasonably predict that more and more heat applied to that water in the kettle will ultimately cause it to turn to steam. So if there is a fire under the kettle, that's a key trend to understanding what might happen next.

Trends are guides, nothing more and nothing less. But these macro guides are important to identify. As the futurist John Nasibett once said: "Trends, like horses, are easier to ride in the direction they are going."

As we look forward, there appear to be at least five key trends that matter greatly to that future story of cybersecurity. None of these trends is definite, and indeed, there will be many more that will emerge. These trends are driven by a number of factors that we can begin to observe. Hardware has gotten substantially cheaper, making it both easier to concentrate in incredibly powerful data centers, as well as diffuse into our everyday lives. New uses will emerge that take advantage of this broader capacity, and new generations of users around the world will find new paradigms for understanding how cyberspace can expand into their lives.

The first among the most fascinating and important trends emerging now is the rise of "cloud computing," where computing resources are managed outside the individual or organization's control. Essentially, the cloud moves personal computing from hardware you purchase to a service you buy online. In some ways, this new development echoes the birth of the Internet itself. Cloud empowers individuals by providing practically limitless computational resources and by sharing powerful computing resources over the network with many users. A new startup, for example, no longer needs to worry about buying and running its own web servers, HR sales records, or even data storage—it can be rented from a cloud provider, saving as much as 40 to 80 percent, depending on the situation. The militaries of the world are also greatly interested in the cloud. General Martin Dempsey, the top US military officer at the time, told us in 2013 that he wanted to move the force from running some 15,000 different computer networks to a "joint information environment" in the cloud. He saw that this would not only cut costs, but also reduce the number of human systems administrators, the potential Bradley Manning and Edward Snowden types who had been behind so many recent data breaches. The result is that the cloud field has boomed in recent years, with the global industry growing from roughly $79 billion in 2010 to an estimated $149 billion in 2014.

Beyond cost savings and size, cloud computing is deeply important to the future of the Internet, potentially altering the very architecture and power balance of cyberspace. Individual machines become less important, and instead the companies that control the data and access to it play an increasingly essential role. This can actually solve some security issues: the average individual consumer or even IT security worker is probably not as good as the security engineers at the large firms like Amazon or Google who specialize in the cloud and can bring scale to the problem. The incentives also align better. Just as banks had to grow better at differentiating between legitimate and fraudulent transactions, cloud providers will have to learn to detect illicit behavior if they hope to be a successful business.

At the same time, cloud computing introduces a host of new security policy concerns. The risk is much more concentrated, but comes with less certainty. As data flows between the cloud provider and the user, who, exactly, is responsible for different aspects of security? International boundaries become even more important, but more challenged. As a Brookings report explored, "What [one] state might see as an opportunity for law enforcement or public safety intervention could very well be viewed as a flagrant violation by the data owner, used to operating under a different set of laws." Will every state demand its full rights into the cloud, balkanizing the Internet, or will countries follow a free-trade model that sacrifices closely held traditional values in the name of greater efficiency?

Cheaper and more accessible storage and computation will inspire new uses, particularly the collection and analysis of data. This leads to the second important trend: "Big Data." As data sets have grown ever larger and more complex, new tools and methods have been needed to understand them. These tools, in turn, continue to support a qualitative shift in what we can learn from information collected. This has driven everything from the NSA's controversial collection of "meta-data" about the wider public's Internet contact points in the hunt for terrorist links to fundamental shifts in business models. For example, Netflix started as a company that rented movie and TV show DVDs that were shipped primarily via the postal system. With the rise of the Internet and online media, it shifted to a streaming digital model. But as Netflix sent out its online movies and TV shows, it gathered vast data on the preferences of the individual consumer and the wider collection of viewers they were part of. The collection and analysis of this new scale of data allowed Netflix to approach the market in a whole new way, even using it to produce and shape the very content and cast of its own hit series *House of Cards*.

The sweep of Big Data is immense. More and more decisions and analysis, even of the most human concerns, begin to be made based off of links and associations. As a result, Big Data can also lead to big problems. The revelation of NSA meta-data collection caused an immense scandal that is still shaking out, with implications for everything from the future of counterterrorism to broader public trust in government. But even the seemingly innocuous use by Netflix also demonstrates the dangers of Big Data for privacy. After releasing a de-identified list of user movie preferences to crowd-source an improvement to their recommendation algorithm, executives were shocked to learn that researchers could tie this data to real identities. In one instance, a list of what movies someone liked was enough to determine his or her closeted sexual orientation. More data, and better tools to understand it, can yield unprecedented knowledge, but they may also break down human social, legal, and ethical boundaries we aren't yet ready to cross.

Better and cheaper technology will not only concentrate computational power, it will also distribute it across the globe. This is the essence of another key trend, what has been called the "mobile revolution." From one perspective, telecommunications going mobile is not that new a trend. The process arguably began in 1973, when Motorola engineer Martin Cooper stood on a New York City street and called his rival at Bell Labs to crow about beating him to the invention of a mobile telephone (meaning the "revolution" started with a prank call). But as phones became "smart" and added Internet functionality, the Internet itself went wireless and mobile (for instance, the percentage of visitors to websites using mobile devices jumped from 1.6 percent in 2010 to 20.2 percent in 2012).

The shift of personal computing from the desktop to mobile devices will only increase as devices get cheaper and smaller. And innovation in this space shows no sign of stopping. One 2013 study found that a full quarter of all patents were for mobile technology.

But as the digital extends further into the physical world, there are other limits. Today's mobile devices depend on radio communication, which is built on a finite spectrum, a binding constraint for the number of devices and how much data they can send. This is the battle of bandwidth. A key challenge is whether technical advances such as cognitive radio will allow more dynamic and context-sensitive use of radio frequencies, which is necessary to opening up the airwaves to more devices and applications.

As we use phones and tablets more, the security risks are also going mobile. By the start of 2013, over 350,000 unique variants of malware had been created to target mobile devices; there were none just a few years earlier. This increase is natural, but the real danger is that our understanding of the risk has not grown at the same rate. Mobile devices have smaller interfaces that offer less security information, and have fewer computational resources for defense. Unlike your desktop computer, mobile devices also usually travel between the workplace and home, making organizational security boundaries harder to define. Users currently have less control over their devices and are thus more dependent on vendors for security. Yet, as we saw earlier, that market is fragmented, with multiple makers, from the phone to the operating system to the mobile apps, each with a role in security but often lacking any sense of responsibility for it. And, finally, similar to the broader security issue, mobile platforms present governance questions: which government organizations have oversight, and which market actors are responsible for countering mobile threats? Just as with the desktop world, all these issues will have to be resolved.

Mobile technology can transform the world by putting data directly into our hands, but what makes it even more powerful is the number of hands the devices reach, especially outside the developed world. Whereas the mobile phone started as an expensive device that only those rich drug dealers on *Miami Vice* could afford, now it spreads computing power across the income spectrum, with immense consequences. In East Africa, mobile technology has revolutionized banking and commerce; anyone with a mobile phone can pay anyone else with a phone using M-Pesa, which doesn't require access to a bank or credit system. This growing role in the developing world economy, however, means that security becomes even more important, and unfortunately it becomes most pressing in places least able to afford high-end security solutions.

This demographic shift in the makeup of those who consider cyberspace home points to a fourth important trend when considering the future of cybersecurity. When the Internet started out, it linked together a small set of American researchers, mostly Californians (who are even more of a peculiar species). Today, an ever-shrinking percentage of cyberspace is American, and even Western in terms of its users, the content they put on it, and the use they make of it. The UN, for example, predicts that Chinese-speaking users of the Internet will outnumber English speakers by 2015, while there are more mobile smartphone users in Africa than in the United States and the EU.

This shift matters greatly in ways both big and small. For example, the dominance that cute cats have had over online videos (an Internet meme we have had so much fun with in this book) may be ending. Google researchers have noticed an explosion of cute goat and cute Panda bear videos that have risen in parallel with the greater number of users coming online in sub-Saharan Africa and China. More important than the breaking of cats' monopoly over Internet cuteness, the very language is shifting. For the first few decades of the Internet, no standards-conforming browser could access a website without using Latin characters. This has been recently broken, meaning you now find the Egyptian Ministry of Communication at http://موقع.وزارة-الأتصالات.مصر/.

Beyond content, this trend may see cyberspace increasingly fragment to reflect the values of these new netizens and their governments. The Internet, and its structures and norms, grew out of the worldviews of that early mix of mostly American computer scientists who first built it. Their approach was shaped by the mix of academic freedom and hippie mentality that characterized the era, with a strong emphasis on the power and importance of connection, sharing, and openness. However, that worldview may not be the new norm of the evolved Internet. We've already seen these tensions come to a head in the debates over cybersecurity and Internet freedom in realms like the ITU, and they can be expected to continue. It also opens the risk that the Internet may become more and more divided. As *The Economist* observed, "A growing number of such countries have an internet that each of them can call their own, walled off as much or as little as suits them."

There is a caveat to this danger. The current and future users of the Internet may not have much politically or culturally in common with the long-haired early developers in places like 1960s Berkeley, California. But these founders' values are exactly what created the online world that the new generation of users so want to enter. And once these new users are inside it, their worldviews are increasingly shaped by this world. Cyberspace reflects the characteristics and needs of its users, but as we've seen, these users also grow to reflect its characteristics and needs.

The final trend that will likely have serious cybersecurity implications builds on both cheaper computation and a more mobile world. The future blurring of cyber and physical will come to fruition when digital systems are fully embedded in the real world, also known as the "Internet of Things."

Like so many aspects of cyberspace, the Internet of Things can best be illustrated with a cat. Steve Sande was a man living in Colorado who worried about Ruby, his feline companion, when he was away. His particular concern was that Ruby might get too hot in his home that lacked air conditioning. However, Steve was environmentally conscious (or cheap) and didn't want to waste power on a fan when it wasn't needed. So he linked his fan to an Internet-connected device called a WeMo and wrote a script that monitored an online weather website. Whenever the website said the weather was over 85 degrees Fahrenheit, the WeMo switched the fan on. With no direct human instruction, the "things" in Steve's house worked together via the Internet to keep Ruby the cat cool.

More broadly, the Internet of Things is the concept that everything can be linked to a web-enabled device to collect or make use of data. So many physical objects in our lives, from cameras to cars, already have computer chips built in. What happens when they can all "talk" to each other? And then, what happens when literally anything from the wristband you wear to wall of your bathroom to fruit at the grocery store can have tiny cheap chips put on them, and also join the conversation? In this vision, distributed sensors can detect street traffic, enabling your GPS to route your car home from work, while communicating to your home's thermostat how far away you are, so that it can power back up the heat from its most efficient setting, determined off its link to the smart power grid; sensors can detect how crowded different restaurants are to make you a reservation, and your exercise bike at the gym will talk to your credit card to find out what you ordered at that restaurant, and decide how long you have to work out the next day to burn that cheesecake off.

One of the main obstacles to this vision is interoperability. The Internet exploded because of shared, open standards that anyone could build on. Without the unruly but effective governance structures, however, the many other devices that may be linked into the Internet of Things still lack standardized, open inputs and outputs that share and interpret instructions and data in seamless, automated exchanges. Common formats are required to understand data, and some mechanism is needed to gather and interpret data in the first place, which can be an expensive proposition. And while turning Ruby's fan on was a simple function of knowing the temperature, not everything is so easy. Far more decisions need complex analysis and technical negotiations, requiring incredibly sophisticated software agents trying to interpret our wants and needs, and, in turn, complex human decisions and negoatiations about them.

The other key challenge for the future of connected "things" is that it also enables cyberattackers to penetrate far deeper into our lives than ever before. If everything around us makes important decisions based on computerized data, we'll need to work long and hard to make sure that data is not corrupted. As we've seen there have already been attempts at everthing from "car hacking" to tampering with an Internet-enabled toilet.

Like the cybersecurity questions discussed throughout this book, each of these potential future trends offers a set of challenges that go beyond the technical to issues of governance, markets, and international affairs. Moreover, they will likely interact with each other to create even more questions.

What Do I Really Need to Know in the End?

Given what we've seen happen in cyberspace already, it is certainly daunting to imagine such a world. And it's even more overwhelming when we can be certain that there are more trends that lie beyond.

Undoubtedly, new technologies and applications will emerge that will revolutionize our conceptions, just as the explosive growth of cyberspace over the last two decades has upended much of what we knew about security. Former US Secretary of Defense Donald Rumsfeld had a famous laugh line that explained the world as being made up of three categories: "Known knowns, there are things we know we know. We also know there are known unknowns, that is to say we know there are some things we do not know. But there are also unknown unknowns, the ones we don't know we don't know." It may not have been the most eloquent way to say it, but he was actually right.

The extent of present and future known and unknown knowns makes the world of cyberspace seem an incredibly intimidating and even scary place, both today and maybe more so tomorrow. As we saw, however, it need not be. Whatever plays out, the answer is the same: building proper understanding and enacting thoughtful responses.

To bring this story full circle, in the beginning of this book, we explained how we were first introduced to computers as young kids. The idea that these machines would one day do everything from steal a person's identity to literally become weapons of mass disruption would have scared the wits out of our younger selves. The prospect of entering such a dangerous online world likely would have reduced us to tears and spurred pleas to our parents not to hit the "power" button.

Today, we wouldn't have it any other way. Our journey into the world of cyberspace has given us, and the rest of humanity, fantastic powers that were then unimaginable. We have gained everything from the ability to track down the answer to almost any question we might have to the opportunity to become friends with people whom we have never met.

The same as it was back then is how it will be in the future. We must accept and manage the risks of this world—both online and real—because of all that can be achieved in it. And that really is *What Everyone Needs to Know*.

ACKNOWLEDGMENTS

Writing a book is often described as a lonely effort, but in reality our journey would not have been possible without a community of supporters behind the scenes.

We would like to thank our editor, David McBride, who first approached us with such a wonderful and important concept and then guided the process to success. The Smith Richardson Foundation and the Brookings President's Special Initiatives Fund were crucial enablers of the type of long-term work a book project requires, and we particularly appreciate their recognition of the importance of both cybersecurity and collaboration across programs and disciplines. Martin Indyk and Darrell West, respectively the Directors of Foreign Policy and Governance Studies at Brookings, guided our work and, along with Strobe Talbott, the President of Brookings, provided an atmosphere that is all too rare, in which scholarship can be applied to the most pressing issues of the day. A tireless team of staff provided research and editing support, including Emerson Brooking, Joshua Bleiberg, Kevin Li, Jin Rang, and especially Tim Peacock, notable for being never afraid to challenge our thinking and improve upon it. Of particular importance was the role of the remarkably talented and able Brendan Orino, who not only provided support on the research, writing, and editing, but also masterfully organized the entire cyber book campaign. He is an APT wrapped into one person. Jordan and Abby Clayton provided their visual wizardry. A number of colleagues were incredibly generous with their advice and expertise, which sharpened both our thinking and writing, including Ian Morrison, Michael O'Hanlon, Ian Wallace, Tammy Schultz, Mark

Hagerott, Tyler Moore, Jean Camp, Herb Lin, Noah Shachtman, Ken Lieberthal, Beau Kilmer, and Bruce Schneier. We are in deep appreciation of the scores of interviewees, meeting participants, and event and trip hosts who took their time out of busy schedules to aid this work.

On a personal level, Allan would like to thank the unflagging support and love of his wife, Katie, who agreed to marry him in spite of his insistence on talking about cybersecurity constantly and writing about it late into the night.

Peter would like to thank Susan, Owen, and Liam, who make it all worth it, every single moment.

And finally, we would like to thank our parents for many things, but especially for buying those first clunky computers so many years ago.

NOTES

INTRODUCTION
WHY WRITE A BOOK ABOUT CYBERSECURITY AND CYBERWAR?

1 *convinced us to write this book* Cyber Terrain Conference, Spy Museum, Washington, DC, May 18, 2011.

2 *30 trillion individual web pages* Google, "How Search Works," http://www.google.com/insidesearch/howsearchworks/, accessed April 15, 2013.

2 *gadgets not yet imagined* Rod Soderbery, "How Many Things are Currently Connected to the 'Internet of Things' (IOT)?" *Forbes*, January 7, 2013, http://www.forbes.com/fdc/welcome_mjx.shtml.

2 *gearing up to fight battles* Keith Alexander, "Cybersecurity and American Power," remarks at the American Enterprise Institute, Washington, DC, July 9, 2012.

3 *"national security challenges of the 21st century"* Gordon Crovitz, "Cybersecurity 2.0," *Wall Street Journal*, February 27, 2012, http://online.wsj.com/article/SB10001424052970203918304577243423337326122.html.

3 *leaders in countries from Britain to China* "A Strong Britain in the Age of Uncertainty: The National Security Strategy," UK Government document, 2010, http://www.direct.gov.uk/prod_consum_dg/groups/dg_digitalassets/@dg/@en/documents/digitalasset/dg_191639.pdf, accessed July 31, 2013.

3 *a time of "cyber anxiety"* George R. Lucas, Jr., "Permissible Preventive Cyberwar: Restricting Cyber Conflict to Justified Military Targets," presentation at the Society of Philosophy and Technology Conference, University of North Texas, May 28, 2011.

3 *"single greatest emerging threat"* "The FP Survey: The Internet," *Foreign Policy* (September–October 2011): p. 116.

3 *"bloody, digital trench warfare"* David Tohn, "Digital Trench Warfare," *Boston Globe*, June 11, 2009, http://www.boston.com/bostonglobe/editorial_opinion/oped/articles/2009/06/11/digital_trench_warfare/.

3 *fight and win wars in cyberspace* "Fact Sheet: Cybersecurity Legislative Proposal," White House press release, May 12, 2011, http://www.whitehouse.gov/the-press-office/2011/05/12/fact-sheet-cybersecurity-legislative-proposal.

3 *"welfare in search of security"* Joseph S. Nye, "Power and National Security in Cyberspace," in *America's Cyber Future: Security and Prosperity in the Information Age*, vol. 2, edited by Kristin M. Lord and Travis Shard (Washington, DC: Center for a New American Security, June 2011), p. 15.

3 *disconnect from the worldwide Internet* Ibid., p. 16.

3 *"free exchange of ideas"* Rebekka Bonner, "Arms Race in Cyberspace?" *Rebekka Bonner's Blog* (blog), Information Society Project, Yale Law School, May 24, 2011, http://www.yaleisp.org/2011/05/arms-race-in-cyberspace.

4 *"command and control of warships"* Mark Clayton, "The New Cyber Arms Race," *Christian Science Monitor*, March 7, 2011, http://www.csmonitor.com/USA/Military/2011/0307/ The-new-cyber-arms-race.

Why Is There a Cybersecurity Knowledge Gap, and Why Does It Matter?

4 *"any decision we might make"* Joseph S. Nye Jr., "Nuclear Lessons for Cyber Security?" *Strategic Studies Quarterly* 5, no. 3 (Winter 2011): p. 18.

5 *"I just don't use e-mail at all"* Janet Napolitano, "Uncovering America's Cybersecurity Risk," speech at National Journal Cybersecurity Summit, Newseum, Washington, DC, September 28, 2012.

5 *"workings of a computer"* Mark Bowden, *Worm: The First Digital World War* (New York: Atlantic Monthly Press, 2011), p. 7.

6 *"policy in the world of cyberspace"* Sandra Erwin, "Cyber Command Wrestling With Unresolved Technology and Policy Issues," *National Defense* (March 2, 2011): p. 198.

7 *never even heard of Tor* "Top Gillard IT Security Czar Has Never Heard of Tor," Delimiter.com, May 29, 2013, http://delimiter.com.au/2013/05/29/top-gillard-it-security-czar-has-never-heard-of-tor/.

7 *"preparations to fight the Internet war"* Eyder Peralta, "Chinese Military Scholars Accuse U.S. of Launching 'Internet War,'" *NPR*, June 3, 2011, http://www.npr.org/ blogs/thetwo-way/2011/06/03/136923033/chinese-military-scholars-accuse-u-s-of-launching-internet-war.

8 *"policy in the smoky backrooms"* Cyber Terrain Conference, Spy Museum, Washington, DC, May 18, 2011.

How Did You Write the Book and What Do You Hope to Accomplish?

10 *the broader world is all the more informed* Daniel E. Geer, Jr., "How Government Can Access Innovative Technology," in *America's Cyber Future: Security and Prosperity in the Information Age*, vol. 2, edited by Kristin M. Lord and Travis Shard (Washington, DC: Center for a New American Security, June 2011), p. 187.

Part I: How It All Works
The World Wide What? Defining Cyberspace

12 *"It's a series of tubes"* Liz Ruskin, "Internet 'Tubes' Speech Turns Spotlight, Ridicule on Sen. Stevens," *Common Dreams*, July 15, 2006, http://www.commondreams.org/head-lines06/0715-06.htm.

12 *"clusters and constellations of data"* William Gibson, *Neuromancer* (New York: Berkley Publishing Group, 1984), p. 128.

13 *humble beginnings* Scott W. Beidleman, "Defining and Deterring Cyber War," strategy research project, US Army War College, 2009, p. 9.

13 *light from the sun* Ibid.

13 *"embedded processors and controllers"* Ibid., p. 10.

14 *the infrastructure that powers and uses it* Ibid.

14 *sovereignty, nationality, and property* Joseph S. Nye, "Power and National Security in Cyberspace," in *America's Cyber Future: Security and Prosperity in the Information Age*, vol. 2, edited by Kristin M. Lord and Travis Shard (Washington, DC: Center for a New American Security, 2011), pp. 14–15.

14 *"the click of a switch"* Ibid., p. 9.

15 *registered sites hit 550 million by 2012* Jon Russell, "Importance of Microblogs in China Shown as Weibos Pass 500 Million Users," *The Next Web*, last modified November 11, 2011, http://thenextweb.com/asia/2011/11/11/importance-of-microblogs-in-china-shown-as-weibos-pass-550-million-users/.

15 *"supervisory control and data acquisition"* Beidleman, "Defining and Deterring Cyber War," p. 6.

15 *"the control system of our economy"* Ibid., p. 1.

16 *"knowingly or not, it is life"* Ben Hammersley, "Speech to the UK's Information Assurance Advisory Council," remarks at the Information Assurance Advisory Council, London, September 6, 2011, http://www.benhammersley.com/2011/09/my-speech-to-the-iaac/.

WHERE DID THIS "CYBER STUFF" COME FROM ANYWAY? A SHORT HISTORY OF THE INTERNET

16 *the Stanford end of the network crashed* Chris Sutton, "Internet Began 25 Years Ago at UCLA; Forum to Mark Anniversary Oct. 29," *UCLA Newsroom*, September 14, 2004, http://newsroom.ucla.edu/portal/ucla/Internet-Began-35-Years-Ago-at-5464.aspx? RelNum=5464.

17 *"hostilities should longer exist"* Tom Standage, *The Victorian Internet: The Remarkable Story of the Telegraph and the Nineteenth Century's On-Line Pioneers* (New York: Walker, 1998), p. 83.

19 *a majority of traffic across the network* Stephen Segaller, *Nerds 2.0.1: A Brief History of the Internet* (New York: TV Books, 1999), p. 109.

19 *independently organized infrastructure* National Science Foundation, "The Launch of NSFNET," http://www.nsf.gov/about/history/nsf0050/internet/launch.htm, accessed March 15, 2013.

20 *quicker privatization of the network* Rajiv Shah and Jay P. Kesan, "The Privatization of the Internet's Backbone Network," *Journal of Broadcasting and Electronic Media* 51, no. 1 (March 2007): pp. 93–109, http://www.governingwithcode.org/journal_articles/pdf/Backbone.pdf.

20 *the smut industry* Jerry Ropelato, "Internet Pornography Statistics," *Top Ten Reviews*, 2006, http://internet-filter-review.toptenreviews.com/internet-pornography-statistics. html, accessed November 13, 2006.

20 *"the process of growing up"* Mike Musgrove, "Technology's Steamier Side: Fates of Pornography and Internet Businesses Are Often Intertwined," *Washington Post*, January 21, 2006, p. D1.

21 *"their customers and their suppliers"* Peter H. Lewis, "U.S. Begins Privatizing Internet's Operations," *New York Times*, October 24, 1994, http://www.nytimes.com/1994/10/24/business/us-begins-privatizing-internet-s-operations.html?src=pm.

HOW DOES THE INTERNET ACTUALLY WORK?

21 *video-sharing website YouTube* Martin A. Brown, "Pakistan Hijacks YouTube," *Renesys* (blog), *Renesys*, February 24, 2008, http://www.renesys.com/blog/2008/02/pakistan_hijacks_youtube_1.shtml.

24 *over 40,000 AS nodes* Tony Bates, Philip Smith, and Geoff Huston, "CIDR Report," http://www.cidr-report.org/as2.0/, accessed April 2013.

WHO RUNS IT? UNDERSTANDING INTERNET GOVERNANCE

26 *first coup d'état of the Internet* Cade Metz, "Remembering John Postel—and the Day He Hijacked the Internet," *Enterprise* (blog), *Wired*, October 15, 2012, http://www.wired.com/wiredenterprise/2012/10/joe-postel/.

26 *controlled by the US government* Rajiv Chandrasekaran, "Internet Reconfiguration Concerns Federal Officials," *Washington Post*, January 31, 1998, http://songbird.com/pab/mail/0472.html.

26 *"couldn't wrest control of the Internet"* Metz, "Remembering John Postel."

26 *"experiment in anarchy"* Eric Schmidt and Jared Cohen, *The New Digital Age* (New York: Knopf, 2013), p. 263.

28 *the system's evolution*   Vint Cerf, "IETF and the Internet Society," Internet Society, July 18, 1995, http://www.internetsociety.org/internet/what-internet/history-internet/ietf-and-internet-society.

US government's central involvement   Jack Goldsmith and Tim Wu, *Who Controls the Internet? Illusions of a Borderless World* (New York: Oxford University Press, 2006).

29 *"diversity of the Internet"*   United States Department of Commerce, "State of Policy on the Management of Internet Names and Addresses," National Telecommunications & Information Administration, June 5, 1998, http://www.ntia.doc.gov/federal-register-notice/1998/statement-policy-management-internet-names-and-addresses.

29 *continue to perform this role today*   AFRINIC, "AFRINIC History," http://www.afrinic.net/en/about-us/origins, accessed February 2013.

29 *sucks.com*   Adam Goldstein, "ICANNSucks.biz (and Why You Can't Say That): How Fair Use of Trademarks in Domain Names Is Being Restrained," *Fordham Intellectual Property, Media and Entertainment Journal* 12, issue 4 (2002), http://ir.lawnet.fordham.edu/cgi/viewcontent.cgi?article=1237&context=iplj.

30 *represented among the decision-makers*   Eric Pfanner, "Ethics Fight over Domain Names Intensifies," *New York Times*, March 18, 2012, http://www.nytimes.com/2012/03/19/technology/private-fight-at-internet-naming-firm-goes-public.html?_r=0.

30 *"rough consensus and running code"*   David Clark, "A Cloudy Crystal Ball- Visions of the Future," in *Proceedings of the Twenty-Fourth Internet Engineering Task Force*, Massachusetts Institute of Technology, Cambridge, MA, July 13–17, 1992, http://ietf.org/proceedings/prior29/IETF24.pdf.

ON THE INTERNET, HOW DO THEY KNOW WHETHER YOU ARE A DOG? IDENTITY AND AUTHENTICATION

32 *cute, bear-shaped candy*   Tsutomu Matsumoto, Hiroyuki Matsumoto, Koji Yamada, et al., "Impact of Artificial 'Gummy' Fingers on Fingerprint Systems," in *Proceedings of SPIE Vol. #4677, Optical Security and Counterfeit Deterrence Techniques IV*, San Jose, CA, January 24–25, 2002, http://cryptome.org/gummy.htm.

32 *contact trusted friends*   Stuart Schechter, Serge Egelman, and Robert W. Reeder, "It's Not What You Know, but Who You Know: A Social Approach to Last-Resort Authentication," in *CHI '09: Proceeding of the Twenty-Seventh Annual SIGCHI Conference on Human Factors in Computing Systems*, New York, April 9, 2009, http://research.microsoft.com/apps/pubs/default.aspx?id=79349.

WHAT DO WE MEAN BY "SECURITY" ANYWAY?

34 *the presence of an adversary*   Institute for Security and Open Methodologies, *The Open Source Security Testing Methodology Manual: Contemporary Security Testing and Analysis*, 2010, http://www.isecom.org/mirror/OSSTMM.3.pdf, accessed August 11, 2013.

WHAT ARE THE THREATS?

37 *Idaho National Laboratory*   Mike M. Ahiers, "Inside a Government Computer Attack Exercise," CNN, October 17, 2011, http://www.cnn.com/2011/10/17/tech/innovation/cyberattack-exercise-idaho.

37 *"cyber Pearl Harbor"*   Google search, August 2013.

37 *Iranian nuclear research*   Joe Lieberman, Susan Collins, and Tom Carper, "A Gold Standard in Cyber-Defense," *Washington Post*, July 7, 2011, http://www.washingtonpost.com/opinions/a-gold-standard-in-cyber-defense/2011/07/01/gIQAjsZk2H_story.html.

38 *ultimate goal of financial theft*   Nelson D. Schwartz and Eric Dash, "Thieves Found Citigroup Site an Easy Entry," *New York Times*, June 13, 2011, www.nytimes.com/2011/06/14/technology/14security.html.

39   *much lower profit margins*   Cormac Herley, "The Plight of the Targeted Attacker in a World of Scale," in *The Ninth Workshop on the Economics of Information Security (WEIS 2010)*, Harvard University, Cambridge, MA, June 2010, http://weis2010.econinfosec. org/papers/session5/weis2010_herley.pdf.

ONE PHISH, TWO PHISH, RED PHISH, CYBER PHISH: WHAT ARE VULNERABILITIES?

40   *key fob digital ID*   Jason Torchinsky, "Watch Hackers Steal a BMW in Three Minutes," *Jalopnik*, July 6, 2012, http://jalopnik.com/5923802/watch-hackers-steal-a-bmw-in-three-minutes.

40   *paper leaflets on all BMWs*   BBC One, "BMW: Open to Car Theft?" *Watchdog*, September 12, 2012, http://www.bbc.co.uk/programmes/b006mg74/features/bmw-car-theft-technology.

40   *call up a low-level employee*   Kevin D. Mitnick and William L. Simon, *The Art of Deception: Controlling the Human Element of Security* (Indianapolis, IN: Wiley Books, 2002).

40   *cooperation through psychological mechanisms*   Michael Workman, "Gaining Access with Social Engineering: An Empirical Study of the Threat," *Information Security Systems* 16, issue 6 (November 2006), http://dl.acm.org/citation.cfm?id=1451702.

40   *fear of exposure can motivate payment*   Nicolas Christin, Sally S. Yanagihara, and Keisuke Kamataki, "Dissecting One Click Frauds," Carnegie Mellon University Technical Report, April 23, 2010, http://www.andrew.cmu.edu/user/nicolasc/publications/ TR-CMU-CyLab-10-011.pdf.

41   *a shocking number of users*   There are even numerous websites that catalog these for the convenience of the forgetful honest user and the lazy malicious user.

42   *misconfigured applications*   M. Eric Johnson and Scott Dynes, "Inadvertent Disclosure: Information Leaks in the Extended Enterprise," in *Proceedings of the Sixth Workshop on the Economics of Information Security*, June 7-8, 2007, http://weis2007.econin-fosec.org/papers/43.pdf.

43   *managed to cripple networks*   Robert Lemos, "'Good' Worm, New Bug Mean Double Trouble," *CNet*, August 19, 2003, http://news.cnet.com/2100-1002-5065644.html.

44   *500 accounts in a single day*   Symantec, "Highlights from Internet Security Threat Report, Volume 18," http://www.symantec.com/security_response/publications/threatreport. jsp, accessed May 20, 2013.

44   *defraud online advertisers*   Zhaosheng Zhu, Guohan Lu, Yan Chen, et al., "Botnet Research Survey," in *Computer Software and Applications, 2008. COMPSAC '08. 32nd Annual IEEE International*, July 28, 2008–August 1, 2008, http://ieeexplore.ieee.org/xpl/login.jsp?tp =&arnumber=4591703&url=http%3A%2F%2Fieeexplore.ieee.org%2Fxpls%2Fabs_all. jsp%3Farnumber%3D4591703.

45   *supporters of the Syrian regime*   OpenNet Initiative, "Syrian Electronic Army," http://opennet.net/syrian-electronic-army-disruptive-attacks-and-hyped-targets, accessed April 2013.

45   *the adolescent Internet in the 1980s*   C. Cowan, P. Wagle, C. Pu, et al., "Buffer Overflows: Attacks and Defenses for the Vulnerability of the Decade," in *DARPA Information Survivability Conference and Exposition, 2000. DISCEX '00. Proceedings*, vol. 2, 2000, http://ieeexplore.ieee.org/xpl/login.jsp?tp=&arnumber=821514.

45   *a detailed how-to guide*   Aleph One, "Smashing the Stack for Fun and Profit," *Phrack Magazine* 7, issue 49 (August 11, 1996), http://www.phrack.org/issues.html?issue=49& id=14#article.

HOW DO WE TRUST IN CYBERSPACE?

46   *tamper-resistant seals*   J. Alex Halderman and Ariel J. Feldman, "PAC-MAN on the Sequoia AVC-Edge DRE Voting Machine," https://jhalderm.com/pacman/, accessed March 15, 2013.

46   *key building block in cryptography*   Why did the cryptographer send his breakfast back? His hash wasn't salted.

49 *a Dutch CA's keys* Kim Zetter, "Google Certificate Hackers May Have Stolen 200 Others," *Threat Level* (blog), *Wired*, August 31, 2011, http://www.wired.com/threatlevel/2011/08/diginotar-breach/.

49 *it may even be impossible* Sara Sinclair and Sean W. Smith, "What's Wrong with Access Control in the Real World?" *IEEE Security & Privacy* 8, no. 4 (July–August 2010): pp. 74–77, http://www.computer.org/csdl/mags/sp/2010/04/msp2010040074-abs.html.

50 *trade secret law* Evan Brown, "Password Protection Not Enough to Protect Trade Secrets," *Internetcases*, April 8, 2005, http://blog.internetcases.com/2005/04/08/password-protection-not-enough-to-protect-trade-secrets/.

50 *crucial dots unconnected* Stewart Baker, *Skating on Stilts: Why We Aren't Stopping Tomorrow's Terrorism* (Stanford, CA: Hoover Institution Press, 2010), PDF e-book, http://www.hoover.org/publications/books/8128, accessed April 2013.

FOCUS: WHAT HAPPENED IN WIKILEAKS?

51 *"ive made a huge mess"* Evan Hansen, "Manning-Lamo Chat Logs Revealed," *Threat Level* (blog), *Wired*, July 13, 2011, http://www.wired.com/threatlevel/2011/07/manning-lamo-logs/.

51 *"exposing corruption and abuse"* Yochai Benkler, "A Free Irresponsible Press: Wikileaks and the Battle over the Soul of the Networked Fourth Estate," *Harvard Civil Rights–Civil Liberties Law Review* 46, no. 1 (2011): p. 315, http://harvardcrcl.org/wp-content/uploads/2011/08/Benkler.pdf.

52 *evidence of their wrongdoing online* Alasdair Roberts, "WikiLeaks: The Illusion of Transparency," *International Review of Administrative Sciences* 78, no. 1 (March 2012): p. 116, http://papers.ssrn.com/sol3/papers.cfm?abstract_id=1801343.

52 *"corruption, malfeasance, or ineptitude"* Benkler, "A Free Irresponsible Press," p. 316.

52 *"threat to the U.S. Army"* Stephanie Strom, "Pentagon Sees a Threat from Online Muckrackers," *New York Times*, March 17, 2010, http://www.nytimes.com/2010/03/8/us/18wiki.html.

52 *"gender identity disorder"* Hansen, "Manning-Lamo Chat Logs Revealed."

52 *"risk to himself and possibly others"* Kim Zetter, "Army Was Warned Not to Deploy Bradley Manning in Iraq," *Threat Level* (blog), *Wired*, January 27, 2011, http://www.wired.com/threatlevel/2011/01/army-warned-about-manning/.

53 *"everything that they were entitled to see"* Marc Ambinder, "WikiLeaks: One Analyst, So Many Documents," *National Journal*, November 29, 2010, http://www.nationaljournal.com/whitehouse/wikileaks-one-analyst-so-many-documents-20101129.

53 *"Information has to be free"* Hansen, "Manning-Lamo Chat Logs Revealed."

53 *overwrite the music with data* Kevin Poulsen and Kim Zetter, "U.S. Intelligence Analyst Arrested in WikiLeaks Video Probe," *Threat Level* (blog), *Wired*, June 6, 2010, http://www.wired.com/threatlevel/2010/06/leak/.

53 *"american history"* Hansen, "Manning-Lamo Chat Logs Revealed."

54 *"shutting the barn door"* Eric Lipton, "Don't Look, Don't Read: Government Warns Its Workers Away From WikiLeaks Documents," *New York Times*, December 4, 2010, http://www.nytimes.com/2010/12/05/world/05restrict.html?_r=1&.

54 *dissident listed in the cables* Mark MacKinnon, "Leaked Cables Spark Witch-Hunt for Chinese 'Rats,'" *Globe and Mail*, September 14, 2011, http://www.theglobeandmail.com/news/world/asia-pacific/leaked-cables-spark-witch-hunt-for-chinese-rats/article2165339/.

54 *called for Assange to be tried* Dianne Feinstein, "Prosecute Assange under the Espionage Act," *Wall Street Journal*, December 7, 2010, http://online.wsj.com/article/SB10001424052748703989004575653280626335258.html.

54 *"I think fairly modest"* Secretary of Defense Robert M. Gates and Chairman, Joint Chiefs of Staff Adm. Mike Mullen, "DOD News Briefing with Secretary Gates and Adm. Mullen from the Pentagon," remarks at the Pentagon, Washington, DC, November 30, 2010, http://www.defense.gov/Transcripts/Transcript.aspx?TranscriptID=4728.

55 *prominent high school football players* Alexander Abad-Santos, "Local Leak Tipsters Allege Steubenville Victim Was Drugged," *Atlantic Wire*, January 4, 2013, http://

www.theatlanticwire.com/national/2013/01/local-leaks-tipsters-allege-steubenville-victim-was-drugged/60597/.

55 *"modicum of legal protection"* Hansen, "Manning-Lamo Chat Logs Revealed."

WHAT IS AN ADVANCED PERSISTENT THREAT (APT)?

56 *"finding them once a day"* Cybersecurity CEO, interview with the authors, Washington DC, May 23, 2013.

57 *"The most impressive tool"* Gary McGraw, private communications with authors, April 26, 2011.

57 *Keep on trucking* Brian Grow and Mark Hosenball, "Special Report: In Cyberspy vs. Cyberspy, China has the Edge," Reuters, April 14, 2011, http://www.reuters.com/article/2011/04/14/us-china-usa-cyberespionage-idUSTRE73D24220110414.

58 *compromised with hidden instructions* Dmitri Alperovitch, *Revealed: Operation Shady RAT* (white paper, Santa Clara, CA: McAfee, 2011), p. 3.

58 *Admiral James Stavridis* James Lewis, "How Spies Used Facebook to Steal NATO Chiefs' Details," *Telegraph*, March 10, 2012, http://www.telegraph.co.uk/technology/9136029/How-spies-used-Facebook-to-steal-Nato-chiefs-details.html.

58 *seek out sensitive information* Alperovitch, *Revealed*, p. 3.

59 *eavesdrop on conversations* Grow and Hosenball, "In Cyberspy vs. Cyberspy, China Has the Edge."

59 *"phone home" phase* Ibid.

59 *thermostat and printer* "Resisting Chaos," Strategic News Service, February 4, 2013.

HOW DO WE KEEP THE BAD GUYS OUT? THE BASICS OF COMPUTER DEFENSE

60 *110 million different species* Pat Calhoun, "The Next Cyber War Is Already in Progress: Security Expert," *Hacking America* (blog), CNBC, February 27, 2013, http://www.cnbc.com/id/100501836.

61 *0.34 percent of signatures* Sang Kil Cha, Iulian Moraru, Jiyong Jang, et al., "SplitScreen: Enabling Efficient, Distributed Malware Detection," *Journal of Communications and Networks* 13, no. 2 (April 2011): pp. 187–200, http://users.ece.cmu.edu/~sangkilc/papers/nsdi10-cha.pdf.

61 *12 new detections resulted* Ed Bott, "The Malware Numbers Game: How Many Viruses Are Out There?" *ZDNet*, April 15, 2012, http://www.zdnet.com/blog/bott/the-malware-numbers-game-how-many-viruses-are-out-there/4783.

63 *rather snazzy paperweights* Katie Hafner, "Altered iPhones Freeze Up," *New York Times*, September 29, 2007, http://www.nytimes.com/2007/09/29/technology/29iphone.html.

64 *operations network successfully separated* House Committee on Oversight and Government Reform, Subcommittee on National Security, Homeland Defense, and Foreign Operations; Cybersecurity: Assessing the Immediate Threat to the United States, testimony of Sean McGurk, Director of the National Cybersecurity and Communications Integration Center, May 26, 2011, http://oversight.house.gov/wp-content/uploads/2012/04/5-25-11-Subcommittee-on-National-Security-Homeland-Defense-and-Forei gn-Operations-Hearing-Transcript.pdf.

64 *"skating on thin ice"* Center for a New American Security conference, June 13, 2013, Washington, DC.

64 *"a couple of minutes of peace and quiet"* Dave Paresh, "Some Companies Looking at Retaliating against Cyber Attackers," *Los Angeles Times*, May 31, 2013.

WHO IS THE WEAKEST LINK? HUMAN FACTORS

65 *US presidential helicopter* Loren B. Thompson, "Cyber Remedies Likely to Limit Liberties," Lexington Institute, April 27, 2010, http://www.lexingtoninstitute.org/cyber-remedies-likely-to-limit-liberties?a=1&c=1129.

66 *lessons of proper caution* David A. Fulghum, "Cross-Training: Cyber-Recruiters Look for Specialists with Expertise in Many Fields," *Aviation Week & Space Technology* 173, no. 18 (May 23, 2011): p. 48.

PART II: WHY IT MATTERS
WHAT IS THE MEANING OF CYBERATTACK? THE IMPORTANCE OF TERMS AND FRAMEWORKS

67 *meeting of diplomats* Neil King, Jr. and Jason Dean, "Untranslatable Word in U.S. Aide's Speech Leaves Beijing Baffled," *Wall Street Journal*, December 7, 2005.

68 *"millions of cyber attacks"* Testimony before the House Armed Services Subcommittee, Cyberspace Operations Testimony, testimony of Keith Alexander, Commander of US Cyber Command, September 23, 2010.

68 *Internet-related technology* See, for example, William Lynn, "Defending a New Domain," *Foreign Affairs* 89, no. 5 (October 2010), http://www.foreignaffairs.com/articles/66552/william-j-lynn-iii/defending-a-new-domain.

68 *"alter, disrupt, deceive, degrade, or destroy"* William A. Owens, Kenneth W. Dam, and Herbert S. Lin, eds., *Technology, Policy, Law, and Ethics Regarding U.S. Acquisition and Use of Cyberattack Capabilities*, Committee on Offensive Information Warfare, National Research Council (Washington, DC: National Academies Press, 2009).

69 *two fundamental differences* Ibid.

70 *"scale and impact are absolutely key"* Dmitri Alperovitch, "Deterrence in Cyberspace: Debating the Right Strategy with Ralph Langner and Dmitri Alperovitch," remarks at the Brookings Institution, Washington, DC, September 20, 2011, http://www.brookings.edu/~/media/events/2011/9/20%20cyberspace%20deterrence/20110920_cyber_defense.

70 *"something we want to try to deter"* Ibid.

70 *designs of combat aircraft stolen* Christopher Drew, "Stolen Data Is Tracked to Hacking at Lockheed," *New York Times*, June 3, 2011, http://www.nytimes.com/2011/06/04/technology/04security.html.

72 *an essential human right* Hillary Rodham Clinton, "Remarks on Internet Freedom," remarks at the Newseum, January 21, 2010, http://www.state.gov/secretary/rm/2010/01/135519.htm.

72 *free flow* Joseph Menn, "Agreement on Cybersecurity 'Badly Needed,'" *Financial Times*, October 12, 2011.

72 *undermine state stability* Alperovitch, "Deterrence in Cyberspace." Alperovitch references discussions with the Chinese Foreign Ministry, where they declared that rumor-spreading on Facebook that causes social unrest in China would be considered a cyberattack.

72 *Western "information war"* Richard Fontaine and Will Rogers, "Internet Freedom and Its Discontents: Navigating the Tensions with Cyber Security," in *America's Cyber Future: Security and Prosperity in the Information Age*, vol. 2, edited by Kristin M. Lord and Travis Shard (Washington, DC: Center for a New American Security, June 2011), p. 152.

WHODUNIT? THE PROBLEM OF ATTRIBUTION

72 *"Holy Grail of a botnet"* Mark Bowden, *Worm: The First Digital World War* (New York: Atlantic Monthly Press, 2011), p. 228.

73 *whoever designed it was Ukrainian* For more on this, see Bowden, *Worm*.

73 *over 12 million computers* Teresa Larraz, "Spanish 'Botnet' Potent Enough to Attack Country: Police," Reuters, March 3, 2010, http://www.reuters.com/article/2010/03/03/us-crime-hackers-idUSTRE6214ST20100303.

74 *deniable, but directed, attack* Jeff Carr, "Russia/Georgia Cyber War—Findings and Analysis," Project Grey Goose, October 17, 2008, http://www.scribd.com/doc/6967393/Project-Grey-Goose-Phase-I-Report.

74 *"Attacks can be 'crowd sourced'"* Bryan Krekel, "Capability of the People's Republic of China to Conduct Cyber Warfare and Computer Network Exploitation," Northrop Grumman Corporation, October 9, 2009.

75 *2008 Olympics in Beijing* Brian Grow and Mark Hosenball, "Special Report: In Cyberspy vs. Cyberspy, China Has the Edge," Reuters, April 14, 2011, http://www.reuters.com/article/2011/04/14/us-china-usa-cyberespionage-idUSTRE73D24220110414.

75 *compelling proof Commonwealth vs. Michael M. O'Laughlin,* 04-P-48 (A. C. MA 2005), http://www.truthinjustice.org/o'laughlin.htm.

75 *"We could not poinpoint the attacks"* Ronald Deibert, "Tracking the Emerging Arms Race in Cyberspace," *Bulletin of the Atomic Scientists* 67, no. 1 (January–February 2011): pp. 1–8, http://bos.sagepub.com/content/67/1/1.full.

76 *lacked "absolute certainty"* Office of the National Counterintelligence Executive, "Foreign Spies Stealing US Economic Secrets in Cyberspace," October 2011, http://www.ncix.gov/publications/reports/fecie_all/Foreign_Economic_Collection_2011.pdf, accessed August 11, 2013.

76 *"Harry Pota"* "'Harry Pota' and the Wizards of Unit 61398," *Australian*, February 23, 2013, p. 1.

WHAT IS HACTIVISM?

78 *"World Wide Web War I"* Craig S. Smith, "May 6–12; The First World Hacker War," *New York Times*, May 13, 2001, http://www.nytimes.com/2001/05/13/weekinreview/may-6-12-the-first-world-hacker-war.html.

78 *Ohio high schools* Jeffrey Carr, *Inside Cyber Warfare* (Sebastopol, CA: O'Reilly Media, 2009), p. 2.

78 *"potentially harmful consequences"* Nancy R. Mead, Eric D. Hough, and Theodore R. Steney III, "Security Quality Requirements Engineering (SQUARE) Methodology CMU/SEI-2005-TR-009," Software Engineering Institute, Carnegie Mellon University, Pittsburgh, PA, November 2005, http://www.cert.org/archive/pdf/05tr009.pdf, accessed August 11, 2013.

79 *Stop Huntingdon Animal Cruelty* Chris Maag, "America's #1 Threat," *Mother Jones*, January–February 2006, http://www.motherjones.com/politics/2006/01/americas-1-threat.

79 *caterers and cleaners* Kate Sheppard, "Are Animal Rights Activists Terrorists?" *Mother Jones*, December 21, 2011, http://motherjones.com/environment/2011/12/are-animal-rights-activists-terrorists.

79 *"every critical relationship"* Christopher Schroeder, "The Unprecedented Economic Risks of Network Insecurity," in *America's Cyber Future: Security and Prosperity in the Information Age*, vol. 2, edited by Kristin M. Lord and Travis Shard (Washington, DC: Center for a New American Security, June 2011), p. 172.

80 *sprayed in the eyes* Senate Committee on Environment and Public Works, "Eco-terrorism Specifically Examining the Earth Liberation Front and the Animal Liberation Front," testimony of John E. Lewis, Deputy Assistant Director, Federal Bureau of Investigation, May 18, 2005, http://epw.senate.gov/hearing_statements.cfm?id=237817.

FOCUS: WHO IS ANONYMOUS?

81 *"a world of hurt"* Spencer Ackerman, "'Paranoia Meter' Is HBGary's Plot to Find the Pentagon's Next WikiLeaker," *Danger Room* (blog), *Wired*, April 3, 2011, http://www.wired.com/dangerroom/2011/04/paranoia-meter-hbgarys-plot-to-find-the-next-pentagon-wikileaker/.

81 *"don't mess with Anonymous"* Ibid.

81 *"embarrassing laundry"* "Aaron Barr: Pervert or Vigilante?" *Crowdleaks*, last modified March 24, 2011, http://crowdleaks.org/aaron-barr-pervert-or-vigilante/.

81   "*beatdown*"   Quinn Norton, "How Anonymous Chooses Targets," *Threat Level* (blog), *Wired*, July 3, 2012, http://www.wired.com/threatlevel/2012/07/ff_anonymous/all/.

82   "*Anyone who wants to can be Anonymous*"   Chris Landers, "Serious Business: Anonymous Takes On Scientology (and Doesn't [sic] Afraid of Anything)," *Baltimore City Paper*, April 2, 2008, http://www.citypaper.com/columns/story.asp?id=15543.

82   "*ultra-coordinated motherfuckery*"   Norton, "How Anonymous Chooses Targets."

82   *supposedly secretive group*   Mike Isaac, "Facebook and Twitter Suspend Operation Payback Accounts," *Forbes*, December 8, 2010, http://blogs.forbes.com/mikeisaac/2010/12/08/facebook-and-twitter-suspend-operation-payback-accounts/.

82   "*Internet vigilante group*"   Gus Kim, "Internet Justice?" Global News, CanWest Global Communications, December 8, 2007.

83   *websites knocked offline*   Matthew Lasar, "KISS Frontman on P2P: Sue Everybody. Take Their Homes, Their Cars," *Ars Technica*, December 20, 2010, http://arstechnica.com/tech-policy/news/2010/10/kiss-frontman-we-should-have-sued-them-all.ars.

84   "*Two clandestine non-state groups*"   Paul Rexton Kan, "Cyberwar in the Underworld: Anonymous versus Los Zetas in Mexico," *Yale Journal of International Affairs*, February 26, 2013, http://yalejournal.org/2013/02/26/cyberwar-in-the-underworld-anonymous-versus-los-zetas-in-mexico/.

84   "*noisy political demonstration*"   "WikiLeaks Cyber Backlash All Bark, No Bite: Experts," *Vancouver Sun*, December 11, 2010.

84   "*this is Lexington*"   Steven Swinford, "WikiLeaks Hackers Threaten British Government," *Daily Telegraph*, December 10, 2010, http://www.telegraph.co.uk/news/worldnews/wikileaks/8193210/WikiLeaks-hackers-threaten-British-Government.html.

THE CRIMES OF TOMORROW, TODAY: WHAT IS CYBERCRIME?

85   "*crime which may exist in the future*"   Neil Ardley, *School, Work and Play (World of Tomorrow)* (New York: Franklin Watts, 1981), pp. 26–27.

85   *unique to electronic networks*   European Commission, "Towards a General Policy on the Fight against Cyber Crime," May 2007, http://europa.eu/legislation_summaries/justice_freedom_security/fight_against_organised_crime/l14560_en.htm, accessed August 11, 2013.

86   *clumsy fingers*   Tyler Moore and Benjamin Edelman, "Measuring the Perpetrators and Funders of Typosquatting," in *14th International Conference on Financial Cryptography and Data Security*, Tenerife, Spain, January 25–28, 2010, http://link.springer.com/chapter/10.1007%2F978-3-642-14577-3_15?LI=true.

87   *$100 million business*   Brett Stone-Gross, Ryan Abman, Richard A. Kemmerer, et al., "The Underground Economy of Fake Antivirus Software," in *10th Workshop on the Economics of Information Security*, Fairfax, VA, June 14–15, 2011, http://www.cs.ucsb.edu/~chris/research/doc/weis11_fakeav.pdf.

87   *opiate painkillers*   Damon McCoy, Andreas Pitsillidis, Grant Jordan, et al., "Pharmaleaks: Understanding the Business of Online Pharmaceutical Affiliate Programs," in *Proceedings of the 21st USENIX Conference on Security Symposium*, Bellevue, WA, August 8–10, 2012, http://cseweb.ucsd.edu/~savage/papers/UsenixSec12.pdf.

88   "*wagers for the Super Bowl*"   Gregory J. Rattray and Jason Healey, "Non-state Actors and Cyber Conflict," in *America's Cyber Future: Security and Prosperity in the Information Age*, vol. 2, edited by Kristin M. Lord and Travis Shard (Washington, DC: Center for a New American Security, 2011), p. 71.

88   "*online betting houses*"   Brian Phillips, "Soccer's New Match-Fixing Scandal," *Grantland*, February 7, 2013, http://www.grantland.com/story/_/id/8924593/match-fixing-soccer.

88   *American free speech protections*   European Commission, "Towards a General Policy on the Fight against Cyber Crime."

88 *"100 different sources of data"* Ross Anderson, Chris Barton, Rainer Bohme, et al., "Measuring the Cost of Cybercrime," presented at the 11th Annual Workshop on the Economics of Information Security WEIS 2012, Berlin, June 25–26, 2012, http://weis2012.econinfosec.org/papers/Anderson_WEIS2012.pdf.

89 *bank or paint maker* Dave Paresh, "Some Companies Looking at Retaliating against Cyber Attackers," *LA Times*, May 31, 2013.

89 *more useful endeavors* Ibid.

89 *"Million-dollar crimes"* James Andrew Lewis, "The Threat," *Government Executive* 43, no. 10 (August 15, 2011): p. 19.

89 *"credit card fraud scheme"* *United States of America v. Rogelio Hackett Jr.*, no. 1:11CR96 (E.D. Va.) April 21, 2011.

90 *a mere $200* McAfee presentation to authors, 2011.

90 *"Selection of countries is free"* Thomas Holt, "Exploring the Economics of Malicious Software Markets," National Institutes of Health presentation, 2011.

90 *"toleration if not support"* Ibid.

91 *"clutching a computer cassette"* Ardley, *School, Work and Play*, pp. 26–27.

SHADY RATS AND CYBERSPIES: WHAT IS CYBER ESPIONAGE?

91 *exfiltrating key data* Dmitri Alperovitch, *Revealed: Operation Shady RAT* (white paper, Santa Clara, CA: McAfee, 2011), p. 3.

92 *2008 Beijing Olympics* Ibid., p. 6.

92 *"high-speed connection"* Lewis, "The Threat," p. 18.

93 *digital espionage* Ibid.

93 *Hainan Island in China* Krekel, "Capability of the People's Republic of China to Conduct Cyber Warfare and Computer Network Exploitation."

93 *F-35 fighter jet's design* Lewis, "The Threat," p. 18.

93 *midst of a test flight* Siobhan Gorman, August Cole, and Yochi Dreazen, "Computer Spies Breach Fighter-Jet Project," *Wall Street Journal*, April 21, 2009, http://online.wsj.com/article/SB124027491029837401.html.

94 *"it will kill a lot of us"* Jason Healey, "The Cyber 9/12 Project: The Role of Media in a Cyber Crisis," remarks at the Atlantic Council, Washington DC, June 1, 2012.

94 *"indigenous industry"* Mark Clayton, "The New Cyber Arms Race," *Christian Science Monitor*, March 7, 2011, http://www.csmonitor.com/USA/Military/2011/0307/The-new-cyber-arms-race.

94 *"Fortune Global 2000 firms"* Alperovitch, *Revealed*, p. 2.

94 *$630 iPhone* Horace Dediu, "An iPhone Profit Paradox," *Business Spectator*, February 29, 2012, http://www.businessspectator.com.au/article/2012/2/28/technology/iphone-profit-paradox.

94 *"easiest way to innovate"* Grow and Hosenball, "Special Report."

95 *furniture in China* David Leonhardt, "The Real Problem with China," *New York Times*, January 11, 2011.

95 *direct and veiled accusations* "China Denies Pentagon Cyber-Raid," BBC News, September 4, 2007, http://news.bbc.co.uk/2/hi/6977533.stm.

95 *18 have direct ties* Personal data set from Economic Espionage Act prosecutions.

95 *"96 percent"* Tony Romm, "Report Fuels China CyberSpying Concerns," *Politico*, April 23, 2013, http://www.politico.com/story/2013/04/china-industrial-cyberspy-cybersecurity-espionage-90464.html.

95 *"Cold War mentality"* Ibid.

95 *"unprecedented transfer of wealth"* Alperovitch, *Revealed*, p. 3.

95 *too small to be fatal* Lewis, "The Threat," p. 18.

96 *"death by a thousand cuts"* James Fallows, "Cyber Warriors," *Atlantic*, March 2011.

96 *CrowdStrike* Joseph Menn, "Security Firm CrowdStrike Hires U.S. Air Force Info-Warfare Expert," *Chicago Tribune*, October 29, 2012, http://articles.chicagotribune.com/2012-10-29/business/sns-rt-us-cybersecurity-offensivebre89s17g-20121029_1_crowdstrike-steven-chabinsky-alperovitch.

HOW AFRAID SHOULD WE BE OF CYBERTERRORISM?

96   *"clandestine agents"*   Margaret Rouse, "Cyberterrorism," *Search Security*, May 2010, http://searchsecurity.techtarget.com/definition/cyberterrorism, accessed August 11, 2013.

96   *simulated catastrophic failure*   Scott W. Beidleman, "Defining and Deterring Cyber War," strategy research project, US Army War College, 2009, p. 6.

96   *Guantánamo Bay*   Ibid., p. 7.

97   *"as much clarity as cybersecurity"*   Cyber Terrain Conference, Spy Museum, Washington, DC, May 18, 2011.

97   *Mohmedou Ould Slahi*   Rattray and Healey, "Non-state Actors and Cyber Conflict," p. 72.

97   *1700 percent*   General Martin Dempsey, "Defending the Nation at Network Speed," remarks at the Brookings Institution, Washington, DC, June 27, 2013.

97   *less than a week*   Ken Dilanian, "Virtual War a Real Threat," *Los Angeles Times*, March 28, 2011, p. 28.

97   *"fundamental way of life"*   Cyber Terrain Conference, Spy Museum, Washington, DC, May 18, 2011.

98   *"drinking Red Bull"*   Spencer Ackerman, "Pentagon Deputy: What If al-Qaeda Got Stuxnet?" *Danger Room* (blog), *Wired*, February 15, 2011, http://www.wired.com/dangerroom/2011/02/pentagon-deputy-what-if-al-qaeda-got-stuxnet/.

98   *"Glen Canyon and Hoover Dams"*   George R. Lucas, Jr., "Permissible Preventive Cyberwar: Restricting Cyber Conflict to Justified Military Targets," presentation at the Society of Philosophy and Technology Conference, University of North Texas, May 28, 2011.

99   *"cyber-sophistication"*   Joseph S. Nye, "Power and National Security in Cyberspace," in *America's Cyber Future: Security and Prosperity in the Information Age*, vol. 2, edited by Kristin M. Lord and Travis Shard (Washington, DC: Center for a New American Security, June 2011), p. 16.

SO HOW DO TERRORISTS ACTUALLY USE THE WEB?

101   *$70 a month*   Joby Warrick, "Extremist Web Sites Are Using U.S. Hosts," *Washington Post*, April 9, 2009, p. A01.

101   *Osama bin Laden's lieutenants*   Jacob Fenton, "Student's Web Site Hacked by al-Qaida," *Vanguard*, April 8, 2003, http://psuvanguard.com/uncategorized/students-web-site-hacked-by-al-qaida/.

102   *from Iraq to Afghanistan*   Department of Homeland Security, "Domestic Improvised Explosive Device (IED) Threat Overview," PDF briefing, http://info.publicintelligence.net/DHS-DomesticIED.pdf, accessed January 14, 2013.

102   *four of the helicopters*   "Islamists Destroyed US Helicopters Found in Online Photos," Yahoo! News, March 16, 2012, http://news.yahoo.com/insurgents-destroyed-us-helicopters-found-online-photos-165609778.html.

102   *Fort Benning, Georgia*   Cheryl Rodewig, "Geotagging Posts Security Risks," US Army, March 7, 2012, http://www.army.mil/article/75165/Geotagging_poses_security_risks/.

WHAT ABOUT CYBER COUNTERTERRORISM?

103   *"a link for download"*   Adam Rawnsley, "'Spyware' Incident Spooks Jihadi Forum," *Danger Room* (blog), *Wired*, September 1, 2011, http://www.wired.com/dangerroom/2011/09/jihadi-spyware/.

103   *for terrorists to target and kill*   Ibid.

104   *RAND Corporation*   Warrick, "Extremist Web Sites Are Using U.S. Hosts," p. A01.

105   *"mysteriously resurfaced"*   Rawnsley, "'Spyware' Incident Spooks Jihadi Forum."

105   *Mujahideen Secrets 2.0*   Ibid.

105   *"housewife-next-door" genre*   Fenton, "Student's Web Site Hacked by al-Qaida."

Security Risk or Human Right? Foreign Policy and the Internet

106 *Dutch government in 2011* Loek Essers, "Dutch Minister Changes Patriot Act Stance," *Computerworld*, September 21, 2011, http://www.computerworld.com/s/article/9220165/Dutch_minister_changes_Patriot_Act_stance.

106 *"regardless of frontier"* Fontaine and Rogers, "Internet Freedom and Its Discontents," p. 148.

107 *"a church or a labor hall"* Ibid.

107 *Nazi memorabilia* "France Bans Internet Nazi Auctions," BBC News, May 23, 2000, http://news.bbc.co.uk/2/hi/europe/760782.stm.

107 *blackout of Wikipedia* Allan A. Friedman, "Cybersecurity in the Balance: Weighing the Risks of the PROTECT IP Act and the Stop Online Piracy Act," remarks at the Brookings Institution, Washington, DC, November 15, 2011, http://www.brookings.edu/papers/2011/1115_cybersecurity_friedman.aspx.

Focus: What Is Tor and Why Does Peeling Back the Onion Matter?

108 *surveillance by the NSA* Kurt Opsahl, "Exactly How the NSA is Getting Away with Spying on US Citizens," *Gizmodo*, June 23, 2013, http://gizmodo.com/exactly-how-the-nsa-is-getting-away-with-spying-on-us-c-540606531?

108 *"36 million people"* John Sullivan, "2010 Free Software Awards Announced," Free Software Foundation, March 22, 2011, http://www.fsf.org/news/2010-free-software-awards-announced.

108 *"dark corner of the Internet"* "Monetarists Anonymous," *Economist*, September 29, 2012, http://www.economist.com/node/21563752?fb_action_ids=10152174673925385&fb_action_types=og.likes&fb_ref=scn%2Ffb_ec%2Fmonetarists_anonymous&fb_source=aggregation&fb_aggregation_id=246965925417366.

109 *endpoint of a conversation* The Tor Project, Inc., https://www.torproject.org/, accessed March 17, 2013.

109 *Tor built in* The Tor Project, Inc., "Tor Browser Bundle," https://www.torproject.org/projects/torbrowser.html.en, accessed March 17, 2013.

110 *circumvent each new technique* "How China Blocks the Tor Anonymity Network," *The Physics arXiv* (blog), MIT *Technology Review*, April 4, 2012, http://www.technology-review.com/view/427413/how-china-blocks-the-tor-anonymity-network/.

110 *Skype's importance* Hooman Mohajeri Moghaddam, Baiyu Li, Mohammad Derakhshani, et al., *Skypemorph: Protocol Obfuscation for Tor Bridges* (Waterloo, ON: University of Waterloo, 2010), http://cacr.uwaterloo.ca/techreports/2012/cacr2012-08.pdf.

Who Are Patriotic Hackers?

110 *"Russia is attacking Estonia"* "Statement by the Foreign Minister Urmas Paet," Estonian Foreign Ministry statement, May 1, 2007, http://www.epl.ee/news/eesti/statement-by-the-foreign-minister-urmas-paet.d?id=51085399.

110 *"carried out by my assistant"* R. Coulson, "Behind the Estonia Cyberattacks," Radio Free Europe, March 6, 2009, http://www.rferl.org/content/Behind_The_Estonia_Cyberattacks/1505613.html.

110 *Markov's young assistant* Charles Clover, "Kremlin-Backed Group behind Estonia Cyber Blitz," *Financial Times*, March 11, 2009, http://www.ft.com/cms/s/0/57536d5a-0ddc-11de-8ea3-0000779fd2ac.html.

111 *"anti-Fatherland" forces* J. R. Jones, "*Putin's Kiss*: The Kids Are Hard Right," *Chicago Reader*, March 7, 2012, http://www.chicagoreader.com/chicago/putins-kiss-the-kids-are-hard-right/Content?oid=5787547.

111 *"Nazism and liberalism"* Ibid.

111 *Russian intelligence* Carr, *Inside Cyber Warfare*, p. 3.

112 *"Cyber-space is everywhere"* Ian Traynor, "Russia Accused of Unleashing Cyberwar to Disable Estonia," *Guardian*, May 16, 2007, http://www.guardian.co.uk/world/2007/may/17/topstories3.russia.

112 *hacker magazine Xaker* Khatuna Mshvidobadze, "Is Russia on the Wrong Side of the Net?" *Jane's Defence Weekly* 48, no. 9 (March 2, 2011): p. 22.

112 *Syrian president Assad* Max Fisher and Jared Keller, "Syria's Digital Counter-revolutionaries," *Atlantic*, August 31, 2011, http://www.theatlantic.com/international/archive/2011/08/syrias-digital-counter-revolutionaries/244382/.

113 *hacker group Javaphile* Krekel, "Capability of the People's Republic of China to Conduct Cyber Warfare and Computer Network Exploitation."

113 *"Iranian Cyber Army"* Tim Stevens, "Breaching Protocol," *Janes Intelligence Review* 22, no. 3 (March 2010): pp. 8–13.

113 *170,000 members* Ibid.

114 *"computer network experts"* Krekel, "Capability of the People's Republic of China to Conduct Cyber Warfare and Computer Network Exploitation."

114 *200,000 members* Ibid.

FOCUS: WHAT WAS STUXNET?

115 *"indiscriminate and destructive"* Lucas, "Permissible Preventive Cyberwar." A study of the spread of Stuxnet was undertaken by a number of international computer security firms, including Symantec Corporation. Their report, "W32.Stuxnet Dossier," compiled by noted computer security experts Nicholas Falliere, Liam O'Murchu, and Eric Chien, and released in February 2011, showed that the main countries affected during the early days of the infection were Iran, Indonesia, and India: http://www.symantec.com/content/en/us/enterprise/media/security_response/whitepapers/w32_stuxnet_dossier.pdf, accessed August 11, 2013.

116 *lingering in the wild forever* Lucas, "Permissible Preventive Cyberwar."

117 *replacing the broken centrifuges* Mark Clayton, "How Stuxnet Cyber Weapon Targeted Iran Nuclear Plant," *Christian Science Monitor*, November 16, 2010, http://www.csmonitor.com/USA/2010/1116/How-Stuxnet-cyber-weapon-targeted-Iran-nuclear-plant.

117 *"Chinese water torture"* Ralph Langner, "Better than bunker busters: the virtual Chinese water torture," Langer.com, November 15, 2010, http://www.langner.com/en/2010/11/15/better-than-bunker-busters-the-virtual-chinese-water-torture/.

118 *"Olympic Games"* David Sanger, "Obama Order Sped Up Wave of Cyberattacks against Iran," *New York Times*, June 1, 2012, http://www.nytimes.com/2012/06/01/world/middleeast/obama-ordered-wave-of-cyberattacks-against-iran.html.

WHAT IS THE HIDDEN LESSON OF STUXNET? THE ETHICS OF CYBERWEAPONS

118 *"Its atomic bomb?"* "The FP Survey: The Internet," *Foreign Policy* (September–October 2011): p. 116.

118 *planes and nuclear reactors* Clayton, "How Stuxnet Cyber Weapon Targeted Iran Nuclear Plant."

118 *says Leslie Harris* "The FP Survey," p. 116.

119 *"civilian personnel and infrastructure"* Neil C. Rowe, "Ethics of Cyber War Attacks," in *Cyber Warfare and Cyber Terrorism*, edited by Lech J. Janczewski and Andrew M. Colarik (Hershey, PA: Information Science Reference, 2008), p. 109.

119 *"984 Siemens centrifuges"* Ibid.

120 *"Pandora's box"* Mark Clayton, "From the Man Who Discovered Stuxnet, Dire Warnings One Year Later," *Christian Science Monitor*, September 22, 2011, http://www.csmonitor.com/USA/2011/0922/From-the-man-who-discovered-Stuxnet-dire-warnings-one-year-later.

"Cyberwar, Ugh, What Are Zeros and Ones Good For?": Defining Cyberwar

120 *"hereby formally declared"* Historical Resources about the Second World War, "Text of Declaration of War on Bulgaria—June 5, 1942," August 7, 2008, http://historicalresources. wordpress.com/2008/08/07/text-of-declaration-of-war-on-bulgaria-june-5-1942/.

120 *War on Christmas* Anna Dimond, "O'Reilly: 'War' on Christmas Part of 'Secular Progressive Agenda' That Includes 'Legalization of Narcotics, Euthanasia, Abortion at Will, Gay Marriage,'" *Media Matters for America*, November 21, 2005, http://mediamatters. org/video/2005/11/21/oreilly-war-on-christmas- part-of-secular-progre/134262.

121 *"significant destruction"* Aram Roston, "U.S.: Laws of War Apply to Cyber Attacks," *Defense News*, September 18, 2012, http://www.defensenews.com/article/20120918/ DEFREG02/309180012/U-S-Laws-War-Apply-Cyber-Attacks.

121 *"intensive cyberconflict with us"* Clayton, "The New Cyber Arms Race."

121 *"without triggering a shooting war"* David Sanger, "A New Cold War in Cyberspace, Tests US Times to China," *New York Times*, February 25, 2013, http://www. nytimes.com/2013/02/25/world/asia/us-confronts-cyber-cold-war-with-china. html?pagewanted=2&_r=1&partner=rss&emc=rss.

A War by Any Other Name? The Legal Side of Cyber Conflict

122 *"an attack against them all"* North Atlantic Treaty Organization, "The North Atlantic Treaty," April 4, 1949, http://www.nato.int/cps/en/natolive/official_texts_17120.htm, accessed August 11, 2013.

122 *honoring Russian soldiers* Beidleman, "Defining and Deterring Cyber War," p. 4.

122 *NATO was obliged to defend* "Estonia Hit by 'Moscow Cyber War,'" BBC News, May 17, 2007, ttp://news.bbc.co.uk/2/hi/europe/6665145.stm.

123 *short film about the episode* "NATO tegi filmi Eesti kübersõjast," *Postimees*, March 28, 2009, http://www.postimees.ee/100125/nato-tegi-filmi-eesti-kubersojast/.

123 *"territorial integrity...of a state"* United Nations, "Charter of the United Nations," June 6, 1945, http://www.un.org/en/documents/charter/chapter1.shtml.

123 *Tallinn Manual* Michael N. Schmitt, ed., *Tallinn Manual on the International Law Applicable to Cyber Warfare* (New York: Cambridge University Press, 2013), http://issuu. com/nato_ccd_coe/docs/tallinnmanual?mode=embed&layout=http%3A%2F%2Fskin. issuu.com%2Fv%2Flight%2Flayout.xml&showFlipBtn=true.

123 *reports* Foreign Policy *magazine* Josh Reed, "US Government: Laws of War Apply to Cyber Conflict," *Killer Apps* (blog), *Foreign Policy*, March 26, 2013, http://killerapps.for-eignpolicy.com/posts/2013/03/25/us_govt_laws_of_war_apply_to_cyber_conflict.

124 *Charles Dunlap* Siobhan Gorman and Julian Barnes, "Cyber Combat: Act of War," *Wall Street Journal*, May 31, 2011, http://online.wsj.com/article/SB10001424052702304563104576355623135782718.html?mod=WSJ_hp_LEFTTopStories.

124 *equivalent to the use of guns* Beidleman, "Defining and Deterring Cyber War," p. 13.

124 *"more like a cyber riot"* Shaun Waterman, "Analysis: Who Cyber Smacked Estonia?" United Press International, March 11, 2009.

125 *directness and measurability* Owens, Dam, and Lin, *Technology, Policy, Law, and Ethics Regarding U.S. Acquisition and Use of Cyberattack Capabilities*.

126 *"politics by different means"* Carl von Clausewitz, *On War*, edited by Michael Howard and Peter Paret (Princeton, NJ: Princeton University Press, 1976).

126 *bend the other to its will* Thomas G. Mahnken, "Cyberwar and Cyber Warfare," in *America's Cyber Future: Security and Prosperity in the Information Age*, vol. 2, edited by Kristin M. Lord and Travis Shard (Washington, DC: Center for a New American Security, June 2011), p. 59.

126 *"It's always a judgment"* Jennifer Martinez, "DOD Could Use Force in Cyber War," *Politico*, July 15, 2011, http://www.politico.com/news/stories/0711/59035.html.

WHAT MIGHT A "CYBERWAR" ACTUALLY LOOK LIKE? COMPUTER NETWORK OPERATIONS

127 *confirm the Israeli suspicions* Erich Follath and Holger Stark, "How Israel Destroyed Syria's Al Kibar Nuclear Reactor," *Der Spiegel*, November 2, 2009, http://www.spiegel. de/international/world/the-story-of-operation-orchard-how-israel-destroyed-syria-s-al-kibar-nuclear-reactor-a-658663-2.html.

127 *Israeli jets flew* Sally Adee, "The Hunt for the Kill Switch," *IEEE Spectrum*, May 1, 2008, http://spectrum.ieee.org/semiconductors/design/the-hunt-for-the-kill-switch/0.

128 *Solar Sunrise* Beidleman, "Defining and Deterring Cyber War," p. 3.

128 *enemy's use of cyberspace* Noah Shachtman, "Darpa Looks to Make Cyberwar Routine with Secret 'Plan X,'" *Danger Room* (blog), *Wired*, August 21, 2012, http://www.wired. com/dangerroom/2012/08/plan-x/.

128 *$110 million program* Ibid.

128 *"a new type of warfare"* "A New Kind of Warfare," *New York Times*, September 9, 2012, http://www.nytimes.com/2012/09/10/opinion/a-new-kind-of-warfare.html?_r=2&hp&.

128 *"Western Pacific theater"* Krekel, "Capability of the People's Republic of China to Conduct Cyber Warfare and Computer Network Exploitation."

129 *prototype robotic fighter jet* Dan Elliott, "Glitch Shows How Much US Military Relies on GPS," *Phys.org*, June 1, 2010, http://phys.org/news194621073.html.

129 *inside the enemy's mind* Owens, Dam, and Lin, *Technology, Policy, Law, and Ethics Regarding U.S. Acquisition and Use of Cyberattack Capabilities.*

131 *killed 75 people* David A. Fulghum, "Digital Deluge," *Aviation Week & Space Technology* 173, no. 18 (May 23, 2011).

132 *new can of worms* Fontaine and Rogers, "Internet Freedom and Its Discontents," p. 155.

FOCUS: WHAT IS THE US MILITARY APPROACH TO CYBERWAR?

133 *once sophisticated code* US CERT, "Vulnerability Note VU#836068," December 31, 2008, http://www.kb.cert.org/vuls/id/836068.

134 *"double-hatted"* Zachary Fryer-Biggs, "U.S. Cyber Security Gets Aggressive," *Defense News* 26, no. 34 (September 19, 2011): p. 6.

134 *no decorations or badges* Ibid.

134 *discussed "cyber" 147 times* "Seven Things You Didn't Know about the DoD Budget," *Foreign Policy*, April 12, 2013, http://e-ring.foreignpolicy.com/posts/2013/04/12/seven_things_you_didnt_know_about_the_dod_budget_request.

134 *set to effectively double* Tony Cappacio, "Pentagon Five Year Cybersecurity Plan Seeks $23 Billion," Bloomberg, June 10, 2013, http://www.bloomberg.com/news/2013-06-10/pentagon-five-year-cybersecurity-plan-seeks-23-billion.html.

135 *"admin tech business"* Fryer-Biggs, "U.S. Cyber Security Gets Aggressive," p. 6.

135 *30 pages* Gorman and Barnes, "Cyber Combat."

135 *three types of cyber forces* Ellen Nakashima, "Pentagon to Boost Cybersecurity Forces," *Washington Post*, January 27, 2013.

135 *William Lynn publicly talked* William J. Lynn, "Remarks at the Defense Information Technology Acquisition Summit," remarks at the Grand Hyatt, Washington, DC, November 12, 2009.

136 *"do things offensively"* Fryer-Biggs, "U.S. Cyber Security Gets Aggressive," p. 6.

136 *"we can do better"* Seymour M. Hersh, "The Online Threat," *New Yorker*, November 1, 2010, http://www.newyorker.com/reporting/2010/11/01/101101fa_fact_hersh.

136 *"which could merit retaliation"* Gorman and Barnes, "Cyber Combat."

136 *"one of your smokestacks"* Ibid.

136 *workable in execution* Owens, Dam, and Lin, *Technology, Policy, Law, and Ethics Regarding U.S. Acquisition and Use of Cyberattack Capabilities.*

136   *"Absolute, unambiguous technical proof"*   Ibid.

137   *2.4 times as much*   Jim Michaels, "Pentagon Expands Cyber-Attack Capabilities," *USA Today* April 22, 2013, http://www.militarytimes.com/article/20130421/NEWS/304210016/Pentagon-expands-cyber-attack-capabilities.

137   *"protecting supply chains"*   Gary McGraw and Nathaniel Fick, "Separating Threat from the Hype: What Washington Needs to Know about Cyber Security," in *America's Cyber Future: Security and Prosperity in the Information Age*, vol. 2, edited by Kristin M. Lord and Travis Shard (Washington, DC: Center for a New American Security, June 2011), p. 48.

137   *"bad at defense"*   Senior US military official, interview with authors, April 2011.

137   *months after it had been decided*   "Obama Orders US to Draw Up Overseas Target List for Cyber-Attacks," *Guardian*, June 7, 2013, http://www.guardian.co.uk/world/2013/jun/07/obama-china-targets-cyber-overseas.

138   *"knock the s**t out of them"*   Joseph S. Nye, Jr., "Nuclear Lessons for Cyber Security?" *Strategic Studies Quarterly* 5, no. 4 (Winter 2011): p. 26.

FOCUS: WHAT IS THE CHINESE APPROACH TO CYBERWAR?

138   *"most threatening actor in cyberspace"*   Tony Capaccio, "China Most Threatening Cyberspace Force, U.S. Panel Says," *Bloomberg*, November 5, 2012, http://www.bloomberg.com/news/2012-11-05/china-most-threatening-cyberspace-force-u-s-panel-says.html.

138   *"active and persistent"*   Office of the National Counterintelligence Executive, "Foreign Spies Stealing US Economic Secrets in Cyberspace."

138   *"No. 1 Cyber Threat"*   Bill Gertz, "Cyber Spies Spotted," *Washington Free Beacon*, October 26, 2012, http://freebeacon.com/cyber-spies-spotted/.

138   *clearly placed China*   Department of Defense, "Department of Defense Strategy for Operating in Cyberspace," July 2011, http://timemilitary.files.wordpress.com/2011/07/d20110714cyber.pdf, accessed August 11, 2013.

138   *digital echo*   David Ignatius, "Cold War Feeling on Cybersecurity," *Real Clear Politics*, August 26, 2010, http://www.realclearpolitics.com/articles/2010/08/26/cold_war_feeling_on_cybersecurity_106900.html.

139   *"Cold War mentality"*   "China Denies Pentagon Cyber-Raid," BBC News.

139   *more frequently under attack*   An example is "China was accused time and again for launching cyber attacks abroad but there was never any solid proof. Actually, China has become a victim of such repeated claims." Su Hao, an expert on international security at the China Foreign Affairs University, in Ai Yang, "Nation Needs 'More Internet Security,'" *China Daily*, December 29, 2010.

139   *largest number of cyberattacks*   Yang, "Nation Needs 'More Internet Security.'"

139   *80 percent annually*   S. Smithson, "China Open to Cyber-Attack," *Washington Times*, March 17, 2011, http://www.washingtontimes.com/news/2011/mar/17/china-open-to-cyber-attack/?page=all, accessed September 26, 2011.

139   *10 to 19 million*   "著名IT杂志称：中国已成为黑客攻击热门目标 (Famous IT Magazine Claims: China Is a Heated Target for Hackers)," *Renmin wang*, http://it.people.com.cn/GB/42891/42894/3308326.html, accessed September 2, 2011.

139   *foreign computer hackers*   Tim Stevens, "Breaching Protocol," *Janes Intelligence Review* 22, no. 3 (March 2010): pp. 8–13.

139   *"state-sponsored espionage"*   James Mulvenon, e-mail to authors, March 21, 2013.

139   *Su Hao*   Yang, "Nation Needs 'More Internet Security.'"

139   *cyberattacks from the United States*   "中国是"间谍软件"最大受害国 美国攻击最多 (China Is the Biggest Victim of Spyware, Most Attacks Origin from U.S.)," *Xinhua News*, April 10, 2009, http://news.xinhuanet.com/mil/2009-04/10/content_11163263.htm, accessed September 26, 2011.

139   *90,000 times*   Paul Mazor, "China Alleges Cyberattacks Originated in U.S.," *Wall Street Journal*, March 1, 2013, http://online.wsj.com/article/SB10001424127887323293704578331832012056800?mg=reno64-wsj.html?dsk=y.

139 *20 of the top 50* Noah Shachtman, "Pirates of the ISPs," Brookings Institution, June 2011, http://www.brookings.edu/~/media/Files/rc/papers/2011/0725_cybersecurity_shachtman/0725_cybersecurity_shachtman.pdf, accessed August 11, 2013.

140 *"biggest villain in our age"* "China 'Gravely Concerned' on Cybersnooping by US, Called World's 'Biggest Villain,'" *South China Morning Post,* June 23, 2013, http://www.scmp.com/news/china/article/1267204/us-cyber-snooping-makes-it-worlds-biggest-villain-our-age-says-xinhua.

140 *US government entity* "谁掌控了我们的服务器 (Who Controls Our Servers)," *International Financial News,* August 20, 2009, p. 2, http://paper.people.com.cn/gjjrb/html/2009-08/20/content_323598.htm.

140 *"fight the Internet war"* Eyder Peralta, "Chinese Military Scholars Accuse U.S. of Launching 'Internet War,'" NPR, June 3, 2011, http://www.npr.org/blogs/thetwo-way/2011/06/03/136923033/chinese-military-scholars-accuse-u-s-of-launching-internet-war.

140 *According to government sources* Jan van Tol, Mark Gunzinger, Andrew Krepinevich, et al., "AirSea Battle: A Point-of-Departure Operational Concept," Center for Strategic and Budgetary Assessments, May 18, 2010, http://www.csbaonline.org/publications/2010/05/airsea-battle-concept/.

141 *some 130,000 personnel* William Matthews, "Chinese Attacks Bring Cyber Spying into the Open," *Defense News* (January 18, 2010): p. 4.

141 *10 subdivisions* Gertz, "Cyber Spies Spotted."

141 *"informationized Blue Team"* Krekel, "Capability of the People's Republic of China to Conduct Cyber Warfare and Computer Network Exploitation."

141 *across the newspaper's front page* David Sanger, "Chinese Army Unit Is Seen as Tied to Hacking against U.S.," *New York Times,* February 18, 2013, http://www.nytimes.com/2013/02/19/technology/chinas-army-is-seen-as-tied-to-hacking-against-us.html?hp.

141 *40 other APT operations* "What Mandiant Brings," Strategic News Service, e-mail message to authors, March 11, 2013.

142 *"2003-class"* Nicole Perloff, "Internet Sleuths Add Evidence to Chinese Military Hacking Accusations," *New York Times,* February 27, 2013, http://bits.blogs.nytimes.com/2013/02/27/internet-sleuths-add-evidence-to-chinese-military-hacking-accusations/.

142 *"new strategic high ground"* Ibid.

142 *"enemy information equipment"* Office of the Secretary of Defense, "Annual Report to Congress: Military Power of the People's Republic of China 2009," 2009, p. 27, http://www.defenselink.mil/pubs/pdfs/China_Military_Power_Report_2009.pdf, accessed August 11, 2013.

142 *reduced risk of counterattack* Krekel, "Capability of the People's Republic of China to Conduct Cyber Warfare and Computer Network Exploitation."

143 *"electronic Maginot line"* Qiao Liang and Wang Xiansui, *Unrestricted Warfare* (Panama City, Panama: Pan American Publishing, 2002), cited in Timothy L. Thomas, *The Dragon's Quantum Leap* (Fort Leavenworth, KS: Foreign Military Studies Office, 2009).

143 *"level of informationization"* Bryan Krekel, Patton Adams, and George Bakos, "Occupying the Information High Ground: Chinese Capabilities for Computer Network Operations and Cyber Espionage," Northrop Grumman Corporation, March 7, 2012, p. 25, http://www.uscc.gov/RFP/2012/USCC%20Report_Chinese_CapabilitiesforComputer_NetworkOperationsandCyberEspionage.pdf.

144 *"China has big stones"* Menn, "Agreement on Cybersecurity 'Badly Needed.'"

WHAT ABOUT DETERRENCE IN AN ERA OF CYBERWAR?

144 *"deterrence ladder"* Department of Defense, "Resilient Military Systems and the Advanced Cyber Threat," Defense Science Board task force report, Washington,

DC, January 2013, http://www.acq.osd.mil/dsb/reports/ResilientMilitarySystems. CyberThreat.pdf, accessed August 11, 2013.

145 *"Conventional Prompt Global Strike"* Ibid.

145 *"sums it up the best"* John Reed, "DoD Panel Recommends Special Bomber-Armed Cyber Deterrence Force," *Killer Apps* (blog), *Foreign Policy*, March 6, 2013, http://killerapps.foreignpolicy.com/posts/2013/03/06/dod_panel_recommends_special_bomber_armed_cyber_deterrent_force.

145 *"unacceptable counteraction"* "Deterrence," *Department of Defense Dictionary of Military and Associated Terms Joint Publication 1-02* (Washington, DC: The Joint Staff, November 8, 2010, as amended through December 15, 2012), p. 85, http://www.dtic.mil/doctrine/new_pubs/jp1_02.pdf.

145 *deter or retaliate against* See T. V. Paul, Patrick M. Morgan, and James J. Wirtz, *Complex Deterrence: Strategy in the Global Age* (Chicago: University of Chicago Press, 2009).

146 *"try to harm America"* Leon E. Panetta, "Remarks by Secretary Panetta on Cybersecurity to the Business Executives for National Security," remarks at the Intrepid Sea, Air And Space Museum, New York, October 11, 2012, http://www.defense.gov/transcripts/transcript.aspx?transcriptid=5136.

146 *"analysis of these operations"* Alperovitch, "Deterrence in Cyberspace."

WHY IS THREAT ASSESSMENT SO HARD IN CYBERSPACE?

148 *"just as many nuclear wars"* Nye, "Nuclear Lessons for Cyber Security?" p. 25.

148 *"feasibility of adversaries"* Herbert Lin, "Thoughts on Threat Assessment in Cyberspace," presentation at the Conference on Cybersecurity: Shared Risks, Shared Responsibilities, Ohio State University, April 1, 2011.

148 *"harboring fears"* Smithsonian National Air and Space Museum, "Satellite Reconnaissance: Secret Eyes in Space," http://www.nasm.si.edu/exhibitions/gal114/SpaceRace/sec400/sec400.htm, accessed January 8, 2013.

150 *"never in doubt"* Owens, Dam, and Lin, *Technology, Policy, Law, and Ethics Regarding U.S. Acquisition and Use of Cyberattack Capabilities*, p. 142.

DOES THE CYBERSECURITY WORLD FAVOR THE WEAK OR THE STRONG?

150 *various insurgent groups* Siobhan Gorman, August Cole, and Yochi Dreazen, "Insurgents Hack U.S. Drones," *Wall Street Journal*, December 17, 2009, http://online.wsj.com/article/SB126102247889095011.html.

151 *"preserve of great states"* Lewis, "The Threat," p. 20.

151 *"the most to lose"* Clayton, "The New Cyber Arms Race."

151 *"tons of vulnerabilities"* Ibid.

152 *"power equalization"* Nye, "Power and National Security in Cyberspace," p. 14.

152 *dummy set of centrifuges* William J. Broad, John Markoff, and David E. Sanger, "Israeli Test on Worm Called Crucial in Iran Nuclear Delay," *New York Times*, January 15, 2011, http://www.nytimes.com/2011/01/16/world/middleeast/16stuxnet.html?pagewanted=all&_r=0.

152 *"smaller dogs bite"* Nye, "Power and National Security in Cyberspace," p. 14.

152 *escalation dominance* Malruken, "Cyberwar and Cyber Warfare," p. 61.

WHO HAS THE ADVANTAGE, THE OFFENSE OR THE DEFENSE?

153 *"military law in 1913"* Barbara W. Tuchman, *August 1914* (London: Constable, 1962), p. 44.

153 *"cult of the offensive"* Stephen Van Evera, "The Cult of the Offensive and the Origins of the First World War," *International Security* 9, no. 1 (Summer 1984): pp. 58–107.

154 *offense-dominant for the foreseeable future* van Tol et al., "AirSea Battle."

154 *cheaper and easier* Ibid.

154 *10 million* Defense Advanced Research Projects Agency Director Regina E. Dugan, submitted testimony before the House Armed Services Committee, Subcommittee on Emerging Threats and Capabilities, March 1, 2011, pp. 16–17, www.darpa.mil/WorkArea/DownloadAsset.aspx?id=2929, accessed January 8, 2013.

154 *"less investment by the attacker"* Ibid.

155 *difficult to estimate* Owens, Dam, and Lin, *Technology, Policy, Law, and Ethics Regarding U.S. Acquisition and Use of Cyberattack Capabilities.*

155 *"stop the attack at any step"* Graham Warwick, "Cyberhunters: Aerospace and Defense Primes See Automation of Cyberdefenses as an Opportunity to Apply Their System-Integration Skills," *Aviation Week & Space Technology* 173, no. 18 (May 23, 2011).

155 *even a cyber counterattack* Owens, Dam and Lin, *Technology, Policy, Law, and Ethics Regarding U.S. Acquisition and Use of Cyberattack Capabilities.*

156 *"fight through the intrusion"* Vint Cerf, e-mail message to authors, September 5, 2011.

156 *sow doubt in the offense* Mark Clayton, "10 Ways to Prevent Cyberconflict," *Christian Science Monitor*, March 7, 2011, http://www.csmonitor.com/USA/Military/2011/0307/10-ways-to-prevent-cyberconflict/Start-cyberwar-limitation-talks.

156 *"it doesn't scare you"* Andrea Shalal-Esa, "Ex-U.S. General Urges Frank Talk on Cyber Weapons," Reuters, November 6, 2011, http://www.reuters.com/article/2011/11/06/us-cyber-cartwright-idUSTRE7A514C20111106.

A New Kind of Arms Race: What Are the Dangers of Cyber Proliferation?

156 *"we shall be utterly ruined"* Plutarch, *The Parallel Lives*, vol. 9, last modified May 4, 2012, http://penelope.uchicago.edu/Thayer/E/Roman/Texts/Plutarch/Lives/Pyrrhus*.html#21.

157 *"amassing cybermilitary capabilities"* Clayton, "The New Cyber Arms Race."

157 *Stuxnet-like weapon* Ibid.

157 *"it is very intense"* Michael Nacht, interview with the authors, February 24, 2011.

158 *10 experts* Langner, "Deterrence in Cyberspace."

158 *vulnerabilities that Stuxnet attacked* Ibid.

159 *case of inspiration* Tom Espiner, "McAfee: Why Duqu Is a Big Deal," *ZDNet UK*, October 26, 2011, http://www.zdnet.co.uk/news/security-threats/2011/10/26/mcafee-why-duqu-is-a-big-deal-40094263/.

159 *"copy so much from Stuxnet"* Clayton, "From the Man Who Discovered Stuxnet, Dire Warnings One Year Later."

159 *smoother and more worrisome* "Security in Embedded Devices" presentation, McAfee, June 22, 2011.

Are There Lessons from Past Arms Races?

160 *"world peace or world destruction"* Bernard Baruch, "The Baruch Plan," remarks to the United Nations Atomic Energy Commission, June 14, 1946.

161 *"ill-formed, undeveloped, and highly uncertain"* Owens, Dam, and Lin, *Technology, Policy, Law, and Ethics Regarding U.S. Acquisition and Use of Cyberattack Capabilities*, p. 4.

161 *"millions and millions"* Clayton, "The New Cyber Arms Race."

162 *Rebecca Bonner* Rebecca Bonner, "Arms Race in Cyberspace?" International Security Project, Yale Law School, May 2011, http://www.yaleisp.org/2011/05/arms-race-in-cyberspace.

Behind the Scenes: Is There a Cyber-Industrial Complex?

163 *"the conference for you"* Invitation to Cyber Security Conference, e-mail to authors, May 27, 2013. More at www.cyberarmsrace.com.

163 *65 billion* Guy Andersen, "Cyber Security: Corporate Challenges and Responses to Emerging Opportunities," *Jane's Defence Weekly* 48, no. 36 (September 7, 2011): pp. 30–32.

163 *6 percent to 9 percent* Market Media Research, "U.S. Federal Cybersecurity Market Forecast 2013–2018," http://www.marketresearchmedia.com/?p=206, accessed January 2013.

163 *"$80 billion and $150 billion"* Eric Schmidt and Jared Cohen, *The New Digital Age* (New York: Knopf, 2013), p. 110.

163 *"rare oasis"* Andersen, "Cyber Security," pp. 30–32.

163 *Professor Peter Sommer* Susan Watts, "Proposal for Cyber War Rules of Engagement," BBC News, last modified February 3, 2011, http://news.bbc.co.uk/2/hi/programmes/newsnight/9386445.stm.

163 *"wealth of opportunity"* Invitation to Cyber Security Conference, e-mail to authors.

164 *15 percent of all mergers* Andersen, "Cyber Security," pp. 30–32.

164 *anti-money-laundering specialist* Ibid.

164 *Boeing has spent* Interview with Boeing executive, Annapolis Junction, MD, April 16, 2013.

164 *commercial IT infrastructures* Mark Hoover, "Boeing Inks Partnership for Japanese Cyber Initiative," *Washington Technology*, September 19, 2012, http://washingtontechnology.com/articles/2012/09/19/boeing-partners-with-sojitz-for-japanese-cybersecurity-measures.aspx.

164 *"witnessed in the late 1990s"* Andersen, "Cyber Security," pp. 30–32.

164 *"Good News for Lobbyists"* James Ball, "Good News for Lobbyists: Cyber Dollars," *Washington Post*, November 13, 2012, http://articles.washingtonpost.com/2012-11-13/news/35505525_1_cybersecurity-lobbyists-lame-duck-session.

164 *Ronald Deibert* Jerry Brito and Tate Watkins, "Loving the Cyber Bomb? The Dangers of Threat Inflation in Cybersecurity Policy," Mercatus Center, George Mason University, April 26, 2011, http://mercatus.org/publication/loving-cyber-bomb-dangers-threat-inflation-cybersecurity-policy.

165 *hype the threats* Ibid.

165 *single power supplier* McGraw and Fick, "Separating Threat from the Hype," p. 44.

165 *Cory Doctorow* "The FP Survey," p. 116.

PART III: WHAT CAN WE DO?
DON'T GET FOOLED: WHY CAN'T WE JUST BUILD A NEW, MORE SECURE INTERNET?

166 *"the wily hacker"* William R. Cheswick and Steven M. Bellovin, *Firewalls and Internet Security: Repelling the Wily Hacker* (Reading, MA: Addison-Wesley, 1994).

166 *"the packet has evil intent"* Steven M. Bellovin, "The Security Flag in the IPv4 Header," RFC Editor, April 1, 2003, http://www.ietf.org/rfc/rfc3514.txt.

166 *"better off without it"* Robert Samuelson, "Beware the Internet and the Danger of Cyberattacks," *Washington Post*, June 30, 2013, http://www.washingtonpost.com/opinions/robert-samuelson-of-internet-threats-and-cyberattacks/2013/06/30/df7bd42e-e1a9-11e2-a11e-c2ea876a8f30_story.html.

167 *consumer banks* Aliya Sternstein, "Former CIA Director: Build a New Internet to Improve Cybersecurity," *National Journal*, May 29, 2013, http://www.nationaljournal.com/nationalsecurity/former-cia-director-build-a-new-internet-to-improve-cybersecurity-20110707.

167 *"secure, protected zone"* J. Nicholas Hoover, "Cyber Command Director: U.S. Needs to Secure Critical Infrastructure," *InformationWeek Government*, September 23, 2010, http://www.informationweek.com/government/security/cyber-command-director-us-needs-to-secur/227500515.

167 *"secure alternative Internet"* David Perera, "Federal Government Has Dot-Secure Internet Domain under Consideration," *Fierce Government IT*, June 21, 2011, http://www.

fiercegovernmentit.com/story/federal-government-has-dot-secure-Internet-domain-under-consideration/ 2011-06-21.

167 *Artemis declared* Dan Goodin, "My Own Private Internet: secure TLD Floated as Bad-Guy-Free Zone," *Ars Technica*, May 10, 2012, http://arstechnica.com/security/2012/05/my-own-private-Internet-secure-tld-floated-as-bad-guy-free-zone/.

Rethink Security: What Is Resilience, and Why Is It Important?

169 *"Hundreds of Thousands May Lose Internet"* "Hundreds of Thousands May Lose Internet in July," Associated Press, April 20, 2012, http://www.azcentral.com/news/articles/20 12/04/20/20120420internet-loss-hackers-virus.html.

170 *"the Internet is broken"* "How to Avoid July 9 'Internet Doomsday': Fix the DNS Charger Malware," Fox News, April 23, 2012, http://www.foxnews.com/tech/2012/04/23/how-to-avoid-july-internet-doomsday-fix-dnschanger-malware/.

170 *steer people to assistance* Ibid.

170 *119 different definitions* Dennis Schrader, "A Practical Approach to Achieving Resilience," *DomPrep Journal* 8, issue 11 (November 2012): pp. 26–28, http://www.domesticpreparedness.com/pub/docs/DPJNov12.pdf.

170 *Dan Geer frames it* Daniel E. Geer, Jr., "How Government Can Access Innovative Technology," in *America's Cyber Future: Security and Prosperity in the Information Age*, vol. 2, edited by Kristin M. Lord and Travis Shard (Washington, DC: Center for a New American Security, 2011), p. 199.

171 *"work under degraded conditions"* Ibid.

171 *shutting the whole thing down* Réka Albert, Hawoong Jeong, and Albert-László Barabási, "Error and Attack Tolerance of Complex Networks," *Nature* 406, no. 6794 (July 2000): pp. 378–382, http://www.nature.com/nature/journal/v406/n6794/full/406378a0.html.

172 *focused on the bottom line* World Economic Forum, "Partnering for Cyber Resilience,"http://www.weforum.org/issues/partnering-cyber-resilience-pcr,accessed August 11, 2013.

173 *adapt or innovate* Richard Cyert and James G. March, *A Behavioral Theory of the Firm*, 2nd ed. (New York: Wiley-Blackwell, 1992).

Reframe the Problem (and the Solution): What Can We Learn from Public Health?

174 *some 5,000 plus* Bill Woodcock and Vijay Adhikari, "Survey of Characteristics of Internet Carrier Interconnection Agreements," Packet Clearing House, May 2011.

174 *more effectively reimagined* Gregory J. Rattray and Jason Healey, "Non-state Actors and Cyber Conflict," in *America's Cyber Future: Security and Prosperity in the Information Age*, vol. 2, edited by Kristin M. Lord and Travis Shard (Washington, DC: Center for a New American Security, 2011), p. 79.

175 *"coordination of preventive actions"* United States Department of Homeland Security, "Enabling Distributed Security in Cyberspace: Building a Healthy and Resilient Cyber Ecosystem with Automated Collective Action," National Protection and Programs Directorate white paper, March 23, 2011, p. 2, http://www.dhs.gov/xlibrary/assets/nppd-cyber-ecosystem-white-paper-03-23-2011.pdf, accessed May 10, 2011.

175 *"slap a cyber in front of it"* Zach, "Cybersecurity Reboot: Two Game-Changing Ideas (Federal Computer Week)," *Cyber Security Law and Policy* (blog), April 8, 2012, http://blog.cybersecuritylaw.us/2012/04/08/cybersecurity-reboot-two-game-changing-ideas-federalcomputerweek/, accessed January 2013.

175 *hospitals, universities, and research centers* Rattray and Healey, "Non-state Actors and Cyber Conflict," p. 79.

175 *shared problems of cybersecurity* Mark Clayton, "10 Ways to Prevent Cyberconflict," *Christian Science Monitor*, March 7, 2011, http://www.csmonitor.com/USA/Military/20 11/0307/10-ways-to-prevent-cyberconflict/Start-cyberwar-limitation-talks.

176 *"mitigate such attacks"*   Rattray and Healey, "Non-state Actors and Cyber Conflict," p. 79. See also Andy Purdy and Nick Hopkinson, "Online Theft of Intellectual Property Threatens National Security," The European Institute, January 2011.

177 *"greater threat to society"*   Steve Ragan, "Microsoft Proposes a Cyber CDC to Address Web Threats," *Tech Herald*, October 5, 2010, http://www.thetechherald.com/articles/Microsoft-proposes-a-cyber-CDC-to-address-Web-threats/11535/.

LEARN FROM HISTORY: WHAT CAN (REAL) PIRATES TEACH US ABOUT CYBERSECURITY?

178 *they compelled negotiations*   American Merchant Marine at War, "American Merchant Marine and Privateers in War of 1812," http://www.usmm.org/warof1812.html, accessed September 5, 2011.

178 *also blasted the Confederates*   William Morrison Robinson, Jr., *The Confederate Privateers* (New Haven, CT: Yale University Press, 1928), p. 14.

178 *50 Internet service providers*   Michel Van Eeten, Johannes M. Bauer, Hadi Asghari, et al., "The Role of Internet Service Providers in Botnet Mitigation: An Empirical Analysis Based on SPAM Data," Organization for Economic Cooperation and Development, November 12, 2010, http://search.oecd.org/officialdocuments/displaydocumentpdf/?doclanguage=en&cote=dsti/doc%282010%295.

179 *"drain the swamp"*   Purdy and Hopkinson, "Online Theft of Intellectual Property Threatens National Security."

179 *greater power and control*   Janice E. Thomson, *Mercenaries, Pirates, and Sovereigns* (Princeton, NJ: Princeton University Press, 1994).

PROTECT WORLD WIDE GOVERNANCE FOR THE WORLD WIDE WEB: WHAT IS THE ROLE OF INTERNATIONAL INSTITUTIONS?

181 *"public order or morals"*   International Telecommunication Union, "Plenipotentiary Conferences," http://www.itu.int/en/history/Pages/PlenipotentiaryConferences.aspx?conf=1&dms=S0201000001, accessed January 14, 2013.

181 *"Declaration of the Independence of Cyberspace"*   John Perry Barlow, "A Declaration of the Independence of Cyberspace," Electronic Frontier Foundation, https://projects.eff.org/~barlow/Declaration-Final.html, accessed January 14, 2013.

182 *"free" part of cyberspace*   Robert Axelrod, e-mail message to the authors, September 5, 2011.

182 *"Nazi memorabilia"*   Internet Governance Project, "Threat Analysis of the WCIT Part 4: The ITU and Cybersecurity," June 21, 2012, http://www.internetgovernance.org/2012/06/21/threat-analysis-of-the-wcit-4-cybersecurity/, accessed January 2013.

182 *"wave of the future"*   Fred Tipson, e-mail message to the authors, December 20, 2010.

183 *"a healthy, orderly environment"*   "China: U.S. 'Internet War Being Waged against Multiple Nations,'" *Huffington Post*, June 3, 2011, http://www.huffingtonpost.com/2011/06/03/china-us-internet-war-bei_n_870754.html.

183 *"international communications technologies"*   Michael Berkens, "Reuters: ITU: Russia Backed by China, Saudi Arabia, Algeria, Sudan, and the UAE Wants to Take Control Away From ICANN," TheDomains.com, December 9, 2012, http://www.thedomains.com/2012/12/09/reuters-itu-russia-backed-by-china-saudi-arabia-algeria-sudan-and-the-uae-wants-to-take-control-away-from-icann/.

183 *"people trying to reach a given website"*   Ibid.

183 *"digital version of the Cold War"*   L. S., "A Digital Cold War?" *Babbage* (blog), *Economist*, December 14, 2012, http://www.economist.com/blogs/babbage/2012/12/internet-regulation?fsrc=scn/tw_ec/a_digital_cold_war_, accessed January 14, 2013.

184 *"treaty agreed in Dubai"*   "New Global Telecoms Treaty Agreed in Dubai," International Telecommunication Union press release (Dubai, United Arab Emirates, December 14, 2012), http://www.itu.int/net/pressoffice/press_releases/2012/92.aspx.

184 *"national bits of the Internet"*   L. S., "A Digital Cold War?"

185 *"banner of security"* Internet Governance Project, "Threat Analysis of the WCIT Part 4: The ITU and Cybersecurity."

"GRAFT" THE RULE OF LAW: DO WE NEED A CYBERSPACE TREATY?

185 *"floating on the water"* The World War I Document Archive, "The Hague Rules of Air Warfare," http://wwi.lib.byu.edu/index.php/The_Hague_Rules_of_Air_Warfare, accessed January 2013.

185 *"regulation of air warfare"* Scott W. Beidleman, "Defining and Deterring Cyber War," strategy research project, US Army War College, January 6, 2009, p. 21.

185 *"what constitutes normal behaviour"* Joseph Menn, "Agreement on Cybersecurity 'Badly Needed,'" *Financial Times*, October 12, 2011.

185 *American West* Beidleman, "Defining and Deterring Cyber War," p. 21.

186 *"unofficially the answer is no"* Menn, "Agreement on Cybersecurity 'Badly Needed.'"

186 *vulnerable civilian infrastructure* Ibid.

187 *"an entire domain"* Ronald Deibert, "Tracking the Emerging Arms Race in Cyberspace," *Bulletin of the Atomic Scientists* 67 (January-February 2011): pp. 1–8.

187 *increase your chances of success* Martha Finnemore, "Cultivating International Cyber Norms," in *America's Cyber Future: Security and Prosperity in the Information Age*, vol. 2, edited by Kristin M. Lord and Travis Shard (Washington, DC: Center for a New American Security, 2011), p. 90.

187 *70 percent* James Fallows, "Cyber Warriors," *Atlantic*, March 2010.

188 *"moving from the Wild West"* Ibid.

188 *"malicious payloads"* Jeffrey Carr, *Inside Cyber Warfare* (Sebastopol, CA: O'Reilly Media, 2010), p. 5.

189 *politics of what might happen next* Dean Cheng, "Chinese Cyber Attacks: Robust Response Needed," Heritage Foundation, February 23, 2013, http://www.heritage.org/research/reports/2013/02/chinese-cyber-attacks-robust-response-needed.

189 *Farwell writes* James Farwell, "Take Chinese Hacking to the WTO," *National Interest*, March 15, 2013, http://nationalinterest.org/commentary/take-chinese-hacking-the-wto-8224.

190 *"China should confront"* James McGregor, "Is the Specter of a 'Cyber Cold War' Real?" *The Atlantic*, April 27, 2013, http://www.theatlantic.com/china/archive/2013/04/is-the-specter-of-a-cyber-cold-war-real/275352/.

190 *common terms and definitions* Robert Radvanovsky and Allan McDougall, *Critical Infrastructure: Homeland Security and Emergency Preparedness*, 2nd ed. (Boca Raton, FL: Taylor & Francis, 2010), p. 3.

190 *easier to protect such infrastructure* Zhang Chenfu and Tang Jun, "信息化风险管理：基本战略与政策选择 (Informationization Risk Management: Basic Strategy and Policy Choices)," *Chinese Public Administration* 260, no. 2 (2007): pp. 52–54.

190 *missiles with multiple warheads* Stanford Arms Control Group, *International Arms Control: Issues and Agreements*, 2nd ed., edited by Coit D. Blacker and Gloria Duffy (Stanford: Stanford University Press, 1976), p. 237.

191 *"to call Russia's bluff"* Jordan Schneider, "Cyberwarfare," paper shared via e-mail, Yale University, May 2011.

191 *"international financial servers"* Ibid.

192 *says Michael Hayden* Menn, "Agreement on Cybersecurity 'Badly Needed.'"

193 *swamp of sanctuaries* Robert Axelrod, e-mail message to authors, September 5, 2011.

193 *no formal rules agreed* Finnemore, "Cultivating International Cyber Norms," p. 90.

UNDERSTAND THE LIMITS OF THE STATE IN CYBERSPACE: WHY CAN'T THE GOVERNMENT HANDLE IT?

194 *no one government could seize* TorrentFreak, "The Pirate Bay: The Site Is Safe, Even If We Lose in Court," January 31, 2008, http://torrentfreak.com/pirate-bay-is-safe-080131/.

195 *without traditional due process*   Ewan MacAskill, "Julian Assange Like a High-Tech Terrorist, Says Joe Biden," *Guardian*, December 19, 2010, http://www.guardian.co.uk/media/2010/dec/19/assange-high-tech-terrorist-biden.

195 *"enemy combatant"*   Shane D'Aprile, "Gingrich: Leaks Show Obama Administration 'Shallow,' 'Amateurish,' " *Blog Briefing Room* (blog), *The Hill*, December 5, 2010, http://thehill.com/blogs/blog-briefing-room/news/132037-gingrich-blames-obama-on-wikileaks-labels-assange-a-terrorist.

195 *traditional channels*   Ewen MacAskill, "WikiLeaks Website Pulled by Amazon after US Political Pressure," *Guardian*, December 1, 2010, http://www.guardian.co.uk/media/2010/dec/01/wikileaks-website-cables-servers-amazon.

195 *registered in Australia*   Hal Berghel, "WikiLeaks and the Matter of Private Manning," *Computer* 45, no. 3 (March 2012): pp. 70–73.

195 *French national banking system*   Loek Essers, "Visa and Mastercard Funding Returns to WikiLeaks via French Payment Gateway," *PCWorld*, July 18, 2012, http://www.pcworld.com/article/259437/visa_and_mastercard_funding_returns_to_wikileaks_via_french_payment_gateway.html.

195 *1989 protests in Tiananmen Square*   Stephen Jewkes, "Milan Prosecutor Wants Jail Terms Upheld for Google Autism Video," Reuters, December 11, 2012, http://www.reuters.com/article/2012/12/11/us-google-italy-idUSBRE8BA10R20121211?feedType=RSS&feedName=technologyNews&utm_source=dlvr.it&utm_medium=twitter&dlvrit=56505.

196 *"98 percent"*   Eric Talbot Jensen, "Cyber Warfare and Precautions against the Effects of Attacks," *Texas Law Review* 88, no. 7 (June 2010): p. 1534.

196 *"zero knowledge"*   The Conficker Working Group Lessons Learned Document, accessed June 23, 2013, http://www.confickerworkinggroup.org/wiki/pmwiki.php/ANY/LessonsLearned.

RETHINK GOVERNMENT'S ROLE: HOW CAN WE BETTER ORGANIZE FOR CYBERSECURITY?

198 *lifetime in the cyber world*   Doug Krueger, "GSA Issues First FedRAMP Certification, Sign of More to Come," Federal Blue Print, http://federalblueprint.com/2013/gsa-issues-first-fedramp-certification-sign-of-more-to-come/, accessed August 11, 2013.

199 *DDoS attacks in 2012*   Ellen Nakashima, "Cyber Defense Effort Is Mixed, Study Finds," *Washington Post*, January 12, 2012, http://articles.washingtonpost.com/2012-01-12/world/35438768_1_cyber-defense-nsa-data-defense-companies.

199 *massive levels of data mining*   Siobahn Gorman, "NSA's Domestic Spying Grows as Agency Sweeps Up Data," *Wall Street Journal*, March 10, 2008, http://online.wsj.com/article/SB120511973377523845.html.

200 *solely defensive focus*   Matt Blaze, "The FBI Needs Hackers, Not Backdoors," *Wired*, January 14, 2013, http://www.wired.com/opinion/2013/01/wiretap-backdoors/.

200 *them being open elsewhere*   Tyler Moore, Allan Friedman, and Ariel D. Procaccia, "Would a 'Cyber Warrior' Protect Us: Exploring Trade-offs between Attack and Defense of Information Systems," in *Proceedings of the 2010 Workshop on New Security Paradigms*, Concord, MA, September 21–23, 2010, pp. 85–94, http://www.nspw.org/papers/2010/nspw2010-moore.pdf.

200 *"coordinate cyber incident response"*   Matthew H. Fleming and Eric Goldstein, "An Analysis of the Primary Authorities Governing and Supporting the Efforts of the Department of Homeland Security to Secure the Cyberspace of the United States," Homeland Security Studies and Analysis Institute, May 24, 2011, p. 18, http://www.homelandsecurity.org/docs/reports/MHF-and-EG-Analysis-of-authorities-supporting-efforts-of-DHS-to-secure-cyberspace-2011.pdf.

200 *eight times as much*   Aliya Sternstein, "DHS Budget Would Double Cyber Spending to $769 million," *Nextgov*, February 13, 2012, www.nextgov.com/cybersecurity/2012/02/dhs-budget-would-double-cyber-spending-to-769-million/50632/.

202 *ability to set security standards*   US Government Accountability Office, "Electricity Grid Modernization: Progress Being Made on Cybersecurity Guidelines, but Key Challenges Remain to be Addressed," Report to Congressional Requester, January 12, 2011, http://www.gao.gov/assets/320/314410.pdf.

202 *"biggest laggers in cybersecurity"*   Cybersecurity CEO, interview with the authors, Washington DC, May 23, 2013.

202 *no power or expertise*   Joseph Kramek, "The Critical Infrastructure Gap: U.S. Port Facilities and Cyber Vulnerabilities," Brookings Institution, July 2013, http://www.brookings.edu/research/papers/2013/07/03-cyber-ports-security-kramek.

202 *"cybersecurity for the Nation"*   Department of Homeland Security, "Fact Sheet: Executive Order (EO) 13636 Improving Critical Infrastructure Cybersecurity and Presidential Policy Directive (PPD)-21 Critical Infrastructure Security and Resilience," posted March 12, 2013, http://www.dhs.gov/publication/fact-sheet-eo-13636-improving-critical-infrastructure-cybersecurity-and-ppd-21-critical.

203 *"legislation or regulation"*   David A. Gross, Nova J. Daly, M. Ethan Lucarelli, et al., "Cyber Security Governance: Existing Structures, International Approaches and the Private Sector," in *America's Cyber Future: Security and Prosperity in the Information Age,* vol. 2, edited by Kristin M. Lord and Travis Shard (Washington, DC: Center for a New American Security, 2011), p. 119.

203 *"0.1 percent"*   Philip J. Bond, "Private Sector Perspectives on Department of Defense Information Technology and Cybersecurity Activities," Testimony before the House Armed Services Committee, Subcommittee on Terrorism, Unconventional Threats and Capabilities, Washington, DC, February 25, 2010, p. 6, http://democrats.armedservices.house.gov/index.cfm/files/serve?File_id=72e44e6b-3f8e-46d6-bcef-b57cd2e0c017. Readers should note that the Department of Defense's total information technology budget increased by approximately 50 percent during the same period.

203 *"$100 million helicopter"*   Katie Drummond, "Military's New Plan to Weed Out Counterfeits: Plant DNA," *Danger Room* (blog), *Wired*, January 20, 2012, http://www.wired.com/dangerroom/2012/01/dna-counterfeits/.

204 *"trusted delivery systems"*   Darrell West, "12 Ways to Build Trust in the Global ICT Trade," *Brookings*, April 18, 2013, http://www.brookings.edu/research/papers/2013/04/18-global-supply-chain-west.

204 *"America's digital infrastructure"*   Executive Office of the President of the United States, "The Comprehensive National Cybersecurity Initiative," March 2, 2010, http://www.whitehouse.gov/sites/default/files/cybersecurity.pdf.

Approach It as a Public-Private Problem: How Do We Better Coordinate Defense?

205 *"cyber-criminal gangs"*   Brian Krebs, "Major Source of Online Scams and Spams Knocked Offline," *Security Fix* (blog), *Washington Post*, November 11, 2008, http://voices.washingtonpost.com/securityfix/2008/11/major_source_of_online_scams_a.html.

205 *up to no good*   Ibid.

205 *"Holy cow!"*   Ibid.

205 *Spam levels*   Vincent Hanna, "Another One Bytes the Dust," *Spamhaus*, November 17, 2008, http://www.spamhaus.org/news/article/640/.

206 *Visa to process payments*   Ron Scherer, "Visa Draws a Hard Line on Child Porn," *Christian Science Monitor*, February 24, 2003, http://www.csmonitor.com/2003/0224/p01s01-ussc.html.

207 *money laundering*   Anne Broache, "E-Gold Charged with Money Laundering," CNet News, April 30, 2007, http://news.cnet.com/E-Gold-charged-with-money-laundering/2100-1017_3-6180302.html.

208 *stewardship of the Internet*   Melissa Hathaway and John Savage, "Stewardship in Cyberspace: Duties for Internet Service Providers," Cyber Dialogue 2012, March 2012,

http://www.cyberdialogue.citizenlab.org/wp-content/uploads/2012/2012papers/
CyberDialogue2012_hathaway-savage.pdf, accessed August 11, 2013.

208 *support of major American ISPs* Federal Communications Commission, "Federal
Advisory Committee Unanimously Approves Recommendations to Combat Three Major
Cybersecurity Threats: Botnet Attacks, Domain Name Fraud and IP Route Hijacking,"
March 22, 2012, http://transition.fcc.gov/Daily_Releases/Daily_Business/2012/
db0322/DOC-313159A1.pdf.

208 *customers and shareholders* Ross Anderson, Chris Barton, Rainer Bohme, et al.,
"Measuring the Cost of Cybercrime," paper presented at the 11th Annual Workshop
on the Economics of Information Security WEIS 2012, Berlin, June 25–26, 2012, http://
weis2012.econinfosec.org/papers/Anderson_WEIS2012.pdf.

209 *an enemy's bomber planes* Paul Rosenzweig, "Cybersecurity and Public Goods: The
Public/Private 'Partnership,'" Task Force on National Security and Law, Hoover
Institution, September 7, 2011, http://media.hoover.org/sites/default/files/docu-
ments/EmergingThreats_Rosenzweig.pdf.

209 *companies have told Congress* Congressional staffer, interview with the authors,
Washington, DC, March 13, 2013.

209 *information assurance agencies* SANS Institute, "A Brief History of the 20 Critical Security
Controls," http://www.sans.org/critical-security-controls/history.php, accessed August
11, 2013.

210 *spend more on protection* Ibid.

210 *steps to reduce risk* Paul David, Rolande Maude-Griffin, and Geoffrey Rothwell,
"Learning by Accident? Reductions in the Risk of Unplanned Outages in U.S. Nuclear
Power Plants after Three Mile Island," *Journal of Risk and Uncertainty* 13, no. 2 (1996).

210 *"meeting government mandates"* Ken Dilanian, "U.S. Chamber of Commerce Leads
Defeat of Cyber-Security Bill," *Los Angeles Times*, August 3, 2012, http://articles.latimes.
com/2012/aug/03/nation/la-na-cyber-security-20120803.

EXERCISE IS GOOD FOR YOU: HOW CAN WE BETTER PREPARE FOR CYBER INCIDENTS?

211 *malicious computer code* Dan Goodin, "At Facebook, Zero-Day Exploits, Backdoor
Code, Bring War Games Drill to Life," *Ars Technica*, February 10, 2013, http://
arstechnica.com/security/2013/02/at-facebook-zero-day-exploits-backdoor-
code-bring-war-games-drill-to-life/.

211 *no major damage* Sean Gallagher, "Facebook Computers Compromised by Zero-Day Java
Exploit," *Ars Technica*, February 15, 2013, http://arstechnica.com/security/2013/02/
facebook-computers-compromised-by-zero-day-java-exploit/.

211 *tried to harm Facebook* Dennis Fisher, "How Facebook Prepared to Be Hacked,"
Threatpost, March 8, 2013, http://threatpost.com/en_us/blogs/how-facebook-prepared-
be-hacked-030813.

212 *offensive tactics and tricks* Samuel L. King, Peter M. Chen, Yi-Min Wang, et al.,
"SubVirt: Implementing Malware with Virtual Machines," University of Michigan, http://
web.eecs.umich.edu/~pmchen/papers/king06.pdf, accessed August 11, 2013.

213 *"Israelis tried it out"* William J. Broad, John Markoff, and David E. Sanger, "Israeli
Test on Worm Called Crucial in Iran Nuclear Delay," *New York Times*, January
15, 2011, http://www.nytimes.com/2011/01/16/world/middleeast/16stuxnet.html?
pagewanted=all&_r=0.

213 *network-based attack* Tucker Bailey, James Kaplan, and Allen Weinberg, "Playing
Wargames to Prepare for a Cyberattack," *McKinsey Quarterly*, July 2012.

213 *McKinsey found* Ibid.

214 *pension database* Estonian defense official, interview with the authors, March 17, 2012,
Washington DC.

214 *"We were warned"* Bipartisan Policy Center, "Cyber ShockWave," http://bipartisan-
policy.org/events/cyber2010, accessed August 11, 2013.

214 *officials from different European countries* "ENISA Issues Report on 'Cyber Europe 2010' Cyber Security Exercise," SecurityWeek News, April 18, 2011, http://www.security-week.com/enisa-issues-report-cyber-europe-2010-cyber-security-exercise.

215 *under poor assumptions* Nick Hopkins, "US and China Engage in Cyber War Games," *Guardian*, April 16, 2012, http://www.guardian.co.uk/technology/2012/apr/16/us-china-cyber-war-games.

215 *Stewart Baker highlighted* "Classified Memo Toughens Cyber-Threat Portrayals in DOD Exercises," *Inside the Pentagon*, January 20, 2011, https://defensenewsstand.com/component/option,com_ppv/Itemid,287/id,2351617/.

216 *Ryan McGeehan said* Goodin, "At Facebook, Zero-Day Exploits, Backdoor Code, Bring War Games Drill to Life."

BUILD CYBERSECURITY INCENTIVES: WHY SHOULD I DO WHAT YOU WANT?

216 *"tangible and demonstrable progress"* Jonathan Krim, " 'We Want to See Results,' Official Says at Summit," *Washington Post*, December 4, 2003, http://groups.yahoo.com/group/unitedstatesaction/message/3317.

217 *FBI repeatedly has found* Devlin Barrett, "U.S. Outgunned in Hacker War," *Wall Street Journal*, March 28, 2012, http://online.wsj.com/article/SB10001424052702304177710457 7307773326180032.html.

217 *banks' individual brand names* Tyler Moore and Richard Clayton, "The Impact of Incentives on Notice and Take-down," in *Managing Information Risk and the Economics of Security*, edited by M. Eric Johnson (New York: Springer, 2008), pp. 199–223.

218 *unpatched vulnerabilities* Lucian Constantin, "Over Half of Android Devices Have Unpatched Vulnerabilities, Report Says," *PC World*, September 14, 2012, http://www.pcworld.com/article/262321/over_half_of_android_devices_have_unpatched_vulner-abilities_report_says.html.

218 *automated security tool* Benjamin Edelman, "Adverse Selection in Online 'Trust' Certifications," *Electronic Commerce Research and Applications* 10, no. 1 (2011): pp. 17–25, http://www.benedelman.org/publications/advsel-trust-draft.pdf.

219 *opt-in model* Eric J. Johnson and Daniel Goldstein, "Do Defaults Save Lives," *Science* 302, no. 5649 (November 2003): pp. 1338–1339, http://www.sciencemag.org/content/302/5649/1338.short.

220 *"extensive mitigation costs"* United States Department of Homeland Security, "Enabling Distributed Security in Cyberspace."

220 *"reduce risks to participants"* Ibid.

221 *keys to the kingdom* SANS Institute, "CSIS: Critical Controls for Effective Cyber Defense, Version 4.1," March 2013, http://www.sans.org/critical-security-controls/, accessed August 11, 2013.

221 *94 percent of security risks* Ibid.

221 *"nefarious entities"* "Cyber-Attacks That Kill, IPv6, and Vulnerability Markets on Tap for 2013," *Infosecurity*, December 7, 2012, http://www.infosecurity-magazine.com/view/29741/cyberattacks-that-kill-ipv6-and-vulnerability-markets-on-tap-for-2013/.

LEARN TO SHARE: HOW CAN WE BETTER COLLABORATE ON INFORMATION?

222 *"To share with everyone"* Jack Johnson, "The Sharing Song," *Sing-A-Longs and Lullabies for the Film "Curious George,"* 2006, Brushfire/Universal, http://www.azlyrics.com/lyrics/jackjohnson/thesharingsong.html, accessed August 11, 2013.

222 *estimated $330 million* Tyler Moore and Richard Clayton, "The Consequence of Non-cooperation in the Fight against Phishing," in *Proceedings of the 3rd APWG eCrime Researchers Summit*, Atlanta, GA, October 15–16, 2008, http://lyle.smu.edu/~tylerm/ecrime08.pdf.

222 *Cyberspace Policy Review explained*   Executive Office of the President of the U.S., "Cyberspace Policy Review: Assuring a Trusted and Resilient Information and Communications Infrastructure," December 2009, http://www.whitehouse.gov/assets/documents/Cyberspace_Policy_Review_final.pdf, accessed August 11, 2013.

224 *inside a trusted group*   Moore and Clayton, "The Consequence of Non-cooperation in the Fight against Phishing."

224 *"provide analytical support"*   Dan Verton, "Interview: Scott Algier, Exec. Director, IT-ISAC," *The Risk Communicator*, January 2013, http://archive.constantcontact.com/fs173/1102302026582/archive/1112298600836.html, accessed August 11, 2013.

225 *"trust and relationships"*   Christopher Schroeder, "The Unprecedented Economic Risks of Network Insecurity," in *America's Cyber Future: Security and Prosperity in the Information Age*, vol. 2, edited by Kristin M. Lord and Travis Shard (Washington, DC: Center for a New American Security), p. 178.

225 *"DoD is compromised"*   Department of Defense, "Defense Industrial Base Cyber Security," Office of the Deputy Secretary of Defense, October 31, 2012, http://www.acq.osd.mil/dpap/policy/policyvault/OSD012537-12-RES.pdf.

225 *maintaining confidentiality*   Advanced Cyber Security Center, "Initiatives," http://www.acscenter.org/initiatives/, accessed August 11, 2013.

225 *malware is studied and defeated*   IEEE Standards Association, "ICSG Malware Working Group," https://standards.ieee.org/develop/indconn/icsg/malware.html, accessed August 11, 2013.

226 *quoting its reports*   David E. Sanger, David Barboza, and Nicole Perlroth, "Chinese Army Unit Is Seen as Tied to Hacking against U.S.," *New York Times*, February 18, 2013, http://www.nytimes.com/2013/02/19/technology/chinas-army-is-seen-as-tied-to-hacking-against-us.html?pagewanted=all.

226 *"respect and credibility"*   Adam Shostack, "Can You Hear Me Now?" *Emergency Chaos*, June 13, 2008, http://emergentchaos.com/archives/2008/06/can-you-hear-me-now-2.html.

226 *"improving our cybersecurity"*   Shawn Osbourne, "Shawn Osbourne to the Honorable Mike Rogers and The Honorable C. A. 'Dutch' Ruppersberger," letter regarding the Cyber Intelligence Sharing and Protection Act, April 17, 2012, http://intelligence.house.gov/sites/intelligence.house.gov/files/documents/041712TechAmericaLetterCISPA.pdf.

227 *pesky lawyers*   Joseph Kramek, "The Critical Infrastructure Gap."

227 *Paul Rosenzweig explains*   Paul Rosenzweig, "The Organization of the United States Government and Private Sector for Achieving Cyber Deterrence," in *Proceedings of a Workshop on Deterring Cyberattacks: Informing Strategies and Developing for U.S. Policy*, edited by the National Research Council (Washington, DC: National Academies Press, 2010), p. 2084.

227 *phishing takedown firms*   Tal Moran and Tyler Moore, "The Phish Market Protocol: Sharing Attack Data between Competitors," in *Proceedings of 14th International Conference on Financial Cyrptography and Data Security*, Tenerife, Spain, January 25–28, 2010, http://lyle.smu.edu/~tylerm/ecrime08.pdf.

DEMAND DISCLOSURE: WHAT IS THE ROLE OF TRANSPARENCY?

228 *Simitian's proposed bill*   Kim Zetter. "California Looks to Expand Data Breach Notification Law," *Threat Level* (blog), *Wired*, March 6, 2009, http://www.wired.com/threatlevel/2009/03/ca-looks-to-exp/.

228 *80 members…40 members*   Ibid.

228 *there were 51*   Alessandro Acquisti, Allan Friedman, and Rahul Telang, "Is There a Cost to Privacy Breaches? An Event Study," paper presented at the 27th International Conference on Information Systems and Workshop on the Economics of Information Security, Milwaukee, WI, December 2006, http://www.heinz.cmu.edu/~acquisti/papers/acquisti-friedman-telang-privacy-breaches.pdf.

229 *A 2011 industry study*   Brian Grow and Mark Hosenball, "Special Report: In Cyberspy v. Cyberspy China Has the Edge," Reuters, April 14, 2011, http://www.reuters.com/article/2011/04/14/us-china-usa-cyberespionage-idUSTRE73D24220110414.

229 *Christopher Schroeder explained*   Schroeder, "The Unprecedented Economic Risks of Network Insecurity," p. 177.

230 *According to the SEC*   US Securities and Exchange Commission, "CF Disclosure Guidance: Topic No. 2: Cybersecurity," Division of Corporation Finance, October 13, 2011, http://www.sec.gov/divisions/corpfin/guidance/cfguidance-topic2.htm.

230 *"more disclosure in this area"*   Sarah N. Lynch, "SEC 'Seriously' Looking at Cybersecurity," Reuters, June 8, 2011, http://www.reuters.com/article/2011/06/08/us-sec-cybersecurity-idUSTRE7576YM20110608.

230 *Melissa Hathaway counters*   Ellen Nakashima and David S. Hilzenrath, "Cybersecurity: SEC Outlines Requirement That Companies Report Cyber Theft and Attack," *Washington Post*, October 14, 2011, http://articles.washingtonpost.com/2011-10-14/world/35279358_1_companies-report-breaches-guidance.

230 *a 2012 study*   Jody R. Westby, "How Boards & Senior Executives Are Managing Cyber Risks," Governance of Enterprise Security: CyLab 2012 Report, May 16, 2012, http://www.rsa.com/innovation/docs/CMU-GOVERNANCE-RPT-2012-FINAL.pdf.

231 *As Tyler Moore explains*   Tyler Moore, "Introducing the Economics of Cybersecurity," National Academies report, 2010, http://www.nap.edu/openbook.php?record_id=12997&page=3, accessed August 11, 2013.

GET **"Vigorous"** about Responsibility: How Can We Create Accountability for Security?

231 *said Bill Braithwaite*   Rob Stein, "Medical Privacy Law Nets No Fines," *Washington Post*, June 5, 2006, http://www.washingtonpost.com/wp-dyn/content/article/2006/06/04/AR2006060400672.html.

231 *not a single case*   Ibid.

231 *Winston Wilkinson*   Ibid.

232 *A consultant summarized*   Ibid.

232 *Dmitri Alperovitch notes*   Dmitri Alperovitch, "Deterrence in Cyberspace: Debating the Right Strategy with Ralph Langer and Dmitri Alperovitch," remarks at the Brookings Institution, Washington, DC, September 20, 2011, http://www.brookings.edu/~/media/events/2011/9/20%20cyberspace%20deterrence/20110920_cyber_defense.pdf.

233 *Michael Assente*   Mark Clayton, "America's Power Grid Too Vulnerable to Cyberattack, US Report Finds," *Christian Science Monitor*, February 3, 2011, http://www.csmonitor.com/USA/2011/0203/America-s-power-grid-too-vulnerable-to-cyberattack-US-report-finds/(page)/2.

233 *40 million users*   "Security Firm RSA Offers to Replace SecurID Tokens," BBC News, June 7, 2011, http://www.bbc.co.uk/news/technology-13681566.

233 *DigiNotar's bankruptcy*   Kim Zetter, "DigiNotar Files for Bankruptcy in Wake of Devastating Hack," *Threat Level* (blog), Wired, September 20, 2011, http://www.wired.com/threatlevel/2011/09/diginotar-bankruptcy/.

234 *A conservative estimate*   Richard S. Betterley, "Cyber/Privacy Insurance Market Survey—2012: Surprisingly Competitive, as Carriers Seek Market Share," Betterley Risk Consultants, June 2012, p. 5, http://betterley.com/samples/cpims12_nt.pdf, accessed August 11, 2013.

234 *commented one analyst*   Ibid.

234 *Joel Brenner explains*   Joel F. Brenner, "Privacy and Security: Why Isn't Cyberspace More Secure?" *Communications of the ACM* 53, no. 11 (November 2010): p. 34, http://www.cooley.com/files/p33-brenner.pdf.

234 *Larry Clinton*   US Government Accountability Office, Testimony before the Senate Judiciary Committee, US Senate; testimony of Larry Clinton, President and CEO of the Internet Security Alliance, November 17, 2009, http://www.judiciary.senate.gov/ pdf/09-11-17Clinton'sTestimony.pdf.

235 *Cyberspace Policy Review put it*   Executive Office of the President of the United States, "Cyberspace Policy Review: Assuring a Trusted and Resilient Information and Communications Infrastructure."

235 *"requirements of the security rule"*   Julie Bird, "Boston Teaching Hospital Fined $1.5M for ePHI Data Breach," *FierceHealthIT*, September 18, 2012, http:// www.fiercehealthit.com/story/boston-teaching-hospital-fined-15m-ephi-d ata-breach/2012-09-18#ixzz2OC67Xiwh.

FIND THE IT CROWD: HOW DO WE SOLVE THE CYBER PEOPLE PROBLEM?

236 *"the same resumes"*   Ellen Nakashima, "Federal Agencies, Private Firms Fiercely Compete in Hiring Cyber Experts," *Washington Post*, November 13, 2012.

236 *add another 600*   Ibid.

236 *one industry consultant explained*   Loren Thompson, "Cyberwarfare May Be a Bust for Many Defense Contractors," *Forbes*, May 9, 2011, http://www.forbes.com/sites/ beltway/2011/05/09/washingtons-cyberwarfare-boom-loses-its-allure/.

236 *3 to 10 percent*   Karen Evans and Franklin Reeder, *A Human Capital Crisis in Cybersecurity: Technical Proficiency Matters*, Center for Strategic and International Studies, November 2010, p. 6, http://csis.org/files/publication/101111_Evans_HumanCapital_ Web.pdf, accessed August 11, 2013.

236 *tens of thousands more*   Brittany Ballenstedt, "Building Cyber Warriors," *Government Executive*, August 15, 2011, p. 40, http://www.nextgov.com/cybersecurity/2011/08/ building-cyber-warriors/49587/.

236 *By one estimate*   Brian Fung, "You Call This an Army? The Terrifying Shortage of U.S. Cyberwarriors," *National Journal*, last modified May 30, 2013, http://www. nationaljournal.com/tech/you-call-this-an-army-the-terrifying-shortage-of-u-s-cyber- warriors-20130225.

236 *cybersecurity expert*   Ralph Langner, "Deterrence in Cyberspace: Debating the Right Strategy with Ralph Langner and Dmitri Alperovitch," remarks at the Brookings Institution, Washington, DC, September 20, 2011, http://www.brookings.edu/events/ 2011/09/20-cyberspace-deterrence.

237 *only 40 percent*   Ballenstedt, "Building Cyber Warriors," p. 40.

237 *explains Alan Palmer*   Ibid.

237 *a 2011 study*   Ibid.

238 *education for free*   Ibid., p. 43.

239 *fellowship program*   Ibid.

239 *vibrant for job prospects*   Fung, "You Call This an Army?"

239 *full-time job after graduation*   Ibid., p. 42.

239 *about 25 percent*   Graham Warwick, "Talent Spotting: Aerospace, Defense Must Compete with Other Sectors to Recruit and Retain Cyberexperts," *Aviation Week & Space Technology* 185, no. 18 (May 23, 2011).

240 *Lynn Dungle*   Ibid.

240 *6-minute intervals*   Ibid.

240 *professional hacker websites*   Ibid.

240 *reach the top*   Ibid.

DO YOUR PART: HOW CAN I PROTECT MYSELF (AND THE INTERNET)?

241 *"123456"*   Mat Honan, "Kill the Password: Why a String of Characters Can't Protect Us Anymore," *Gadget Lab* (blog), *Wired*, November 15, 2011, http://www.wired.com/ gadgetlab/2012/11/ff-mat-honan-password-hacker/all/.

241 *"bad guys can hide in"* Cyber Terrain conference, Spy Museum, Washington, DC, May 18, 2011.

241 *85 percent of targeted intrusions* Ian Wallace, "Why the US Is Not in a Cyber War," *Daily Beast*, March 10, 2013, http://www.thedailybeast.com/articles/2013/03/10/why-the-u-s-is-not-in-a-cyber-war.html.

242 *risks in the realm* Schroeder, "The Unprecedented Economic Risks of Network Insecurity," p. 174.

242 *"security wasn't important"* Steven Bucci, "Looking Forward," remarks at the Washington Post Cybersecurity Summit, November 13, 2012.

242 *"That's pathetic"* Ben Hammersley, "Speech to the UK's Information Assurance Advisory Council," remarks to the Information Assurance Advisory Council, London, September 7, 2011, http://www.benhammersley.com/2011/09/my-speech-to-the-iaac/.

243 *smart and responsible user* "Tips to Avoid Cyber Thieves," *Washington Post*, November 13, 2012, http://www.washingtonpost.com/postlive/tips-to-avoid-cyber-thieves/2012/11/12/fe12c776-28f4-11e2-96b6-8e6a7524553f_story.html.

243 *"damned stupid on computers"* Cyber Terrain Conference, Spy Museum, Washington DC, May 18, 2011.

243 *"database-friendly formats"* Honan, "Kill the Password."

243 *One study of hacked websites* Ibid.

244 *37 percent of the total data* Ibid.

CONCLUSIONS

WHERE IS CYBERSECURITY HEADED NEXT?

247 *122,400 processor cores* Jon Brodkin, "World's Top Supercomputer from '09 is now Obsolete, Will Be Dismantled," *Ars Technica*, March 31, 2013, http://arstechnica.com/information-technology/2013/03/worlds-fastest-supercomputer-from-09-is-now-obsolete-will-be-dismantled/.

248 *John Nasibett once said* Brian Monger, "Knowing Who Your Market Is and What They Want," *SmartaMarketing*, November 11, 2012, http://smartamarketing.wordpress.com/2012/11/11/knowing-who-your-market-is-and-what-they-want/.

249 *40 to 80 percent* Ray, "Cloud Computing Economics: 40–80 percent Savings in the Cloud," *CloudTweaks*, April 9, 2011, http://www.cloudtweaks.com/2011/04/cloud-computing-economics-40-80-savings-in-the-cloud/.

249 *General Martin Dempsey* General Martin Dempsey, "Defending the Nation at Network Speed," remarks at the Brookings Institution, Washington, DC, June 27, 2013.

249 *$149 billion in 2014* Transparency Market Research, "Cloud Computing Services Market- Global Industry Size, Market Share, Trends, Analysis and Forecasts, 2012–2018," http://www.transparencymarketresearch.com/cloud-computing-services-market.html, accessed August 11, 2013.

249 *a Brookings report explored* Allan A. Friedman and Darrell M. West, "Privacy and Security in Cloud Computing," *Issues in Technology Innovation*, no. 3, the Brookings Institution (October 26, 2010), http://www.brookings.edu/research/papers/2010/10/26-cloud-computing-friedman-west.

250 *"allowed Netflix to approach"* David Carr, "Giving Viewers What They Want," *New York Times*, February 24, 2013, http://www.nytimes.com/2013/02/25/business/media/for-house-of-cards-using-big-data-to-guarantee-its-popularity.html?pagewanted=all.

250 *closeted sexual orientation* Ryan Singel, "Netflix Spilled Your Brokeback Mountain Secret, Lawsuit Claims," *Threat Level* (blog), *Wired*, December 17, 2009, http://www.wired.com/threatlevel/2009/12/netflix-privacy-lawsuit/.

251 *prank call* Daniel Thomas, "Mobile Revolution Marks Fortieth Year," *Financial Times*, April 3, 2013, http://www.ft.com/intl/cms/s/0/4efdaf92-9c73-11e2-ba3c-00144feabdc0.html#axzz2QHyT5GGa.

251   *20.2 percent in 2012*   Neil Walker, "The Mobile Revolution 2012," *State of Search,* http://www.stateofsearch.com/the-mobile-revolution-2012/, accessed August 11, 2013.

251   *One 2013 study*   Stephen Lawson, "Study: One-quarter of U.S. Patents Issued This Year Will Be in Mobile," *ITworld,* March 27, 2013, http://www.itworld.com/mobile-wireless/350027/study-one-quarter-us-patents-issued-year-will-be-mobile.

251   *350,000 unique variants*   Proofpoint, Inc., "Cyber-Security Risks Rise with Spike in Spam Variety," March 1, 2013, http://www.proofpoint.com/about-us/security-compliance-and-cloud-news/articles/cyber-security-risks-rise-with-spike-in-spam-variety-397144.

252   *The UN, for example, predicts*   "The State of Broadband 2012: Achieving Digital Inclusion for All," Report by the Broadband Commission, September 2012, http://www.broadbandcommission.org/Documents/bb-annualreport2012.pdf, accessed August 11, 2013.

253   *As* The Economist *observed*   "To Each Their Own," *Economist,* April 6, 2013, http://www.economist.com/news/special-report/21574634-chinas-model-controlling-internet-being-adopted-elsewhere-each-their-own.

254   *WeMo switched the fan on*   Clive Thompson, "No Longer Vaporware: The Internet of Things Is Finally Talking," *Wired,* December 6, 2012, http://www.wired.com/opinion/2012/12/20-12-st_thompson/.

WHAT DO I REALLY NEED TO KNOW IN THE END?

255   *Donald Rumsfeld*   Charles M. Blow, "Knowns, Unknowns, and Unknowables," *New York Times,* September 26, 2012, http://campaignstops.blogs.nytimes.com/2012/09/26/blow-knowns-unknowns-and-unknowables/.

GLOSSARY

advanced persistent threat (APT): A cyberattack campaign with specific, targeted objectives, conducted by a coordinated team of specialized experts, combining organization, intelligence, complexity, and patience.

Advanced Research Projects Agency (ARPA): Formed in 1958 after the Sputnik launch, the American defense agency dedicated to preventing technological surprises for the United States and creating such surprises for its foes. With a focus on expanding the frontiers of science and technology, it provided much of the funding for a series of initiatives that evolved into the modern Internet. It was renamed DARPA (for Defense) in 1972, and continues to focus on long-term defense-related research and development.

Advanced Research Projects Agency Network (ARPANET): The precursor to the modern Internet. Funded by ARPA, it began in 1969 with a first link between UCLA amd Stanford, growing to link forty nodes by 1972 and then exponentially as more universities and research centers around the world joined.

air-gap: To physically isolate a computer or network from other unsecure networks, including the public Internet, to prevent network-enabled attacks. It sounds nice in theory, but it is extremely hard to ensure complete isolation in practice.

Anonymous: A decentralized but coordinated collection of users from various Internet forums, who gather to conduct organized attacks, protests, and other actions using cyber means. The most noted of the hactivist groups, its motives range from political protest to vigilantism to sheer amusement.

asymmetric cryptography: The practice of securing data using a public key, which is shared with everyone, and a private key that remains secret. Data encrypted with the public key can only be decrypted with the private key, and vice versa. This allows secure communications without a shared secret.

Autonomous System (AS): An independent network serving as a node in the inter-connected Internet. Traffic between ASs is governed by the Internet protocols and routing policies.

Bitcoin: A popular digital currency, first developed in 2008, that offers significant anonymity and requires no centralization or coordinated control.

botnet: A network of "zombie" computers controlled by a single actor. Botnets are a common tool for malicious activity on the Internet, such as denial-of-service attacks and spam, since they provide free (stolen) computation and network resources while hiding the identity of the controller.

Centers for Disease Control and Prevention (CDC): A public agency that coordinates research, communications, and information sharing for public health in the United States.

certificate authority (CA): A trusted organization that produces signed digital "certificates" that explicitly tie an entity to a public key. This allows asymmetric cryptography users to trust that they are communicating with the right party.

cloud computing: A shift in control of computing resources from the individual or organization to a shared resource run by a third party. By pooling network-enabled resources, cloud computing enables mobility, scalability, flexibility, and efficiency, but increases the dependency on the cloud provider.

computer emergency response team (CERT): Organizations located around the world that serve as hubs of cybersecurity technical expertise, collaboration, and security information dissemination. Many governments have their own national CERTs, as do an increasing number of industrial sectors and large organizations.

computer network operations (CNO): The military concept of utilizing computers to "destroy, deny, degrade, disrupt, [and] deceive," as the US Air Force puts it, while at the same time, preparing and defending against the enemy's attempts to do the same.

Conficker: A computer worm first discovered in 2008 that targeted Windows operating systems. It is noteworthy for the size and spread of the botnet made from computers compromised by the malware, and the international cooperation required to counter it.

critical infrastructure: The underlying components of the economy that run our modern-day civilization, ranging from power and water, to banking, healthcare, and transportation. Many countries have special policies and regulations for critical infrastructure protection.

Cyber Command (CYBERCOM): The US military organization that brings together the various parts of the US military that work on cyber issues. Its headquarters is at Fort Meade in Maryland, colocated with the National Security Agency.

cyberterrorism: As defined by the FBI, a "premeditated, politically motivated attack against information, computer systems, computer programs, and data which results in violence against non-combatant targets by sub-national groups or clandestine agents." Like Shark Week, it is far more exciting than the data would bear out.

DARPA: ARPA with a D.

Department of Homeland Security (DHS): Created in response to 9/11, the US government agency designated to prepare for, prevent, and respond to domestic emergencies, particularly terrorism. Its National Cyber Security Division (NCSD) is responsible for various public cybersecurity roles and missions in the United States, including being the home of US-CERT.

device driver: A software tool that allows hardware devices to interact with an operating system. Because so many are built into modern operating systems, device drivers are a frequent vector for attacks.

digital currency: Alternate currency (i.e., not accepted or endorsed by national banks) also known as "electronic money." It requires mechanisms to prevent infinite replication and can be used just like other forms of money, provided that you can find someone in the online world to accept it as payment.

digital native: A person who has grown up in a world where networked computers have always existed and seem a natural aspect of the world. This might make those who predate the Web "digital immigrants."

distributed denial of service (DDoS): An attack that seeks to inundate a targeted system's functions or connection to the Internet. Attackers distribute the overwhelming traffic across multiple sources, often using botnets of thousands or even millions of machines.

Domain Name System (DNS): The hierarchal, distributed naming system that translates humanly memorable names (like Brookings.edu) into numeric IP addresses (192.245.194.172). The DNS is global and decentralized, with an architecture that can be thought of as a tree.

doxing: Revealing personal documents publicly, as part of a protest, prank, or vigilante action. Often doxing requires minimal network penetration, relying more on careful research to link hidden personal or embarrassing data to the victim.

Federal Risk and Authorization Management Program (FedRAMP): A certification program launched in 2012 that allowed, for the first time, a government contractor to be cleared just once to provide services for the entire civilian US government.

firewall: A filter that rejects data traffic from entering a specific network or machine following specific rules. The name was taken from the concept of barriers built into cars or buildings to prevent fires from spreading further.

GhostNet: A network of 1,295 infected computers in 103 countries discovered by researchers in 2009. It targeted foreign affairs ministries, embassies, and multilateral organizations in places from Iran and Germany to the Tibetan government in exile. While the origin of the operation was never confirmed, the servers utilized were all located on Hainan Island in China.

grafting: A strategy of international cooperation building. Akin to the horticulture technique of adding a new plant to the roots of an older plant, the idea is to build new initiatives on established frameworks and interests to increase the chances of success.

hacker: Originally a passionate technical expert who ignored rules, the term has evolved to focus on those who discover and exploit vulnerabilities in a computer system or network. It does not always denote malicious intent. For example, a "white hat" hacker is someone who tries to find (and close) weaknesses before a "black hat" criminal can.

hacktivism: Combining hacking and activism, the use of computer means of protest and attack to aid the cause of civil disobedience.

hash: A cryptographic function that takes any piece of data and maps it to a smaller, set-length output, with two specific properties. First, the function is one-way, which makes it very difficult to determine the original data from the output. Second, and even more important, it is incredibly hard to find two input pieces of data that generate the same output hash. This lets the hash function "fingerprint" a document, e-mail, or cryptographic key to verify the integrity of that data.

honeypot (or honeynet): A tactic used by security researchers in which computers, networks, or virtual machines are intentionally exposed to attacks. By observing how different types of malware behave, researchers can identify new types of attacks and devise defenses.

HyperText Transfer Protocol (HTTP): The technical protocol that defines how applications ask for and deliver content on the World Wide Web.

industrial control system (ICS): A computer system that monitors and runs large-scale industrial processes, for everything from factories to pipelines. The hardware controlled is very different, but computers have enabled simplified management and operation.

information security: Safeguarding the flow and access of reliable digital information. Defined by some to include the suppression of harmful information of a political nature, which spurred the rise to the alternative but not identical term "cybersecurity."

Information Sharing and Analysis Center (ISAC): Independent organizations for coordinating security for critical infrastructure sectors of the economy, such as financial services or healthcare, with each sector determining its organizational form and function. ISACs vary in their activity level and relevance, from passive collections of resources to active collaboration of sector risk management.

informatization: A hallmark in the Chinese military's approach to cyber operation, focusing on defending PLA networks and, in turn, targeting the adversary's key nodes of communication, command, and coordination.

integrity attack: Entering a computer network or system with the intent not to extract information but to change it, such that the information on the system can no longer be considered reliable.

International Telecommunications Union (ITU): Formed in 1865 to regulate cross-border telegraph communications, a United Nations agency that coordinates international communication policies and interconnections.

Internet Corporation for Assigned Names and Numbers (ICANN). The private nonprofit created in 1998 to run the various Internet administration and operations tasks that had previously been performed by US government organizations.

Internet Engineering Task Force (IETF): An international, voluntary organization that develops Internet standards and protocols and modifies existing ones for better performance. Part of ISOC.

Internet freedom: The idea of online free expression and the right to access the Internet as a means of connecting to others around the world, and the commitment to work against state censorship and repression.

Internet of things: Superimposing an information environment on top of the real world. As more objects have digital sensors and unique identifiers, the communication and processing powers of cyberspace can be embedded in the real world.

Internet Protocol (IP): The primary principal communications protocol that enables Internet working. It defines addressing methods and how to deliver packets from one point to another solely based on their IP address.

Internet Protocol (IP) address: A numerical label that is assigned to an addressable connection to the Internet; an endpoint.

Internet service provider (ISP): An organization that provides access to the Internet, as well as other services such as web hosting or e-mail. It is a primary control point, since all traffic from an individual or organization flows through its ISP.

Internet Society (ISOC): An international nonprofit organization formed in 1992 that oversees much of the technical Internet standards process, including the IETF. ISOC also serves as a forum for public participation and discussion around Internet governance questions.

intrusion detection systems: A set of sensors that look for invalid behavior, detecting the signatures of known or likely attacks as well as identifying anomalous behavior.

key: In cryptography, a string of data used to encrypt text or to decrypt encrypted text. Longer keys are harder to guess by trial and error, so key length is often correlated with greater security.

malware: Malicious or malevolent software, including viruses, worms, and Trojans, that is preprogrammed to attack, disrupt, and/or compromise other computers and networks. A packaged exploitation of vulnerability, there is often a "payload" of instructions detailing what the system should do after it has been compromised.

metadata: Data about data itself. Information about digital files or actions, such as dates, times, entities involved and other descriptive characteristics, metadata is used to organize and manage data. It became controversial in 2013, when the NSA's large scale metadata collection was disclosed by Edward Snowden.

money mules: Individuals or networks who act as intermediate steps in the transfer of money or goods, undermining detection efforts and reducing risk to the criminals.

multifactor authentication: A layered approach to security uses two or more mechanisms to authenticate identity, such as something the user knows, like a password, something the user has (like a smart card), where the user is, and/ or something the user is physically, such as a biometric characteristic like the fingerprint.

mutually assured destruction (MAD): The military strategy of a "balance of terror" that held during the Cold War. The great powers shied away from direct conflict by MAD guaranteeing that the initiator of any hostilities would also be destroyed.

National Institute of Standards and Technology (NIST): Located in the US Department of Commerce, NIST is the federal agency that works to develop and apply new standards and frameworks, especially for areas where industry has no clear consensus.

National Security Agency (NSA): The US Defense Department intelligence agency that focuses on signals and information intelligence and protection. It is seen as having some of the most advanced cybersecurity capabilities in the world, and works in close partnership with the US military's Cyber Command.

network-centric: A US military concept of utilizing computers bound together in a "system of systems" to coordinate forces across great distances with digital speed.

Operation Orchard: The Israeli strike on the nuclear research facility in al Kibar, Syria, on September 6, 2007, that utilized cyber means both to discover the plans and disable Syrian air defenses.

Operation Shady RAT: A series of cyberattacks that began around 2006, ultimately compromising data confidentiality of at least seventy-two organizations, ranging from defense and oil firms to the United Nations and International Olympic Committee. The name derives from the attacker's use of remote administration tools, enabling full use of system tools such as cameras and microphones.

packet: Digital envelope of data. By breaking up flows of data into smaller components, packets can each be delivered in an independent and decentralized fashion, then reassembled at the endpoint. When conversations are broken into smaller parts, packets from multiple different conversations can share the same network links, without a controlled path or dedicated circuits.

patch: A software code update. Vendors use security patches to mitigate or fix security vulnerabilities.

patriotic hacking: Citizens or groups within a state joining together to carry out cyberattacks on perceived enemies of that state, without explicit, official state encouragement or support.

People's Liberation Army (PLA): The Chinese military.

phishing: An attempt to fool the user into voluntarily supplying credentials, such as a password or bank account number, often by spoofed e-mails or fake web pages. "Spear phishing" attacks are customized to target specific individuals.

protocol: A set of formats and rules that defines how communications can be exchanged.

pwn: Hacker term meaning to "own," or take control of, a rival's systems and networks.

ransomware: A type of malware that restricts access to a target and demands payment to return regular service.

red-team: To examine and/or simulate an attack on oneself, in order to identify and close vulnerabilities before an adversary can do so. Often performed by "white hat" hackers.

RickRolling: The Internet meme of tricking someone into watching a horribly addictive music video by 1980s singer Rick Astley.

root access: The ability to read and write to every file on a system. This ability is necessary for the administration of an operating system, but if adversaries get root access, they "pwn" the system.

Secure Internet Protocol Router Network (SIPRNet): The US military's classified network, used to communicate secret information following the same basic protocols as the broader Internet.

social engineering: The practice of manipulating people into revealing confidential information online.

SQL injection: A common attack vector against web servers. The attacker attempts to trick a website into passing a "rogue" Structured Query Language (SQL) command to the database. If the database program can be compromised, the attacker may be able to gain access to other files or permissions on the server.

Structured Query Language (SQL): A type of programming language used to manage data.

Stuxnet: Created by US and Israeli intelligence agencies, a computer worm specifically designed to sabotage Iranian nuclear research facilities.

supervisory control and data acquisition (SCADA): A type of industrial control system, particularly used to monitor and manage interconnected sensors and control large facilities.

test beds: Extensible models and mockups used to simulate large IT systems, networks, and operational environments, on which attacks and defenses can be mimicked, replicated, and practiced.

Tor: Short for "The Onion Router," an overlay network that provides online protection against surveillance and traffic analysis. Originally developed with US government funding, now maintained and operated by an international group of volunteers and researchers.

Transport Control Protocol (TCP): Paired with the Internet Protocol, one of the foundational protocols of the Internet. Developed by Vint Cerf and Bob Kahn in 1974, TCP manages expectations that each end of a networked communication link has of the other end.

Trojan: A type of malware disguised or attached to legitimate or innocuous-seeming software, but that instead carries a malicious payload, most often opening a backdoor to unauthorized users. Named after a large wooden farm animal.

typosquatting: The practice of registering web domains just one letter off from a popular website, and collecting advertisement revenue from the page visits by those with clumsy fingers.

Unit 61398: Also known in cybersecurity circles as the "Comment Crew" or "Shanghai Group," a key unit in the Chinese military tasked with gathering political, economic, and military-related intelligence on the United States through cyber means. In 2013, it was caught stealing employee passwords to break into the computer networks of the *New York Times*.

virus: A malware program that can replicate itself and spread from computer to computer.

watering hole: A type of attack that targets specific groups by compromising websites frequently visited by that community or occupation.

whitelisting: A security practice that defines a set of acceptable software, e-mail senders, or other components, then bans everything else.

WikiLeaks: An online organization formed in 2006 with the goal of "exposing corruption and abuse around the world." It is also frequently used to refer to a series of scandals in 2010, when a trove of US diplomatic cables were released online.

worm: A type of malware that spreads automatically over a network, installing and replicating itself. The network traffic from rapid replication and spread can cripple networks even when the malware does not have a malicious payload.

zero day: An attack that exploits a previously unknown vulnerability; taken from the notion that the attacks takes places on the zeroth day of the awareness. Knowledge about zero-day exploits are valuable to both defenders and attackers.

zombie: A computer that has been compromised by an outside party, for the purpose of exploiting its computational and network resources; frequently linked into a botnet.

INDEX